Romantic Shades and Shadows

Romantic Shades and Shadows

SUSAN J. WOLFSON

Johns Hopkins University Press
Baltimore

© 2018 Johns Hopkins University Press
All rights reserved. Published 2018
Printed in the United States of America on acid-free paper
9 8 7 6 5 4 3 2 1

Johns Hopkins University Press
2715 North Charles Street
Baltimore, Maryland 21218-4363
www.press.jhu.edu

Library of Congress Cataloging in Publication Control Number: 2017039406

A catalog record for this book is available from the British Library.

ISBN 978-1-4214-2554-2 (hardcover : alk. paper)
ISBN 978-4214-2555-9 (electronic)
ISBN 1-4214-2554-8 (hardcover : alk. paper)
ISBN 1-4214-2555-6 (electronic)

*Special discounts are available for bulk purchases of this book. For more information,
please contact Special Sales at 410-516-6936 or specialsales@press.jhu.edu.*

Johns Hopkins University Press uses environmentally friendly book materials,
including recycled text paper that is composed of at least 30 percent post-consumer
waste, whenever possible.

Frontispiece: Edward Hopper, *Night Shadows* (1921; published 1924). The presence of
this etching in my imagination is a mystery to me. I think that my father, Andrew T.
Wolfson, bought this print, an early striking in a run of 500, when he was a student
at Yale University in the 1930s. With a strong sense of photographic design, he must
have been drawn to Hopper's spectral shadowland of urban modernity, its solitary
figure composed of shadow and substance, small joined shapes approaching the stark
diagonal shadow-shaft cast by an off-frame street pole, the source of the pool of light
in the dark world. Light and dark, shadow and substance, human form and mute,
blank, huge, inhospitable architectural forms seem focalized by some dislocated,
unlocatable observer above, the gaze ambiguously dispassionate or quietly menacing.

William Wordsworth, *The Prelude*. For my readers' convenience, my texts are from the handy Norton Critical Edition; unless otherwise indicated, my text is 1805. I italicize year-texts (*1799, 1805, 1850*) to distinguish these from book and line number(s). For *1850*, Norton uses MS D, the last one that Wordsworth supervised, rather than the posthumous 1850 publication, with which his executor-editors interfered.

John Keats. Unless otherwise indicated, my texts are from *John Keats: A Longman Cultural Edition*, ed. Susan J. Wolfson.

Lord Byron, *Don Juan*. Unless otherwise indicated, my texts are from *Byron, Complete Poetical Works*, ed. Jerome J. McGann, vol. 5.

This list is for frequently cited works. A full bibliography is in the Works Cited.

1839	*Poetical Works of Percy Bysshe Shelley*, ed. Mary Shelley, 1839
BCPW	*Byron, Complete Poetical Works*, ed. J. McGann; cited by volume: page
BL	*Biographia Literaria* (Coleridge, 1817), cited by volume: page
BLJ	*Byron's Letters and Journals*, ed. L. Marchand; cited by volume: page
DJ	*Don Juan*, Lord Byron; cited by Canto.stanza
DW	*The Dramatick Writings of Will. Shakspere*, 1788; cited by page, if relevant
E&I	*Essays and Introductions*, W. B. Yeats
ECCO	Eighteenth-Century Collections Online (database)
EY	*The Letters of William and Dorothy Wordsworth. The Early Years*
K	*John Keats: A Longman Cultural Edition*, ed. Susan J. Wolfson
L	*Letters* (if the author/edition is obvious); sometimes *CL: Collected Letters*
LB	*Lyrical Ballads* (William Wordsworth)
LION	Literature Online (database)
LJK	*Letters of John Keats*, ed. Hyder E. Rollins, cited by volume.page
LY	*The Letters of William and Dorothy Wordsworth. The Later Years*
MS/MSS:	manuscript(s) — ^{r}: recto page; ^{v}: verso page
MSJ	*Mary Shelley's Journals*, ed. Paula Feldman and Diana Scott-Kilvert
MY	*The Letters of William and Dorothy Wordsworth. The Middle Years*
OED	*Oxford English Dictionary*
PL	*Paradise Lost*, John Milton, 2d edition, 1674
RT	*The Round Table*, William Hazlitt
TT	*Table-Talk*, William Hazlitt

Romantic Shades and Shadows

CHAPTER ONE

Setting the Stage

Apparitions of Writing

I. Phantasmics on Purpose to a Life

Letters are dead. Writing survives. Reading is haunted. This may be, contends John Milton in a vigorous rebuke of censorship, because books are not "absolutely dead things,"

> but doe contain a potencie of life in them to be as active as that soule was whose progeny they are; nay they do preserve as in a violl the purest efficacie and extraction of that living intellect that bred them . . . a good Booke is a pretious life-blood of a master spirit, imbalm'd and treasur'd up on purpose to a life beyond life. (*Areopagitica* 4)

The last sentence is blazoned over the entrance to the Reading Room of the New York Public Library, both a motto and an instance of what is still potent in the Book of Milton himself. In this "potencie of life," books are culture's undead, ready for revivifying. Onward a quarter millennium to Joseph Conrad: "It is so hard to realise that I have any readers!" he writes to a correspondent; "To know that *You* could read me is good news indeed—for one writes only half the book; the other half is with the reader."[1] It's not just the book but also this letter, in the imagined present of reading, as pages and sheets come to life, turn into conversation.

Yet for all its vital progeny, reading is a weirdly phantasmic trade: to read is to revivify words, revive an absent or vanished writer. William Wordsworth was keenly tuned to this as both the agent and the privileged reader. At the outset of *The Prelude,* the self-accounting that turned in his mind and on his pages for decades, he confesses his longing to

> endue, might fix in a visible home,
> Some portion of those phantoms of conceit,
> That had been floating loose about so long.   (1.129–31)

It's a strange phrase, "phantoms of conceit." The sense of *conceit* as a wisp in the mind hangs in readiness for legible apprehension, an embodiment in words. Even the sense of *phantoms* is unsettled: nebulous, but also, in the indexical "those phantoms," condensing habit into familiar figures.[2] If Wordsworth wishfully deflects from *phantom* obsolete senses of "unreality . . . vanity . . . delusion; a deception" (OED 1a, 1b), the word is still hospitable to the sense of "notion or idea which plays on the mind or haunts the imagination" (3a). This notion haunts the very grammar of the phrase "phantoms of conceit": *of* may indicate conceit (idea) as the producer of phantoms, or may indicate a conceit in phantom-form or formation. I like the way Timothy Bahti catches the float: a "figure—of meaning, of poetic intention," as yet "without a written sign" ("Rhetorical Theft" 96).

It matters to Wordsworth, however—and to the argument of *Romantic Shades and Shadows*—that phantom status puts pressure on his hope that he "might fix." It is a modal suspense, not just in this moment of wishing, but expanding over the long career of Wordsworth's fixing and unfixing the frames of the autobiographical home so conceived. If poetic formations draw intention from phantoms, formal provisions also solicit phantoms. Years on, Wordsworth recalls one (seemingly actual) vision of a

> frame of social being, which so long
> Had bodied forth the ghostliness of things
> In silence visible and perpetual calm.   (*1850* 6.427–29)

The pause of syntax at "so long" is the effect of poetic form as well as verbal meaning. If "the ghostliness of things / In silence visible" evokes what writing is, nothing is more Wordsworthian than the peculiar fiction of this report. Drafting these lines sometime between 1818 and 1820, Wordsworth recalls having beheld from afar, in August 1790, French forces approaching the Convent of Chartreuse "to expel / The blameless inmates, and belike subvert / That frame of social being" (425–27). It's spectral history squared. It is not just the haze, back then, of a distant sight in an alpine auditorium that seemed to rustle with "Nature's uttered" reproof (431); it's also later Wordsworth's haze of history: the monks were not expelled in 1790 but in 1792.[3] The poetry is a phantasmic anachronism, its frame fractured between Wordsworth's sympathy with the principles of the French Revolution and his retrospective horror at its future effects.[4] This was not just any regicide; it was a regicide, by Revolution, of the monarchy itself. The visible home of writing is, in effect, a ghost story—a phantom of conceit.

The conceit of phantoms is my reciprocal terrain in *Romantic Shades and Shadows*. This is a book about spectral linguistic agencies, both on the field of

Romantic writing and, reflexively, for our reading of the field. It is apt that Wordsworth is not only an arresting subject in this mode but also an avid student of it. Here he is, revisiting the onslaught of London's data (first given in *The Prelude* 7.154–204) with a staging in a Miltonic simile, a re-imagining in which confused experience may be savored as the experience of confusion:

> As when a traveller hath, from open day
> With torches passed into some vault of earth,
>
> . . . .
>
> He looks and sees the cavern spread and grow,
> Widening itself on all sides, sees, or thinks
> He sees, erelong, the roof above his head,
> Which instantly unsettles and recedes—
> Substance and shadow, light and darkness, all
> Commingled, making up a canopy
> Of shapes, and form, and tendencies to shape,
> That shift and vanish, change and interchange
> Like spectres—ferment quiet and sublime.   (8.711–12, 715–23)

Each line poses a dramatic hesitation with such quiet force that "A spectacle to which there is no end" (741) emerges as the master-trope for this unsettling phantasmagoria, both for the eye that sees and for the words that convey it, figuring shadows into poetry's substance, spectres into its spectacles.

Wordsworth later thought to add "ghostly semblance" into the spectacle-poetry (*1850* 8.586), a sensation that verges on but is not quite ghost-seeing. Ghosts are familiars in Gothic genre-literature (ballads and novels) and take memorable turns on the Shakespearean stage. My interest is in the apparitional semblances in verbal textures: chance associations, ruptures of logic, figural recurrences, and overproductions. This irreparable literariness registers in the way Romantic-era writers read Shakespeare and Milton. The responsiveness of S. T. Coleridge, John Keats, William Hazlitt, Wordsworth (et al.) to penumbral nuances in Shakespeare's poetry is not only a tribute to Shakespeare's verbal genius but also a register of *literary* reading: close, slow, careful, and open to various, not necessarily reconcilable, energies in the movements of language. It was the particularities of Shakespeare's poetry that sparked Coleridge's "practical criticism" (*BL* 2:12) and convinced him "how little instructive any criticism cannot be which does not enter into minutiæ" (*Notebooks* 3:3970). Keats admired how Milton could inflect a word with "all its shades of signification": shades that are nuances, shades that are apparitional.[5] Such shades need not compel a dialectical refinement into clarity but may persist as a presence in reading.

My perspective on shades and shadows of language is stimulated by, but also distinct from, two strong claims on modern literary study. The first is the discursive regime Jerome McGann influentially named "The Romantic Ideology": a false consciousness in spiritual consolations that occlude incoherences and disjunctions in historical existence.[6] The second is Jacques Derrida's "Hauntology," an arch pun that not only deconstructs official ontology with its homonymic ghost, but also redefines the Romantic Ideology.[7] Derrida, that is, revises McGann's exposure of complacent fictions into a rival principle of endless slippages and evaporating stories, a history where the time is always already out of joint. Less universalizing than these paradigms, my focus is on apparitional presences in the finely grained textures of writing and their effects on reading—textures too often submerged, or even lost, when literary practice is regarded as a symptom of, or an arsenal against, historical ideologies. Although literature can tell us much about material power and general theories of meaning, its particular textures need to be uncoupled from both in order to discover what the nuances of literary actions might report. This is not to propose "art for art's sake," but to refine our views of both literary imagination and the larger issues to which it can be re-coupled. The surplus energies of literature, in imagination and in events of writing, won't be settled by paradigms of socio-cultural analysis. Nor need these energies be resigned, alternatively, to a deconstructive chain of endless representation.

Vibrating in relays of natural and supernatural, of figure and form, individual inspiration and institutional dictation, the presences that interest me are ones glanced in peripheries. Strange byways of writing, haunted recalls and recognitions, phantasms of a future, spectral pressures on shapes of composition: there are ghosts in these goings-on, too. Not assignable to a metaphysics of evanishment and absence, these work by "under-presence," a sensation for which Wordsworth had to coin this compound (*Prelude* 13.71). Sometimes the phantasmics condense into visible figuring; sometimes these press into thematizing, even theorizing; sometimes it's an effect that draws reading into the sedimented interstices of writing. My chapters report histories from figural shadowlands, social as well as personal. In relays of arrest and recognition, the reports can fall athwart narrative logic, as when Wordsworth's autobiography imprints uncanny self-naming in the accidents of words. Or reports can issue from recoils of intention, as when Hazlitt's fine-tuned poetics of allusion, steeped in literary history, send apparitional surplus into writing's unsuspecting present haunts. Phantoms can be summoned into historiography, as when Shelley's political imagination, casting what is yet unwritten, draws both visions of possibility and specters of impossibility. Shades can double the self, as Byron discovers when his production of ghosts across his career spawns ghost-Byrons, stalking his celebrity and claiming the new-branded housing of *Don Juan* as their epic haunt. Haunting is the grammar of both self and history when Yeats's modernist self-modeling, in disdain of immature "Keats," exposes semblances of Keatsian shades and scenes, with the twinned effect of undermining the modernist and mining a Keats of precursive modernism.

When Wordsworth pauses the verse of *The Prelude* to remark that "oftentimes do flit / Remembrances before me . . . / . . . long in their graves," the trace-line of memory is "phantoms passed / Of texture midway betwixt life and books" (3.608–9, 613–14). In a "passed" that is not past, what is this midway texture? It is writing's shades and shadows, the haunts of the present, lodged in books, with a potency of life.

II. Ghost Story, Ghost History, Ghost Historiography

In the genre of "Ghost Story" a ghost is the retail thrill, but the critical surcharge comes in the uncertainties: oscillations of readable agency and unsettled influence, of phenomenology and psychology, of restless repressions and ruling orders. The genre term may have been coined by Coleridge in 1819. Keats reports conversing with him on April 11 about a "ghost Story" (*K* 245). The genre (in plural) seems to have been in Byron's conceit of phantoms in 1819 as he drafted *Don Juan*. OED's first citation of the term is a canceled line about the narrator's fondness of "supper—punch—Ghost stories—and such chat."[8] He was in the process of exploiting the uncanny for canny sociability. Five years on, in 1824, he dangles "the story of a ghost" to introduce *Canto XVI*, host to the epic's most sustained, most hilarious, most crafty ghostwork. Its muse, Byron quips, is "beyond all contradiction / The most sincere that ever dealt in fiction" (2). From this proto-Wildean riff, he unveils a story of a ghost as the real deal:

> But of all truths which she has told, the most
>   True is that which she is about to tell.
> I said it was the story of a ghost—
>   What then? I only know it so befell.   (XVI.4)

A superlative *most*, rhymed to *ghost*, gives Byron a *meta-ghost* rhyme that draws the story out, on the very wording of the lure. All about to *tell*. Yet the testimony is hedged—"I only know it so befell"—and wrapped around an ambiguity: does *it* refer to a ghost, or to the story of a ghost?

Byron had at hand the public sensation in 1762, the Cock-Lane Ghost, said to haunt this little district in the shadow of London's bastion of belief, St. Paul's Cathedral. The Ghost was a telling as much as a haunting. The "story had become so popular" that in January 1763 sage, sober, judicious Dr. Johnson signed onto an investigative posse. Johnson (reports Boswell) held to "a distinction between what a man may experience by the mere strength of his imagination, and what imagination cannot possibly produce." It was an epistemological crux: "suppose [said Johnson] I should think I saw a form and heard a voice" speaking to matters already "so deeply impressed upon my mind, that I might *imagine* I thus saw and heard." The mind is already impressed, an imprinted template. In such a case, "I should not believe that an external communication had been made to me." Belief is beside the point. But proof is not: "if a form should appear, and a voice should tell me" what "should afterwards be unquestionably proved, I should . . . be persuaded that I had supernatural intelligence imparted to me" (*Life of Johnson*, ætat 54; 1:219). A ghost is at once the author and the subject of the conundrum, "if . . . a voice should tell me." Johnson was not "weakly credulous" (Boswell insists, against "misrepresentations" on this score); he "had a very philosophical mind and a rational respect for testimony" that could be "authentically proved" by sober investigation. "Being thus disposed, he was willing to inquire into the truth of any relation of supernatural agency a general belief of which has prevailed in all nations and ages" (220). Johnson cordoned off the Holy Ghost; but to save such faith, he would expose fraud. His "account of the detection of the imposture in *Cock-lane*" appeared in the very next issue of *Gentleman's Magazine* (February), accompanied by another "account of the rise of this imposture." In this public sphere of rational report, the Ghost-question would seem resolved: imposture, not truth.

Yet as a story, crux it was, in letter no less than in spirit: *willing to inquire* survives *unquestionably proved*. Fifteen years on, Johnson was still "Talking of ghosts":

> It is wonderful that five thousand years have now elapsed since the creation of the world, and still it is undecided whether or not there has ever been an instance of the spirit of any person appearing after death. All argument is against it, but all belief is for it. (ætat 69, 31 March 1778; *Life* 2:190)

That last sentence, no wonder, became famous. Such belief led Joanna Baillie in the 1790s (when *Life of Johnson* came out) to theorize the appeal of
ghost-effects. In her "Introductory Discourse" to *Plays [on] the stronger passions of the mind,* including passions that are hospitable to belief, she makes
this proposal in behalf of mediated vision, one degree removed:

> No man wishes to see the Ghost himself, which would certainly procure him
> the best information on the subject, but every man wishes to see one who be-
> lieves that he sees it, in all the agitation and wildness of that species of terror.
> (8–9)

Among those impressed by Baillie's skillfully mediated aesthetics of wild-
ness and agitation, her deft linking of incredulity to fascinating reports, was
Byron. His was so patently possessed by her dark arts that *Blackwood's* could
confect a ghost story of influence: "the dark shadows of his Lordship's imagination have received a deeper gloom from his early acquaintance with those
wild and midnight forests" in which the passion of demonic De Monfort
"consummated its dreadful purpose, and the dim aisles in which it met its
retribution" ("Celebrated Female Writers" 16:165). Her shadows of writing
fall on Byron's reading, imagination, and writing out.

In the fun of *Don Juan,* a more self-possessed Byron submits a slyly modest
amica curae on Johnson's double-minded skepticism and curiosity. If the poet
questions ghosts, he also questions the powers of reason to explain them away:

> I merely mean to say what Johnson said,
>   That in the course of some six thousand years
> All nations have believed that from the dead
>   A visitant at intervals appears.
> And what is strangest upon this strange head
>   Is that whatever bar the reason rears
> 'Gainst such belief, there's something stronger still
> In its behalf, let those deny who will.   (16,7)

In tune with Johnson's phrasings, Byron's stanza plays it both ways. Belief is
first slotted as a historical curiosity, an oddly durable tradition (Byron ups it
1,000 years). Then history, strangest and stronger, advances a brief on *behalf*
of *belief,* these half-chimed words half-underwriting the case: denial is only
willful and insufficient. It's a deft preview to Byron's impending story—or
its ghost.

Ann Radcliffe's talent was relaying a heroine's dreadful reading into
dynamics for her own readers. Early in *The Mysteries of Udolpho* (1794),

Emily St. Aubert glances apprehensively at papers of import to her father's occluded past, but forbidden by him to read. Radcliffe leverages the lure of the writing before Emily into the phenomenology of our reading the print before us:

> her eyes involuntarily settled on the writing of some loose sheets, which lay open; and she was unconscious, that she was transgressing her father's strict injunction, till a sentence of dreadful import awakened her attention and her memory together. She hastily put the papers from her; but the words, which had aroused equally her curiosity and terror, she could not dismiss from her thoughts. So powerfully had they affected her, that she even could not resolve to destroy the papers immediately; and the more she dwelt on the circumstance, the more it inflamed her imagination. Urged by the most forcible, and apparently the most necessary, curiosity to enquire farther, concerning the terrible and mysterious subject, to which she had seen an allusion, she began to lament her promise to destroy the papers. (*Mysteries* I.XI; 1:275–76)

Under this spectral "allusion," aroused words uncannily echo the word *father* into her urge to enquire *farther*. The father haunts not as a ghost from the past but as sentences on the present page. In this fateful siege of contraries—curiosity and terror, transgression and obedience—Emily puts the papers to the flames. But her imagination, and ours, stay *inflamed*. In the eventfulness of Radcliffe's syntax, distinctions—of past and present, unconscious and conscious attention, papers and imagination, objective subject and subjective mystery—are blurred, condensed, phantomized.[9] Words, for her and for us, haunt, awaken and arouse. "Curiosity to inquire": this is Dr. Johnson in Gothic drag.

In a parody of this siege in *Northanger Abbey* (begun in the late 1790s), Jane Austen foregrounds these Udolphics—but not without intervals of affective intensity that escape sheer parodying. In the love plot, heroine Catherine Morland, stoked on *The Mysteries of Udolpho*, is thrilled at her invitation to Northanger Abbey from General Tilney (who is quietly engineering a match with his son Henry). En route, Henry flirts with Catherine by teasing her about this gothic theme park of her dreams, promising her, in an exuberance of vivid ghost-storying, a violent storm no later than the third night:

> Peals of thunder so loud as to seem to shake the edifice to its foundation will roll round the neighbouring mountains—and during the frightful gusts of

wind which accompany it, you will probably think you discern (for your lamp is not extinguished) one part of the hanging more violently agitated than the rest. Unable of course to repress your curiosity in so favourable a moment for indulging it, you will instantly arise, and throwing your dressing-gown around you, proceed to examine this mystery. (II.5, 237)

Spinning a Radcliffean web around Catherine, Henry fans her credulity for his morning-after amusement. When a storm comes on her very first night, Catherine is amply primed, ready to roll:

she crossed the hall, listened to the tempest with sensations of awe; and, when she heard it rage round a corner of the ancient building and close with sudden fury a distant door, felt for the first time that she was really in an Abbey.—Yes, these were characteristic sounds;—they brought to her recollection a countless variety of dreadful situations and horrid scenes, which such buildings had witnessed, and such storms ushered in; and most heartily did she rejoice in the happier circumstances attending her entrance within walls so solemn. (II.6, 244)

Marking "such buildings . . . such storms" and "characteristic sounds" in able "recollection" of "dreadful situations and horrid scenes" of her reading, Catherine enters the arena of Henry's arch craftwork. What possesses her is not a ghost but ghost stories. It would have been easy enough for Austen to give the rule to parody, cued by Henry's campy preview, and in tune with this merry letter in the *Monthly Magazine* of August 1797, headed *Terrorist System of Novel-Writing*:

There is a great deal in the wind. Indeed, it is one of the principal objects of terror, for it may be taken for almost any terrific object, from a banditti of cut-throats to a single ghost. The tapestry, therefore, must give signs of moving, so as to make the heroine believe, there is something behind it, although, not being *at that time* very desirous to examine, she concludes, very naturally and logically, that it can be nothing but the wind. (103)

This is the well-shopped inventory. The smart send-up of the wind that must have a great deal to signify, and all the system's mechanics, favor the "nothing but" of natural and logical sense for the sensible reader. Yet because parody trades in the medium of its object, it can't avoid attesting to "the power of the thing mocked," comments George Levine; effects may be "parodied but not dismissed" (337, 350).

Skillfully working this kind of doubleness, Austen shifts and sifts Catherine's literacy in the system into real-time remarking, writing a ghost-story as a story of ghostly sensations not reducible to delusion but also not certifiable communication of the supernatural. R. W. Buss grasped this in staging a scene of Catherine reading, arrested in these Udolphics.[10] Even though she has shut her book in apprehension, its pages play out in spectral form, in the rectangles of other books, of doorframe, bedframe, vanity table, walls, window-panes—and not least, a mirror tilted to reflect candlelight on the page and catching an image in Catherine's (but not our) sightline. What you don't see is what you get. Julian Wolfreys reads in scenes like this the dynamics of Gothic rapture: the immersed reader starts to "believe" in a text's figurings, forgetting their status as "apparitions . . . belonging to the phantasmatic dimension of fabulation" (xiii). I suggest that this is an extreme of the potent phantasmics of reading per se: the way words impress and imprint imagination, on the page, and then on textualized space. Apparitions haunt not from the past but in the presence of words.

With Radcliffean skill, Austen opens the indirect discourse of Catherine's apprehension to the reader's participation. As Catherine "looked around the room," informed reading ("Yes, these were characteristic sounds") shimmers into immediate sensations from Austen's pages. The sentences pace out with affective mimesis:

> The window curtains seemed in motion. It could be nothing but the violence of the wind penetrating through the divisions of the shutters; and she stept boldly forward, carelessly humming a tune, to assure herself of its being so, peeped courageously behind each curtain, saw nothing on either low window seat to scare her, and on placing a hand against the shutter, felt the strongest conviction of the wind's force. (II.6; p. 245)

Pressed by a *wind* that at once naturalizes inspiration (*spiritus: wind*) and evokes a supernatural spirit, the *wind*ow curtains stir as Udolphic-curiosity materialized. The blueprint of parody dissolves into phenomenology. "It could be" resonates for Austen's heroine and reader alike in a free indirect style—of which this passage is a fine example—so well tuned that defenses come to seem what's really phantasmic. The coolly tested *nothing but* is vexed by the hot pulse of a self-fortifying bravado, humming against the wind, while *carelessly* is carefully tuned to twin *courageously*: not mindlessly, but affecting a pose. In this theater of words, Austen can leave subtly ambiguous what "felt the strongest conviction" might register: a mind deducing

"Catharine [*sic*] Morland," wood engraving by R. W. Buss. In Reverend Ebenezer Cobham Brewer, *Character Sketches of Romance, Fiction and the Drama, A Revised American Edition of the Reader's Handbook* (New York: Elmer Hess, 1892), vol. 5, opposite p. 66.

only the wind; a body feeling in contact with a strange agency on the other side of the shutter, pressing its physical surplus back into her body by a surplus of wording, a *shudder* of strongest conviction about the *shutter's* signifying. To Robert Miles, this is a novelist haplessly divided: her "inclusive, self-aware, rationally given, ironic consciousness . . . is unable completely to stifle the Gothic's dissonances, which ripple the surface of her text" (133). But instead of this diagnosis of surface symptoms (yes, those were ripples), we might admire able Austen's canny language, might credit her skill in auditing the alogical, apparitional undertone of seeming parody, and giving it a hearing.

Wordsworth—who opened *The Prelude* with an epic muse in the wind, "Oh there is blessing in this gentle breeze" (1.1)—can parody his master-trope in this double register. A few books into it, after recounting a college-era epiphany of spiritual self-consecration, he wends his story into a twilight woods, rippled by a wind that feels supernaturally intent, then he tips a jest:

> The mountain heights were slowly overspread
> With darkness, and before a rippling breeze
> The long lake lengthened out its hoary line,
> And in the sheltered coppice where I sate,
> Around me, from among the hazel leaves——
> Now here, now there, stirred by the straggling wind——
> Came intermittingly a breath-like sound,
> A respiration short and quick, which oft,
> Yea, might I say, again and yet again,
> Mistaking for the panting of my dog,
> The off-and-on companion of my walk,
> I turned my head to look if he were there.   (4.169–80)

Those long dashes are scriptive dramatics. "Now here, now there" eerily taps into *Hic et ubique*, the cellar rumbling of *Hamlet*'s ghost (1.5); but these locators also map the mundane "panting of my dog." Is it inspiration, ghost-gust, or everyday doggy life? Wordsworth presents a decentered webwork rather than an elusive, but potentially discoverable spirit. The grammar of "I turned . . . to look if" oscillates with its own straggling sense between rational testing and conjectural *as if*. Hedging on "breath-like," Wordsworth writes spectral history not against ordinary real time, but in it, where "again and yet again" is both recollected sensation and the poet's present saying— which includes "mistaking."

This is the spectral ledger of *The Prelude* at large. In early fragments, then in *Book First*, Wordsworth gets compositional traction as he reanimates, in real-time syntax, the breath of ghostliness in episodes of boyhood theft.[11] In one lark, stealing birds from others' traps, the boy (or boy-minded narrator) first camps it up as a Gothic parody: "I was a fell destroyer" (327); "when the deed was done" (328). But in a turn of a line, the campy "I" becomes a startled "me," surprised into an eerie auditorium, in rebuke of his jokey theatrics:

> I heard among the solitary hills
> Low breathings coming after me, and sounds

Of undistinguishable motion, steps
Almost as silent as the turf they trod.   (1.329–32)

The forward momentum of this report halts to suspend *sounds* at the line's end, a placement that gives a presence to its sense, just before—in a pretty amazing feat of iambic pentameter—the poetry's own steps pace out, pant out *undistinguishable*. The godfather of this sensation is Milton's Death, that spectral "shape . . . that shape had none / Distinguishable" (*PL* 2.667–68). Milton shifts the line from *shape* to *none,* then, across the enjambment, into a queasy phantasmagoria of *none Distinguishable.* Wordsworth rhymes this phrase into one spectacular six-syllable word, *undistinguishable,* and draws its sense into the sensation, in the very sound of "mo*tion, steps* / Almo*st silent . . . turf . . . trod.*"

Such effects could have come straight out of Gothic Central Casting. But it's a chapter of natural life in the every-night boyhood of William Wordsworth, and in the nature of the autobiographer that he would become. The next verse paragraph in this run of recollection expands a virtual grammar of undistinguishable motion, past and present at once. The event is a plundering, now in daylight, of birds' nests—habitually, it seems, for the spectral thrill of almost floating in a phantom of conceit:

Oh, when I have hung
Above the raven's nest, by knots of grass
And half-inch fissures in the slippery rock
But ill sustained, and almost, as it seemed,
Suspended by the blast which blew amain,
Shouldering the naked crag, oh, at that time
While on the perilous ridge I hung alone,
With what strange utterance did the loud dry wind
Blow through my ears; the sky seemed not a sky
Of earth, and with what motion moved the clouds!   (1.341–50)

The phrase *I have hung* is not only for the past but also for present poetics, hung at the line-end to unfurl one long cadence of ghostly utterances and sensational spectral optics: line by line, clause by clause, in gasps of *oh,* with the paced stresses and pregnant pause of "loud dry wind" (*wind* is a hypermetrical syllable in an already over-stressed line)—and not least, the phantom temporality of that present perfect progressive, *I have hung,* as if the poet were still in the habit.[12] The syntax repeated in "With what . . . with what" is no less phantasmic, seeming to shade an exclamation point with a ghost-question. That Wordsworth's first drafts made no decision about a terminal punctuation spells a haunted uncertainty of mode.[13] Memory in real time is writing's presence, in all its suspense and apprehension.

This poetry's presencing becomes a narrative propulsion with the turn of verse to a boy's boat-boosting. As the little thief, thrilled and apprehensive, rows out from the shore, this apparently happened:

> When from behind that craggy steep, till then
> The bound of the horizon, a huge cliff,
> As if with voluntary power instinct,
> Upreared its head.   (1.405–8)

On the synchrony of the rhymed *When/then,* a rational mind (the adult poet's, ours) can do the math: as the line of rowing lengthens into the lake, the right-triangle hypotenuse shifts, and forms not visible on the foreshortened shorescape now rise on a vertical axis into the boy's sightline.[14] Yet such counter-phantasmic logic scarcely registers. (I often have to diagram it for students.) Even as the mode of *As if* signals the poet's better knowing, its syntax hews to the boy's illusion. Following "Upreared its head" (408), the poetry propels this phenomenology:

> I struck, and struck again,
> And, growing still in stature, the huge cliff
> Rose up, between me and the stars, and still
> With measured motion, like a living thing
> Strode after me.   (1.408–12)

"With measured motion" is a proto-poetic signature. In this syntax, the remorseless irony of Wordsworth's repeated *still* is that it does not mean *not-moving;* it's the sheer opposite, *not to be arrested.* It's a lost cause by now to recall the rational geometry of these terror-optics. Hung at the line-end, *still* is suspense itself. The self-wrought spectacle is a counter-reality that haunts, informs, and radically transforms the world:

> and after I had seen
> That spectacle, for many days my brain
> Worked with a dim and undetermined sense
> Of unknown modes of being. In my thoughts
> There was a darkness—call it solitude

Or blank desertion—no familiar shapes
Of hourly objects, images of trees,
Of sea or sky, no colours of green fields,
But huge and mighty forms that do not live
Like living men moved slowly through my mind
By day, and were the trouble of my dreams.   (1.417–27)

Mind and brain: haunted psychology has a physiology.[15] A "change took place in my dreams; a theatre seemed suddenly opened and lighted up within my brain, which presented nightly spectacles of more than earthly splendour," De Quincey writes of his opium dreams, ones all the more haunting for being composed from the field of waking probability: "whatsoever things capable of being visually represented I did but think of in the darkness, immediately shaped themselves into phantoms of the eye" (*Confessions* II, p. 372).

In such brain-theater, what is the cue of Wordsworth's rhetorical pause at "call it" (1.421)? It is not just a reach for words but a call to the shapes of these present words. Writing of "forms that do not live / Like living men" (435–36), Wordsworth declines the past tense "did not live." These forms "do not live" only until the end of the line. Then at the turn, they do live, but like specters. Call it apparitional poetics. It's a ghost story with a vengeance.

III. Ghost-Reading

In 1773, Anna Aikin (later Barbauld) was meditating "On the Pleasure Derived from Objects of Terror":

> A strange and unexpected event awakens the mind, and keeps it on the stretch; and where the agency of invisible beings is introduced, "of forms unseen, and mightier far than we," our imagination, darting forth, explores. (125–26)

As her sounding of Pope's *Essay on Criticism* may tell, she allows even a supernatural seduction by Superstition.[16] Writing on *Udolpho* in 1794 for *Critical Review*, Coleridge (soon to be Wordsworth's collaborator in supernatural poetics) was smitten by phantom-effects that were not just presented, but gripped the reader into participation:

> mysterious terrors are continually exciting in the mind the idea of a supernatural appearance, keeping us, as it were, upon the very edge and confines of the world of spirits, and yet are ingeniously explained by familiar causes; curiosity is kept upon the stretch from page to page, and from volume to

volume, and the secret, which the reader thinks himself every instant on the point of penetrating, flies like a phantom before him, and eludes his eagerness till the very last moment of protracted expectation. (361)

That stretch again. Describing the technique, Coleridge's extravagantly protracted sentence is itself a drama. It scarcely matters that Dr. Johnson's *Dictionary* defines *ingeniously* as "wittily," "subtly," with a shade of artful contrivance. As Coleridge's present tenses suggest, Radcliffe's "art of escaping the guesses of the reader" (361) is an escape artistry that ingeniously phantomizes the reader. The simile for reading's pursuit, "flies like a phantom before," gives the stretch of curiosity both in the tale and on the page.

By 1816, Coleridge will worry about, and theorize, the paucity of language as no more than a "phantom proxy" of a notion, weaker than sensate impressions by "apparitions of matter." His reading of Radcliffe testifies to an immediacy of effect from the material page, a poetic faith that, far from being "buried in the dead letter," is vivid imagination.[17] Radcliffe's *Udolpho* had no need to import the supernatural or its ally, embodied superstition. Her sentences induced readers by their natural gradations into an apparitional interiority. She achieved this by capitalizing on common reading practices: sometimes social, but often alone (as Buss's image shows), when half-lit shadows can seem to rise from the words on the page.

This effect is what Coleridge admired, an artistry infiltrated by conditions of nature and probability:

> Without introducing into her narrative any thing really supernatural . . . the reader experiences in perfection the strange luxury of artificial terror, without being obliged for a moment to hoodwink his reason, or to yield to the weakness of superstitious credulity. . . . within the limits of nature and probability, [her art is] well contrived to hold curiosity in pleasing suspense, and at the same time to agitate the soul with strong emotions of sympathetic terror. (*Monthly Review* 15:280)

The possession by verbal power gives a probable sensation, argues Margaret Russett, that is "no less compelling for being repeatedly unveiled" (159–60).[18] Curiosity in the arena of reason, the luxury of terror agitated into sympathetic terror: it is not improbable that Coleridge's famous aesthetic contract, a "willing suspension of disbelief," grew out of his attention to the popular press of "suspence." In the year that *Northanger Abbey* was published (1817), he reported a conversation with Wordsworth in 1797–98 (when Austen started writing the novel) that theorized this effect. In the plan for *Lyrical Ballads*, Coleridge would conjure "incidents and agents . . . in part at least, supernatural" in order to convey "a human interest and a semblance of truth sufficient to procure for these shadows of imagination that willing suspension of disbelief for the moment, which constitutes poetic faith" (*BL* chapter 14; 2:1–2).

In such faith, Coleridge objected to the either/or regime of Enlightenment philosophy, its exile of shadows and apparitions to the land of untrue:

> If to destroy the reality of all, that we actually behold, be idealism, what can be more egregiously so, than the system of modern metaphysics, which banishes us to a land of shadows, surrounds us with apparitions, and distinguishes truth from illusion only by the majority of those who dream the same dream? "*I* asserted that the world was mad," exclaimed poor Lee, "and the world said, that I was mad, and confound them, they outvoted me." (*BL* chapter 12, 1:262)[19]

The legislation of truth and illusion by majority rule is an egregious fiction to Coleridge (and surely an insult to Byron's muse of sincere fiction). Coleridge's related theory is "willing illusion," which (elsewhere) he takes pains to desynonimize both from the poles of "delusion" and the Dr. Johnson–rationalism of being undeluded.[20]

The medial mode of aesthetic illusion, especially for the mind's shades and shadows, coincides with the "uncanny movement from mental image to spectral reality" that Terry Castle discusses as the incomplete project of Enlightenment rationalism—incomplete, because it did not so much dispel the apparitional as psychologize it.[21] How far a "spectral reality" reaches for the nineteenth century is reflected in the way writers read dislocations in the historical world at large. Derrida's *Specters of Marx*, describing tremors in a global historiography of unresolved ruptures and ineluctable repetitions, takes its cue from the opening of Karl Marx's *Communist Manifesto*: "A spectre is haunting Europe—the Spectre of Communism" (1), an epic invocation to the ghost-story within official history. Mindful of gothic novels and gothic theater, Burke troped the French Revolution of 1789 as an infernal specter. Shelley replied with glorious phantoms of a future day. Phantoms and specters emerged as shaping spirits in the literary, political, social, and historical world. Audiences and readers were disturbed into a broad, volatile spectacle of modern life itself. "The theatre becomes most profoundly unsettling at the uncanny moment when the imagination finds its own shapings realized—represented back to it in satisfaction of hitherto unconscious desires." So Mary Jacobus writes of Wordsworth's haunting by Macbeth's regicide during the proto-regicidal violence in Paris in 1791 ("That Great Stage" 355).

Jacobus's focus is that hallucinatory dagger, *avant le meutre*, hovering between a "vision, sensible / To feeling" and a "dagger of the mind, a false creation" (*Macbeth* 2.1.36–39). Macbeth is possessed by a phantom of a *fait accompli*, as if a nebulous possibility were already a certain fate. No wonder that Wordsworth, reading *Macbeth* at night in his room in Paris in 1792 as the Revolution was going to hell, feels "substantial dread /. . . conjured from tragic fictions" (*Prelude* 10.66–67). Ghosts return via reading and precipitate into Macbeth's words just after the regicide of 1793 that is on Wordsworth's mind as he writes about Paris in 1804:

> With unextinguished taper I kept watch,
> Reading at intervals.
>
> . . . .
>
> And in such way I wrought upon myself,
> Until I seem'd to hear a voice that cried
> To the whole city, 'Sleep no more!'   (10.61–62, 75–77)

It's not just that Wordsworth speaks as haunted Macbeth (2.2), feeling complicit in regicide. It's also that this voice still possesses him as he writes *Book Tenth* in 1804: *I wrought* is literal, its sound and root wound with *wrote*. With "the phantom ear of memory" (the phrase is Hartman's), this poet knows what the young man of 1792 fears: Louis XVI's fate at the guillotine.[22] Shakespeare's ghost-work supplies the haunt of Romantic modernity. "I awoke in struggles, and cried aloud—'I will sleep no more!'" is De Quincey's reckoning with opium hell (*Confessions* II. 378). "The world looks often quite spectral to me," Carlyle confessed when he was writing his *French Revolution*, gripped by a sensation that the "babble, babble" of modern London life was veering into a De Quinceyan pageant of darkness.[23]

Austen localizes the spectral world in a modernized Northanger Abbey. As with so many estate names, this one is scarred by historical trauma. Abbeys laid to ruin or appropriated for the Protestant ascendancy during the Reformation were not secured (it was said) from ghosts of the dispossessed. Byron exploited this lore for theatrical revels at Newstead Abbey, his ances-

19

tral haunt, and for artistry of all kinds at Norman Abbey, his setting for that "story of a ghost" (1823). Austen's *Northanger Abbey* harbors gothic shades not from the historical past, but from the gothic everyday, especially in patriarchal shades. Catherine Morland's projection of a Gothic novel onto General Tilney's manner errs only in its superstructure (the dead wife was neither prisoned nor poisoned). She is right on base: the gentleman is not gentle. He is a common specter in the polite veneer of modern life, its veiled master trope. Haunting about the shape of *Northanger Abbey* is the backstory of his marriage-hunting rich heiress Miss Drummond, who seems to have endured (by Henry's awkward admission, no less) something less than wedded bliss.

In the destiny of Austen's marriage plot, the next Mrs. Tilney is Miss Morland. Is the ghost of the first an uncanny, ominous double? While Henry seems the genial antitype of his avaricious father, there are affiliations in the social system in which both exercise power. Henry dangles Gothic bait to tease Catherine, and when she takes it into speculative overdrive, he flexes his discipline in the armature of patriarchy, in a full-throttle bust (II:9):

> If I understand you rightly, you had formed a surmise of such horror as I have hardly words to—Dear Miss Morland, consider the dreadful nature of the suspicions you have entertained. What have you been judging from? Remember the country and the age in which we live. Remember that we are English, that we are Christians. Consult your own understanding, your own sense of the probable, your own observation of what is passing around you . . . (II:9; p. 274)

Henry cites only the superstructure, not accounting for a plausible basis in the social norm. But in Austen's social-text, his "probable" is so inwrought with what's "dreadful" that Miss Morland's suspicions, however mortified, are arguably credited by the real nightmare of what is passing around her: men hunting in the marriage market, specters of national unrest, and the complacency of a father appointed clergyman, in whose Christian England violence, as state policy, is the spirit of the age in which they live.[24] If Miss Morland's *Udolpho*-cast suspicions are errors of apparition, they are also, by Austen's lights, canny apprehensions.[25]

How canny comes to proof four chapters on. The harbinger is a strange disturbance at the Abbey, a "perturbation of surprise," then a long silence, then "the noise of something moving close to the door" of Catherine's bedchamber that "made her start":

it seemed as if some one was touching the very doorway—and in another moment a slight motion of the lock proved that some hand must be on it. She
trembled a little at the idea of any one's approaching so cautiously. (II:13; p. 300)

The Gothic index is legible, but chastened Catherine is a more sober, rational
respondent to "it seemed" and "as if." Disciplining a tremble, she opens the
door, to discover "only Eleanor," her dear friend and Henry's sister. Yet if her
own trembles are allayed, not so for "only Eleanor": more than trembling, she
is "pale, and her manner greatly agitated" (300), as if a specter sprung from
pages of horror. She has been sent to report the General's mandate that Catherine leave early the next morning, with no provision for safety or comfort.
When Eleanor cries in despair, "My real power is nothing" (302), Catherine
realizes Gothic Northanger after all. Soon to be "driven from the door" of
her host, she endures a night of "disturbed imagination," torments, "agitated
spirits and unquiet slumbers" (307, 305). These spirits are no issue from
ghost-lore, and the disturbance is no fanciful supposition but news "mourn-
fully superior in reality and substance" (305):

> Her anxiety had foundation in fact, her fears in probability; and with a mind
> so occupied in the contemplation of actual and natural evil, the solitude of her
> situation, the darkness of her chamber, the antiquity of the building were felt
> and considered without the smallest emotion; and though the wind was high,
> and often produced strange and sudden noises throughout the house, she
> heard it all as she lay awake, hour after hour, without curiosity or terror. (305)

In these dark lights, Mr. Tilney loses status as the probabilist critic of Catherine's fancies and is exposed as the complacent fancier of his own social
narrative. It is Catherine who registers fact, probability, the actual, for which
any fictional thrills are sheer supererogation.

If Austen proves the gothic register of female social existence, Keats
proved this on the pulses of life at large. Like Austen, he could spoof gothic
tropes, gleefully flaunting the "fine mother Radcliff names" he coined for
The Eve of St. Agnes (K 238)—even do this side by side with a gothic, ghost-
haunted marriage plot in *Isabella; of the Pot of Basil*, with such a sharply
delineated economic base that George Bernard Shaw saw shades of Marx.
Both these "romances" were published in 1820, just a few years after
Northanger Abbey.[26] Keats was always reading dark shadows, even in worlds
of light, nowhere more incisively than in *Tintern Abbey*. While this is not an
"Abbey" poem (Wordsworth is *"a few miles above Tintern Abbey . . . on the*

banks of the Wye"), it is a haunted poem. Keats marks the tracks in a letter from a spring morning (May 3, 1818) to a friend and fellow poet J. H. Reynolds. He is pressed by his brother's horrid suffering from tuberculosis (he would die by the end of the year): "after a Night without a Wink of sleep, and over-burdened with fever," Tom has managed "a refreshing day sleep" (*K* 127). Conscious of Wordsworth's memory of relief from the "fever of the world" in *Tintern Abbey* (54), Keats quotes its poetry a few sentences on when he explains why he has kept his medical books after forgoing the career: "an extensive knowledge is needful to thinking people—it takes away the heat and fever; and helps, by widening speculation, to ease the Burden of the Mystery"—including Tom's night "overburdened with fever" (*K* 127). He is alluding to Wordsworth's cherishing of those blessed moods

> In which the burthen of the mystery,
> In which the heavy and the weary weight
> Of all this unintelligible world
> Is lighten'd.   (39–42)

For Wordsworth this relief, such as it is, comes from memory's book of life:

> Though absent long,
> These forms of beauty have not been to me,
> As is a landscape to a blind man's eye.   (23–25)

This is how "our own best images come back to us: like words on the page, prompts that summon not the absent or lost but . . . a pure potential in the now," so Garrett Stewart reads this revisiting (*Deed* 58). Yet this poetry's "in the now" is simultaneously a temporality of *again*—again and again (2, 4, 9, 15), all set against an absence that feels just as present as "now." After "five long years" (1), *absent long* is describing both *these forms* and *me*.

When revenant status can be granted both to the world and to conscious-ness, perception becomes phantomized. It is in a weirdly spectral light of revival that the first event of the word *now* in *Tintern Abbey* plays:

> And now, with gleams of half-extinguish'd thought,
> With many recognitions dim and faint,
> And somewhat of a sad perplexity,
> The picture of the mind revives again.   (59–62)

As a surgeon's assistant before anesthesia, let alone modern cures, and as a boy who had suffered the death of both parents, with a beloved brother's life failing as he wrote this letter, Keats could appreciate intervals of relief from world-weights and weariness. This is what *Tintern Abbey* registers in lines 39–41 (above), in prepositional extensions of the world, 15 weighted syllables, before the predicate, "Is lighten'd" (42). For Keats, the force of this poetry is the sensation of lightening as antithesis, within antithesis. And so "it is impossible to know how far knowledge will console us for the death of a friend and the ill 'that flesh is heir to,' " he sighs to Reynolds (*K* 128), as Wordsworth's verse will soon sigh of "the fretful stir / Unprofitable, and the fever of the world" (53–54). For both poets, Hamlet's alienation (3.1.63) is not just re-heard; it is rehearsed from a ghost in the mind into present sensation.

Keats's letter returns to the phrase "the burthen of the mystery," now shorn of the predicate in Wordsworth's syntax, "is lighten'd." Retuning this syntax for a "world . . . full of Misery and heartbreak, pain, Sickness and op-pression," Keats marks this as poetic knowledge, which he feels as the true "burthen" of Wordsworth's lines (*K* 130) and for which ease of speculation is no certainty:

> We are in a Mist. We are now in that state — We feel the "burden of the Mys-tery," To this Point was Wordsworth come, as far as I can conceive when he wrote "Tintern Abbey" and it seems to me that his Genius is explorative of those dark Passages . . . he can . . . shed a light in them. (*K* 130)

Wordsworth's "light" entails "dark Passages." Keats was possessed by the phrase "burden of the Mystery."[27] Two years on, in *The Fall of Hyperion,* he renders an intense dream-witnessing of epochal misery and "all its bur-thens." Its poet-dreamer ever "More gaunt and ghostly" (1.389–96), the bur-then of the mystery becomes psychological ghost-genetics, poor Tom's.

In his letter to Reynolds, Keats cites Wordsworth's calling his mind as "My haunt, and main region of my song" (*Excursion* xii; *K* 129). It is a region of ghosts, late and soon: a discharged soldier of "uncouth shape . . . ghastly in the moonlight" (*Prelude* 4.402–11)—*ghastly*: "like a ghost" (Johnson, *Dic-tionary* 898); a spectral blind beggar wearing his story in brief on a placard (*Prelude* 7); a reading-haunted dream of a book-crazed Arab, and a Boy of Winander spirited into death before age ten, his grave a frequent haunt for the poet (both in *Prelude* 5); "presences in Nature . . . through many a year / Haunting . . . my boyish sports" (*Prelude* 1.494–95) and later drawing him to "listening to sounds that are / The ghostly language of the ancient earth" (2.328–29), the line cut holding the present time of writing (*sounds that are*) in the echosphere. This is a poet's mind ever "haunted by itself"

(6.180). A mundane old Leech-gatherer is both "in my mind's eye," and in Wordsworth's reading, as a ghost of Hamlet's haunting (*Resolution and Independence* 136; *Hamlet* 1.2). As early as 1802, Wordsworth felt his vocation as self-haunted: "conjuring up in himself passions" for the writing (Preface to *Lyrical Ballads* xxviii). If his poetic devotion is emotion recollected in tranquility, his recurring sensation is that memory itself is haunted. A creature of "thoughts and things/In the self-haunting spirit" is how he named himself as late as the 1850 *Prelude* (14.283–84). Traced through time and history, this is phantasmic Romanticism, epic scale.

IV. Shades of Hamlet

"He is a momentary visualization of the unseen forces which dominate the action and is a clear command from Shakespeare that the men of the theatre shall rouse their imagination and let their reasonable logic slumber," writes Edward Gordon Craig about the ghost in *Hamlet* (266). For all his theoretical savvy on our contract of a willing suspension of disbelief, Coleridge wrote an escape clause for "the case of the King in *Hamlet*," which, in its sublime, apparently embodied presence, one could feel "purporting instant danger to ourselves." "The fact really is," he adds with absolute aplomb, "as to apparitions, that the terror produces the image instead of the contrary; for *in omnem actum perceptionis influit imaginatio*" (Lecture XII, 204).[28] "The fact" is rendered in scholarly Latin (standard for conjuring ghosts) with the affect of absolute authority.

Marjorie Garber's *Shakespeare's Ghost Writers: Literature as Uncanny Causality* reads ghosts (Shakespeare's especially, especially *Hamlet*'s) as deconstruction-theory embodied, and in action: absence as presence, past as present.[29] Derrida's *Specters of Marx*, it is fair to say, counts as a sequel to Hamlet: "the time is out of joint" is his epigraph (xxi); "everything begins by the apparition of a specter," so he sums the muse—for Hamlet, for Marx's *Manifesto*, and into *Specters*. With a long first chapter that makes a refrain of the epigraph (1–60), Derrida might be nominated as the latest case of Romantic addiction to Hamlet: iconic consciousness of alienation from present time and history, possessed by a ghost with a plan for repair. In *Hamlet*, the Ghost is a tellingly communal spectacle before its aim at a private interview. Though named as one character, it refracts into multiple shades. To the anxious rampart guards, it portends war. To scholar Horatio— whose very name, in a time out of joint, means *timekeeper*—it is an insult to philosophy; *Horatio* is also burdened by the words *ratio: reason* and *oratio:*

speech. To Hamlet, the Ghost is all this and more, echoing his misgivings about a regime-change and his mother's realigned affections.

Legend has it that Shakespeare acted the Ghost, authorizing this specter of imagination. The Ghost comes as a call to language, first to Horatio and the guards—"Thou art a scholar, speak to it, Horatio . . . mark it, Horatio . . . Question it, Horatio (1.1.52–55)[30]—then comes the next night to Hamlet alone, a prompt in the shape of language:

> *Enter Ghost.*
> Thou com'st in such a questionable shape
> That I will speak to thee.   (1.4.43–44)

Sensing an open franchise, Radcliffe conjures Hamlet's Ghost into *The Mysteries of Udolpho* as she winds towards its serial revelations. This is her epigraph for IV.VII (p. 150):

> "Be thou a spirit of health, or goblin damn'd,
> Bring with thee airs from heaven, or blasts from hell,
> Be thy intents wicked or charitable,
>
> ———
>
> ———I will speak to thee."———————
>
>   HAMLET.

By eliding the stage direction and Shakespeare's text, "Thou comest in such a questionable shape / That . . . ," Radcliffe's paring sets open Hamlet's anxiety for her heroine and all readers. At the same time, her blanked lines are haunted by what they efface, the questionable shape that disturbs Hamlet into speech.[31]

Filling in the lines behind Radcliffe's blanks, Wordsworth's *Ode: Intimations of Immortality* ponders the "Blank misgivings" that beset a boyhood of "Moving about in worlds not realised" (IX). Hamlet's ghost-startled words echo in this boy's bent to "those obstinate questionings" (*those* are familiars) of "sense and outward things": it is the pull of "shadowy recollections" to affiliation elsewhere. The "Freudian uncanny is a sort of phantom," Castle proposes; it arises from repression in spectral formation (*Female Thermometer* 7). Wordsworth figured this out before Freud, and perhaps recalled, as Freud surely did, that what follows "I will speak to thee" is "I'll call thee Hamlet"— his father's name, and his own. It is identity in the shape of a ghost.

In *The Prelude*, Wordsworth substantiates Hamlet's confrontation in a ghostly formation that emerges out of a landscape, as if a dreamlike spectral portent. This is a haunting memory of himself as a schoolboy, waiting impatiently for his father's horses to take him home for the holidays. Keeping watch on two likely roadways from a ridge above, he sees "the mist / Which on the line of each of those two roads / Advanced in such indisputable shapes" (*1799* I.365–67). The syntax is strangely fraught, with a specifying "such" that has no consequence. A brief annotation by Ernest de Selincourt (615) suggests a conjuring with the ghost of Hamlet's father, that "questionable shape"—but with a difference. Where Hamlet's "questionable" indexes both uncertainty and provocation, Wordsworth's "indisputable" distills Hamlet's ghost into the antonym, unquestionable. The line of knowing bends back to the "early childhood" Wordsworth casts for the Boy of the *Intimations* Ode, whose spectral imagination symptomizes a metaphysical disturbance. He trembles in the material world "like a guilty Thing surprised," because he senses that his allegiance is radically beyond this world— in effect, with Hamlet's ghost, who at the break of daylight "started like a guilty thing / Upon a fearful summons" (1.1.163–64). Within material being abides a spectral identity, anchored elsewhere.

Radcliffe summons Hamlet's ghost less as a spectral shape than as a potent voice. An early chapter in *Udolpho* (I.II; p. 79) has the epigraph "I could a tale unfold, whose lightest word / Would harrow up thy soul" (*Hamlet* 1.5). Citing just "Shakespeare," Radcliffe conjures the ghost's narrative promise for her own. And not for the first time; it's a revenant from the title page of her first success, *A Sicilian Romance* (1790), where, untagged, it advertises a capital genre. "I could a Tale unfold": *unfold* not only as narrative but also with the material pages of the book at hand. The ghost's voice supplies Radcliffe with her authorial motto, her genre and its genetic lineage and, not least, her call to her reader. Epigraph and allusion come in a tight complementarity of revenance, the epigraph the more fully embodied apparition, the allusion more spectral and intuitive. Commenting in 1818 on Radcliffe, master-allusionist Hazlitt goes for this ghost, too: "in harrowing up the soul with imaginary horrors, and making the flesh creep, and the nerves thrill, with fond hopes and fears, she is unrivalled."[32] Unrivalled indeed: Hamlet's ghost is Radcliffe's signature alter ego.

In an essay on supernatural poetry (written about two decades after *Udolpho* and published in 1826), Radcliffe parsed the real-time phantasmics in Shakespeare's ghost-writing. Along with Coleridge, who pondered this affect with her novels in mind, Radcliffe produced the first sustained theory of apparitions as common apprehension. I quote from her essay at length because it's a ghost-story in itself. Shakespeare's "supernatural beings" may arrive "wild and remote . . . from common apprehension," but they "never compel us, for an instant, to recollect" any "licence for extravagance" (147). They precipitate from already present foreboding:

> Above every ideal being is the ghost of Hamlet, with all its attendant incidents of time and place. The dark watch upon the remote platform, the dreary aspect of the night, the very expression of the officer on guard, 'the air bites shrewdly; it is very cold'; the recollection of a star, an unknown world, are all circumstances which excite forlorn, melancholy, and solemn feelings, and dispose us to welcome, with trembling curiosity, the awful being that draws near; and to indulge in that strange mixture of horror, pity, and indignation, produced by the tale it reveals. Every minute circumstance of the scene between those watching on the platform, and of that between them and Horatio, preceding the entrance of the apparition, contributes to excite some feeling of dreariness, or melancholy, or solemnity, or expectation, in unison with, and leading on toward that high curiosity and thrilling awe with which we witness the conclusion of the scene. (147–48)

Radcliffe's phrasing, "produced by the tale it reveals," names a narrative agency that provokes "trembling curiosity"—a ghost's tale, and her own genre, in relay with the genetic agency of words in bringing a story to life. The theatrical agency of producing a play on "the scene . . . on the platform" for those "watching" at Elsinore extends the scene to the theater's audience. The cue for "the entrance of the apparition" is both Hamlet-time and *Hamlet*-time: "we witness" it and "we immediately feel it" from "the first question of Bernardo, and the words in reply, 'Stand and unfold yourself'" (148). By this time of writing, as Radcliffe knows, "unfold" is destined for repetition by the Ghost, the great unfolder who remands "you" to list: "I could a tale unfold." This is not only a superb reading of Shakespeare's verbal artistry; it is also Radcliffe's verbal theater. Her own story, threaded with Shakespeare's, inhabits the dramatic haunt of act 1's repetition and return:

> When Horatio enters, the challenge—the dignified answers, "Friends to this ground, and liegemen to the Dane,"—the question of Horatio to Bernardo, touching the apparition—the unfolding of the reason why "Horatio has consented to watch with them the minutes of this night"—the sitting down together, while Bernardo relates the particulars of what they had seen for two nights; and, above all, the few lines with which he begins his story, "Last night

of all," and the distinguishing, by the situation of "yon same star," the very point of time when the spirit had appeared—the abruptness with which he breaks off, "the bell then beating one"—the instant appearance of the ghost, as though ratifying the story for the very truth itself—all these are circumstances which the deepest sensibility only could have suggested, and which, if you read them a thousand times, still continue to affect you almost as much as at first. (148)

In the syntactic drama of this one, long, amazing sentence, Radcliffe hardly needs to add, "I thrill with delightful awe, even while I recollect and mention them, as instances of the exquisite art of the poet" (148). Recollecting, present thrilling, reading a thousand times and still feeling the cue to a latest affect: these returns are the shades and shadows of words animated into a spectral reality that doesn't usurp everyday reality, but inhabits it throughout in the presence of language for the reading, and for the writing.

V. Ghost-Theory, Theory's Ghosts

Ghosts so readily symptomize transgression, the return of the repressed, uncanny doublings and historical anxiety, as to provoke ghost theory. In oscillations between past and present, absence and presence, closure and deferral, origin and repetition, the death of the author and the life of writing, the ghost theory most legibly in the works is deconstruction. The nineteenth century's ghost-figurings became magnetically readable with the rise of deconstruction, and deconstruction found a prehistory in Romantic ghost-figurings. Coleridge was a prime agent in this discovery. At the outset of a January 1819 lecture on *Hamlet,* he pondered Shakespeare's skillful stage-management of slippage, both temporal and epistemological:

> The preparation *informative* of the Audience, just as much as was precisely necessary—how gradual first, and with the certain appertaining to a question, What? has *this* THING appeared *again* to-night? (even the word *again* has its credibilizing effect). . . . Then this "thing" becomes at once an APPARITION, and that too an intelligent Spirit that is to be *spoken* to. — (*Lectures* 2:295)

Coleridge's precisely necessary coinage, *credibilizing* (OED), registers the artful effect for all Audience: on the stage, in the theater, in reading, and in recall. His note-scripts play along, with capital letterings miming fictive presences: APPARITION not only signifies a thing but also signifies as a

THING, in tune with the upgraded *S* of *Spirit* that reifies communicable intelligence. "Add to that" (Coleridge returns to subject in his next lecture),

> the Apparition itself has by its frequent previous appearance been brought nearer to a Thing of this World. This accrescence of Objectivity in a Ghost that yet retains all of its ghostly attributes & fearful Subjectivity, is truly wonderful. (2:299)

A "Ghost-Theory" about the sensation of a Thing of this World was a subject that Coleridge had been developing at least since 1809 (and already entertaining in his poetry).

The theory unfolds in Essay III in *The Friend*, by a deft accrescence of optical illusions, spectral fantasy, dream sensations, a jest, and at its close, a sudden sigh of bereavement on ghost-sensations.[33] Coleridge begins with an optical illusion that offers "a fair resemblance of an apparition" (246): a hearth-fire reflected on a windowpane at twilight seeming like a fire in the landscape outside. From such resemblance (phenomenal twin of the noumenal image), Coleridge moves on to dream scenes, a mode in which thoughts "become at times perfectly *dramatic*," with the effect that "the *Form* of the vision appears to talk to us its own thoughts in a voice as audible as the shape is visible" (246–47). This is the deep psychology of Hamlet's ghost-seeing. Coleridge is thinking about illusory form along the logic of Dr. Johnson's ghost-tracks, how impassioned imagination can "make a vivid thought consubstantiate with the real object, and derive from it an outward perceptibility" (247). The ambiguous grammar of *consubstantiate* is to the point, seeming both a modifier of *thought* and as a verb compounding with *make*.

Yet like Wordsworth in the breezy twilight woods, Coleridge cannot resist a jest (as if to pull back from his deepest discovery). Instead of a homey dog, an unnamed lady is the straightman:

> A lady once asked me if I believed in ghosts and apparitions, I answered with truth and simplicity: *No, Madam! I have seen far too many myself.* (248)[34]

Freud uses similar materials to a different end in *Jokes and Their Relation to the Unconscious* when he probes the malleability of belief in "nonsensical form": "Not only did he disbelieve in ghosts; he was not even frightened of them" (108). The Oscar Wildey syntax of the joke gets its force as a release from disciplines of repression.[35] Freud's "not even frightened" puts affect above disbelief. Coleridge suspends both belief and disbelief by invoking objective seeing, and then a record for reading. "I have indeed a whole memorandum book filled with records of the Phænomena," he assures his readers, half in jest. But only half: it is "data" for a projected treatise developing a "Psychology . . . for a theory of perception and its dependence on the memory and imagination" (248).[36] Coleridge quotes again that Latin phrase headlined in Lecture XII of the same year. If ghosts are psychology, then psychology might credibilise, even credit, a ghost.

By 1813, one of Coleridge's contemporaries, Dr. John Ferriar, was articulating a theory of "recollection" as a "faculty of spectral representation"—or ghost-production:

> From recalling images by an art of memory, the transition is direct to beholding spectral objects, which have been floating in the imagination. . . . The simple renewal of the impressions of form or voice in the case of particular friends is the most obvious, and most forcible of these recollections. (*Theory of Apparitions* 100)

Recall, as Coleridge could, Wordsworth's possession by "phantoms of conceit, / That had been floating" in his imagination, getting an anchor in what memory can "call to mind" (*Prelude* 1.130–31, 308). The faculty of memory, long regarded as spatial housing of mental images, can conjure among these images ghosts of those gone. Meditating his "Ghost-Theory," Coleridge is moved to mention someone "who would have realized this idea: who had already established the foundations and the law of the theory" (Essay III, 248). He seems to be turning his essay here from aesthetic imagination to cognitive science, but it is from this same sentence, which begins "But HE is no more, who would have," that he swerves into, and never back from, haunted, pained grief. It is not "Ghost-Theory," but a ghost-memory of this lost friend and patron (Tom Wedgewood) that swells Coleridge's last paragraph, and with such lyric intensity that this loss, this absence, seems to have been his motive and occasion all along. By the final sentence, this friend is not just an apparition in the text but a simulacrum of the Holy Ghost, with disbelief impossibly, fatally sad: "Were it but for the remembrance of him alone and of his lot here below, the disbelief of a future state would sadden the earth around me, and blight the very grass in the field" (250). This is ghost-belief needing no willing suspension of disbelief.

The poignancy of spiritual consolation is that it does not displace the art of memory. This, Ferriar proposed, works through spectral conjurings. Consolation is a temporary stay against confusion and melancholy that can, at any moment, revive half-glimpsed specters and affective shadows. This lonely experience links a wide range of Romantic-era thinkers and poets. Walter Cooper Dendy, a physician, poet, and student at Guy's hospital just before Keats's term, writes a ghost story on this template in *The Philosophy of Mystery* (1841).[37] Sited at neo-Gothic Abbotsford, it is an anecdote about the intimate connection of "spectral forms," of images in a mind bereft, and of "hand-writing on the wall" (or on the page):

> Not long after the death of Byron, Sir Walter Scott was engaged in his study during the darkening twilight of an autumnal evening, in reading a sketch of his form and habits, his manners and opinions. On a sudden he saw as he laid down his book, and passed into his hall, the *eidòlon* of his departed friend before him. He remained for some time impressed by the intensity of the illusion, which had thus created a phantom out of skins, and scarfs, and plaids, hanging on a screen in the gothic hall of Abbotsford. (61)

In the liminal "real" of twilight (*darkening* and *reading* are vivid present participles), Scott sees a phantom of departed Byron—distilled, in the mode of Coleridgean phantasmics, from reading, and projected onto ready material (*eidòlon* is a term in Greek philosophy analogous to *phantasmata*: a dream-image drawn from the material of sense perception). To describe Scott as "impressed" by an intense illusion is to cast his twilit mind as a text, marked and imprinted, in Cicero's trope, "as a wax writing-tablet and the letters written on it."[38]

Phantoms reside in imagination this way, especially in the impress of passions. On track to Dendy's discussion of ghost-illusions, Ferriar was drawn to the famous fifteenth-century anecdote of the "apparition of Ficinus to Michael Mercato," friends who agreed that whoever died first would return to the other, to report on the afterlife. "I have no doubt," Ferriar writes, "that Mercato had seen what he described": "the idea of his friend, and of their compact, had been revived, and had produced a spectral impression, during the solitude and awful silence of the early hours of study" (100–102). The double force of "impression" as affect and as imprinting is a recurrent trope. Ferriar frequently cites poetry as if it were documentary this way; so, too, does Coleridge, favoring quasi-occult Latin, the default for ghost-converse (*Friend* 244). The title page of *Theory of Apparitions* conjures this report:

> A thousand fantasies
> Begin to throng into my memory,
> Of calling shapes, and beck'ning shadows dire,

And airy tongues, that syllable men's names
On sands, and shores, and desert wildernesses.
These thoughts may startle well, but not astound.

COMUS, 1.205

Milton's scene of "memory" is a haunt of proto-scriptive figurings—shapes and shadows that work like language, beckoning, calling, syllabling—because memory takes this form, too.

In the 1802 Preface to *Lyrical Ballads* Wordsworth makes a vocational claim for a poet's "disposition" to be "affected . . . by absent things as if they were present" (xxviii). In the poetry, it seems symptomatic that the word *absent* appears just twice: once in that notation of life away from the Wye ("Though absent long") that reverses into presence; once for a man whose "absent brother was still at his heart" (*The Brothers, LB* 2:40), *at* marking a present pressure rather than habitual residence *in*. That this absent brother is radically so, dead at the moment of this expression, suggests why Mary Shelley would turn to Wordsworth's haunts of grief to find a voice for her own liminal status between life and death. In her journal for 7 October 1822, about three months after Percy Shelley drowned at sea, she writes:

> I have been . . . reading my letters to mine own Shelley during his absences at Marlow. What a scene to recur to! My William, Clara, Allegra are all talked of—They lived then—They breathed this air & their voices struck my sense, their feet trod the earth beside me—& their hands were warm with blood & life when clasped in mine. Where are they all? This is too great an agony to be written about. I may express my despair but my thoughts can find no words—Where are ye all?
>
> ———— 'Tis falsely said
> That there was ever intercourse
> Between the living and the dead.
>
> But they live . . . They are all gone & I live—(*MSJ* 435)

"They" are in the shades "my letters" and in Shelley's memory, which includes the words from Wordsworth that she quotes, in a reflex of contradiction. In "The Affliction of Margaret—— of ——" (57–60) Wordsworth voices a mother's mourning for her a lost son, unconsoled by any ghost. The blanks in his title are not a prompt to decode the particulars of Margaret's identity but a lodge for a reader's sympathetic supplement.[39] Shelley insists on absent presences in her own shadow-life:

But they live—Tell me truth, Beloved, where are you? And shall I join you?
They are all gone & I live—if it be life to be as I am. But it is not—I am in the
valley of the shadow of death. (*J* 435)

This is ghost-writing in is deepest haunting, and Shelley could guess this was
every mourner's haunted life.

She recalls Wordsworth's poem, with fuller quotation, for the epigraph to
her essay "On Ghosts" (1824):

I look for ghosts—but none will force
Their way to me; 'tis falsely said
That there was ever intercourse
Between the living and the dead.—*Wordsworth.* (253)

This afflicted ghost-search stays on the essay's horizon of *ubi-sunt* laments
on the demise of ghost-belief in a disenchanted modernity, and it comes into
play in Shelley's setting of scenes of reading hospitable to ghosts: "Let it be
twelve at night in a lone house," she conjures; let the cue for a ghost "be assisted by solitude, flapping curtains, rushing wind, a long and dusky passage,
an half open door," ghost-storying for sure. Catherine Morland (or Dendy's
Scott, for that matter) might have sighed this sentence. Then Shelley pivots
the patent genre in the realm of genuine sensation. Reader, you "decide
whether there be such a thing as a ghost in the world" (254). For her part, the
essayist will testify to her own ghost-seeings: "once in a dream," and once in
a waking scene.

The pang of Shelley's essay is the way it spectralizes this distinction in the
medium of memory. She tells of being alone at twilight in an empty house
where she had last seen a lost friend, "filled with sensations of the most poignant grief," *filled with,* as if sensations were substantial living beings. In this
intercourse between the living and the dead, memory is a ghost-haunt. "He
had been there; his living frame had been caged by those walls, his breath
had mingled with that atmosphere, his step had been on those stones."
Grief-history is a ghost-story: "The wind rising in the east rushed through
the open casements, making them shake;—methought, I heard, I felt—I
know not what—but I trembled." Cicero trained the art of memory to store
"images in . . . places, so that the order of the places will preserve the order of
the things, and the images of the things will denote the things themselves," as
if the mind were a library of images, for a mental "writing tablet."[40] Shelley

phanomizes this mnemonic, infusing it into syntaxes that blur distinction of sensation and thinking, the uncertainties of knowing then and what she still can't "know" for certain. While *methought* might be the topos of medieval dream vision,[41] she makes it waking cognition, "I thought." It is a spectral chiasmus of phenomenal world and ghost-world: "I thought:—the earth is a tomb, the gaudy sky a vault, we but walking corpses" (254).

Or a ghost: "Am I indeed Mary Shelley?" she writes to her friend E. J. Trelawny in March 1824, that is, the carefree soul he knew in Genoa, "untamed as she was by any sorrow?—Mary Shelley now is but a ghost of that" (*L* 1:415). This transformation had taken hold in her first alarm at the thought of Percy Bysshe Shelley's death at sea. Having sped with Jane Williams to Pisa to prove her fears, she imagines their appearance to Byron as "poor, wild, aghast creatures"; he told her later that "I looked more like a ghost than a woman—light seemed to emanate from my features, my face was very white   I looked like marble" (15 August 1822, *L* 1:247).

This shimmer into ghost and then inanimate marble (the space in Shelley's letter is a visual mimesis) embodies the "threat of a deeper logical disturbance" that Paul de Man reads in prosopopoeia ("Autobiography as De-facement" 928). His prompt is the line from Milton's super-sonnet, "On Shakespear," that Wordsworth couldn't bring himself to write when he summoned it to close "Epitaphs" (*Friend* 416). Wordsworth quotes Milton's reverence for the "live-long Monument" of Shakespeare's words but he stops before the radically reciprocal effect that Milton punningly gives for a reader's "astonishment": "Dost make us Marble with too much conceaving" (7–8, 14). Did Mary Shelley become such marble in conceiving Percy Shelley's death? Set in an essay on epitaphs, the line that Wordsworth truncated, remarks de Man,

> cannot fail to evoke the latent threat that inhabits prosopopeia, namely by
> making the death speak, the symmetrical structure of the trope implies, by
> the same token, that the living are struck dumb, frozen in their own death
> not only the prefiguration of one's own mortality but our actual entry into the
> frozen world of the dead. (928)

Marjorie Garber twice quotes this as "making the dead speak"; her mistake has logic, and perhaps de Man slipped. But he kept the wording in a reprint;[42] and she kept hers in a reprint (185, 196). Garber's *dead* brings a different inflection: it denotes revenant bodies rather than the unimaginable disembodiment that de Man's repetition of "the death" in "their own death" literally spells, and phantomizes for death-haunted imagination. De Man speaks of, and speaks out for, apparitional verbal power.[43]

Chartreuse had this effect on Matthew Arnold, whose "Stanzas from the Grande Chartreuse" was haunted by Wordsworth's phantasm. Arnold beholds a lodge of "spectral vapours" (13), "where, ghostlike in the deepening night, / Cowl'd forms brush by in gleaming white" (35–36). "*What dost thou in this living tomb?*" the poet asks himself (72), already knowing his passport (in a now famous passage) to its "Brotherhood austere" (65):

> Wandering between two worlds, one dead,
> The other powerless to be born,
> With nowhere yet to rest my head,
> Like these, on earth I wait forlorn. (85–88)

This suspended animation is a memorable record of Victorian paralysis, the forlorn spirit of the age; it is also a haunting from Wordsworth's haunted arrest, with the power of present sensation. And more: "it represents that moment for ever," said T. S. Eliot (*Kipling's Verse* 7).

VI. Romanticism's Shades: Seeing through Shadows

This book might have ranged across a wide *terra cognita*: Gothic novels, Gothic theater, ghost-stars in just about every genre.[44] We know the score. *The Prelude* is an epic of haunting. There is Blake's *Ghost of Abel* and visions, early and late, in the form of specters and emanations. Shades hover over Charlotte Smith's melancholy sonnets and come to visit in Charles Lamb's homey essays on witches and night-fears. A spectral crew rises in Coleridge's *Rime of the Ancient Mariner,* and a ghost-mother haunts *Christabel.* Wordsworth's *Thorn* is a primer of apparitional imagination, and a ghost is the love-pang of "Laodamia." A nightmare-ghost is the lurid muse of Keats's *Isabella*, and a phantom parade the amusement of his daytime *Ode on Indolence.* Shelley writes *Prometheus Unbound* as a phantom-fantasia. Felicia Hemans's poetry wheels through haunted sites and haunted homes, no more poignantly than in *A Spirit's Return.* De Quincey's *Confessions* and *Suspiria de Profundis* open into a phantasmagoria of dream-ghosts, uncanny doubles, haunted houses, urban labyrinths, and supernatural fields. Romantic haunting is no news, then. Coexisting with Enlightenment rationalism, modern science, and the material world is its vast converse with spirits near and far, apparitions, ghosts seen, dreamed and dreamed up, old mythologies, specters in historical catastrophes, in high theory and in low culture. However one maps "Romanticism," the challenge would be to avert from its phantoms, shades and specters.[45]

My chapters bring a sharper focus to ghostly semblances and ghostlier demarcations that press as presences for reading: structural ruptures, disturbances of syntax and grammar, skewed tracks of argument or narrative, verbal stresses of perception and self-representation in undertones and under-presences, overtones and over-determinations. These are remarkable, arresting, important word-workings.

Chapter 2 begins close up (with wider stakes) with weird slants of syllables from Wordsworth's name in the autobiography that he began in 1797 and kept at for decades. In so self-conscious a mode, these syllables operate beyond mere coincidence with words about other business. At cross-purposes with narrative recollection, name-words collect a lexical apparition of uncanny cooperation. Spelling out the story of his life, Wordsworth exposes this philology, too, literally a "love of words" stirring in surprisingly strange registers.

If this looks like a form of self-alluding, the effect is still different from the more audible orchestrations of allusion, conjurings with intentional recall. In chapter 3, I read Hazlitt's allusioning as Milton's proof, a library ever activated. Allusions play as memory's gloss, its biographia literaria, with Hazlitt texturing his great and moving recollection of 1823, "My first Acquaintance with Poets," into what looks like a typology of allusion itself. The "first" moment of "1798" oscillates between recollection so vivid as to be present again and a consciousness of historical difference that shades allusion into elegy.

Hazlitt's present-past relay is haunted by Coleridge's political apostasy (sad ashes of the 1790s firebrand). In chapter 4, I read Shelley's political poetry of 1819 as a theorized phantasmics with a double intent, signifying a fraudulent, alienating present and conjuring an antithetical "unwritten story" for future realization (*The Mask of Anarchy* 148). But if these phantasmic projections within and beyond the here and now seem on track to Marx's spectral politics—a present haunted by unresolved history and conjuring unresolved futures—Shelley's explorations in the pre-fixtures of "un-" can't help worrying its questionable shapes: ghosts of futurity may also be bearing news from nowhere.

Chapter 5 reads Byron's poetry as a ghost-working of presence, suffusing the world. His accumulating company of ghosts spins a surplus that whirls into a complementary cult: writers seeking Byron's ghost and its haunts (especially at Newstead Abbey), in order to keep company with "the spirit of Byron." Byron himself led the way. In the production of ghosts, he discovers what amuses him, troubles him, parodies him, propels him: it is the spectral logic of modern aesthetic life, a fully present scene where a poet's personality negotiates the larger world through what phantasmics can supply.

"A poet writes always of his personal life," but "he never speaks directly . . . there is always a phantasmagoria," states Yeats, with great self-possession, as "The First Principle" of a "General Introduction for My Work" (509). It's the first sentence, even. Yet Phantom-Theorist Yeats is not always the designer. The subject of my last chapter is Yeats's phantasmagoria of Keats. Call Keats/Yeats a "ghost rhyme."[46] Yeats's indirect speaking is haunted by a "Keats" that haunts his "modernism"—to disturb, as Yeats's contemporary Freud would put it, something "familiar . . . in the mind" that "has been estranged . . . by the process of repression" and comes back in unexpected forms ("The Uncanny" 148). This is not just a history of poetry; it is poetry as history.

My "After Wording" is a short story about my own haunts of reading. The argument developing across my chapters, that language is apparitional, points more broadly to a way of reading (I state with conviction and from experience) for which some new methods of reading today—all salient, provocative attempts to accommodate our rapidly expanding canons and technologies of reading, or to clean house—strike me as inadequate. Data-driven "distant reading" seems to me no reading at all, if the value of reading is attention to words, discovered in complex contexts and in the literary aesthetics of particulars. Surface-reading's refusal of depths and its call for "just description" seem to me a narrow legislation, with more than a few begged questions about description as surface reporting, and about what constitutes or measures surface anyway. Another adventure, "post-critical reading" (a "critique of critique") regards critical reading as a stricture against open reading, and deems thinking through depths and in contexts as perversion; its patent disdain of reading against the grain implies that there is only one direction in which words can cut.[47] My attention to apparitions of words and wordings, of latencies and depths, proceeds in antithesis to these calls. This study reads apparition as a subtle presence in literary writing—a stress on and in words, in syntaxes, in imagination itself, where apparitions are not fugitive wisps but immediate sensations.

Some time ago, yet with durable force, Cleanth Brooks distinguished description (the business of paraphrase) from literary reading, a critical attention to "the pressure of context": "the word . . . has to be conceived of, not as a discrete particle of meaning, but as a potential of meaning, a nexus of cluster," in a play of language that is "warped and bent . . . deflected away from a positive straightforward formulation" (*The Well Wrought Urn* 210–11). Such attention, notwithstanding the story often transmitted, isn't just so much "chitchat about irony, paradox, and ambiguity."[48] It is the care for thick verbal structure, and for the agencies of construction, that distinguishes literary aesthetics from informational communication. Such care is not derealizing. Far from it. It is what animates the "potencie of life" that mattered to Milton's defense of writing, not only in the moment, but in readiness, "on purpose to a life beyond life." The generous life of reading for me is this uncanny capacity (Keats would say, "negative capability") for renewal, as it activates shades, shadows, phantoms of conceit, within the textures of writing in its subtlest, most intimate, formations.

CHAPTER TWO

Shades of *Will* + *Words* + *Worth*

What's in a Name?

I. Seeking and Hiding a Name

In William Wordsworth's autobiographical epic there is a book titled *Books,*
and within this, a dream about books, and within this, a word-chain even
more self-reflexive than has been noticed in the rich archive of critical attention to this episode. *Book Fifth: Books* opens in a crisis about the material
survival of "things worthy of unconquerable life" (5.19), including this book.
Is there an under-presence of *Wordsworth* in *worthy*? I wouldn't ask, but for
having caught both syllables of the name *Wordsworth* in a crucial line in the
dream soon at hand. Even though *1850* shifts "things worthy of" to "things
that aspire to" (20), the dream-narrative recovers the name-pressure, because
the poet now claims it as his own.[1] Thomas De Quincey was alert to the can-
nily formative field:

> the form of the dream is not arbitrary; but, with exquisite skill in the art of
> composition, is made to arise out of the situation in which the poet had pre-
> viously found himself, and is faintly prefigured in the elements of that situa-
> tion. He had been reading 'Don Quixote' . . . (*Tait's* 97)

De Quincey means the elements of prefigurative reading: "the errant
knight / Recorded by Cervantes" (5.60–61). The form-field is more than this
record, however. As it turns out, elements figure, more than faintly, into the
dream-poetry, not only in the title of one book therein, but also, with apparitional legibility, in syllable-elements of the name *Wordsworth* in the line of
verse that introduces the other book. In this strange art of dream composition, the poet finds himself here, too.[2]

This is how it happens in *1850.* The dreamer is lost in a desert, when suddenly, "Close at my side, an uncouth shape appeared / Upon a dromedary,
mounted high" (5.75–76). The shape is more than ghostly, not just in the aspect
of a dream-figuring, but within the dream, as a shape unoriginated in sudden presence, in the sheen of "uncouth . . . appeared," and with a textual
conjuring from a near-specter in the nightscape of *Book Fourth:* "lo! an un-

couth shape" (*1850* 4.386). The shape in "the *dream*" (5.87) is spectralized in the poetry itself in a near-rhyming to its medium: "He *seemed* an Arab of the Bedouin tribes" (77, my italics). Tucked under one arm is a stone, and in his opposite hand, a shell. To the already "self-questioned" beholder (84) the shape marks these shapes, the narrator pausing his relation to concede the arbitrary signifying, a figuring about figuring:

> the Arab told me that the stone
> (To give it in the language of the dream)
> Was 'Euclid's Elements'; and 'This', said he,
> 'Is something of more worth'; and, at the word
> Stretched forth the shell.   (5.86–90)

Halting my eye one day in reading, it was line 89 that prompted the adventure of this chapter. Here, in sequence, is *worth . . . word*. The pentameter stress on both syllables, the caesura at *worth,* the pause of *word* at the line-end, the two nearly rhyming: all this sets *word* to claim *worth* as its referent. The syllables of the waking name *Wordsworth*, in the lawless forgery of a dream-machine, mirror in reverse.[3] These are literally "Wordsworth's Elements." As this geometry-charmed poet knows, *Euclid's Elements* is a work in 13 books, like the 1805 form of the autobiography. On this field, *worth . . . word* seemed to me no uncouth shape, but a legible kin of the poet's signature to his debut publication in 1787, "Axiologus."[4] With a glance at Euclidian "axiom," this classy Greek-Latin code name spells "worth of words," or in English syntax, *words' worth.*[5] The pun-pseudonym announces vocation. And vocation, temporal and eternal, is the crisis of worth and words in *Books.*

Poets are not unknown forgers of name-games. "Names! What's in a name?" jests a voice in front of Dublin's library, ringing Juliet's protest to Romeo to challenge the notion of coded autobiography in Shakespeare's works. Stephen Dedalus briskly parries:

> He has hidden his own name, a fair name, William, in the plays   as a
> painter of old Italy set his face in a dark corner of his canvas. He has revealed
> it in the sonnets where there is Will in overplus . . . (Joyce, *Ulysses* 209–10)

Whether hidden in corners of play or blazoned for display, Will reads out. "Overplus" is not just Dedalus-accounting; it is a recounting of Shakespeare's own petition, in Sonnet 135, to a mistress oversupplied: "Whoever hath her wish, thou hast thy *Will,* / And *Will* to boot, and *Will* in overplus" (1–2). In 14 lines, *Will* plays as many times, pumped up to a capital *W* and flaunted in italics.[6] All this is amplified by the pun-plush neighbors, Sonnet 134—"I my-self am mortgaged to thy will" (2)—and a flagrantly promiscuous Sonnet 136:

> Swear to thy blind soul that I was thy *Will*,
> And will thy soul knows is admitted there.   (2–3)

> *Will* will fulfill the treasure of thy love,
> Ay, fill it full with wills, and my will one.   (5–6)

> And then thou lovest me for my name is *Will*.   (14)

Here, too, are 14 imprints of the fair name, also blazoned with capital *W*s and italics. In the quarto, the imperative, "Ay, fill it full," is a first-person declara-tive: "I fill it full."

Even short of such overplus, writers can score happily in the chances of a name, blessed with semantic capital, pointless to hide. It pays off handsomely in *Phil*ip Sidney's Astro*phil* sonnets to Stella, and in John Donne's "Hymne to God the Father": "When thou hast done, thou hast not done, / For, I have more" (he advises) from a life that will end only "when I have spunne" it all. This verb of production holds *pun*, the trope at hand, nicely rhyme-paired with *done* and lettered (*—unne*) to evoke *Donne*. Then there's Thomas Hood's quip, "I have to be a lively Hood for a livelihood," and its rueful rep-etition as he lay dying, with greetings to "the undertaker, who wished to urn a lively Hood."[7] S. T. Coleridge unabashedly plundered the pun-phonetics of S.T.C. across his career, splaying the initials into word-sounds as early as 1801, ΕΣΤΗΣΕ becoming his regular newspaper signature.[8] In 1802, he glossed the happy tenor:

> Ἐστησε signifies—He hath stood—which in these times of apostasy from the principles of Freedom . . . is no unmeaning Signature, if subscribed with hu-mility, & in the remembrance of, Let him that stands take heed lest he fall—. However, it is in truth no more than S.T.C. written in Greek. Es tee see—
> (10 September 1802)[9]

And no less: the signature is still subscribing a letter to William Godwin, late 1818.[10]

Coleridge the reflexive punster, Coleridge the philosophical reader, Coleridge the principled theorist: all converge in the "truth" of S.T.C. In 1819, he summoned the macaronics for a poem he titled "A Trifle," which he circulated to friends.[11] It was clearly more than a trifle, "more than S.T.C. written in Greek." "A Character" is the forthright title given in his 1834 *Po-*

etical Works. The initial occasion explains the upgrade: a pained defense against Hazlitt's published serial of outrage at the seeming apostasy of *The Statesman's Manual* (1816) and *A Lay-Sermon* (1817), twin defections from the principles of Coleridge's firebrand polemics of the 1790s.[12] Stung by the charge, Coleridge parries the word "Character" as his ethical core, fortu-itously endorsed by the characters of his "no unmeaning Signature"—in sound, syllables, the very letters (OED 3a). On all these circuits, he protests,

> Our bard pursued his old A. B. C.
> Contented if he could subscribe
> In fullest sense his name ᾿Εστησε;
> ('Tis Punic Greek, for 'he hath stood!')[13]

Happy, too, is the way the lettering of *Pu*nic Greek subscribes to the trans-lated *pun*-Greek in Coleridge's signature. As Coleridge knew, "Punic Greek" had no standing except as a literary language: it's Punic translated into Greek.[14] Yet the author of a Biographia Literaria will stand with it and by it, underwrite it and subscribe to it with his initials. He was "an Author . . . better known by the initials of his Name than by the Name itself—which he fondly Graecized": "better known" not just in public persona but also in the core self.[15] He set his "Epitaph" in this accord, "O, lift one thought in prayer for S.T.C.," signing "ΕΣ ΤΗ ΣΕ" to one copy.[16]

The semantic fielding of proper names into meaningful words is a distraction to theories of the arbitrary attachment of signifier to signi-fied. "What's in a name? That is what we ask ourselves in childhood when we write the name that we are told is ours," adds young Dedalus to his Shakespeare-riff (210). The name-question petitions "William Wordsworth" as slants of *word(s)* and syllable-kins *worth* and *will* chance, willy-nilly, into the composition of his autobiography.[17] I admit that these slants strike my eye with a critical difference from the designings of Will's Will, Donne's done, Hood's hoods, and Coleridge's crafty initials. Wordsworth's syllables seem accidents. Even so, as the accidents accumulate, they begin to precipi-tate "a figure of reading" that Paul de Man has described as endemic to au-tobiography. Reversing the notion that "life *produces* autobiography as an act produces its consequences," de Man reads autobiography as a "specular structure" that generates a "specular model of cognition." In this aspect, the "autobiographical project may itself produce and determine the life and that whatever the writer *does* is in fact governed by the technical demands of self-portraiture and thus determined, in all its aspects, by the resources of his medium."[18] Because the specular model is self-divided, (re)cognition can only be ghostly, apparitional. De Man's terms press to an extreme, casting off *may* for a rigorous legislation—*determine(d), in fact governed, demands, in all its aspects*—and ultimately fatal deprivation: "Death is a displaced name for a linguistic predicament" (930). Mary Jacobus emphasizes this death-sentence: by "turning on itself . . . to reflect on the peculiar status of autobiographical inscription," autobiography exposes "the impossibility of autobiographical self-encounter," a blockage that "ultimately spells death to the subject."[19] There are more productive outcomes, however.

Wordsworth was not innocent of the spell of death and actually conjures it into his accounting. Quite early in his drive to write about himself, he reflects on the specular non-coincidence between a "self-presence in my heart" (*1799* 2.28)—a compound he had to invent for this sensation[20]—and a reflex of thinking about a past self:

> I seem
> Two consciousnesses—conscious of myself,
> And of some other being.   (*1799* 2.29–31)

To these two, add the "I" that arrays "myself" and "some other." This "I" is inevitably disparate, too, across the multiple versions of this passage from 1799 on. No argument, then, with the fractioning and fracturing that distribute these self-encounters into multiples of self. But is this splay only the specter of a death-sentence in the autobiographical venture?

Wordsworth's wordings are often productively double. The very verb that de Man summons for the genre-force, *determine*, is itself disturbed, oscillating between fate and subjective resolve.[21] This ambiguity registers at the formal outset of *The Prelude*: "speedily a longing in me rose / To brace myself to some determined aim" (1.123–24). Here, *determined* solicits senses both volitional and destined, which dovetail at the end of *Book First* as the poet embraces his "theme / Single and of determined bounds" (668–69). That these are the only two events of *determined* in *The Prelude* makes them seem tuned for this relay, tuned even across a spectral antonym: what the poet calls, in his recollection of the boy haunted by that boat-boosting, an "undetermined sense / Of unknown modes of being" (419–20). The antonym appears only once more in *The Prelude*, and it is linked to the poet's name-word: "undetermined to what plan of life / I should adhere," he indulged a "self-willed" vacation from "all ambition" and "dangerous passions" (7.63–64, 69–72).[22]

The name-stakes in *Will I am Words Worth* (and close kin) weave this kind of shadow-text of strange figurings into the autobiography of William Wordsworth. In such shadings, de Man's question, "does the referent determine the figure, or is it the other way around?" (921), is not sortable into *either/or.* Referent and figure are activated into a mutual generativity. Name-syllables haunt the textual field of *The Prelude* with readable signs for self-reflection; and reading gets tuned by the encounters. The haunts range from aural to scriptive, can figure as homonyms, sight puns and rhymes, in surprises of vertical array and linear syntax (as in the dream). Such workings are not out of character for a poem in which accidents tend to spring open scenes for self-reading.[23] Accidents are so "co-relative" with plotwork in *The Prelude* as to seem its narratological spell.[24] From earliest drafts to latest revisions, "external accidents" work to "plant, for immortality, images of sound and sight, in the celestial soil of the Imagination"—so Wordsworth glosses the "gentle shock" by which a Boy of Winander gets "surprised" into sublimity. This, Wordsworth says, reflects "one of my own primary consciousnesses."[25] No surprise that the first draft of these lines (MS JJ:Sʳ) shifts the local third-person legend into a first-person recollection.[26] Among the accidents planted in the textual field of autobiography are name-images of sound and sight, ready for a para-narrative word-processing that didn't know it was going there, but once there, takes root: *nomen est omen.*

The ricochet between accident and spectral punning traces an undecidability that directs us deep into language itself as a theater of the unconscious beneath its own stagings of theme.[27] Not by design or lexical system, and athwart grammatical logic, this is apparitional production. The accumulating namescape feels at once canny and uncanny, along lines that Freud would theorize, a century or so on, in the intimate double-play of "what is familiar and congenial" with "what is concealed and kept out of sight." Both sensations are in "the word *Heimlich,*" a coincidence that "develops towards an ambivalence, until it finally coincides with its opposite, *unheimlich*" ("Uncanny" 129, 131). Nothing more spectral-lexical. In the cadences of Wordsworth's autobiography, canny and uncanny come to seem so coincident in name-character events as to tremble into a pretext, a linguistic archeology, of the Freudian poetics. Names in common words are not only prone to coincidences of signifying—of familiar words and strangely sighted (and sited) signs—but are over-ready, in overplus, for specular reading.

It's hard to imagine Poe (for another instance) missing the *Poe*-prints in his essay on the genre, vocation, and effect of poetry: "We shall reach . . . a distinct conception of what the true *Poetry* is, by mere reference to a few of the simple elements which induce in the *Poet* himself the true *poetical* effect" (*Poetic Principle* 246). Before turning more fully to Wordsworth-elements, it will help to survey some related groundwork. An ally in my venture is Garrett Stewart's audit of the *imp*-syllables in Poe's own "The Imp of the Perverse," as well as Stewart's signature method in *Reading Voices* of sounding out "a signifying force" that "underlies, and at times surfaces within, the syntax of textual succession, obtruding lexical alternatives to the graphic text."[28] For namework, there is J. H. Prynne. Though cautious about Stewart's liberal phonotexts, he is fascinated by how Ferdinand de Saussure, master-theorist of the arbitrary linguistic sign, can disturb, even suspend, this notion when he discerns in some classical authors word-forms and syllables (verbal and phonetic anagrams) that coincide with theme-words, "characteristically . . . a proper name, of a god or hero, considered as generative in relation to the sequence of its narrative context."[29] While Saussure could scarcely tolerate a pun, he could pause, in the field of such a name, over "combinatory features devised so as to present to the reader an apparently motivated system of words and word-forms which converged towards the effect of a connected, intrinsic significance" (21). Sequences of dispersed syllables, even discrete letters, seemed to be at work in sub-syntactic spelling.

Still, Saussure is nagged by a key question: how (in Prynne's paraphrases) to assess "the *status* of the evidence which he thought he had found to support his anagram hypothesis." This is the "crucially indeterminate factor." Is this an apparently motivated system, or a too apparently motivated reader: "would the effect merely *imitate the appearance* of significance, or might the work of such selection in fact have *installed* significance?" Prynne circumvents this "or" with a soft appeal to Coleridge's poetics of procurement: "the reader is induced (perhaps by generic considerations) to make a willing suspension of disbelief."[30] But Coleridge's field is spectral psychology, "shadows of imagination," while Saussure's data-analysis guarantees Prynne's question: Can design govern in a thing so small, or is this a manic overplus of sign-reading? "Instead of being the guiding motif of poetic creation, the hypogram might be only a retrospective phantom evoked by the reader," whose pains are "always assured of 'success'": so Jean Starobinski phrases Saussure's hesitancy with these ghostlier demarcations, just short of conceding "mere chance encounter" (105).

With more legible word-marks in his name, Wordsworth needed no minutely fascinated Saussure in order to entertain specular formations. Writer and sign-reader both, he is poised for thematic payoff, even on the most sober of occasions. "It is well known how fond our ancestors were of a play upon the name of the deceased when it admitted of a double sense," he observes in an essay on ancient epitaphs that he drafted in 1810. Such name-play "brings home a general truth to the individual by the medium of pun" and (glancing at his forename) "*will* readily be pardoned, for the sake of the image suggested by it."[31] In his own epitaph on Charles Lamb, he defended a para-punning on "Lamb."[32] He was probably unaware that Lamb had beaten him to the name-punch, smartly bleating to a friend in a letter of late February 1801, about "a **Word's**-worth of good Poetry" in the newly expanded *Lyrical Ballads* (*Letters* 1:276).

As Lamb's bolded jest shows, Wordsworth proved a kind of muse himself for fresh coinages on his name and character. When Coleridge sent him "The Nightingale" for *Lyrical Ballads,* he enclosed a playful couplet: "dear Wordsworth / You'll tell me what you think my Bird's worth" (Mays, 1.1.521). In a letter to John Murray, 19 January 1821, referring to a satirical quatrain he had sent the week before, Byron quips,

The lines were even worthy

"Of Turdsworth the great Metaquizzical poet
A man of great merit amongst those who know it.["]   (*BLJ* 8:66)

The couplet, tuned on the double-coined name and adjective, launches the quatrain mentioned. Byron had debuted the naughty name for Murray in a letter of 12 August 1820, on a roll mocking Felicia Hemans as "Mrs. Hewoman's," a "Tadpole of Poet Turdsworth" (*BLJ* 7:158). He gleefully lobbed "Turdsworth" over to his friend Douglas Kinnaird, 31 August, back to Murray the same day (167–68), and on to his friend Francis Hodgson on 22 October (253). While the namesake could not have read "Turdsworth" when the letter-cum-quatrain above was first published (1830, with polite asterisks in lieu), the word just prior, *worthy* was cue enough.[33] *Don Juan IV* (1821), gave a preview: "poet Wordy" (clx)—this, the one forming of the name-syllable that managed to escape Wordsworth's wordings.

Byron minted two sides in coinage: *Turdsworth* and *Metaquizzical.* In another first-striking, in 1803, Coleridge described and decried "Self-involution in Wordsworth." To get at what irked him, he had to coin the compound and double the syllable *in* (*in*volution *in*).[34] This is a notable indulgence for the language-monitor who in 1817 would append a long footnote to the very second paragraph of *Biographia Literaria* on the dubious propriety of "new coined double epithets":

The rule for the admission of double epithets seems to be this: either that they should be already denizens of our Language, such as . . . self-applauding: or when a new epithet, or one found in books only, is hazarded, that it, at least, be one word, not two words made one by mere virtue of the printer's hyphen. A language which, like the English, is almost without cases, is indeed in its very genius unfitted for compounds. (1:5n)

But what is, and isn't, in the genius of an intrusive compound? A case-poor language such as English may be flexed, even richly fitted out, by non-grammatical impingement, maverick compoundings. Coleridge knew this from his own exercise, and Wordsworth was not shy of experimenting. Contemporary grammarian William Cobbett argued that the "compounding of nouns" to which (*pace* Coleridge) "our language is very prone" actually holds "an advantage peculiar to our language. It enables us to say much in few words, which always gives strength."[35] A hyphen brands this operation: "A note of conjunction," Dr. Johnson's *Dictionary* puts it (p. 1032), in effect planting a logic for "Self-involution."

By reciprocity, a word that reads like conjunction is prone to separating its discrete elements.[36] "William Wordsworth" beckons this way, with double-sense reserves in the syllables *Will Words Worth*. All are denizens of the poem that by 1804 Coleridge himself was calling (with another double epithet, even) "his divine Self-biography."[37] And all are ready (ready and willing) to be aroused into self-formation. The semantic potentials of lexical formation angle into Wordsworth's formal reflexes, which, early and late, are self-regarding. "My own voice cheared me," he writes about the breezy confidence rehearsed in the opening verse-paragraph of *The Prelude* (1.64). Just as characteristically, such a reflex can go into reverse (and re-verse), with no small consequence for name-words and his very medium. Some books on, the poet remarks that he hasn't always been a good "judge of . . . words" (6.124ff); and yet he recognizes how a mind such as Coleridge's, in a passion of "subtle speculations," uses "words for things—/ The self-created sustenance of a mind" that may have no resources beyond words (6.308–12).

The critical complications of words, not for, but as, things have been finely sifted by William Keach for the Romantic era: words can be eventful things of expressive power; but as cherished things on a material page, words are sadly perishable; moreover, if the word-making mind is what really matters, then words are just agents, not the point.[38] F. W. Bateson made an end run around the whole Wordsworthian quandary when he proposed that with this poet, anyway, "a more inclusive and a more rarefied meaning" for the poetry "lay between the words" (38), in gaps and fissures, silences and absences. This Wordsworthian poetics (a metaphysics related to what de Man measures into privation) is legion, legendary. More spectral yet is the presence of words laid with the poet's name-syllables. That this opens to puns may be because, as Jonathan Culler remarks, puns are "an exemplary product of language or mind" (*On Puns* 4). Catherine Bates will even raise the pun-stakes to a "microcosm of literariness": "ambiguity, polysemy, and frequently metaphor, all within a single word" (425).[39] The effect described by Geoffrey Hartman has consequence for "Wordsworth": whether you "define a pun as two meanings competing for the same phonemic space or as one sound bringing forth semantic twins," it is "a crowded situation" that "makes poetry radically oblique in terms of sign function" ("Voice" 347). What is the information: spectral or inspected?[40] How much more perplexing a question this is in autobiography.

While *The Prelude* isn't proactively punning, its many convergences of name-syllables and ordinary words write a scene of semiotic possibilities—a Wordsworthian poetics (or theory) that nominates "Words," as Wordsworth himself put it in a sequel essay on epitaphs, as "a constituent part and power or function in the thought" (Grosart 2:4). Name-syllables in autobiography "can be seen not as an author's appropriation of the world but as a dissemination or dispersal of the proper name, the transformation of it into the elements of a world—in short, a foundation of letters." This is Culler on the gains to be realized by "a punning exfoliation" of a proper name (*On Puns* 10). If I don't see Wordsworth rolling up his sleeves to pour such a foundation, long or short, I'll conjecture that his writerly mind wasn't averse to imprints. Neither a Freudian slip (an index of latency) nor the overplus of a pun, the elements stir in "William Wordsworth" with the lure of baked-in folk etymology.[41] Literally with words, this is a poet who can write the poem and haunt the poem at the same time, and do so in a non-referential way that makes the author function (a discursive role) into a new kind of functioning author. As early as 1800, Wordsworth twice sounds a surname-syllable into his vocational discourse: "*Words*, a Poet's *words* more particularly," may attach to the mind as "*things*, active and efficient."[42] Words may be immaterial signifiers or may be material presences.

One exuberant heir to this field of activity is Jacques Derrida, who plays in *Signéponge* with semantics in the name of French prose-poet Francis Ponge. Derrida blames sponge-worthy Ponge for the wringing game: "he is *himself* engaged, has engaged *himself . . . engaged in his name"* (28). Derrida is just playing along in what Christopher Norris calls "a species of massive and wilful impropriety, discounting the rule that would regard word play on an author's name as the merest of impertinent jokes" (10). Tempted as I am to call *wil(l)* and *word* out of this sentence, I'll just say that Wordsworth didn't have to wait for his Derrida. Sometimes the name-shades halt a line for the eye, as when he muses on the sorts of men (potentially a poet, too) able, with native passion, to generate

> Encouragement, and energy, and *will*,
> Expressing liveliest thoughts in lively *words*.   (12.262–63)

Hung at these vertically sequential line-ends, *will* and *words* deposit a worthy currency for self-investment. The poet of *The Prelude* may not seem profligate with such word-capital (versus flagrant punsters Shakespeare, Donne, Hood), but the poetry can plumb the resource.

The shimmer is charged with what Coleridge assigns to the genius of *Lyrical Ballads*: everyday "characters" come to life "where there is a meditative and feeling mind to seek after them, or to notice them, when they present themselves." This is a different accounting from the story of deconstruction: reading turns material marks into signs, indicators of immaterial meanings; all language, then, is figural, because it presents and represents. What Coleridge guesses is that in a material world that presents, Wordsworth can also care for the material presence of information. In the temporality that he ascribes to the Wordsworthian electrometer, seeking after, noticing, reading and writing are not dispersed into difference but condense into one event. This immediacy holds a power "to excite a feeling analogous to the supernatural" in a natural present, shaking into visibility apparitional information in that "film of familiarity," under which "we have eyes, yet see not, ears that hear not." On a film of familiar words obliquely angled, autobiographer Wordsworth is poised to see and hear his name, even with the divine riff that Coleridge's allusion to scripture summons (*BL* chapter 14; 2:2–3).[43] Coleridge himself meditated on this kind of verbal force, from his first appreciations of poetry to his late spiritual reflections. Words are not just agents of thought but events of power:

> Reflect on your own thoughts, actions, circumstances, and . . . accustom yourself to reflect on the words you use, hear, or read, their birth, derivation and history. For if words are not things, they are living powers, by

which things of most importance to mankind are actuated, combined, and humanized.

This is a concluding exhortation in the Preface to *Aids to Reflection* (xi), but it could just as well describe the latency of self-reflection in Wordsworth's encounters with words embedded in his birth and history, ready to be actuated, combined, humanized in writing out. Though not inevitable, it is also not implausible.

The vertical serendipity of *will* / *words* in the lines above traces what De Quincey describes when he wonders about the uncanny oracular effect when a reader catches "sudden angular deflexions of words, uttered or written, that had not been originally addressed to himself." He even thinks that Wordsworth is "the first person to notice" and to have written poetry about this kind of communication (*Autobiographic Sketches* 113–14). Averting the extremes of perverse reading or elected receptivity, such "angular deflexions of words" chance into name syllables in *The Prelude*, with Wordsworth doubled as the agent of what is "written" and the subject "addressed." De Quincey has metaphysical (or supernatural) stakes in the readerliness of these verbal "scintillations": they are "providential lights oftentimes arresting our attention, from the very centre of what else seems the blank darkness of chance and blind accident." We don't have to get this metaphysical—divination as divine—to grasp the key of reading, and reading requires literacy-readiness. The arrested reader, comments De Quincey, "had to some extent co-operated" in order to be "startled by a solitary word, lying, as it were, in ambush, waiting and lurking for *him*, and looking at him steadily as an eye searching the haunted places in his conscience" (114). This lurking-looking is eye-opening, apparitional, and wholly present in the literary texture.

It's also, accidentally, a great gloss of Wordsworth's autobiography of self-wording.

II. Spreading the Word

This intimacy of reading—the eye that reads the word and the word that awaits its reader abides in *The Prelude*'s texture of *Wordsworth* name-markings. The convergences that De Quincey catches in "co-operated" had been spelled out (as he knew) by Wordsworth himself, in the 1815 *Poems*. In the Preface he discusses his design to represent "internal feelings cooperating with external accidents" in the work of "Imagination" (1:xxxii); an "Essay, Supplementary" urges "the exertion of a co-operating *power* in the mind of the Reader" (1:370). He had sketched the grammar the decade before, in a strange interval in *Book Seventh: Residence in London*. Meditating on the arresting effect of Shakespeare's words embodied on the stage as "gross realities" of "incarnation" (509–10), Wordsworth could have turned anti-theatrical—on the same page as his lament on seeing the summit of Mont Blanc, only to register an "image on the eye / Which had usurped upon a living thought" (6.454–56). Yet here in London's theater, embodied words work with a difference, making

> me recognise
> As by a glimpse, the things which I had shaped
> And yet not shaped, had seen and scarcely seen.   (7.513–15)

That this effect comes by glimpse rather than from patent shaping makes it all the more impressive. Like the para-narrative accumulation of name-word signs, recognition works from a latency that embodiment literally makes legible. John Locke was interested in how "Names heard" (not proper names, but words for ideas and ideas of objects) can work by a force of association that "affects the Senses."[44] While Wordsworth's relay of words and names is more tenuous, more spectral, it is not excluded from this interest.

It is the cross-writing of *The Prelude*. Sometimes it appears in deflection. Sometimes it comes on like a deluge, as in the dreamscaped shape of words in *Books*, to which I now return for fuller attention. One of its name-elements, *worth*, has a constituent part to play in the essay on epitaphs that Wordsworth published in 1810 and again in 1814. It appears in an anecdote of a Greek Sage, newly arrived on a strange shore: coming upon a random corpse, he scorns it as "of no more value than the worthless Shell." Bird-shell, that is, but the seashell borne by the phantom Arab of the dream is homologous, a homophone, even: "see the Shell . . . !" the Sage smirks, the dream's measure of "more worth" just "worthless" here, the poet's name-syllable welded to a negating suffix. It is the radical antithesis of "an Epitaph, (in the ordinary meaning attached to the word)," whose purpose, says Wordsworth, is a "record" of "tribute due to . . . individual worth."[45] But epitaphs fade, and their tributes are more generic than individual. Can any life, in its posthumous presence, secure its words' worth, or must it fall to a worthless Shell?

One dire answer emerges in the dream of *Books*. When Wordsworth writes that the phantom Arab "Stretched forth the shell" (5.90), the gesture puts in English the Latin elements of "intention" (*in* [toward] + *tentus* [stretched]), including a stretch of an eye-rhyme from *forth* back to *worth* in the line just prior (89). An intention for poetry comes with a vengeance when the dreamer is commanded to hold the shell to his ear. He does so,

> And heard that instant in an unknown tongue,
> Which yet I understood, articulate sounds,
> A loud prophetic blast of harmony;
> An Ode, in passion uttered, which foretold
> Destruction to the children of the earth
> By deluge, now at hand.   (5.93–98)

In the shell's "articulate sounds," the expectation of "more worth" (89) turns round as with the might of waters: *worth* now echoes, in devastating strains, into a rhyme with the end-word *earth*. As dire news for *earth* puts *worth* in doubt, *ear*th literally resounds, and spells again, the poet's receptor *ear*.

The self-spelling spirals into crazed self-accounting. On the paradox of "unknown tongue" that is yet "understood" is the dream-logic of Wordsworth's writing: unknown consciously but understood in articulation, because the words are his own. The hand that writes this poetry, no less than the hand that holds the shell to the ear, gives the involuted acoustics: the shell isn't any oracle; it's an echo-chamber of the ear's chamber. In the dreamer's ear, moreover, is an echo of a *worth*-rhymed phrase "child of *earth*," the epithet for man in the crisis induction to *Books*. Even though the poet knows that mortal destiny is "immortal being" (5.23), it is the plight of every man that he,

> As long as he shall be the child of earth,
> Might almost 'weep to have' what he may lose,
> Nor be himself extinguished.   (5.25–27)

The quotation is another echo, of Shakespeare's Sonnet 64: as the ruins of "Time's fell hand" tell the fate of everything loved, "This thought is as a death, which cannot choose / But weep to have that which it fears to lose." *Books* relays the distress of a categorical "child of earth" into the dream's emergency for all "children of the earth," the death of all and all their works, including the material pages of poetry, not sparing the poem at hand. No wonder, then, that a poem of vocational doubt and self-reckoning from Wordsworth's midlife (1807), "Resolution and Independence," would set the phrase "a happy Child of earth am I" in a syntax that veers into a fear of survival neither resolute nor independent in its "pain of heart" (35): *earth* (and *ear*) is lettered within this thought's very *heart*.[46]

In 1828, Wordsworth devised a radical upgrade on *word* for the final line of another *Ode* played in "the cell of hearing," *Stanzas on the Power of Sound*. This concludes (stanza 14):

> though Earth be dust
> And vanish, though the Heavens dissolve, her stay
> Is in the WORD, that shall not pass away.

Wordsworth's draft underlined what the 1835 printing sets in full capitals.[47] Against the dream-trauma of dissolution in *Books*, WORD is a fortified presence on the page, not just as a word but for the author who writes it. It is perfectly correspondent that *Earth* doesn't exactly vanish, but holds *Ear* in readiness. "The Ear addressed" introduces the "Argument" (p. 310) and the *Stanzas* begin, "THY functions are etherial" (I.1), the word *Ear* anagrammed into *are* and sounding into *ethereal*. This poetry addresses the ear in the most literal way: "a Spirit *ae*rial / Informs the cell of h*ear*ing" (I, 3–4). Not long after composing this literal, ear-fidelity to the Word, Wordsworth returned to *Books* to retune his praise of book-power as second only to "Nature's self" (5.222 and 230), or "God's own Will."[48] He tuned some more, revising the last phrase to "his pure Word" (222). Either way, it's the poet's account, putting his name-share (*Will* / *Word*) on the books. The poet of divinely authorized *will* and *word* seems a chosen sound.

Yet just as symptomatic is the way *Books* can host a word-rogue that Christopher Ricks calls an "anti-pun": an obtrusive association against apparent sense that has to be ruled out, denied admission, annulled by context.[49] Ricks has in sight that Arab phantom "hurrying o'er the illimitable waste, / With the fleet waters of a drowning world / In chase of him" (*1850* 5.136–38), the accidental noun-sense of naval *fleet* (blame the waters) having to be deflected from the proper adjectival sense, *swift*.[50] This is rational reading, but a dreamscape could well be hospitable to the homonym as an irrational figural deformation in apocalyptic anxiety. The very heart of the dream beats with assent to strange signings:

> I wondered not, although I plainly saw
> The one to be a stone, the other a shell;
> Nor doubted once but that they both were books,
> Having a perfect faith in all that passed.   (*1850* 5.111–14)

This is the dreamer's faith, but poet Wordsworth's double negative, "Nor doubted," is a double-minded word-processing. With signs so arbitrary, the identity of the dream's naming authority is also in doubt: "This Arab phantom . . . / This semi-Quixote" (5.142–43); "Of these he was neither, and was both at once" (125). Every authority doubled, signs slip before our eyes. In the wake of it all, the name-syllable *words* returns in a question of doubtful tone, hovering between rhetorical confidence and a spasm of vocational doubt:

> Why call upon a few weak words to say
> What is already written in the hearts
> Of all that breathe?   (*1850* 5.185–87)

A rhyme-stressed *all* would seem to make any word-*call* redundant. In *1805*, near the close of *Books*, the poet seems to polish up the register by recalling a time, somewhere between ages 10 and 13, when "words themselves / Move us with conscious pleasure" (5.567–68):

> My ears began to open to the charm
> Of words in tuneful order, found them sweet
> For *their own sakes*—   (5.577–79, his emphasis)

Yet if this early romance is consciously antiphonal to the sounds of doom in the dreamer's ear, the arc of verse from line 567 has been no tuneful order. It is interrupted by the sad present of writing, the poet having "To think of, to read over, many a page" of poems that used to entrance, "and are now / Dead in my eyes" (571–74), maybe this page too, in futurity.

Books, for all its anomaly as anthology of genres (an imported lyrical ballad, a dream-narrative, a rant on modern system of education), is not so much a pause in the narrative path of *The Prelude* as a registration of everything at hazard on it. These are the stakes of its haunted (and haunting) summary meditation on what endures "in works / Of mighty poets" (5.619–20), the vocation elevated with a capital on Poets in *1850* (595):

> Visionary power
> Attends the motions of the viewless winds,
> Embodied in the mystery of words:
> There, darkness makes abode, and all the host
> Of shadowy things work endless changes there,
> As in a mansion like their proper home.   (*1850* 5.595–600)

On the chord of *winds/words/work,* Wordsworth sounds a ghostly rhyme of vital alliance. This is the full presence in the frame of "There / there" (598–99). The deep etymology of *host* as "stranger, foreigner" (OED n. 2) gets re-routed to the pending value in the double analogy, "As in a mansion like their proper home" (*there* shades this *their,* too). In the logic and flux of these very lines, the "mystery of words" is this kind of ever-working visible embodiment. Changing in time, in poetic time and tempo, *words*—in plural, and in endless potential—are not equivalent to a single, eternal WORD, and deliver more. With new dynamic formings, this verse proposes, words return— even create—visionary power in present reading.

What might otherwise register as a vague claim of word-power is embodied in the course of *words* across *The Prelude.* It "Words are but under-agents" in "the language of the heavens" (*1805* 12.270–72), in practice, Wordsworth has been doing the surface work. Readers (including him) become ever more engaged with the poet not just as protagonist, but also as wordsmith. He will sometimes catch and mute the self-signs in revision; but he often lets them stand, with stakes to play. *Book First*'s opening verses are already playing high stakes on the glint of name-words, as if building the poet's proper home. Here is Wordsworth announcing himself free to settle "where I will," a volition weighted at the end of the line (10), ready for "Long months of peace—if such bold word accord" with the prospect (26). The "if" of this *word* petitions on a claim to have "shaken off . . . / That burthen of my own unnatural self ": "Not mine . . . not made for me" (22–25).

Yet the contradiction of "Not mine" to a "my own" so familiar as to get tagged with *That* cannot but weigh on "the very words which I have here / Recorded" (1.58–59): the first event of the full word *words*. The record that Wordsworth gives in the next verse paragraph opens a mini-saga of default, with a tortured, name-laden litotes: "not unwilling now to give / A respite to this passion" (68–69), the poet dallies and defers. This is the only instance of the phrase "not unwilling" in *The Prelude.* Such a calibrated litotes of *will* soon converges with another name-element in this delay, "What need of many words?" (113): the second event of the full word *words,* now line-end weighted, with a question-mark that airs a flourish without believing it. The "burthen" said to be shaken off adheres to the poetry in name-signs, to regenerate *burthen* in the sense of undersong, a refrain, even a theme (OED IV) against self-composure. It presses again in *Book Second,* on the "Hard task," not naturally guaranteed, in the core mandate of autobiography: how to put into "words of reason deeply weighed" any certain accounting of the origin of general habits and desires, let alone each particular thought (232–36). Not the breezy blow-off of "What need of many words?" this is a blow to the very need of words. Wordsworth had written the dilemma into his earliest drafts.[51]

The question can't deflect a related one: how to distinguish "things / Which we perceive, and not which we have made" (2.223–24). Is the making of word-things that reflect "Wordsworth" a peculiar reflex of this autobiography? "The lexicon glosses names while thinking constitutes signs." So A. C. Goodson (54) comments on William Empson's method in *The Structure of Complex Words*. While Goodson doesn't pause over how names may constitute signs, this potential is in "the background of ideas" in Empson's structure (270). It unfolds brilliantly in Empson's chapter, "Sense in *The Prelude*," a challenge to the widely held view that Wordsworth's poetry doesn't depend on "a concentrated richness of single words." Empson doesn't mean the big-ticket items, "'key' words like Nature and Imagination," with "a sturdy effort to expound them in discursive language." His quarry is "little" words "with a more curious part to play" (289), what Wordsworth's essay on epitaphs calls a "constituent part." In *The Prelude*—this "thing, unprecedented in Literary history" (so he dubs his addiction, that "a man should talk so much about himself")—such curious play sets self-naming words vibrating. "It is not self-conceit, as you will know well," Wordsworth assures George Beaumont about his poem, with a *will/well* rounded to enlist assent (1 May 1805; *EY* 586).

Even so, this is a poet whose forms of denial tend to admit what he himself will know. That double-epithet, "self-conceit," gets used only once in *The Prelude*, in 1850's *Book Thirteenth*—too aptly, in a *words*-laden passage about how "books mislead us" (208),

> flattering self-conceit with words,
> That . . . most ambitiously set forth
> Extrinsic differences, the outward marks
> Whereby society has parted man from man
> From man.   (13.216–20)

Wordsworth revised to give *words* this line-end placement, hanging it over *forth*.[52] The vertical deflexion of *words / forth* is the antonym of *words-worth*. Is this chastened self-conceit, or its meta-poetry? Its formation comes late in a project that can't stop rehearsing its originating unease, especially when name-syllables hit the poetry's syntax.

The pulse is more than originating; it's originary. After recounting in *Book First* an epic writer's block, Wordsworth breaks through with those vivid recollections of juvenile delinquency. He then pauses to tune-up the mainframe: "The calm existence that is mine when I / Am worthy of myself"

(1.360–61). But what a strange tune, its worthy calm at odds with the thrills just written out. This is the poem's first event of *worthy*, initiated by the line-turning *I/Am*: the last syllables of Will*iam*. The emerging argument is that "The mind of man is framed" (351) with a dark

> Invisible workmanship that reconciles
> Discordant elements, and makes them move
> In one society.   (1.353–55)

The poetry's visible workmanship moves elements in name-society. Wanting to be "worthy" of his native fields (1.508), Wordsworth reclaims the "willing heart" with which he had begun his poem in 1799.[53] Willing comes in aid of willing. Not for nothing had he worked in two early drafts to distinguish a willing heart from caprices of a "*will/... not worthy* to be deemed/Our being."[54]

From these name-haunts Wordsworth manages to conjure a worthy will to bring *Book First* to a close, but not without a reflex of doubt:

> My mind hath been revived—and if this mood
> Desert me not, I will forthwith bring down
> Through later years the story of my life.   (1.665–67)

Negotiating mood into a willed story, *if* sounds that undersong troubling "composed ... thoughts" (1.281). Revival pivots on *I will* (*I will forth*, even), joined to "certain hopes" that a provisional "labour will be welcome" to the friend he addresses, Coleridge (673–74), who had been pumping for a different, philosophical epic ever since 1799.[55] Wordsworth soon casts a more hopeful *will* to another audience. Recalling times when he and a dear schoolmate shared lake walks, he allows himself to fancy, "With heart how full/Will he peruse these lines, this page" (2.353–54).

III. Turning the Word

Wordsworth knows the tradition of avoided nominal literalism, from Shakespeare on; knows, too, the variable potential of names hidden and names revealed (to recall Stephen Dedalus's topography) that can turn name-words into alien agents. On this axis, Wordsworth turns new ways to discover "Wordsworth" in *The Prelude*: not spelled to death by auto-narratology, but present in "Wordsworth's Elements." *Book Third* recalls a Cambridge student decked out in "signs of manhood," "As if by word/Of magic or some fairy's power" (33–39). Poet Wordsworth must have winced; this *word*-agency

got revised to "the change" of "some Fairy's wand" (*1850* 35–36). Further vexing this farce, even in *1805*, is a serious argument for differentiating "words,
signs, / Symbols or actions"—those "outward things / Done visibly for other
minds"—from what is "within" (174–76). But if inward "theme" is the "heroic
argument" (173–82), it is also dislodged, in the very sentence that stakes it, by
a sensation that "It lies far hidden from the reach of words" (185).

What is within word-reach is the story of the outward self, and it can turn
anti-heroic. Such turns are not a dialectical toward resolution but a recurring
composition and decomposition of Wordsworth-elements. The end of *Book
Third* finds him spelling one into an alien spectacle of life at Cambridge. The
sorry upshot, with line-end featuring, is "meek Worth / Left to itself unheard
of and unknown" (642–43), a potential negated. Pausing over the patent per-
sonification, Norton's editors mark its exception to the rubric in Preface to
Lyrical Ballads (124n).[56] Wordsworth must have been deliberate about this
artifice, then, casting a name-syllable abstraction not equivalent to the person but readable to the poet. The name-tracking advances to parodic brio in
Book Fourth, as the poet recounts the college man's homecoming to the
Lakes, setting the stage with a cartoon:

> that unruly child of mountain birth,
> The froward brook, which, soon as he was boxed
> Within our garden, found himself at once
> As if by trick insidious and unkind,
> Stripped of his voice, and left to dimple down
> Without an effort and without a will
> A channel paved by the hand of man.
> I looked at him and smiled, and smiled again,
> And in the press of twenty thousand thoughts,
> 'Ha', quoth I, 'pretty prisoner, are you there!'   (4.39–48)

If a "mountain birth" would seem disposed (by genetics, thematics, and phonics) to romance a rhyme-ready "Wordsworth," the sequel, "without a *will*,"
turns the parody. The hand that paves this verse is the poet's, set "to pen
down / A satire on myself" (54–55), his pen tacitly pointing a synonym for the
brook's pent "box."

Such parodies do not diffuse other tones, but play along. With London
looming in the prospect of *Book Seventh*, Wordsworth opens this chapter
with the counterpoint of *will* in overplus. It is sweet vernal promise, birds
a-singing, the poet in correspondent breeze:

> listening, I half whispered, 'We will be,
> Ye heartsome choristers, ye and I will be
> Brethren, and in the hearing of bleak winds
> Will chaunt together.'   (7.34–37)

To prove this triple *will*, the verse paragraph whispers rhymings into *hills* (38, 45), before ending in determination: "We *will* now resume with chearful hope" (54). Thus fortified, the poet recalls a "self-willed" return to London (70); this is restaged with *will* in *Book Eighth*: "I willingly return" (679).[57] Yet nothing is more characteristic of the spells of *will* in *The Prelude* than its zones for ironic change. In *Book Seventh*, the turn is severe and self-satiric.

The herald is an anecdote of a local boy, a cripple, returned from London. Boy Wordsworth, primed for "Some change, some beams of glory," was mocked by disappointment, word-betrayed: "every word he uttered, on my ears / Fell flatter than a caged parrot's note" (7.103–6). Poet Wordsworth still hews to the "wondrous power of words, how sweet they are / According to the meaning which they bring" (121–22), but in the record of London sweet power is nowhere. The "most imposing word" waves in the "masquerade" of an advertising poster (213–14). And the most absurd is borne by Jack the Giant-killer at Sadler's Wells. Even though his "garb is black," to signify (and mime) invisibility, it is contradicted by visible workmanship: "the word / IN- VISIBLE flames forth upon his chest" (303–10). This is the only word in *The Prelude* that Wordsworth puts all in capitals, in travesty of Milton's hellish sublime, "darkness visible," and its specter Death, "Black it stood as Night" (*PL* 1.63, 2.670). Woven into Wordsworth's travesty, *word . . . forth* is visible script to the reading eye, with no sensation of worth.[58] When Wordsworth goes on to say that an audience's "faith must needs be coy" to sustain the pantomime's "Delusion bold" (7.308), he stages, without a shadow of imagi- nation, Coleridge's desynonimizing of delusion and illusion.[59] Illusion requires, and delusion stretches too far, "that willing suspension of disbelief" that procures "poetic faith" (*BL* 2:2).

The flagrant nonsense of sign and referent is a travesty in Jack's garb, but non-sense finds a dire corollary in the epitaph-essay "Celebrated Authors," where Wordsworth warns about trifling with words as costuming: "If words be not . . . an incarnation of the thought, but only a clothing for it, then surely will they prove an ill gift." In distinguishing the spirit and "counter-spirit" of word use, the language at hand strips *will* to *ill* with a vengeance, naming the power of words "to consume and to alienate" an abuser (call it an unworthy self) "from his right mind" (2.65). Another London stage in *Book Seventh*, more pretentious, is a grand travesty of ill gifts abounding: "that great stage/Where senators, tongue-favored men, perform" (7.522–23). Wordsworth describes one wordy actor in a real-time, present tense:

> The enchantment spreads and rises—all are rapt
> Astonished—like a hero in romance
> He winds away his never-ending horn:
> Words follow words, sense seems to follow sense—   (7.537–40)

In syllables spread for self-recognition, "Words follow words"; but the tune grows "tedious even in a young man's ear" (7.543).

From this sham of sense, can a poet's—this poet's—words be saved? The apparition of name-words, however parodised, is never exorcised. In *Book Eighth*, Wordsworth recalls how, in his first enthusiasms of his poetic faculty, a wet black rock might glister with meaning, a recollection he draws into name-indexing:

>   sometimes were the shapes
> Of wilful fancy grafted upon feelings
> Of the imagination, and they rose
> In worth accordingly.   (8.583–86)

The factitious *graft* taps into the root, *graphion,* a stylus for writing. As the poetry describes the process, it graphs down a vertical deflexion of intimate name-syllables: shapes of *Wil*ful fancy (proto-words) move through feeling imagination down to (rising) *worth*.[60] If this is a confessed fancy, its worth is thickened by a precedent in this same book, a recollection that flashes with the glory of an "aerial cross" stationed in the Chartreuse (no less) (8.408–10): a Lakeland Shepherd, a "human form" which imprinted boy Wordsworth as "an index" of "worthiness" (414–16). The index is consulted again, in *Book Ninth*, as Wordsworth meditates on having been "formed" to tell his "story" by boyhood tutoring in "individual worth" (243–49). The story in present forming tells this with elements of the poet's name.

What of a word shaped in no glister or splendor, but totalized darkness? Iconic in Geoffrey Hartman's census of Wordsworth's skewed "correspondence . . . between word and wish" is the call on "Darkness" in *1850*'s *Book Thirteenth* ("Words, Wish" 200). The scene is a midnight crossing of Sarum Plain, and it is doubly dark. One vector is an apostrophe to "Darkness," a poet's ready "word," but the other is a vast darkness that pre-empts any call:

I called on Darkness—but before the word
Was uttered, midnight darkness seemed to take
All objects from my sight.   (*1850* 13.327–29)

Traveller Wordsworth is stunned, as if truly facing Milton's Death: "Black it
stood as Night." Poet Wordsworth can, at last, stage the call. There is sublime
poetic power, even, in the line's pause at "before the word."[61] Before the syntax temporalizes *before,* this line sets it as a spatial presence: *the word* before
the eye. How more dramatic, then, is the turn of verse and sense to a totalized, word-robbing "midnight darkness." Obliterated *sight* is literally underneath a rhymed *midnight.* Before this clinch, Wordsworth lets *take* hover at
the line-end to host the intransitive sense of "have an impact" (OED 13a)
or, better yet, "adhere" (OED 15)—a suspense in the syntax destined for the
transitive sense of "lay claim to."

The nightmare of no words is recurrent in *The Prelude.* In *Book Ninth*
(France, in the early 1790s) an inset tale ends, precisely, with the end of
words. For readers in the twentieth century who learned of Wordsworth's
affair with Annette Vallon, this registers as a ghost-chapter of displaced autobiography, turned into a "tragic tale" (9.591) of young lovers. Soul-mates
since infancy, Vaudracour and commoner Julia secretly marry, their union
doomed by the opposition of Vaudracour's aristocrat father, with full *ancien
régime* support. After several arrests and harassments, Vaudracour finally
accepts an annulment and disgraced Julia's sentence that "she must
retire / Into a convent . . . there immured" for the rest of her life (839–40).
Vaudracour receives the news in "calm despondency" (851),

Composed and silent, without outward sign
Of even the least emotion. Seeing this,
When Julia scattered some upbraiding words
Upon his slackness, he thereto returned
No answer.   (9.852–56)

Wordsworth brings the verb *upbraids* into his own voice in *Book Tenth,* comparing Paris in the Terror to a volume

written in a tongue he cannot read,
So that he questions the mute leaves with pain,
And half upbraids their silence.   (10.52–54)

These are the only two events of *upbraid* in *The Prelude,* the poet's pain before a book, silent and discomposed, that defeats reading, halfway to defeated

Julia's pained scatter of "upbraiding words." Vaudracour marks the dead-end of words. Having sacrificed Julia, and then, "by some mistake / Or indiscretion" having let their son die, "From that time forth he never uttered word" (9.907–8, 912)—the last three words repeated in line 921, to sound a rime riche of poverty. The poet's name-stakes mark the sentence's calendar of arrest: "*forth . . . word.*"⁶² And the stake may have been coded, as David Erdman noticed, in "Vaudracour," for which "worth of heart" reversed to "Heartsworth" is fair English (15)—not quite "Wordsworth," but close enough.

At the outset of *Book Tenth: Residence in France and French Revolution,* Wordsworth takes heartfelt pains to say that, amid his great agitation, he fantasized himself issuing a global call to all souls "Worthy of liberty" to help restore the Republic to its "work of honour" (119, 124): "I willingly" would have joined up (134). This stamp of self-enlistment plays into the further pains that he takes to say, "I both was and must be of small worth" had anything other "than absolute want / Of funds" turned *him* back to England (189–92). He was half Vaudracour in this plea, having abandoned Annette Vallon, pregnant with their daughter, in 1792. This question of *worth,* too close to home, was soon changed to *weight,* a phrasing that held through *1850* (226).⁶³ But the question is sufficiently weighty for Wordsworth to return to a defense in his *Conclusion*: "Let one *word* more of personal circumstance—/ . . . / Since I withdrew *unwillingly* from France" (13.332, 334); *1850* puts these two lines together, even (14.348–49). The embedded syllable *will* sounds the one *word* (amid an implied several) for an "I" *un*-selfed, wrenched at its core. Haunted by Madame Roland's heroic "last words" on the scaffold (10.354), *Book Eleventh* has the poet back in England reclaiming his "worthy theme," disdaining aberrations "Unworthily" indulged, and soon drawing on those "passages of life" when a she-mind was shaping "outward sense" to "her *will,*" her object of action and volition (132, 153, 272).

Theme is one thing, verse-passages another, and the gambit wavers on the force of words. If the theme is a beneficent "will" that forms a poet with "renovating virtue" in reserve (11.259), its foundation is laid in trauma. The poetry spools back to Boy Wordsworth, lost, stumbling on a site of a murderer's execution. With gothic renovation, the convict's name on nearby turf, "engraven / In times long past" by "Some unknown hand," is legible "to this hour / . . . fresh and visible" (293–98), the hour of the boy's displendour in the grass doubled in the hour the poet's writing:

> at length
> I chanced to espy those characters inscribed
> On the green sod.   (11.299–301)

No grave, but engraving visible for the reading, scintillated like a revenance cut off from the inscriber. The immediate sequel to this extraordinary inscription is "an ordinary sight" (308); but this proves a distinction without a difference. Words repeat the "unknown hand" of the inscriber as agents "unknown" even for poet Wordsworth:

> I should need
> Colours and words that are unknown to man
> To paint the visionary dreariness . . .   (11.308–10)

This concession was in an early draft and it held through latest revisions.[64] The limit is always "as far as words can give" (11.339; *1850* 12.283), but the inspiration of this poetry, at a loss for words, is what its poet is willing to give in words.

IV. Willing Words, Worth the Record

The soon-ensuing opening of *Book Twelfth* (the *"Same Subject"* as *Eleventh*: *Imagination How Impaired and Restored*), restores words for an ode to "Nature" as the guarantor of "genius, which exists by interchange / Of peace and excitation" (8–9). In the happiest relay, "words find easy way, inspired" (18). Writing the *Conclusion*, Wordsworth, with easy sway, sounds name elements into a symphony. Those "Willing to work and to be wrought upon" (13.100), goes the story with this capital-W name-launched alliteration, have to put it all to the test, to gain the prize of

> sovereignty within and peace at will,
> Emotion which best foresight need not fear,
> Most worthy then of trust when most intense;
>
> . . . .
>   .   .   . and delight
> That fails not, in the external universe.   (13.114–19)

Line-end placed, *will* (with foresight) projects to the superlative *Most worthy* and success in "the external uni*verse*": the vast field that echoes a vocational *verse* as this long verse paragraph's last syllable. In *1850*, *Most worthy* abides, while *will* and *universe* yield to an even worthier alliance, "words of Holy Writ" (14.123–25).

Willing Words: Words may be willing in inclination, may be willing to act a constituent part, and willing in bequests for times to come. Yet shadowing the multiple values of will is a restless question of worth: innate or attributed value, from the external universe and in the verse of a name. Wordsworth is ever worrying the question, and *The Prelude* is the magnetic site. In its *Conclusion*, the poet insists that he never "did wilfully / Yield . . . to mean cares and low pursuits" (13.134–35); *1850* promotes *Wilfully* to head the next line (14.154). The total accounting enters "words" in memory of an early benefactor:

> The name of Calvert; it shall live, if words
> Of mine can give it life.   (13.350–51)

The pause of line 350 implies words in general; the turn particularizes Wordsworth's hope. The debt involves larger claims, and larger uncertainties, about the life of words, and the life that will give them value. With a new verse paragraph, the poet confesses the question, speaking its keyword, *worth* (again with line-end signing) for Coleridge's endorsement:

> Whether to me shall be allotted life,
> And with life power to accomplish aught of worth
> Sufficient to excuse me in men's sight
> For having given this record of myself,
> Is all uncertain.   (13.386–90)

Coleridge, the monitor ever in mind, gets hailed as a poet of "delicious words" (395), the phrase sounding what it describes, to infuse sympathy

> that the history of a poet's mind
> Is labour not unworthy of regard:
> To thee the work shall justify itself.   (13.408–10)

For Wordsworth, Poet Laureate of Litotes, *not unworthy* joins the roster in a truly supreme meta-formation.[65] The address to Coleridge, replete with phrasings of "we will," held through every revision, long after the happy friendship ceased to be.[66]

Another partner haunts William Wordsworth, however: a shade of private, regenerate self-doubt. Around the time he was completing the 1805 form of this self-qualifying, self-authorizing epic, he wrote "Ode to Duty." Its fifth stanza closes with this longing:

I feel the weight of chance desires:
My hopes no more must change their name,
I long for a repose which ever is the same.   (*1807* 1:72)

A linked *name/same,* beyond change, is prelude to the goal, name-inscribed, that ends the next stanza:

Yet not the less would I throughout
Still act according to the voice
Of my own wish; and feel past doubt
That my submissiveness was choice:
Not seeking in the school of pride
For "precepts over dignified,"
Denial and restraint I prize
No farther than they breed a second Will more wise.   (*1807* 1:73)

How strange a risk in poetic drama is the line-cut at "feel past doubt." The phrase will distill into "a feeling without doubt"; but the pause flirts with the specter of feeling a doubt from the past, partner to "I feel the weight of chance desires"—a feeling no more easily shaken off than "That burthen of my own unnatural self" (*Prelude* 1.23). Will is an ideal invested against accidents and vicissitudes, defined against pompous precepts (the quotation is from Milton's refusal of the genre[67]). Although Wordsworth revised his first draft's "wish more wise" to "will more wise," then to "Will," he canceled the whole stanza after 1807, perhaps wincing at "Will more wise," because he didn't feel past doubt.[68]

But he liked the sound. He brought it back in the 1850 *Prelude,* appreciating the "wise men, willing to grow wiser" from Edmund Burke's "most eloquent tongue" (7.516–17); and he reworked a passage about his deep despair in France in 1792, to state, with the same wordings, his enduring faith in the ideal of "Liberty" (11.253):

I feel
(Sustained by worthier as by wiser thoughts)
The aspiration.   (11.255–57)

Yet even the aspirant to Wiser Will can't shake off the shade of a Will who has to write an "Ode to Duty" in the first place—the poet of restless will that may be less wise but also more dynamic. The second Will may never "feel past doubt," because doubt is the pulse of the poet's lived, enlivening past.[69]

As able Latinist Wordsworth knows, to *doubt* is to be of two minds, two wills, more or less wise. His words do this work, tell it, record it.

More than will-power, it was word-power that prompted Coleridge to one revision of his tribute to Wordsworth's recitation of the whole epic to an intimate circle at Grasmere. In rapture at its close, Coleridge drafted lines of praise (sometime between 1807 and 1808), giving the title "Ad Vilmum Axiologum," a Latin nod to Wordsworth's first signature, "Axiologus."[70] Sometime in the next decade, even with the friendship on the rocks, he added a line to another tribute on how Wordsworth's genius "often quickens in the Heart / Thoughts all too deep for words!"—turning the close of the "Intimations" *Ode*, "Thoughts that do often lie too deep for tears," into a lexical metaphysics.[71] The paradox, tacit but acute in Coleridge's ear, is that it takes words to plumb depths beyond words.

In one order of theoretical accounting, this is deficiency, the non-coincidence of name and referent: words are only a factitious approximation, intermediary or impotent. But in Coleridge's audit, assets accrue in a formation aptly mapped in Wordsworth's *Conclusion* by that compound that he invented for Coleridge's ears: "under-presence" (13.71). The substrate, allied to the inspirations of "under-song," is the deep ground of accidental reading—say, in the boy who discovers that site of execution, where "I chanced to espy those characters inscribed" (11.300). This place of death and the writing that survives without agency could be written up for Derrida's brand-line, but only at the price of Derrida's house rules. The law is this: the "academic conventions of literary biography" presuppose "the link" (*le rapport*), "be it natural or contractual, between a given text, a given so-called author, and his name designated as proper" (24–25); but if an author does not keep "the signature . . . outside the text . . . as an under-signed subscription," and violates the boundary by "inserting it into the body of the text," the investment shifts into a project to "monumentalize, institute, and erect it into a stony object"; and when the proper name "becomes a moment or a part of the text, as a thing or a common name/noun," it is to "lose the identity, the title of ownership over the text."[72] In a slippage of proper to common, the signature of identity cannot but surrender to the free play of textual inscription and wanton semantic potential. Whip out the *Signéponge*.

On the ledger of loss, we might enter Wordsworth's stony shrines and epitaphs, signifiers of absent, even unremembered lives. But on another ledger, we could enter Wordsworth's intuitive swerves around deconstruction and

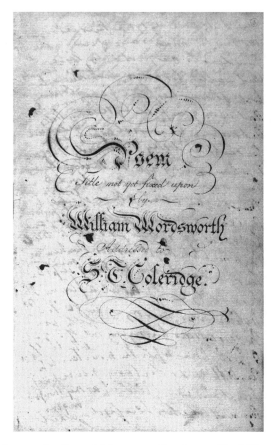

Provisional title page for *Poem/Title not yet Fixed upon/By William Wordsworth/ Addressed to Samuel Taylor Coleridge* Dove Cottage MS. B (DC MS. 53), 4ʳ. Courtesy of the William Wordsworth Trust, Grasmere England.

its perils of Derridian thanatopraxis. He achieves this not only by casting himself as reader-spy of characters inscribed, but also by keeping his proper name off the main turf of *The Prelude*, sounding it only in syllables tuned to other missions. His full name appears only on provisional title-pages, and though written with monumentalizing flourishes, not even in his own hand.[73] The title later affixed, *The Prelude*, was not even his.[74] As late as 1847, Wordsworth's working title was "the Poem of my own Life," with a mere flicker of his name in a subscript: "what seemed best to me *worth* recording" (*Autobiographical Memoranda* 1:15). The name comes in Wordsworth's Elements, and with no monumental inscription.

Hedged on unfixed reception (and only figural audience after Coleridge's death in 1834), *Addressed to* is an open, spectral bid. Its hazard ripples in a punning litotes that one review of the 1850 *Prelude* could not resist, describing the poet's deft aversion of the charge of "egotism" this way: "The walk which Wordsworth selected was . . . by no means unworthy" (*Tait's* 526). A sheerly accidental marking comes with a triple-word hit by Stanley Cavell's meditation on unknowable reception: "whether our *words will* go on meaning what they do depends upon whether other people find it *worth* their while to continue to understand us." In the same year (1979), Mary Jacobus sounded the syllables to review the anxiety marked throughout *The Prelude*: "Wordsworth's nostalgia for . . . the *word* made Logos . . . hardly needs dwelling on. What does seem *worth* exploring is the troubling status of both books and writing."[75] This may be the overplus of my ready eye, but it also has the look, in my retrospect, of inevitability when anyone writes about Wordsworth and worth of written words.

Mindful of his medium, troubled import and all, Wordsworth allows name-signifiers to dwell in the field of writerly self-inscription. This overdetermined register of receptivity is not immune to misgiving, a caution the poet voices in verse near the end of *Book First*, to shadow a primary claim about providential communication:

> The earth
> And common face of Nature spake to me
> Remembereable things; sometimes, 'tis true
> By chance collisions and quaint accidents——   (1.614–17)

Attenuating the romance of prosopopoeia, "sometimes, 'tis true" reviews its elements of communication. If "remembereable things" include quaint accidents of name wordings, the question is not narratological. It's apparitional: what to make of the collisions and quaint accidents of words that look remembereable for "me"? To remember words this way is to write autobiography in words that don't have to be narratologically plotted. In *1799*, Wordsworth had mused just briefly about "quaint associations" (1.421); by 1805 he had more to say on this qualification.

In writing ostensibly about becoming the writer-self, apparitional naming sidesteps the fictional construction of self, to plant identity in the chance collisions of immediate writing, alive to, and vitally alive in, the accidents of words. These are nodes of "power / That does not come unrecognised" but works with "redundant energy, / Vexing its own creation" (*1805* 1.46–48). Redundant energy has its own productivity—and over-productivity:

if I may trust myself, this hour
Hath brought a gift that consecrates my joy;
For I, methought, while the sweet breath of heaven
Was blowing on my body, felt within
A corresponding mild creative breeze.   (*1805* 1.39–43)

Readers (iconically, M. H. Abrams) mark figural inspiration in the corresponding breeze (*spiritus* in Latin). But there is another correspondence, in material poetry, an accident of rhyme. "I, methought" may seem, in the flow of the lines, to be just a polite concession to fantasy; but it rhymes with "Hath brought," visually aligned in the line above, to give the phrasing a slight, counterpointed brake on the venture of "Hath brought." In *1850* Wordsworth cancels "Hath brought" to let "I, methought" breeze more easily by as a happy fantasy. Can he trust himself?

In his earliest draft he continued the line about "redundant energy" this way: "Creating not but as it may / disturbing things created.—"[76] The question about what was prior, creation or disturbance (put another way: writing or reading), is elusive, slippery, unstable, and unappeasably productive. It was on Wordsworth's mind in May 1805 when he confessed to his friend Beaumont his incurable addiction to "the Poem on my own life":

> If when the work shall be finished it appears to the judicious to have redundancies they shall be lopped off, if possible. But this is very difficult to do when a man has written with thought, and this defect, whenever I have suspected it or found it to exist in any writings of mine, I have always found incurable. The fault lies too deep, and is the first conception. If you see Coleridge before I do, do not speak of this to him. (*EY* 586–87)

Too deep for tears, but not for words. For *redundant,* the second definition in Dr. Johnson's *Dictionary* is "using more words . . . than are useful." If this is Wordsworth's name-word worry, the first definition is the one that authorizes the venture from which the poet made a name for himself: "Superabundant; exuberant; superfluous"—in effect, words in overplus, activated into a peculiar Wordsworthian grammar of first conceptions that couldn't then, and still can't, avoid disturbing things created—including writings that incurably mine a name.

* * *

Quaint associations. This may be autobiography in its primary formation and deepest fortuity, a self-allusion. "Allusion is a two-in-one, like a hyphenation," remarks Christopher Ricks, though not with Words-worth in mind (*Force* 332). To Hazlitt, however, Wordsworth seemed to be the antagonist of allusion, inclined to self-regard over bringing another "into play." He recalls a conversation in which he "hinted" to Wordsworth that he seemed to have "borrowed the idea of his *Poems on the Naming of Places* from the local inscriptions of the same kind in Paul and Virginia." Wordsworth shrugged this off, offering "some distinction without a difference, in defence of his claim to originality. Any the slightest variation would be sufficient for this purpose in his mind; for whatever *he* added or omitted would inevitably be worth all that any one else had done," Hazlitt recalls, with a barbed indirect discourse that includes *worth*.

The site of this anecdote is *My first Acquaintance with Poets* (36–37), a funny, poignant, elegiac essay, dense and lively with allusions. The Poets are Wordsworth and Coleridge. Hazlitt's Wordsworth, the self-proposed genius—by turns pompous, mysteriously withdrawn, or just absurd in his striped pantaloons, chanting in a northern *burr*, wreaking havoc on half a Cheshire cheese—is memorable, but not haunting. The essay's core is haunted and animated by Coleridge—in vibrant life in Hazlitt's scene of 1798, but by 1823 (when the essay was written) shaded by what Coleridge would (and wouldn't) become. Allusion is the haunted housing for this historical difference, and Hazlitt is obsessed with, possessed by, what it brings into play. At the same time, an unexpected ghost haunts one allusion called up toward the end of the essay, on behalf of Coleridge and, Hazlitt thinks, from one of Coleridge's works, but its source is deeply elsewhere—a misprision (as we shall see) that exposes more than Hazlitt can bear to hear.

CHAPTER THREE

Hazlitt's Conjurings

First Acquaintance & "Quaint Allusion"

I. Alluding to Allusion

And recollect the work is only fiction
And that I sing of neither mine nor me,
Though every scribe in some slight turn of diction
Will hint allusions never meant.

So sings Byron in Canto XI (88) of *Don Juan* (1823), by which point in the career of this serial epic, the protest comes with ironic flair. Even as this poet goes on to say that he doesn't deal in hints but speaks out plain, it's clear that his turns of diction at once hint allusions and insist that these were "never meant."

The logic of allusion is that it is meant, whatever the affectation. The first thing that Michael Drayton, "Author," speaks of in his headnote to *Poly-Olbion*, "Of The *Illustrations*" (1612), is the performance of allusion: "What the Verse oft, with allusion, as supposing a full knowing Reader, lets slip" (xx-vii). Joseph Pucci smartly notes the two agents: the Verse-slip and "the reader in the process of unraveling allusive meaning"—particularly, a "full-knowing Reader" who "spies the allusion and constructs a meaning for it" (xi).[1] Such a reader is pleased to be so ready, so literate. This literacy is literary memory, remembering a story, and the history around its words and wordings. "Literary uses of language," as J. J. Prynne puts the case for full knowing, bear "a heightened sense of the accumulated layers and aspects of association which form the significatory resonances of previous usage: the whole prior history . . . can be tuned to allow and invite the vibrations of sense and suggestions of historical retrospect" (18). While all language, as received and reiterable, is a form of revenance, allusion is the self-aware formation and orchestration.

Pucci was thinking hard about this in 1998, even earlier in his doctoral thesis in the mid-1980s (xii), and Prynne was lecturing on the subject in 1993—just as internet searchability was emerging. Allusion is not now as it hath been of yore. Formerly culled from a library of one's own and relayed for recognition, allusion used to vibrate in full-knowing transactions, counting even as a literacy test.[2] No more. Phrase, trope and turn, now and in time to be, whenever the screen is on, are no sooner sensed than searched. All is changed, changed utterly with the terrible beauty of the World Wide Web: "no quotation, however recondite, will be difficult to recognize," Adam Kirsch remarks of the search-enginuity. And if "every reader can tune in, allusion is no longer a privileged channel of communication" (75). Kirsch is waxing elegiac, but I confess my happy tuning. The old channels were not restricted to privilege, moreover, if by this you mean elite subscription. Literacy and memory issued a general passport.

Even so, a passport is just a pass; and a find function, at best, a golden retriever in the field of research. Golden, yes: quick to turn up a phrase. But retrieval stops short of interpretation. And this is allusion's vital turn, its possession, even: *ad ludere*, toward something in play. William Hazlitt was the readiest of alluders. He had libraries, at hand, in his head, ready to conjure. Not just a "full knowing Reader," Hazlitt seems a "full knowing Author." Drayton's cute phrase, "lets slip," describes an artfulness that passes for reflex. Hazlitt's allusioning is this kind of affair, calling on past scenes for present import and reflection. His ease can make allusion seem more like a spontaneous association than a conscious riff; but it's art, cued to "ready knowledge" of original text and context—to use Earl Wasserman's phrase for Alexander Pope's art of allusion.[3]

Wasserman's account of the operation is different from John Hollander's in *The Figure of Echo: A Mode of Allusion*. Hollander's echo-chamber cordons off questions of intention and "overt allusion," along with any measures of "the degree of self-awareness, of conscious design" on an audience in reflecting "the very words of an earlier text" (ix). So, too, James Chandler audits Romantic-era allusion as unconscious association (intertextuality in random access memory), and Sarah Annes Brown deepens the echo-chamber into an interior psychology of the uncanny.[4] Hazlitt's allusiveness is otherwise. It's typically controlled play—but not always, and sometimes in the midst of his game, can come with disturbances from unsuspected depths. There is a remarkable slip, or slip-up, at the end of *My first Acquaintance with Poets*—all the more arresting for its shadow on the routes of allusion that Hazlitt's art has so capably, if painfully, laid out.

I postpone turning to this scene, to begin with what the title of Hazlitt's luminously touching essay sets in play: the winding of "acquaintance" with what persona W.H. calls "quaint allusion." The syllable-echo is no accident. From Anglo-Norman to Old French, *acquaintance* and *quaint* tap a Latin

root in knowing: *ad cognitum* (toward knowing), *cognitus* (known)—the relay of allusion's field. Wistfully nostalgic, wittily new-angled: Hazlitt's call to
"quaint allusion" to conjure an art routed across time. While philologist
Walter Whiter commented in 1794 that "the ancient prevalence and familiarity" of some allusions are betrayed by "quaint language" (49n), it is telling
that Dr. Johnson wanted to cite Swift's phrase "quaint modernisms" in his
Dictionary's entry "Modernism."[5] "Quaint" can be retro-modernism in style.
At the same time, as this editor of Shakespeare also knew, Shakespeare's
reputation for *"far-fetched or quaint allusions"* required some defense from
modern editors.[6] When *My first Acquaintance* was published, in 1823, *quaint*
still had this oscillation: a modern recognition of a style skewed, out of style.

We catch this reverberation in Hazlitt's day. For a fantasy in Spenserian
adventure, Wordsworth wryly regards the boy of "Nutting" (1800), "trick'd
out" in "a Figure quaint" (7). Around the same time (1797), Anna Barbauld's
"Washing Day" described hard labor unrelieved by any "quaint device of
mirth" (15). In Barry Cornwall's *Sicilian Story,* we're advised that, "for the
moral," we may "trace it in the quaint and antique text" (xxxviii; p. 136). In
Jane Austen's *Emma* (1815), fashionista Mrs. Elton coos about Mr. Wood-
house's charm: "all that quaint, old-fashioned politeness; it is much more to
my taste than modern ease" (2:17), the affection for "quaint" a nouveau riche
affectation. For his part, Hazlitt regretted Edward Young's hashing of his
moral reflections with "all the smart turns and quaint expression of an
enigma or repartee in verse," and he mocked Leigh Hunt's salon-stockpiling
of "quaint allusions always at hand to produce a laugh."[7]

Quaint is arty this way, but it can raise the stakes to artful skill. In *The
Tempest,* "quaint Ariel" uses a "quaint Device" to make a sumptuous feast
disappear (1.2.316; 3.3.sd). Keats underscored the last phrase (*Dramatic Works*
1814, 1:45) and recalled it in *The Eve of St. Agnes* to describe window-panes of
"quaint device" (xxiv). Over this very stanza Hazlitt had paused in 1821, with
a sigh for imagery he knew would have throbbed his young romantic heart
("On Reading Old Books" 132). In *My first Acquaintance with Poets,* "quaint"
is the muse of indulgence aware of this train of art:

> Would that I could go back to what I then was! Why can we not revive past
> times as we can revisit old places? If I had the quaint Muse of Sir Philip Sid-
> ney to assist me, I would write a *Sonnet to the Road between W—m and
> Shrewsbury*, and immortalise every step of it by some fond enigmatical con-

ceit. I would swear that the very milestones had ears, and that Harmer-hill stooped with all its pines, to listen to a poet, as he passed! (34)

Indulging a fond allusion to Orphean poetic power, W.H. tunes his sigh for reviving and revisiting to a "quaint Muse" from another era.

The Muse of quaint allusion can prove unchary in its indulgences, however, may take on more than might be useful. Hazlitt's friend T. N. Talfourd worried about the way the "force" of Hazlitt's "argument" could be "diverted (unconsciously to himself) by figures and fantasies, by fine and quaint allusions."[8] Yet even as he elaborated this worry some years on (anticipating Chandler and Brown), he couldn't resist the pleasurable diversion, nor could he restrain his own allusive riff on "figures and fantasies" (one of Hazlitt's own allusions, we'll see, in *My first Acquaintance*). If Hazlitt "frequently diminished the immediate effect of his reasonings by the prodigality and richness of the allusions with which he embossed them," mused Talfourd, the indulgence is something more than unconscious pressure. It is a "vivid sense of pleasure, and an intense consciousness of his own individual being," even as the call of allusion "sometimes produced obstacles to the current of speculation, by which it was broken into dazzling eddies or urged into devious windings."[9] The liability only half-troubles Talfourd. And he may have underestimated the devious work in Hazlitt's production of allusion for Samuel Taylor Coleridge—at once a memory and a ghost, shaded with affection pained by regret, and ready to be animated by the life of words.

II. Coleridge in Allusion

My first Acquaintance is so conscious of its operations of allusion as to produce a typology of allusiveness. The essay opens with the arrival of Coleridge in Shrewsbury, January 1798, to assume charge of its Unitarian congregation. Hazlitt, just shy of 20 and a newly avowed infidel (dismaying his father, a dissenting minister),[10] recalls the moment as the advent of his aesthetic education, and he writes in 1823 as if experiencing it all over again. 1798 is always present when Hazlitt writes about it. Coleridge enters Shrewsbury and the essay in a late afternoon coach, "talking at a great rate to his fellow-passengers. . . . He did not cease while he staid; nor has he since, that I know of" (23). Then as now, Coleridge is a ravishment of language: "a sound was in my ears as of a Siren's song; I was stunned, startled with it, as from deep sleep," W.H. recalls (24), waking the sound into his writing.

Fresh from *The Rime of the Ancyent Marinere* and *Kubla Khan* (Hazlitt may soon have heard him recite both[11]), Coleridge burst like sunshine into wintry Shropshire, his talk so captivating that only extravagant allusions will do for W.H. He riffs *Coriolanus*, refitting Shakespeare's contemptuous crab into affable Coleridge, "fluttering the *proud Salopians* like an eagle in a dove-cote."[12] Coleridge didn't just spark allusion but embodied historical recovery, filling the air with "mystic sounds" not heard ("the Welch mountains . . . agree") "since the days of 'High-born Hoel's harp or soft Llewellyn's lay!'" (23). W.H. is quoting Thomas Gray's Bard mourning the extermination of the bards in Edward I's conquest of Cambria (*The Bard* I.2, last line). Tuned to what Wasserman describes—"the relevances of the entire allusive context and its received interpretation" (444)—W.H.'s allusion hails a revival: resounding the music, Coleridge reverses the historical catastrophe.[13]

This allusion is supercharged into what Garrett Stewart wittily dubs "metallusion": an allusion that writes "autoparables of citational transmission."[14] On the wings of allusion's transmissive power, Coleridge generates a chapter of W.H.'s own life in words:

> I had no notion then that I should ever be able to express my admiration to others in motley imagery or quaint allusion, till the light of his genius shone into my soul, like the sun's rays glittering in the puddles of the road. I was at that time dumb, inarticulate, helpless, like a worm by the way-side, crushed, bleeding, lifeless; but now, bursting from the deadly bands that "bound them,
> > "With Styx nine times round them,"
> my ideas float on winged words, and as they expand their plumes, catch the golden light of other years. (24)

The extravagant abjection of Hazlitt "at that time" is licensed by the *now* of the articulate essayist, still catching the glow of first acquaintance. "His thoughts had wings," W.H. will soon say, the figure matched to his own word-winged ideas. He flies to the sheer memory of it, taking a cue from Pope's *Ode for musick on St. Cecilia's Day*:

> Thus song could prevail
> O'er death and o'er hell,
> A conquest how hard and how glorious!
> Tho' fate had fast bound her
> With *Styx* nine times round her,
> Yet music and love were victorious.   (87–92)

The singer is Orpheus; the "her," Eurydice, unsentenced from death by his gorgeous song. As enrapt auditor, W.H. hazards aligning himself with this *her*, to honor the force of Coleridge's voice. His allusion comes in the succession and success of this debt. If this stanza could embarrass some (famously, Joseph Warton[15]), W.H. revels in it. Unchained, word-winged W.H. is the antithesis of the poet of *Epipsychidion* (1821), who laments:

> The winged words on which my soul would pierce
> Into the height of Love's rare Universe,
> Are chains of lead around its flight of fire—
> I pant, I sink, I tremble, I expire!   (588–91)[16]

W.H. finds new life, and Coleridge is the spark: "*I was to visit Coleridge in the Spring* . . . I had been reading . . . his fine *Ode on the Departing Year*, and I applied it, *con amore*, to the objects before me" (36).[17] It was love at first sound.

By 1814, the glow of first acquaintance around Wordsworth had faded, though with some beams of respect. At the end of the second installment of his long review of *The Excursion* for *The Examiner* (August 1814), Hazlitt gave a political spin to his allusion, in the form of quotation, to Wordsworth's elegy for the lost gleam of childhood consciousness:

> though we cannot weave over again the airy unsubstantial dream, which reason and experience have dispelled—
>
> > What though the radiance, which was once so bright,
> > Be now for ever taken from our sight,
> > Though nothing can bring back the hour
> > Of glory in the grass, of splendour in the flower:—[18]

Pluralizing Wordsworth's "my sight" for the Republican hopes of the 1790s, Hazlitt revises Wordsworth's continuing syntax: "We will grieve not, rather find / Strength is what remains behind" (*Ode, Poems* 1807; 2:157). Hazlitt's main clause is a declaration of strength in his original convictions:

> yet we will never cease, nor be prevented from, returning on the wings of imagination to that bright dream of our youth; that glad dawn of the day-star of liberty; that spring-time of the world, in which the hopes and expectations of the human race seemed opening in the same gay career with our own; when France called her children to partake her equal blessings beneath her laughing skies; when the stranger was met in all her villages with dance and

Samuel Taylor Coleridge, 1797. © National Portrait Gallery, London.

festive songs, in celebration of a new and golden era; and when, to the retired
and contemplative student, the prospects of human happiness and glory were
seen ascending like the steps of Jacob's ladder, in bright and never-ending succession. (111)

Hazlitt's prose verges on poetry—in rhymes and half-rhymes, in the swell of
alliteration and reiteration in the anaphora—and on the scrim of Wordsworth's Great Ode it is poised for elegy, not for lost youth, but for the loss of
Wordsworth, fallen into Tory anthems and Tory service:

> The dawn of that day was suddenly overcast; that season of hope is past; it is
> fled with the other dreams of our youth, which we cannot recal, but has left
> behind it traces, which are not to be effaced by Birth-day odes, or the chaunt-
> ing of *Te Deums* in all the churches of Christendom. To those hopes eternal
> regrets are due: to those who maliciously and wilfully blasted them, in the fear
> that they might be accomplished, we feel no less what we owe—hatred and
> scorn as lasting! (112)

William Hazlitt, self-portrait, 1800. © Maidstone Museum and Art Gallery.
Provided by Bridgeman Images.

It's a bitter end to one of the "Poets" of *My first Acquaintance*. By the melancholy winter of 1823, when Hazlitt was writing this essay, his love for Coleridge had gone on the rocks, too.

Twenty-five years on from the vernal promises of winter-spring 1798, Hazlitt's turn to "quaint allusion" conjures first affections in the shades of elegy, memory's phantasm. "He . . . was bitter, sprightly, and full of political and personal allusions," Henry Crabb Robinson noted of an earlier performance, Hazlitt's lecture on the English poets, 17 February 1818 (1:219). When Robinson read the printed lecture in May, he caught the wild swings of betrayal: "He bepraises Coleridge with outrageous eulogy, at the same time that he reproaches him bitterly" (222). *My first Acquaintance* splays a spectrum of these extremes, radiant in the light of 1798, when everything seemed possible for poetry, for liberty, for love, and haunted by that light in 1823. W.H.'s own allusion to *Comus* says it all: "We are no longer wrapped in *lamb's-wool*, lulled in Elysium" (38). He has compressed this from the full score in Milton's poetry: Circe and her Sirens, "Culling their Potent hearbs, and balefull drugs, / Who as they sung, would take the prison'd soul, / And lap it in *Elysium* . . . / . . . in pleasing slumber lull'd the sense" (253–60). Hazlitt adds the sequel of awakening from this slumber, its Coleridge a vanishing dream, for which ghost is the inevitable figure: "nothing is left but the phantoms, the lifeless shadows of what *has been!*" (38).

A dark awakening marks the Christmas Eve finale of Hazlitt's lectures of 1819 at the Surrey Institution (on "Dramatic Literature"). With first acquainted Coleridge and Wordsworth evaporated into Regency remnants, with Hazlitt's Republican hopes shattered (sharply, with the fall of Napoleon), with his marriage a cold collapse by the fall of 1819, and himself target of vicious persecution in the Tory press, he closes the lecture in prospects lost, voicing a first-person plural as the dispirit of the age:

> In youth we borrow patience from our future years: the spring of hope gives us courage to act and suffer. A cloud is upon our onward path, and we fancy that all is sunshine beyond it. The prospect seems endless, because we do not know the end of it. (355)

Hazlitt loads all this into antithesis, a youth of delusion revised into matured knowing:

> Life is a continued struggle to be what we are not, and to do what we cannot. . . .
> We stagger on the few remaining paces to the end of our journey; make perhaps one final effort; and are glad when our task is done! (355–56)

The last words punctuate more than the "done" of this lecture series (a task done in Want of Money). The narrative is so existentially jaded as to turn the lecturer into a wry and rueful embodiment of this vernal vestige. Napoleon, doomed to die in exile, would do so in May 1821, following Hazlitt's father, the Reverend Mr. Hazlitt, who had died in July 1820, two days after Bastille Day, the news not reaching his erratic son for almost two weeks (so reclusive was he that no one knew how to reach him).[19] Already pained to the soul by a son turned infidel, he at least did not live to see his namesake arrested for debt in February 1823.

III. Illusion, Allusion, and the Book of Love

By 1823, that allusive glance at *Epipsychidion* in *My first Acquaintance* was shaded not only by a Coleridge no more, but also by a closed personal season of hope: Hazlitt's recent panting, sinking, and expiring in love's rare universe—all exposed in *Liber Amoris,* the book of love that he published a few weeks after *My first Acquaintance.*[20] It looked like a sequel, glossing the essay's cryptic field of self-allusions in passages such as this:

> My soul has indeed remained in its original bondage, dark, obscure, with longings infinite and unsatisfied; my heart, shut up in the prison-house of this rude clay, has never found, nor will it ever find, a heart to speak to. (24)

With this self-allusion is a loaded allusive sigh from Wordsworth-land, the same poem that haunted Mary Shelley's essay "On Ghosts"—the mother's sigh for her lost son: "I wait for day and night / With love and longings infinite" ("The Affliction of Margaret" 61–63). So, too, W.H.'s semi-cryptic love and longings infinite. "I have wanted only one thing to make me happy," he sighs a few pages on, "but wanting that, have wanted every thing!" (37).

To read any essay by Hazlitt, remarks Virginia Woolf, is to become "familiar with the whole gamut of his grudges and his grievances" (173), which "oddly often break into the context," as if "broken off from some larger book" (180). Here, the larger book is the roman à clef of love and longing's disaster, *Liber Amoris: Or, the New Pygmalion.* This is Hazlitt's chronicle of his infatuation with a coy or reluctant Sarah Walker, the daughter of the landlady in his post-marriage London lodgings. She was about the same age as young Hazlitt in the era of his "first acquaintance" with those poets. Hazlitt's obsession with her, wending through London lodging houses and then divorce-enabling Scotland, would possess two full years, until all hope failed in the summer of 1822.[21] For the record, Hazlitt uses H. for the hero, and S. for Sarah (so she should know).[22] The "or" title, *"the New Pygmalion,"* bids fair as an allusion to Rousseau's hugely popular novel of heartache, *La Nouvelle Héloïse,* which Hazlitt adored, read and reread, had large swaths by heart. The allusion to Pygmalion is bitterly ironic. Beloved S., who looked like "some graceful marble statue," proves a "Cruel girl" (12). H. is left to sculpt only a book of love.

"I don't believe that any woman was ever courted more passionately than she has been by me," H. cries to a friend (*Liber,* Letter IV), then plays an allusive hand of alliance: "As Rousseau said of Madame d'Houptot (forgive the allusion) my heart has found a tongue in speaking to her, and I have talked to her the divine language of love" (62–63).[23] The allusion is unforgiving. The citation is about allusion, its capacity to give a tongue, a talk, a language, to key a resonant field. H. calls on Rousseau (not *Héloïse* but *Confessions*) to confess a mouthful of self-affirming courtly love, winding from Rousseau back to Dante and Petrarch, and of course everyone's Pygmalion.[24] *Liber Amoris* is so rife with allusion and quotation as to count as a "book of love" in the anthology sense.[25] There is nothing to "forgive" in its allusions, every-thing to recognize. Even *Héloïse* will come round, in "Letter the Last," re porting H.'s proposal to S. that they honeymoon in Switzerland, living out the novel, his reciting "to her on the spot the story of Julia and St. Preux" (122).

A proxy in H.'s Pygmalion-dream is another statue, his prized bronze statuette of Napoleon (his political hero). When S. first beheld it on H.'s man-tle, saying that it reminded her of a former beau (though "he was taller"), H. presented it to her, grumbling *"that the God of my idolatry should turn out to be like her Idol"* (37). A few pages on, he revisits the story to say that "She ca-joled me out of my little Buonaparte" (50). Back from exile in Scotland while he waited for his divorce, with hopes high for a future with S., he was touched when she returned the statue, leaping to interpret a loving "proof of her fidel-ity" (136). But when an unsuspecting S. met his tenderly incubated hopes with cool rejection, he dashed "the little Buonaparte on the ground, and stamped upon it, as one of the instruments of her mockery," compounding himself with the deposed (and now dead) Idol: "She has destroyed me for ever!" (142–43). All that's left to do after this "uncontroulable" tantrum (142) is to gather "the fragments . . . strewed about the floor" and send them to heartless S., with a grief-fringed legend: *"Pieces of a broken heart, to be kept in remembrance of the unhappy.   Farewell"* (150). When S., to make mate-rial amends at least, "got the Buonaparte mended," H. shored himself up against the ruins, in a heartbeat: "This was like healing old wounds indeed! My heart, my poor fond heart, almost melted within me" (170–71).[26]

If such patent, pathetic allegorizing (*heart* even rhymes *Buonaparte*) pre-empts any work for allusion, far more edgy is the drama of H.'s self-exclusion from allusive company. Allusion, proposes Christopher Ricks at the outset of *Allusion*, calls upon dead company as a "living resource" (1). Love-sick Hazlitt won't even indulge this company of misery because, against the fresh anima-tions of allusion, he knows, deep in his heart, that his desire knows its dead end. He and a friend had been debating the question of the "least evil" kind of broken attachments: mutual love? or love with "no return"? H. says *mutual*, because it still offers (as does allusion) "a companion" in "consciousness" (128):

> there was a secret sweetness that took off the bitterness and the sting of regret, and "the memory of what once had been" atoned, in some measure, and at intervals, for what "never more could be." (128–29)

Delivered in a marked quotation, Hazlitt's allusion is to the measure in Wordsworth's poem "Three years she grew . . . ," which wends to this epitaphic close:

> She died and left to me
> This heath, this calm and quiet scene,
> The memory of what has been,
> And never more will be.   (39–42)

In H.'s history with S., the allusion is skewed by alienation from Wordsworth's lyric. H. contracts its wistful "what has been" to a bitter "what once had been," and refits the temporality of its "never more will be" to the fatal ache of a lover's heart: there is no shadow of possibility in "never more could be." This pathos not taken is a perfect example of what Ricks describes in "feats of allusion that run not parallel but at pertinent cross-purposes" (109n25). Here it's a spectral feat, because the "absent definitions . . . hover like ghostly revenants over the text" (Stewart, *Reading Voices* 47).

With Wordsworth as the poet par excellence of elegy, H.'s dis-allusion conjures again what readers know already from the *Advertisement* at the front of *Liber Amoris*:

> *The circumstances . . . happened a very short time ago to a native of North Britain, who left his own country early in life, in consequence of political animosities and an ill-advised connection in marriage. It was some years after that he formed the fatal attachment which is the subject of the following narrative. The whole was transcribed very carefully with his own hand, a little before he set out for the Continent in hopes of benefiting by a change of scene, but he died soon after in the Netherlands—it is supposed, of disappointment preying on a sickly frame and morbid state of mind.*

This isn't a friend-editor's account. It's Hazlitt, writing in this persona, enrolling his biography into pathos-registers of the day: Charlotte Smith's (unsigned) rendition of *Manon L'Escaut; or, The Fatal Attachment*; Byron's ill-advised marriage and soon self-exile; Keats's supposed collapse from bad reviews (Shelley's story in *Adonais*).[27]

At the same time, the editor's *envoi* to *"the amusement or sympathy of the reader,"* is a riff loaded with *or*, the phrase *fatal attachment* having left tracks into bathos as well as pathos.[28] Although Shelley did not intend this, the vulnerable "Keats" of *Adonais* was readable as a sad case of unmanly collapse, meanly and memorably re-epitaphed by Byron as "snuffed out by an Article."[29]

In *Liber Amoris*, Keats is revived in Hazlitt's reading, a ghost-brother in his trial of love. After the end of Part I is a separate page (45). The asterisks are H.'s elements of style, signaling thoughts unutterable, unwritable.

WRITTEN IN A BLANK LEAF OF ENDYMION.

I WANT a hand to guide me, an eye to
cheer me, a bosom to repose on; all which
I shall never have, but shall stagger into
my grave, old before my time, unloved and
unlovely, unless S. L. keeps her faith with
me.

          * * * * * * * * * * * *

          * * * * *

—But by her dove's eyes and serpent-
shape, I think she does not hate me; by
her smooth forehead and her crested hair,
I own I love her; by her soft looks and
queen-like grace (which men might fall
down and worship) I swear to live and die
for her!

Wanting S. L.'s hand, what W.H. has in hand is Keats's "Book of Love," its de-spairing hero-lover, saved by "Cupid's dove" (IV.988), the portent of his god-dess gained, returned to spiritualize it all. The other figure is not from this romance, but from a later tale by Keats, about a fatal attraction: *Lamia*, its eponym a serpent-shape turned woman, for whom Lycius falls and dies. One letter toward the end of *Liber Amoris* seems ready to write a "New Lamia," and is not shy about alluding to Milton's Satan, also an allusion in *Lamia*:

It was a fable. She started up in her own likeness, a serpent in place of a woman . . . her proper shape . . . but her form lost none of its original bright-ness by the change of character, but all was glittering, beauteous, voluptuous grace. (163–64)

Milton writes of Satan in Hell that "his form had yet not lost / All her Original brightness" (*PL* 1.591–92). Hazlitt exploits the Latin gendering of "form" to array female S. as Satan's avatar, a recognizable serpent but also an addictive seduction.

On the obverse of the page inscribed by *Endymion,* H. prints lines from Shakespeare, in which he casts himself, patently, as Troilus to Sarah's Cressida, truelove to fated inconstancy:

A PROPOSAL OF LOVE
(Given to her in our early acquaintance).

"Oh! if I thought it could be in a woman
(As, if it can, I will presume in you)
To feed for aye her lamp and flames of love,
To keep her constancy in plight and youth,
Outliving beauties outward with a mind
That doth renew swifter than blood decays:
Or that persuasion could but thus convince me,
That my integrity and truth to you
Might be confronted with match and weight
Of such a winnowed purity in love—
How were I then uplifted! But alas,
I am as true as truth's simplicity,
And simpler than the infancy of truth." TROILUS AND CRESSIDA [3.2]

Given to her early on, with no subtle proposal to S. that she prove herself no Cressida, and then published postmortem to cry his pathos and her inconstancy, *Liber Amoris* Part II is without suspense. No surprise, then, to find H. dead earnest about another identification: Othello's love-anxiety, which H. means to top in agony. This bitterest allusion is threaded in *Liber Amoris* into a letter to a friend, who had scolded H. for his suspicions of S. while he was away in Scotland.

Your reproofs of me and your defences of her are the only things that save my soul from perdition. She is my heart's idol; and believe me those words of yours applied to the dear saint—"To lip a chaste one and suppose her wanton"—were balm and rapture to me. I have *lipped her,* God knows how often, and oh! is it even possible that she is chaste ... Could I but think the love "honest," I am proof against all hazards. (II, Letter IV; pp. 61–62)

The first allusion is to Othello's anxiety about his wife, a fully present, devoted Desdemona:

Excellent wretch! Perdition catch my soul,
But I do love thee! and when I love thee not,
Chaos is come again.   (*Othello* 3.3.168–70)

The next allusion, by marked quotation, is from Othello's agonized fall to Iago's insinuations:

O, 'tis the spight of hell, the fiend's arch-mock,
To lip a wanton in a secure couch,
And to suppose her chaste!   (4.1.82–84)

A sharp arrow in Iago's quiver is "honest," already it seems, a proof against reproof.[30] Hazlitt's allusive field proved a melodramatic hazard. "He now utterly out Othello's Othello," smirked *Blackwood's* (13:644), coining *Othello* into verb, having already smirked at the inscription on *Endymion* as "egregious drivel" (643).

With a more measured allusion on the last page of *Liber Amoris,* H. attempts some mastery when he finds that S. has taken up with another:

Her image seems fast "going into the wastes of time," like a weed that the wave bears farther and farther from me. (192)

The vehicle of the simile alludes to Othello's public trashing of Desdemona: "O thou weed, / Who art so lovely fair." (4.2.391–92). It is one of those channels, says David Bromwich, on which Hazlitt "lived out the drama of his allusions" (436n10).[31] Its full run involves Shakespeare's Sonnet XII ("When I do count the clock that tells the time"), which H. wields for the contextual vengeance of its third quatrain. H. shifts its forecast time to a present report. What the sonnet-poet projects in distress for a beautiful young man—

Then of thy beauty do I question make,
That thou among the wastes of time must go,
Since sweets and beauties do themselves forsake,
And die as fast as they see others grow . . .   (9–12; *Poems* 127)

—H. embraces for immediate consolation, soliciting readers to turn the allusion to analogy.[32] Writing of the beautiful S., H.'s echo is nothing if not gloating: time seems already to be wasting her beauty, mortifying her power. H. may at least claim the pathos of tragic fidelity:

Alas! thou poor hapless weed, when I entirely lose sight of thee, and forever, no flower will ever bloom on earth to glad my heart again!

THE END (192)

The breeding that would brave Time in Shakespeareland will be the leaves, from heart-barren earth, of H.'s *Liber Amoris*. Building on Othello's anguish, H. tunes a double-pity of it (for her and him), with a tinge of Shakespeare's Imogen—she who would have strained her eyes to follow her banished husband Posthumus, sea-born out of sight:

> I would have broke mine eye-strings, crack'd them, but
> To look upon him; 'till the diminution
> Of space had pointed him sharp as my needle;
> Nay, follow'd him, 'till he had melted from
> The smallness of a gnat to air: and then
> Have turn'd mine eye, and wept.   (*Cymbeline* 1.4.279–84)

In another gamble of gender extravagance, H. patterns himself on the faithful wife, for the sake of casting S. as heir to faithless Posthumus.

Wrought by grief and grievance, *Liber Amoris* is the off-stage, repeatedly cued, experiential prequel and the print sequel to *My first Acquaintance with Poets,* its field of allusion tuned not only by personal disappointment but also for epochal political elegy. Rousseau is in the wings—not with a blueprint for romance, but with language for revival.

IV. The Arts of Allusion

This is not how it begins. *My first Acquaintance* comes into print on the glow of expectation in 1823 for the second volume (third number) of *The Liberal,* a new periodical of hope, managed by Leigh Hunt, P. B. Shelley, and Lord Byron, the generation in exile from an England of personal perils (the scandals and domestic trials of Byron and Shelley), political contempt (especially for Hunt) and defeats of political hopes amid severe government repression. Its first pages recall Coleridge's arrival in Shrewsbury and his first (and only) sermon at his new post.[33] The return of memory to 1798, a time of political reaction and peril for progressive voices, also stages an apparitional revival meeting for liberals in 1823:

> A poet and a philosopher getting up into a Unitarian pulpit to preach the Gospel, was a romance in these degenerate days, a sort of revival of the primitive spirit of Christianity, which was not to be resisted. (25)

"These degenerate days," present as well as past, set the stage for W.H.'s extended allusion to Rousseau's romance of *Julie*:

It was in January, 1798, that I rose one morning before day-light to walk ten
miles in the mud, to hear this celebrated person preach. Never, the longest day
I have to live, shall I have such another walk as this cold, raw, comfortless one,
in the winter of the Year 1798.—*Il y a des impressions que ni les tems ni les cir-
constances peuvent effacer. Dusse-je vivre des siècles entiers, le doux tems de ma
jeunesse ne peut renaitre pour moi, ni s'effacer jamais dans ma mémoire.* (25)

These sentences seem less an allusion (though they are that, in the book of
loving Coleridge) than an effortless assimilation, a confluence of W.H.'s
recollection and Saint-Preux's "recalling the days of . . . first loves."[34] "There
are, indeed, impressions which neither time nor circumstance can efface,"
Hazlitt had glossed in English, in 1816, his reading of *Julie* in his own happiest years.[35] *My first Acquaintance* writes the French, distinguished only by italics, as W.H.'s own voice. W.H. renders his own biographia literaria, threaded
with what Marjorie Garber nicely terms a "return of the expressed."[36]

So dazzled was young infidel Hazlitt by the opening words of Coleridge's
anti-war sermon that W.H. summons an allusion to the enraptured
Shepherd-Spirit of *Comus*: his "voice 'rose like a steam of rich distilled per-
fumes'" (25). Milton's simile bears the full knowing effect of astonishment:

> a soft and solemn breathing sound
> Rose like a steam of rich distill'd Perfumes,
> And stole upon the Air, that even Silence
> Was took e're she was ware, and wish't she might
> Deny her nature and be never more
> Still to be so displac't. I was all eare,
> And took in strains that might create a soul
> Under the ribs of Death.   (*Comus* 555–62)

This is radical revival, death animated back to life. The *Air* of climate evokes
air of song. Milton makes it so, sounding *Air* into *e're* and *ware*, and then the
spell, phonic and lettered, on the *eare*, with a devastating pun-reversal on
Still—the temporal extension that even Silence "was took" from her very
identity, prefiguring the Shepherd-Spirit's "I . . . took in." But this Spirit
quickly realized that the sweet strains were ribbed into a "deadly snare!"—
the end of the rhyme-chord begun by *Air* (567). On this field of allusion,
Coleridge's voice is regenerate life in these degenerate days, bravery itself in
the deadly snares of 1798, rife with peril for conscientious objectors to a war-
mongering, domestic-surveilling state.

But in 1823, this Coleridge is also a ghost. W.H. insets this elegy:

"Such were the notes our once-lov'd poet sung"   (26)

Such were is no simple past. It conjures its source, a couplet from a dirge that goes this way:

Such were the notes thy once lov'd Poet sung,
Till Death untimely stopp'd his tuneful tongue.

Such were the notes that began Pope's *Epistle to Robert, Earl of Oxford*. The *Epistle* is "Prefixed to Parnelle's Poems," which Pope edited (1722). In the figure of Dr. Thomas Parnelle, dead from drink, W.H. shades the Coleridge who would fall to opium death-in-life and fall dead to liberal hope. The shift from Pope's *thy* to *"our* once lov'd poet" speaks volumes of generational loss for W.H. in 1823.

If Coleridge's fiery sermon made the pale January sun of 1798 seem a harbinger of "hope and youth in all nature," W.H.'s sentence goes on to say that this is a closed chapter, betrayed in the Regency by Coleridge and others into a Tory political arrogance of a piece with *ancien régime* tyranny. On that morning in January 1798, young Hazlitt took hope from faint sunshine and melting ice, as a political harbinger:

The face of nature had not yet the brand of JUS DIVINUM on it:
"Like to that sanguine flower inscrib'd with woe"   (26)

W.H.'s simile plays across a complex sequence of tonal cues into another elegiac allusion. The sigh of "not yet" is the temporality of 1823, shading over the "emblem of the *good cause*" in the sun visible behind mists after Coleridge's sermon (26). The simile "Like to" is from Milton's *Lycidas* (106), describing Camus, the spirit of the Cam, in Cambridge's academic robes, edged with figurings like a hyacinth flower. This vehicle holds its own pained tenor: Hyacinth, a beautiful youth beloved of Apollo, the very god of poetry, who accidentally killed him. From his blood sprang the flower, and on its petals grieving Apollo marked the letters of "woe."[37] W.H.'s allusive coils whisper that Regency Coleridge is both beloved Hyacinth and this Apollo, killing his own youthful promise ("lov'd" of W.H.) when he endorsed the odious *Jus Divinum*, the stigma of the Bourbon tyranny.[38]

The whisper would be an audible for readers of Hazlitt's letter to the editor of *The Examiner*, 12 January 1817, or its reprinting in Hazlitt's *Political Essays* (1819). Over the pseudonym SEMPER EGO AUDITOR (another allusion: the opening words of Juvenal's Satire I),[39] Hazlitt raged in *The Examiner* about Coleridge's recent, conservative, Church-honoring, working man-placating *Lay Sermon,* bitter at the betrayal by *"this* sermon" of *"that* sermon" 19 years earlier. A virtual first draft of *My first Acquaintance,* the letter seethes from the allusion to *Lycidas* into two paragraphs that Hazlitt kept for *Political Essays* (138–39) but couldn't bear to reprise in *My first Acquaintance:*

> Now, Sir, what I have to complain of is this, that from reading your account of the "Lay-Sermon," I begin to suspect that my notions formerly must have been little better than a deception: that my faith in Mr. Coleridge's great powers must have been a vision of my youth, that, like other such visions, must pass away from me; and that all his genius and eloquence is *vox et pretera nihil*: for otherwise how is it so lost to all common sense upon paper?
>
> Again, Sir, I ask Mr Coleridge, why, having preached such a sermon as I have described, he has published such a sermon as you have described? What right Sir, has he or any man to make a fool of me or any man? I am naturally, Sir, a man of plain, dull, dry understanding, without flights or fancies, and can just contrive to plod on, if left to myself: what right then has Mr C., who is just going to ascend in a balloon, to offer me a seat in the parachute, only to throw me from the height of his career upon the ground, and dash me to pieces?

Even suppressed, however, these paragraphs (and Hazlitt goes on and on) inflect *My first Acquaintance,* haunting about its shape for readers who recall what W.H. could have said.

Between the letter to *The Examiner* and the publication of *My first Acquaintance,* Hazlitt voiced a lament for Coleridge, using Wordsworth's poetry to write it. Closing his lecture "On the Living Poets" (1818), Hazlitt elegizes a still living Coleridge, turning the lines from the "Intimations" *Ode* that he had summoned in 1814 for Wordsworth's failing, into a gloss for lost Coleridge. The allusion works as postscript to the era of "first acquaintance" and (in effect) a prescripting of the essay about it in *Lectures on the English Poets:*

> And shall I, who heard him then, listen to him now? Not I! . . . That spell is broke; that time is gone for ever; that voice is heard no more: but still the recollection comes rushing by with thoughts of long-past years, and rings in my ears with never-dying sound.

"What though the radiance which was once so bright,
Be now for ever taken from my sight,
Though nothing can bring back the hour
Of glory in the grass, of splendour in the flow'r;
I do not grieve, but rather find
Strength in what remains behind;
In the primal sympathy,
Which having been, must ever be;
In the soothing thoughts that spring
Out of human suffering;
In years that bring the philosophic mind!"—   (*Lectures* 330–31)

Hazlitt sounds the great resolution toward which Wordsworth's Great Ode strives, with a double clench: the need for a philosophic mind to deal with the loss of Coleridge's glory, back in the day. Earlier in the lecture is an allusion for this pang of his heart. "There is one fine passage in his Christobel, that which contains the description of the quarrel between Sir Leoline and Sir Roland de Vaux of Tryermaine, who had been friends in youth" (328). Hazlitt quotes it whole, the verse recounting, in a series of cryptic adages, a painful rupture.[40]

My first Acquaintance conjures this era of youth, knowing the shades to come. "His complexion," writes W.H.,

was at that time clear, and even bright—
        "As are the children of yon azure sheen."   (27)

Visiting Thomson's *Castle of Indolence* (popular in Hazlitt's day), the analogy joins young Coleridge to the unsullied children of these quaint Spenserian stanzas, with value added from its tenor, a sweet-souled house Bard,

Of wither'd Aspect; but his Eye was keen,
With Sweetness mix'd. . . .
. . . unpromising of mein.
Gross he who judges so. His Soul was fair,
Bright as the Children of yon Azure sheen.
True Comeliness, which nothing can impair,
Dwells in the Mind: all else is Vanity and Glare.   (II.xxxiii)

As W.H. elaborates his portrait of Coleridge with an earlier line in *The Castle*—"A certain tender bloom his face o'erspread" (27)—the shift is at hand. Its referent is not the Bard, but an unpromising scribbler, rendered in this mingled measure:

> Of all the gentle Tenants of the Place,
> There was a Man of special grave Remark:
> A certain tender Gloom o'erspread his Face,
> Pensive not sad, in Thought involv'd not dark,
> As soot this Man could sing as Morning-Lark,
> And teach the noblest Morals of the Heart:
> But these his Talents were ybury'd stark;
> Of the fine Stores he Nothing would impart,
> Which or boon Nature gave, or Nature-painting Art.   (I.LVII)

This special "grave Remark" is not set for the allusive upgrade of *Gloom* to *bloom,* as a compliment to the bright-Child Coleridge of 1798. In *The Castle of Indolence,* the Man of buried Talents previews later-Coleridge, as the allusive glance at the Parable of the Talents (Matthew 25) may have hinted already:

> Ten thousand glorious Systems would he build,
> Ten thousand great Ideas fill'd his Mind;
> But with the Clouds they fled, and left no Tract behind.   (I.LIX)

My first Acquaintance implies this verse, which Hazlitt had already sounded aloud in an article in *London Magazine,* June 1820, Coleridge transparent:

> The man of, perhaps, the greatest ability now living, is the one who has not only done the least, but is actually incapable of ever doing any thing worthy of him . . . Set him to write a book and he belies all that has been ever said about him—
>
> > Ten thousand great ideas filled his mind,
> > But with the clouds they fled, and left no trace behind.   (*TT* I:646)

The quaint allusion of one line in *My first Acquaintance,* set to bloom for Coleridge, gets crossed by further allusion to Prospero's farewell to cloudy works that "Leave not a rack behind" (*Tempest* 4.1.170). Catching this line in Thomson's "left no Tract behind," Hazlitt's chord of "left no trace behind" writes a record of imagination, apparition, and evanishment—a quaint allusion if ever there was one, to a history of leavings and losses.

So it is poignant to discover that in W.H.'s syntax of lost promise, on the scene of *My first Acquaintance,* is a re-acquaintance with another lost to time, though not for any "instability of purpose or involuntary change of principle" (as W.H. will soon allegorize Coleridge's zigzag walking [32–33]). This second figure is named in the essay's first words: "My father was a Dissenting Minister at Wem" (23), epitome of steadfast purpose. Just mentioned here, he returns to W.H.'s affectionate memory in Coleridge's effect on him. In "the heats of the Unitarian controversy, and squabbles about the American war," outspoken Reverend Mr. Hazlitt "had been relegated to an obscure village, where he was to spend the last thirty years of his life, far from the only converse that he loved, the talk about disputed texts of Scripture and the cause of civil and religious liberty" (28)—writes Londoner W.H., fashioning a poignant allusion from the political trauma of *Julius Caesar:*

> Here he passed his days, repining but resigned . . . Here were "no figures nor no fantasies,"—neither poetry nor philosophy, nothing to dazzle, nothing to excite modern curiosity. (28)

The quotation alludes to the peaceful slumber of Brutus's boy Lucius on the morning of the Ides of March.[41] Hazlitt reverses the scene, in poetry and philosophy. The negatives that breathe the boy's calm are reset for the bereavements of Hazlitt's father, and W.H. finds a way to reacquaint his memory with this figure, too, through the medium of Coleridge's visit.

The Dissenting ministers, separated by miles of unpaved road, were determined to keep up an epic "line of communication," thin, though hot with Republican hope,

> by which the flame of civil and religious liberty is kept alive, and nourishes its smouldering fire unquenchable, like the fires in the Agamemnon of Æschylus, placed at different stations, that waited for ten long years to announce with their blazing pyramids the destruction of Troy. (24)

Troy for them; perhaps a coded Tory regime for the still exiled Dissenters of Pitt's England—and still alive in W.H.'s persistent present tense "is kept alive." This is the apparitional revival of "the year 1798" (23). Coleridge arrives to the Unitarians of Shrewsbury as a flame of liberty—its epic emissary from a new political generation to cheer the Reverend Mr. Hazlitt, a "veteran in the cause, and then declining in the vale of years" (28). Hazlitt plays a chord of complex serial allusions: Othello's pathos—"I am declin'd / Into the vale of years" (3.3.364–65)—reworked into Cowper's allegorical sage "Discipline," a figure of "Paternal sweetness, dignity and love," a "faithful servant long, / Declined at length into the vale of years," now fallen into sad disrespect.[42]

In the memory of Coleridge arriving as a flame of excitement, figures, and fantasies, W.H. reads himself into a history of generations, with no shade of shame on later Coleridge:

> So if we look back to past generations (as far as eye can reach) we see the same hopes, fears, wishes, followed by the same disappointments, throbbing in the human heart; and so we may see them (if we look forward) rising up for ever, and disappearing, like vapourish bubbles, in the human breast! (28)[43]

One heart across generations, from the Reverend Mr. Hazlitt to young Coleridge to W.H., writes this human biography. W.H. returns to his father not only in this life but also in literary life: "He used to be very much dissatisfied that I preferred his Letters to his Sermons," but W.H. will argue for the letters: for "ease, half-plays on words, and a supine, monkish, indolent pleasantry, I have never seen them equalled" (29). Such half-plays are also a line of communication, to W.H.'s love of allusions.

Both Hazlitts fell in love with Coleridge—back then. Hazlitt's father "could hardly have been more surprised or pleased, if our visitor had worn wings. Indeed, his thoughts had wings" (29). It might as well have been Raphael visiting Adam. The very allusion is in the wings: "Kind and affable to me had been his condescension, and should be honoured ever with suitable regard" (35). The allusion does not fall far from the Tree. W.H. echoes Adam's farewell to his "heavenly guest": the visit "shall be honoured ever / With grateful memory" and a hope (readers know, a doomed hope) that he may "oft return" (8.646–51). It is the first paradise lost, the end of a sociable day with a being of both wings and winged thoughts. Yet W.H.'s slant-phrasings, "should be" (for Milton's *shall be*) and "suitable regard" (for Milton's "grateful memory"), reflect what he knows in 1823, that his parting from Coleridge was not just that day, but a parting across the years: his own paradise lost.

Paradise Lost comes round again when W.H. recounts his visit to Coleridge in the spring. On one evening walk, Coleridge's

> voice sounded high
>
> > "Of Providence, foreknowledge, will, and fate,
> > Fix'd fate, free-will, foreknowledge absolute,"
>
> as we passed through echoing grove, by fair stream or waterfall gleaming in the summer moonlight! (39)

Hazlitt knew Coleridge's affection for these lines, from the colloquy in Hell that the fallen angels indulge while they await Satan's return from his reconnaissance (2.559–60). In chapter 1 of *Biographia Literaria* (1817), Coleridge had summoned these lines along with the damning sequel of the next line (561) to recall his boyhood delight in encountering any clergyman on his "leave-days" from school, and in eager conversation,

> directing it to my favorite subjects

> Of providence, fore-knowledge, will, and fate,
> Fix'd fate, free will, fore-knowledge absolute,
> And found no end in wandering mazes lost.

> This preposterous pursuit was, beyond doubt, injurious, both to my natural powers, and to the progress of my education. It would perhaps have been destructive, had it been continued. (*BL* 1:17)

If Coleridge's ironizing preempts any critic's smirk, it also abides as a sweet, poignant pain in the moment of telling. In an otherwise scathing review of *Biographia* (August 1817), Hazlitt cared to quote this passage, and more: a substantial portion of Coleridge's recollection of his lonely, intellectually appetitive school days as an orphan in London (*Edinburgh Review* 28:489–90). When he summons the same lines from *Paradise Lost*, more than five years on, into *My first Acquaintance*, they are filtered by, haunted by, Coleridge's retrospect from 1817 on his school days, by Hazlitt's irritation at *Biographia*, and not least, by what Coleridge had become.

In the scene from 1798 that Hazlitt recalls in 1823, with the effect of a conjuring into vibrant presence, he bends Coleridge's fantasy of being part of this angel-colloquy, fallen as it is, back into his own fantasia: in different roles, both he and Coleridge are there, together at the best philosophy seminar ever. Coleridge's allusion to Milton's lines in 1817 (for his boyhood excitements) becomes Hazlitt's affectionate allusion for Coleridge's conversation in 1798, with Hazlitt the auditor, back then, and reconjured in 1823. Hazlitt quietly stops before line 561's "wandering mazes lost." Aborting this sequel, he gets even more out of the allusion, blending his rapt listening into Adam's listening to Raphael. Yet even sheared away, "lost" still lingers, for full-knowing readers, as a spectral shade. In the structure of allusion, it is a willingly suspended option. This ghost is a touchingly complicated allusion, one that skips a beat by leaving the loss that Milton writes and that Coleridge rehearses to the recall of any reader who wants to go there, without Hazlitt. Hazlitt in effect revises, even re-verses, Coleridge's fuller allusion into a partial absence, potentially, but only potentially, present. Hazlitt surely does remember, but excuses himself from the obligation to bring this matter into the field. The allusion plays as both a memory and a remembering that is otherwise.

The last sounding of Coleridge in *My first Acquaintance* is his reciting some lines that beckon as an allusion to nostalgia itself. Appearing from memory, the lines also figure memory, the shades of the past on the present:

> The next day we had a long day's walk to Bristol, and sat down, I recollect, by
> a well-side on the road, to cool ourselves and satisfy our thirst, when Coleridge
> repeated to me some descriptive lines from his tragedy of Remorse; which I
> must say became his mouth and that occasion better than they, some years
> after, did Mr. Elliston's and the Drury-lane boards,—
>
> "Oh, memory! Shield me from the world's poor strife,
> And give these scenes thine everlasting life."   (46)

W.H.'s memory writes an allusion as apostrophe, the voice that summons presence.[44] Memory is the agency of allusion, the agency of spectral history, recasting "these scenes" with apparitions from elsewhere, tinged with remorse.

In an uncanny emergence in the controlled zone of W.H. well-tuned allusions, memory errs in giving the lines to *Remorse*.[45] Hazlitt's language is haunted by a mistake, the phantasm of a repressed story. Whiter's account of association, developed in the era of Hazlitt's first acquaintance, describes this operation, in effect, as an antonym of allusion: "words and sentiments . . . prompted by a cause" that is "concealed" from consciousness "contain no *intentional* allusion to the source from whence they are derived" but are "forced on the recollection of the writer by some accidental concurrence" (68). This accident is a critical shift into apparitional figuring, an underpresence in Hazlitt's gesture of comprehension. The couplet verse, proffered as an allusion in tribute to Coleridge, comes to Hazlitt by haunted accidence, its ground a deeper "memory" so askew as to seem an evasion.

Not from Coleridge's *Remorse*, the couplet is Robert Bloomfield's, closing an ode, "On revisiting the place of my Nativity," inserted at the end of the second edition of his unexpected best-seller, *The Farmer's Boy* (1800).[46] Yearning for "my distant home," the revisitor sighs, and then signs off (p. 100),

O Memory! Shield me from the World's poor strife;
And give those scenes thine everlasting life!

LONDON, MAY 30, 1800.   ROB. BLOOMFIELD.

Revisiting this call to "Memory," W.H. mistakes this voice as unforgettably Coleridge's, then sighs it for himself in 1823, for himself in 1798, and for all nostalgia. W.H. reconjures his earlier wish for quaint allusion—that it can revive as well as revisit—by translating the distance of Bloomfield's yearning *those scenes* as a present *these*.[47] In the craft of his allusion, Hazlitt renders a poetry that he wants to attribute to Coleridge, in the glow of a remembered idyll, resonant with the call of memory. In the gesture of revival, nothing is ever really lost, when language renders absent presence in its purest manifestation.

Yet the voice that calls to "memory" is ironically misattributed, misremembered, and so impure in this work. I shall improve the editorial tradition of tagging the lines as "untraced" or following W.H. by citing *Remorse*.[48] Hazlitt's contemporaries, I think, would know the source, given Bloomfield's celebrity. Yet having cited Bloomfield in *Lectures on the English Poets* (1818) as a case of "original genius" hampered by both a want of education's cultivation and a consciousness of this want (187–90), Hazlitt repressed the credit of the couplet that clearly possessed him. He had quoted it, inset even, in "On Reading Old Books" (1821), recalling his books in the spirit of Milton's revivifying force:

> Let me still recal you, that you may breathe fresh life into me, and that I may live that birthday of thought and romantic pleasure over again! Talk of the *ideal!* This is the only true ideal—the heavenly tints of Fancy reflected in the bubbles that float upon the springtide of human life.

> "Oh! Memory! shield me from the world's poor strife,
> And give those scenes thine everlasting life!"   (*London Magazine* 3:130)

This is allusion that turns out to be something almost antithetical, a possession that is felt without a delusory trace of origin. For this phantasmic moment, we can summon De Quincey's now famous distinction between "literature of knowledge" and "literature of power" (*North British* 164–66), its "power" sometimes registering in formations other than the conscious operation of allusion. In a bow to this kind of power, De Quincey declares that he owes to the impassioned books which he has read, many a thousand more of emotions than he can consciously trace back to them. Dim by their origination, these emotions yet arise in him, and mould him through life like the forgotten incidents of childhood. (167)

Dim to forgetting, the origin of Hazlitt's language is Bloomfield, not the "Coleridge" that he wants to signify the call of "memory." It is "Memory" misremembered, but no less powerful in its rising in Hazlitt, and its moulding of language that is in his utmost care.

What Hazlitt could not know in this coil of quotation in early 1823 was that by August the world's poor strife would claim Bloomfield, too, dead from poverty and debilitating illness, never matching his brilliant debut. No wonder that in his move to shield himself from his own worldly strife, W.H. finds what he wants in Wordsworth's voice, not Coleridge's, as he projects future writing in the genre of *My first Acquaintance with Poets*:

> Enough of this for the present.
>   "But there is matter for another rhyme,
>   And I to this may add a second tale."   (46)

Yet there is already a surplus of spectral matter: Wordsworth did give the rhyme (these are last lines of *Hart-leap Well*, Part One (*LB* 1800, 2:7), and he had Part Second ready to go (2:8), as Hazlitt knew (and he loved it).[49] In this expectation, Wordsworth's poem reads "I to this would add another tale." Hazlitt's slight mis-memory, promising a second to match Wordsworth's "Part Second" but also shifting Wordsworth's confirmed "would" with a hazier "may," is telling. For Hazlitt, the matter for a sequel never materialized, leaving Wordsworth's line of communication, in the essay's final allusion, to become a quaint epitaph. In after-effect, this is the tale that the summary quaint allusion tells.

There "is always something divided and discordant" in his essays, Woolf finely perceives of Hazlitt, "as if two minds were at work who never succeed save for a few moments in making a match of it" (177). The two minds are never more striking in this match than when, within the words of one writer, we hear the recursive words of another, the precursor. Such a match-up never closes the gap, never makes identity of echo. But it can make a presence of something that won't stay absent. W.H.'s personal audition extends to literary history. While phrases shaped long ago get drawn into and held in memory, the temporal span remains the measure of time's loss, and the measure of writing is time's gain. Call it "Spectral Romanticism." Call it literary history, lived from within. Or call it the mindful play of quaint allusion in the vibrant returns of *My first Acquaintance with Poets*.

* * *

The genre of "Dejection" was to become Coleridge's signature, and a self-haunting. It shapes the exotic, tortured enchantments of *Kubla Khan: or, A Vision in a Dream* and *The Pains of Sleep*, the two poems in the 1816 volume that also housed the spectral fragment of *Christabel*. The genre is a poignant presence in a letter that Coleridge wrote to his brother-in-law Robert Southey in August 1803, a month before he sent him, in another letter, *The Pains of Sleep*. The first letter recounts a dream with a voice telling Coleridge that he is "an involuntary Imposter—that I had no real Genius, no real Depth / —— / This on my honor is as fair a statement of my *habitual Haunting*" (*CL* 2:959). Wordsworth could make an epic of self-haunting, confident, at least some days of the week, of real genius in its depths. Habitual haunting can also turn outward to the world, and phantoms can report positives as well as negatives. This is Shelley's futuring, with stakes high, ungraspable, and unknowable. By another name, this is the way with "words of hope and fear" arising with the phantoms of Shelley's political visions in the year 1819.

CHAPTER FOUR

Shelley's Phantoms of the Future in 1819

I. Writing the "unwritten story"

A long war; economic devastation; abused workers; a horrific climate crisis; floods; massive starvation; an indifferent elite; the emergence of working-class consciousness and violent repressions; calls for law and order; liberals in despair; oppositional journalists arrested, tried, fined imprisoned. Welcome to England in 1819. What's a poet to do? "Painful to read." That's how Shelley's *Defence of Poetry* (drafted 1821) struck Raymond Williams when he took this general measure of "The Romantic Artist" as a political visionary:

> The bearers of a high imaginative skill become suddenly the "legislators," at the very moment when they were being forced into practical exile; their description as "unacknowledged," which, on the theory, ought only to be a fact to be accepted, carries with it also the felt helplessness of a generation. (*Culture and Society* 47)

The *Defence* rested on the ringing declaration, "Poets are the unacknowledged legislators of the World" (57), a sentence Shelley first drafted in 1819 to close chapter 1 of *A Philosophical View of Reform*, there with commendable company: "Poets and philosophers are the unacknowledged legislators of the world" (30). Unacknowledged, because not yet confirmed, but also because authority is written in shadows: poets are "the mirrors of the gigantic shadows which futurity casts upon the present" (*Defence* 57). And neither essay materialized into publication. All this, on the heels of Shelley's procedure to "dismiss" inquiry into "the principles of society itself, and restrict our view to the manner in which the imagination is expressed upon its forms" (4): if philosophers are, in the nineteenth-century lexicon, scientists, Shelley's *Defence* seemed to be fine-tuning poetic science, not political science.

The gap between theory and practice in Williams's story weighed on Shelley, too, who in the crisis year 1819 began writing some popular poetry on the principles of society itself, in language that even Marxists might recognize. "The system of society as it exists at present must be overthrown from the foundations with all its superstructure of maxims & of forms," he told Leigh Hunt in May 1820. He was warming up to pressing him about finding a "bookseller who would like to publish a little volume of <u>popular songs</u> wholly political, & destined to awaken & direct the imagination of the reformers" (*L* 2:191). His dossier held "Lines Written during the Castlereagh Administration," "Song to the Men of England," "Similes for Two Political Characters," "What Men Gain Fairly," "A New National Anthem," "England in 1819," and "Ballad of the Starving Mother."[1] Likely at hand was a fresh plea for the fervently visionary master plan, *The Mask of Anarchy: Written on the Occasion of the Massacre at Manchester*. Writing is one thing, publishing another.

That "Occasion" was 16 August 1819; Shelley sent *The Mask* to Hunt in time for the September 23 *Examiner*, but eight months on, it was still cooling on the shelf. No wonder: even before Parliament passed the repressive Six Acts in December 1819, the peril to publishers was clear.[2] Veteran of a two-year prison term (1813–14) for libeling the Regent in *The Examiner*, Hunt in London, not Shelley in Pisa, would be the one to take the heat for poetry mocking the Monarchy (5–85), and urging the rights of the "Men of England" in 226 lines of rousing oratory (147-372).[3] Shelley knew this, but kept noodging: "I see you smile, but answer my question" (*L* 2:191). A few weeks on, he was pressing Hunt again, now about that *Philosophical View of Reform*: "Do you know any bookseller who w^d publish for me [this] octavo volume . . . ? It is boldly but temperately written—& I think readable—It is intended for a kind of standard book for the philosophical reformers politically considered" (2:201). He had tapped his usual publisher, Charles Ollier, about the prospect back in December, assuring him that this was "an instructive and readable book, appealing from the passions to the reason of men" (2:164). Mindful of the Acts, Ollier took a breath, then took a pass. In 1839, Mary Shelley's "Note on Poems of 1819" cast these ventures as a poet's political romance:

> Shelley . . . believed that a clash between the two classes of society was inevitable, and he eagerly ranged himself on the people's side. He had an idea of publishing a series of poems . . . but in those days of prosecution for libel they could not be printed . . . they show his earnestness, and with what heartfelt compassion he went home to the direct point of wrong—that oppression is detestable. (*1839* 3:207)

But Shelley didn't go home to England to stand on the people's side.

This is the zigzag of Shelley's political poetics. The epitome is that *Mask*, exhorting the people in a dream-vision from Italy. Even as Paul Foot heroizes

"Red Shelley"—the voice hailed in the 1830s by Friedrich Engels and canon-ized by Chartists in the 1840s, resounding in Victorian labor halls and ever after, in protest anthems around the world—he can't fully censure Hunt as "censor" of "some of the most powerful political writing in the English lan-guage" because Shelley, recreating in Italy, "risked nothing."[4] Lobbing popu-lar poetry from a redoubt beyond the grasp of English law in 1819 can look like self-indulgent venting, something less than "wholly political"—especially compared to the on-site moxie of Richard Carlile, William Cobbett, Tom Wooler, or Henry Hunt.[5] As "a public poem with revolutionary intentions," its "generating consciousness, the poet's mind, is in no position to do more than write a poem," is Thomas Edwards's verdict (160). Roger Sales tries a game spin: by 1819, Shelley was theorizing dormant activism, detached from the "political arena," in a dream ultimately "more important than the politi-cian's programme" (196). Leaving agency to a "somehow," Michael Scrivener reasons that in England 1819, politics is necessarily symbolic rather than practical (207, 198). Anne Janowitz argues that the poetry *is* the program, sounding a voice not of individual agency but of class aspiration (92).

But even theory and practice so explained must confront some rather whimsical turns. Edwards can only wince at "the sing-song of instructive nursery-rhymes or routine political oration" and the quaint "gentleman's code" in Shelley's fantasy theater of non-violent resistance, the brutal attack-ers rebuked and disarmed by polite, firm resolve, social contempt, and their own hot shame.[6] These fantasies play even into the language of the most fa-mous stanza of *The Mask,* which Shelley gives two soundings. The first comes in the opening call to "Men of England" (147):

> "Rise like Lions after slumber
> In unvanquishable number
> Shake your chains to Earth like dew
> Which in sleep had fallen on you—
> Ye are many—they are few . . ."   (151–55)

Shelley implies the poetry's numbers as the apparitional muse of the labor-ers' numbers, and makes good on this when he reprises the stanza to close this long address, simultaneously the close of *The Mask* itself (368–72), and positioned there to play wide into public broadcast. It is a rousing call, but even for a figurative politics, the simile for chains is a tad fantastic: mere dew, just shake it off. It's as if Shelley, the schoolboy who liked to concoct chemical explosions, thought political change could work this way, too, by sudden transformation. "Shelley the political revolutionary expected miracle, the Kingdom of God in the twinkling of an eye, like some Christian of the first century," sighed W. B. Yeats, Shelleyan though he was, in the unsettled days of 1932, about *Prometheus Unbound*.[7]

This is the tenor of dissatisfaction with Shelley's romance of politics and its vehicles of poetic victory. While I can't prevent that murmur (I feel its impulse), I want to consider more deliberately than I had in *Formal Charges* (1997) the potent temporality of the genre that Shelley dubs "unwritten story." He names this just before the first "Rise like Lions . . ." stanza:

"Men of England, heirs of Glory,
Heroes of unwritten story . . .   (147–48)

Shelley hails a genre for the horizon of imagination: unwritten, but not un-writeable. He writes *heirs,* phonically and thematically, into *Heroes,* and rhymes *Glory* to *story,* tracing the arc of the Glorious Revolution of 1688 into a declared future. Shelley poses this as a present sensation, said for imagi-nation in a language of imagination. There were helpful antecedents for "unwritten"—not least, Milton, who in an anti-establishment tract of the 1640s cited "unwritten lawes and Ideas which nature hath ingraven in us," an un-official rule resonant in the links of "*un*written," "*in*graven," and "*in* us."[8] In 1765, the great legal theorist William Blackstone began *Commentaries on the Laws of England* by observing that "municipal law" abides not only in "the *lex scripta,* the written, or statute law" but also in "the *lex non scripta,* the unwritten, or common law" (I:63).[9] Shelley takes all this on board and lever-ages it into the future, yet "unwritten" but not unimaginable: "In the world unknown / Sleeps a voice unspoken" (*Prometheus Unbound* 2.1.190–91).

In *Specters of Marx,* Jacques Derrida argues that "Haunting belongs to the structure of every hegemony" as a latency for the "future to come" (46); because hegemony is structured repression, latency must register in appari-tional form. In *The Mask of Anarchy,* its herald is a phantasm, "A mist, a light, an image" (103). Marx gives the gothic form in 1848, when he opens *Manifesto of the Communist Party* with news that "A spectre is haunting Europe—the Spectre of Communism," which European powers are intent "to exorcise." Its information "already acknowledged," this Spectre is ready to manifest its "views . . . aims . . . tendencies" (29). As Shelley was projecting "unwritten story," the trials of English Reformists were beginning the writing, with a force that Ernesto Laclau calls "constitutive dislocation" (69).[10] What Marx names as *Spectre* Derrida theorizes as *hauntology* (10) and Laclau analyzes as *dislocation*. All are in Shelley's unwritten story.

Shelley's visionary poetics—from *Hymn to Intellectual Beauty*, to *Ode to the West Wind* and *To a Sky-lark*, to *The Triumph of Life*—know the force of negating the known into the apparition. The generative grammar is "unseen presence." The poet doesn't just indicate this, Shelley argues in *A Defence*; poetry "marks the before unapprehended relations of things" and from materials that otherwise would "be dead" lettering (5) produces "unapprehended combinations of thought" (16). The action of *marks* draws on multiple senses: *remarks, identifies, renders legible*. It is a success of "words" in new situations: "instinct with spirit . . . many yet lie covered in the ashes of their birth, and pregnant with a lightning which has yet found no conductor" (40).[11] In Shelley's visionary grammar, *yet* cooperates with *un-*. Over the course of *A Defence* poets animated by "an unapprehended inspiration" advance into those "unacknowledged legislators" (57). In the Preface to *Prometheus Unbound*, Shelley cites "great writers" (himself implicit) as "companions and forerunners of some unimagined change in our social condition or the opinions which cement it" (xii)—*unimagined* keyed to *Unbound* in politics no less than in poetics and metaphysics. Is this still too tenuous a stretch? In tune with Williams's critique is the impatience of radical political journalist H. N. Brailsford with the resort to subtractions in the visions of *Prometheus Unbound*: "There is something amiss with an ideal which is constrained to express itself in negatives" (241–42).[12]

If the deep truth is imageless, Shelley will imagine superstructures in the negatives. I read these not as amiss but as tactically aimed, and in ways that Shelley himself theorized: if you want to deny "subjection to the laws of all inferior existences," you need figuration "described or defined by negatives."[13] While his subject in this sentence is negative theology, the logic of political hope is here, too. Negative prefixing (as Garrett Stewart puts the case) is "a present force in consciousness—and thus in reading. It is here that wordplay itself could be seen to do the work of philosophy," including political philosophy.[14] In *The Mask of Anarchy*, Shelley works this into writeable, readable, audible wordplay, in which a negative lexicon is flexed into positive vision—and in no simple optimism, either, but with an "indignant" genesis, "shuddering" into "words of joy and fear" (138–41).[15]

II. "Something must be done"

The flashpoint was on August 16, at St. Peter's Fields. This was the largest peaceful assembly in modern memory. Some 100,000 laborers and their families met for parading (rehearsed for weeks) and speeches. Henry "Orator" Hunt, the first speaker, declared their right of assembly, sounded their grievances, and called for the reform of Parliament. Alarmed at the spectacle and intent on suppression with clarion warning, a saber-wielding local gang, fortified with British Hussars (regular cavalry, among them, Waterloo veterans) charged into the crowd.[16] Wreaking 15 deaths and 400–700 injuries, the attack may have been urged by Home Secretary Lord Sidmouth, or just cheered after the fact, with the Prince Regent's endorsement, for its preservation of public peace. On August 22, *The Examiner* made the outrage front-page news, thickened within by reports from the *Times* and seven "Letters from Manchester." Subsequent issues kept the story front page, along with letters and trenchant verses on "Peter-Loo"—*Manchester Observer*'s sardonic riff, quickly branded, on the alliance of domestic brutality with the cant of Waterloo triumphalism.[17]

Reading the *Examiner* and other papers sent by his friend T. L. Peacock, Shelley was livid. "The torrent of my indignation has not yet done boiling in my veins," he fumed to Ollier on September 6; "I wait anxiously hear how the Country will express its sense of this bloody murderous oppression of its destroyers. 'Something must be done . . . What yet I know not'" (*L* 2:117). He was "writing the Cenci, when the news . . . reached us; it roused in him violent emotions of indignation and compassion," recalled Mary Shelley (*1839* 3:205). He knew what Beatrice Cenci had done. It was no stretch to reiterate lines he had written for her, just after a rape by her father (an event in the gap between the end of act 2 and the opening of act 3):

> I shall go mad. Aye, something must be done;
> What, yet I know not . . . something which shall make
> The thing that I have suffered but a shadow
> In the dread lightning which avenges it.   (3.1.86–89)

Shelley's hypermetrical ellipsis is one of those constitutive dislocations, a pause for conjuring. Published in 1820, *The Cenci* summoned a post-Peterloo phantom. Nominally about events in Rome at the end of the sixteenth century, it relayed political allegory and murmured contingency. "Tyrants . . . leave a path to freedom but through their own blood," Shelley cautioned in

The Examiner, front page, 22 August 1819. Private collection.

A Philosophical View (4). Reflecting on France in 1794, Mary Wollstonecraft gave the map: "if the degeneracy of the higher orders of society be such, that no remedy less fraught with horrour can effect a radical cure, . . . the people are justified in having recourse to coercion, to repel coercion" (*French Revolution* 70). Shelley worried about the radical cure looming in the long shadow into 1819.[18]

The Cenci is a master-specter of philosophical conflict. Its scenes are rife with tyranny and degeneracy, yet tremble at radical remedies. It is a politics of words, with words. Shelley depicts a regime ably invoking *parricide,* along with ample legal commentary, to vilify what Beatrice has "done," while finding no word, let alone law, for what has been done to her. "Days of outrage" would be Mary Shelley's epithet for England in 1819 (*1839* 3:205); in *The*

George Cruikshank, *The Massacre of Peterloo, or "Britons Strike Home!!!"* (London, 1819).

Cenci, the "outrage" to Beatrice hovers only in "half conjectures," "obscure hints . . . darkly guessing" (3.1.348, 357–58).[19] Even God has made it "unutterable" (5.3.81). Beatrice defies this lexical choke: "I am more innocent of parricide / Than is a child born fatherless," her last adjective, in effect, a parricide of "parricide" (4.4.113–14). To her brother Giacomo, "avenging of such a nameless wrong . . . turns black parricide to piety" (5.1.44–45), *nameless* doing the same work as *fatherless*. G. H. Lewes would contest any judgment of her "criminality": "Common notions of right and wrong . . . do not here apply" (*Westminster* 173). Or if they do, judgment was uncommonly strained. To the *Monthly Review*, "incest committed by a father, and murder perpetrated by a daughter" (162) weighed equally in moral reflection and its syntax.

But Oedipal anxiety is palpable. "That word parricide, / Although I am resolved, haunts me like fear," Shelley has this same Giacomo murmur before the murder (3.1.340–41), and afterward, "It was a wicked thought, a piteous deed, / To kill an old and hoary-headed father" (5.1.9–10). Shelley writes recoils of this Macbeth-laced horror for the two stone-cold assassins. "We dare not kill an old and sleeping man," shudders one; "the calm of innocent sleep in which he lay, / Quelled me. Indeed, indeed, I cannot do it" (4.3.9, 12–13).

The other—even as he hears the Count laughing in his dreams of having God's blessing on his curse of his sons—is halted by "the ghost / Of my dead father speaking through his lips, and so "could not kill him" (4.3.20–22). Reciprocally, Shelley conjures a ghost of Lady Macbeth in master-planner Beatrice as she rebukes their cowardice, snatches the dagger, and later reviles these deputies for caving under torture. These gothic and Oedipal tremors reverberate from the French Revolution. Not sequestered to fifteenth-century Catholic Rome, parricide was, as Shelley's generation would know, the lynchpin in Edmund Burke's *Reflections on the Revolution in France* (1790) of the infernal trinity, "Regicide, and parricide, and sacrilege"—a vast image out of the Revolution's Spiritus Mundi. One "should approach to the faults of the state as to the wounds of a father, with pious awe and trembling sollicitude," Burke admonished (114), should "look with horror on those children of their country who are prompt rashly to hack that aged parent in pieces" (143). Extension to Peterloo hardly needed spelling out.

Shelley himself gave the cue, crafting *The Cenci*'s "Dedication to Leigh Hunt Esq." on this score. Although this is dated "*May* 29. 1819" (v), it was on September 3, after Peterloo, that Shelley decided on the honor (*L* 2:112). Hero of Reform and target of serial persecution well before 1819, Hunt could have become a Beatrice. Shelley makes a point of citing him for being "patient" in his "irreconcileable enmity with domestic and political tyranny and imposture" (v). Beatrice is previewed by this measure and reviewed more sternly in the Preface: "the fit return to make to the most enormous injuries is kindness and forbearance, and a resolution to convert the injurer from his dark passions by peace and love"; "Revenge, retaliation" are "pernicious mistakes" (ix–x). If this judgment seems conspicuously warped by a regard of Beatrice as only reactive rather than proactive, only mistaken rather than set on safety, it is because it is not about Beatrice. It is about Peterloo. While Shelley says that his "dramatic purpose" was to "contemplate alike her wrongs and their revenge . . . what she did and suffered," by September there was a political shade on the "tragic character" (x). The boiling of Peterloo in Shelley's veins had cooled to a caution. Writing to Peacock on the 21st, he voices Beatrice again, but without quotation marks (muting the *Cenci* outrage) and with admiration for the composure of Orator Hunt amid the "infernal business": "What is to be done? Something assuredly. H. Hunt has behaved I think with great spirit & coolness in the whole affair" (*L* 2:120).

Arrested and thrust into a brutal gauntlet on the steps of the Manchester Magistrate's house, then packed off for trial in London, Hunt kept his cool and did not rage for retaliation.[20] This was a relief to Shelley's growing anxiety about England's "very disturbed state": "I wonder & tremble," he had confided to Peacock on 24 August (before he learned of Peterloo), hoping that the movement for Reform would "commence among the higher orders, or anarchy will only be the last flash before despotism" (*L* 2:115). Flash where? What Shelley names "The Spectre of Anarchy" in *A Philosophical View of Reform* (84) looms all over the place: despotism in the higher orders; violence from the repressed; retaliation by the higher orders.[21] Hence the zigzags that try Foot's patience with *The Mask*—now "counselling the people to behave constitutionally, and to protest within the system," then "openly advocating revolution" (*Revolutionary Year* 16). From his perch in Ravenna, Lord Byron jeered at the populist leaders, wishing that the "Manchester Yeomanry had cut down <u>Hunt</u>"—so he wrote to his friend John Cam Hobhouse, MP. While he felt for "the poor starving populace" (he was not "an illiberal . . . not against <u>reform</u>"), he reviled the leaders as "scoundrels . . . blackguards . . . dirt . . . miscreants" (22 April 1820; *BLJ* 7:80–81).

With a disingenuous smirk, Byron could say, "<u>radical</u> is a new word since my time—it was not in the political vocabulary in 1816—when I left England—and I don't know what it means—is it uprooting?" (*BLJ* 7:81). This was not just a lexical question; it was a political one. Hunt's arrival in London on 13 September to stand trial turned into a triumphal parade, thronged with cheering crowds, among them, Keats.[22] There was no reform movement led by the higher orders, the middle orders were shifting, and restlessness from below was erupting everywhere. From Italy, one could only wonder and tremble—dream the worst and the best.

III. Apparition in Preview: "As I" to "As if"

It is in a dream-mode that Shelley's *Mask of Anarchy* gets to the fields of Manchester:

> As I lay asleep in Italy
> There came a voice from over the Sea,
> And with great power it forth led me
> To walk in the visions of Poesy.   (1–4)

While the long plan is to Lionize this slumber, this herald is not exactly auspicious, even in an aura of power. A sleepy phonotext slides from the languid locator, *As I lay asleep,* to the dream-site *Italy,* lapping over the *Sea,* a passive *me,* and the medium, *Poesy.* The voice is a phantom, pacing to "visions of

Poesy" in a symptomatic ambiguity of double grammar.[23] In a genitive, "of" casts Poesy as visionary agency; as a preposition, "of" situates Poesy as an object in a visionary dreamscape. What kind of preview is this? *The Mask* invokes a muse of power, from a dreamland in the head that might as well be an ocean away.

Poesy envisions England, with the poet's proxy "I" a virtual comrade of Hunt and Carlile: "I met" (5), "I saw" (36), rendering a report that chimes with Leigh Hunt's August 22 *Examiner*: "Men in the Brazen Masks of power" operating "against an assemblage of Englishmen irritated by every species of wrong and insult."[24] A "ghastly masquerade" (27) is what the dream-orator will call out as "dim imagery" and "impostors" (211–12). Anarchy pomps in a sham "kingly crown" (34), patent twin to Milton's Death, in "the likeness of a Kingly Crown" (*PL* 2.673). Travestying the seventeenth-century masque—pageants of divinely graced monarchy—*The Mask of Anarchy* arrays the artifice of tyranny, no less specious, no less factitious in 1819 than in "the reign of Charles II., when all forms in which poetry had been accustomed to be expressed became hymns to the triumph of kingly power over liberty and virtue" (*Defence* 24).[25] Lord Chancellor Eldon saw in Manchester a "shocking choice between military government and anarchy."[26] Refusing the distinction, Shelley's *Mask* unhymns the triumph of monarchy as a spectacle of anarchy.

His mordant trope is a reversed simile, categorical tenors with the political actors of 1819 as the specter-vehicles:

I met Murder on the way—
He had a mask like Castlereagh— (5–6)

Next came Fraud, and he had on,
Like Eldon, an ermined gown . . . (14–15)

Clothed with the Bible, as with light,
And the shadows of the night,
Like Sidmouth, next, Hypocrisy . . . (22–24)

Murder is the substantive power and Castlereagh its convenient expression. Fraud is vested as Eldon because Eldon is fraudulent. Hypocrisy's choice avatar is shadowy Sidmouth.[27] Anarchy blazons the lexical tautology of power: "I AM GOD, AND KING, AND LAW!" (37), echoed by "hired Murderers who did sing / 'Thou art God, and Law, and King'" (60–61). Cued by the couplet *sing/King*, this chorus is constrained to rhymes, slant-rhymes, and repetitions:

Lawyers and priests, a motley crowd,
To the earth their pale brows bowed;
Like a bad prayer not over loud,
Whispering— "Thou art Law and God."—

Then all cried with one accord;
"Thou art King, and God, and Lord;
Anarchy, to Thee we bow,
Be thy name made holy now!"   (66–73)

In *A Defence*, Shelley proposes that "sounds as well as thoughts have relation both between each other and towards that which they represent" (9–10). This poetry stages tyranny's representation, as words accumulate into a chord of sound and submission: *crowd, brows bowed; not over loud; God; accord; Lord; bow, now!*

Against the tightly ringed declaration and assent of "I AM / Thou art," Shelley moves the poet's proxy "I" from dreamer ("I lay asleep"), to field reporter ("I met," "I saw"), and ultimately into the dreamer's epipsyche, the "I speak" of the orator (171). The dream-state syntax, *"As I lay asleep,"* shifts, correspondingly, into an *As if* to set the stage of imagination:

These words of joy and fear arose

As if their own indignant Earth
Which gave the sons of England birth
Had felt their blood upon her brow,
And shuddering with a mother's throe

Had turned every drop of blood
By which her face had been bedewed
To an accent unwithstood,—
As if her heart had cried aloud:

"Men of England, heirs of Glory,
Heroes of unwritten story . . ."   (138–48)

Hans Vaihinger is a great help on the conceptual potency of "As if": the simile-cue *as* gains an *if* that, while conceding "something unreal or impossible," advances an "apperceptive construct" (91–93); an "impossible case" gets "posited for the moment as possible or real" (258–59).[28] Writing about "surmise," Geoffrey Hartman describes its "capacity for the virtual, a trembling of the imagined on the brink of the real, a sustained inner freedom in the face of death, disbelief, and fact" (*Wordsworth's Poetry* 11). Shelley writes this into a collective imagination, an "accent unwithstood" (144), an "unvanquishable number" (152) ready for "unvanquished war" (322), all antithetical to the *un-* of oppression: "untrue" complacencies (240) wielded by priestly comforters against "woes untold" (295). The high stakes charge these words along multiple rhetorical channels. Tyrants may be unsettled; *Examiner*-readers called to reform; workers roused to resist.[29]

Negation is the conceptual rhetoric from which Shelley draws the unwritten story:

> "What is Freedom?—ye can tell
> That which slavery is, too well—
> For its very name has grown
> To an echo of your own."
>
>   (156–59)

In the subtle engine of slavery, *groan* sounds in *grown,* which spreads its own letters into a rhymed "you*r own.*" Shelley sounds this in antithesis to "Freedom." Antithesis is what Fredric Jameson, in *Marxism and Form,* calls a "political hermeneutic" for the "concept of freedom": "an ontological impatience in which the constraining situation itself is for the first time perceived in the very moment in which it is refused" (84–85). In spring 1819, Shelley had closed Act III of *Prometheus Unbound* (spring 1819) in just such a moment. The Spirit of the Hour unveils what is "called life" as a "loathsome mask" (a mask of anarchy) and a vision by verbal antithesis: "Sceptreless, free, uncircumscribed, . . . / . . . unclassed, tribeless, and nationless" (3.4.190–95). OED cites this passage for the first instances of these antonyms.[30] In microstylistics no less than in macro-ideas, Shelley was shaping political reflection with phantasmic language.

In *The Mask of Anarchy,* the awful specter for labor in 1819 is a cruelly alliterative (as if cognate) "Ghost of Gold": a "paper" travesty of any "substance" of payment. Slavery takes hold of labor in this remorseless way:

> " 'Tis to work and have such pay
> As just keeps life from day to day
> In your limbs, as in a cell
> For the tyrants' use to dwell
>
> "So that, ye for them are made
> Loom, and plough, and sword, and spade . . ."
>
>   (160–65)

The couplet that ends this exposition compresses the ambiguity that Empson calls "double-grammar" into the bitterest of puns: even as tools "are made" for workers' use, workers "are made" into tools for tyrants' use. "What is slavery—" was Shelley's definitional project of *A Philosophical View of Reform*: "It is a system of insecurity of property, and of person" (22–23) under "fraudulent forms of government" (33). To name system and forms is to propose a temporal contingency, reform already at work, with subtractive negatives, in the "just and successful revolt in America" (16): "no king . . . no hereditary oligarchy . . . no established Church . . . no false representation" (12–13).

Yet a *Cenci*-shaded reflex of this vision haunts *The Mask,* registered in swerves that could have been ghost-written by Sidmouth, to sedate unrest:

> "Science, Poetry, and Thought
> Are thy lamps; they make the lot
> Of the dwellers in a cot
> So serene, they curse it not."   (254–57)

Patient Leigh Hunt approved. When *The Masque of Anarchy* finally saw print, in 1832, he paused in his Preface over this "delicious stanza" as "a most happy and comforting picture in the midst of visions of blood and tumult" (x). No surprise that in this year of the Reform Act, he was also happy to cheer, with italics, Shelley's *"political anticipation"* in advising against "active resistance, come what might." In "the spirit of the thing, the success he anticipates has actually occurred, and after his very fashion. . . . The battle was won without a blow" and without the insurrection advocated by "the Political Unions" (x–xi). In this spirit, he and publisher Edward Moxon fashioned a polite *Masque,* scrubbing the *Massacre*-blaring subtitle along with the names Eldon and Sidmouth and the lines about the Bible as the cloak of Hypocrisy.[31] The stanzas were classed up with roman numerals, and italics for the three that issue the appeal to "the old laws of England" (331).[32] Hunt's sole footnote gave an old-school cheer for "the sober, lawful, and charitable mode of proceeding advocated and anticipated by this supposed reckless innovator . . . a picture and a recommendation of '*non-resistance,*' in all its glory" (41). A Shelley-friendly *Athenæum* reflected this mode in its front-page review on 3 November: if *The Masque* was "political," Shelley was "too much of a poet to be a good politician," "too lofty in his conceptions." For all the "strong and simple words," the "account of the Peterloo affair . . . is not in the customary style of reports" (705). This audit enabled it to publish (in December) "LINES / *Written during the Castlereagh Administration.*" In his headnote, Medwin would concede "something fearful in the solemn grandeur," but he marked this as aesthetic indulgence, "without the chance of exciting either personal or party feeling" (794), and, in any event, the full title specified a bygone era.

On Shelley's manuscript, however, the title was categorically "England." The lines opened in a terse tercet of present tenses, congruent with the customary style of the reports:

> CORPSES are cold in the tomb;
> Stones on the pavement are dumb;
> Abortions are dead in the womb . . .   (1–3)

The verdict is "Albion, free no more" (5), just a graveyard:

> Her sons are as stones in the way;
> They are masses of senseless clay;
> They are trodden and move not away,
> The abortion with which *she* travaileth
> Is Liberty, smitten to death.   (6–10)

"Masses of senseless clay": while the demographic sense of *masses* would not emerge until the late 1830s, William Keach reads an anticipation here.[33] With performative contempt, Shelley points the trope at both the trodders and the trodden:

> Then trample and dance, thou Oppressor!
> For thy victim is no redresser;
> Thou are sole lord and possessor
> Of her corpses, and clods, and abortions,—they pave
> Thy path to the grave.   (11–15)

This is a contrapuntal voice, or sidebar, to the more "charitable" mode of *The Mask*. Shelley rings these hard words again in *Song to the Men of England*, his pithy abstract on labor oppression. The first four stanzas issue a barrage of couplet-punctuated challenges:

> MEN of England, wherefore plough
> For the lords who lay ye low?
> Wherefore weave with toil and care,
> The rich robes your tyrants wear?   (1–4)

And so forth, into a set of blunt recapitulations, hinged on medial caesurae:

> The seed ye sow, another reaps;
> The wealth ye find, another keeps;
> The robes ye weave, another wears;
> The arms ye forge, another bears.   (17–20)

Poetically potentiated, these repetitions also evoke the horrific repetitions of labor-history and its dehumanizing mechanizations. Shelley unwrites the story into its reverse:

> Sow seed,—but let no tyrant reap;
> Find wealth,—let no imposter heap;
> Weave robes,—let not the idle wear;
> Forge arms,—in your defence to bear.   (21–24)

The alternative is fatally alienated labor:

> Shrink to your cellars, holes, and cells;
> In halls ye deck another dwells.
> Why shake the chains ye wrought? Ye see
> The steel ye tempered glance on ye.   (25–28)

The steel that glances on them clips them back, and, in a dire pun, reads them.

> With plough and spade, and hoe and loom,
> Trace your grave, and build your tomb,
> And weave your winding-sheet, till fair
> England be your sepulchre.   (29–32)

The couplets are trenchant links: *loom* forecasts the *tomb*; the cant of *fair England* is their *sepulchre*. It is telling that when the President of the National Secular Society read this *Song* on the centenary of Shelley's birth in 1892 to a large audience of "working men who took Shelley quite seriously," it met "thunders of applause."[34] Hear the voice of the Lords!

The voice that commands *The Mask of Anarchy* proceeds toward labor reform by calling a "vast assembly" (295) into a public poetry of speech-activism:

> "Declare with measured words that ye
> Are, as God has made ye, free—

Be your strong and simple words
Keen to wound as sharpened swords . . ."   (297–300)

The analogy is there for the reading, *words* visibly lettered into s*words* (with
an edge from "sword!": an old oath, "by God's word!").[35] These measured
words are political poetry, and readers could join the collective word weap-
onry.[36] This call may be no more than words, a poet's phantom-wooer, but
the Oppressor of 1819 was already hearing words as arms and reviewing the
parades at St. Peter's Field as a well-honed, proto revolutionary formation.

To conclude *The Mask*, Shelley transforms the genre of dream-vision toward
this end. In the convention, the dream evaporates into a frame of ordinary consciousness. Shelley casts off this framework, to reprise the call, "Rise like Lions,"
its "words . . . / Ringing through each heart and brain, / Heard again—again—
again" (364–67), the word *again* performing a cue for a new national anthem:

"Rise like lions after slumber
In unvanquishable number—
Shake your chains to earth like dew
Which in sleep had fallen on you—
Ye are many—they are few."   (368–72)

Shelley must have sensed that he had spun gold. The stanza is now readable
as proleptic historicity, fully present in poetry for ordinary consciousness.
Sensing what Shelley must have, Hunt, for all his prefatory caution, went for
capitals and an exclamation point at "NUMBER!" and he set the last lines as
an upper-case banner: "YE ARE MANY—THEY ARE FEW" (*Masque* 42). One
of Shelley's drafts shows no closing quotation mark, just a prospective dash, as
if marking the way to futurity.[37] "If then my words had power," muses Prometheus (*Prometheus Unbound* I.69): almost 200 years on, Jeremy Corbyn
could tap this stanza for British Labour, calling it to an audience of 120,000 in
Glastonbury, with such roars of approval (at other sites the crowds chanted
along) that on 27 June 2017 the *New Statesman* had to call Shelley into a
front-page article about his utterly present poetry—an unwritten story not
just negatively imaginable but in positive event.

IV. Simile to Simultaneity

Her sons are as stones in the way. In Jameson's analysis of political herme-
neutics is the "temporal form" of a "new idea," a "sudden perception of an
intolerable present" that glimpses "another state in the name of which the

first is judged." This "formal character" tends toward "analogy," he says, because it operates as "a kind of transformational equation whereby the data characteristic of one may be converted into the terms of another" (85). In the formal character of another poem from 1819, Shelley elides the work of conversion to produce a vast critical equation in the multivalence of the word *as*. This is the startling drama:

> As from an ancestral oak
>   Two empty ravens sound their clarion,
> Yell by yell, and croak by croak,
> When they scent the noonday smoke
>   Of fresh human carrion:—
>
> As two gibbering night-birds flit
>   From their bowers of deadly yew,
> Through the night to frighten it,
> When the moon is in a fit,
>   And the stars are none, or few:—
>
> As a shark and dog-fish wait
>   Under an Atlantic isle,
> For the negro-ship, whose freight
> Is the theme of their debate,
>   Wrinkling their red gills the while—
>
> Are ye, two vultures sick for battle,
>   Two scorpions under one wet stone,
> Two bloodless wolves whose dry throats rattle,
> Two crows perched on the murrained cattle,
>   Two vipers tangled into one.[38]

When he published this, Medwin cast it as a poet's exercise, giving it the workshop title *Similes*. He may have missed the way Shelley was mobilizing *As* for political work. The anaphora seems to array similes, but at the final stanza's *Are ye*, the scenes open into simultaneity: all are indictments of tyranny, its emanations and practices. The predatory partners of one intent climax with vipers in the form of a caduceus, Mercury's aegis for reciprocal actors—such as merchants (his namesake).[39]

  The Mask turns this equation around, from a story already vastly written to the prospect of unwritten story. Staging a crisis of despair in the path of

Caduceus.

the Mask's parade of power, Shelley pivots into an event where senses of *like* and *as* cooperate in a counter-vision, joining phantoms of conceit to a tumult of events in the natural world.[40] The herald Shape comes in this progress. First "an image rose, . . . / Like the vapour of a vale" (103–5), then

> as clouds grow on the blast,
> Like tower-crowned giants striding fast
> And glare with lightnings as they fly,
> And speak in thunder to the sky . . .   (106–9)

A temporal shimmer in the analogical *as* conjures a new story, a revitalized process in the world. This double grammar plays wide:

> As flowers beneath May's footstep waken
> As stars from Night's loose hair are shaken
> As waves arise when loud winds call
> Thoughts sprung where'er that step did fall.   (122–25)

In this expanse, even the grammar of "an image rose . . ." (103ff) seems transformed by the figural energy of the awakened "flowers"—a sub-syntactical phantom of conceit that carries forward to the voice from England's heart: "These words of joy and fear arose" (138).

V. Conjectures of *As if* to Conjurings of *May*

What can rise from England's grave? Shelley sent an untitled sonnet, a news rant with a visionary climax, to Leigh Hunt on 23 December (*L* 2:167).[41] Undeluded about the possibility of publishing it in 1819, or any time soon after, Shelley liberated his most revolutionary apparition:

An old, mad, blind, despised, and dying king,—
Princes, the dregs of their dull race, who flow
Through public scorn,—mud from a muddy spring—
Rulers, who neither see, nor feel, nor know,
But leech-like to their fainting country cling,
Till they drop, blind in blood, without a blow.
A people starved and stabbed in the untilled field,—
An army, which liberticide and prey
Makes as a two-edged sword to all who wield;
Golden and sanguine laws which tempt and slay;
Religion Christless, Godless—a book sealed;
A Senate,—Time's worst statute, unrepealed,—
Are graves from which a glorious Phantom may
Burst, to illumine our tempestuous day.

Linked to the negated potential *untilled* is the regime of annihilation, *liber-ticide*. This noun was coined in 1790s France for counter-Revolutionary factions and agents, then imported by English Reformers (Francis Burdett in the 1790s and Jeremy Bentham in 1817) to censure Ministry and Monarchy, and summoned by Coleridge the year after Waterloo to brand the "satanic pride and self-idolatry" characterizing "the Liberticides and mighty Hunters of Mankind, from NIMROD to NAPOLEON."[42] Concentrating the politics of *The Mask* into one intensifying bill of indictment, Shelley's sonnet meets liberticide with his own sword of words. Each wrong is end-punctuated and pulsed into new forms of sonnet-rhyme. Shelley presses his syntax into the action, accreting (in mimicry of Burke's famously swelling periods) an epic catalog for revolution, all converging on the blunt predicate: "Are graves." It's a propulsive *tour de force*, with the line-pause at *may* poised to burst mimetically at the volta, with infinitive power "to illumine."

The designated agent is "a glorious Phantom." The glory speaks implicitly back to the "unformed spectre" of Revolution apocalypse in Burke's *Letters . . . on the Proposals for Peace with the Regicide Directors of France* (1796):

out of the tomb of the murdered Monarchy in France, has arisen a vast, tremendous, unformed spectre, in a far more terrific guise than any which ever yet have overpowered the imagination . . . Going straight forward to it's end, unappalled by peril, unchecked by remorse, despising all common maxims and all common means, that hideous phantom overpowered those who could not believe it was possible she could at all exist. ("Letter I" 6–7)

Assigning phantoms was a political question. When *The Prelude* was published in 1850, *Gentleman's Magazine* could assign it to the *ancien régime* on the register of Wordsworth's Revolution-sympathies in 1790–91: "Men had already asked themselves the question, shall we continue to obey phantasms, or shall we search for realities?" (466).[43] In 1819, Shelley points the sonnet's "glorious Phantom" toward this search.

A blueprint was in a pamphlet of 1817 that he did publish (a limited pseudonymous printing), under a title drawn from a famous phrase in Tom Paine's satire on Burke's swoon for the fall of France's monarchy: "We Pity the Plumage but Forget the Dying Bird."[44] The closing sentence of Shelley's polemic juxtaposes national grief over Princess Charlotte's death in childbirth (and the death of hope for a reformed monarchy) to the brutally cheered execution of the leaders of the Pentridge Rebellion (fomented by an *agent provocateur*):

> Let us follow the corpse of British Liberty slowly and reverentially to its tomb: and if some glorious Phantom should appear, and make its throne of broken swords and sceptres and royal crowns trampled in the dust, let us say that the Spirit of Liberty has arisen from its grave and left all that was gross and mortal there, and kneel down and worship it as our Queen. (380)

The grammatical apparition *if* projects a glorious Phantom to redeem the Spirit of Liberty, with precise political logic: a rising on the debris of the old order (*spectres* of *scepters*). The conjuring of Queen Liberty is the pun of Shelley's *New National Anthem*, its refrain of "God save the Queen" meaning Queen Liberty, in rebuke to the present King, her ruiner. The imperative *save* turns the old-anthem sense, *preserve*, to a call to *rescue, redeem* Liberty from what *God save* has to rhyme with in 1819, "England's *grave*."[45] On such critical stresses, James Chandler goes so far as to argue for Shelley's "notion of changing history *by* interpreting it," activating reading for revolutionary "resurrection" (*England in 1819*, 31).

This is teacherly hope, but it's telling (and winningly honest) that Chandler admits his students' skepticism. The problem is not just the romance of reading-as-action but also the sort of symptom in the climax of "England in 1819": its hinge on that auxiliary, *may / Burst*. The *may* is a complication of both sense and form, with philosophy at stake, and the status of Phantom, too. Exactly at the point where a Shakespearean sonnet would formally clinch its case, Shelley's enjambment is so muting that the couplet-rhyme *day* is scarcely heard, scarcely (even) registered. One of Shelley's most careful readers, Stuart Curran, finds the effect poetically and politically resonant, risking all:

> Shelley pivots his poem on a syntactic potentiality—"may"—that yields to the bursting of its formal bonds in a movement parallel to the revolutionary explosion that will invert the anti-forms repressing contemporary society. The form symbolically consumes itself, as surely as does the society it catalogs. (*Poetic Form* 55)

This is the strong allegory, but I find the mode of *may* uncertain: *perhaps? is enabled? is empowered to?* a tactful underplaying of the phantom-hand? To F. R. Leavis, the "oddly ironical stress" that "results from the rime position" is a "pathetic weakness" (159–61)—revenant of Arnold's Shelley, "ineffectual angel."[46] Timothy Webb, admitting a slant of "improbability," admires a brave "intellectual honesty" in the "ironical and limiting" mode (*Voice* 107–8). Shelley sent the sonnet to Hunt in a letter that wavers on its own *may*: "I do not expect you to publish it, but you may show it to whom you please" (*L* 2:167). Giving *may* to Hunt, Shelley leaves it open. And so *may* rhymes and unrhymes, issues a vision without knowing who'll see it.

This is the shadow-grammar of unwritten story: a phantom-screen to illuminate the not impossible. I appreciate Jerome McGann's reading of *may* as a "glimpse of some far goal in time" but I wouldn't say that Shelley's "ideology of hope" is "deeply allied . . . to his sense of hopelessness," let alone at a "sad" and "dreadful" depth (*Romantic Ideology* 112). Shelley's temporality is historical possibility, beyond the material here and now, and he risks the trope of "Phantom" on this proposal.[47] Always mindful of *The Tempest*, he knew that "tempestuous" involves the etymology of *time*: for this day, not for ever. In the *Mask*, Anarchy's triumph is time-stamped this way, as a "tempestuous cry" (56). The counterpart in *Prometheus Unbound*, Jupiter, incites a "strange tempest" in the sea, and his furies are "tempest-walking hounds," while Ruin charges "Like a tempest through the air" (1.166, 331, 786). All these tempests are tropes, temporary states, and so can be recast. Early in Act II, Asia is hailing Spring "Cradled in tempests" (1.6); and at the climax of Act III, Jupiter falls and burns into the "tempest-wrinkled Deep" (2.9). Hope for man appears as a "tempest-wingèd ship," to be ruled by love; "the tempest is his steed" (4.410, 421). This is visionary writing; but it is also a vision in writing, for reading and imagination.

Shelley's persistence in writing a future day, if the French Revolution is any reminder, often, quite often, resides in the compromise of what poetry may "illumine" at the moment. This is the verb used in the last line of "England in 1819" to disclose the hell on earth in the mask of Law and God, with a glance at the only two instances in *Paradise Lost*—ones that radiate into French Revolutionary language, even into Wordsworth's counter-cultural mythology. The first is Milton's famous plea to his Spirit: "What in me is dark / Illumine" (1.22–23). The second is an ironizing sequel, a betrayal from the rebels' swords, whose "sudden blaze / Far round illumin'd hell" (1.665–66). Milton gives *illumine* to hope and to error. In *Prometheus Unbound*, it is this mental light. Prometheus cries of his "woe-illuminèd mind" (1.637), and when tyrant Jupiter falls, "The terrors of his eye illumined Heaven / With sanguine light, through the thick ragged skirts / Of the victorious Darkness" (3.3.4–6). The political orbit involves various spins. A secret anti-monarchal society dubbed themselves "The Order of the Illuminées" (or Illuminati) and gave the founding principles for the French Revolution.[48] In 1795 Coleridge hailed "William Godwin, Author of *Political Justice*" as "form'd t'illume a sunless world forlorn" in a sonnet he published in the *Morning Chronicle*.[49] In 1814, Wordsworth gave a counter-cultural slant in imagining how "the unenlightened Swains of pagan Greece," hearing a noontime wind, could fancy a sun-god whose "golden lute . . . filled the illumined groves with ravishment" (4.859–60; p. 179).

Thirty years after the French Revolution, Shelley sounds all these chords for poetic imagination. The day-star of liberty seeming as remote as the old mythology, the immediate days were not heartening. "Every thing seems to conspire against Reform," he sighed to Peacock in March 1820, just weeks after sending Hunt "England in 1819" (*L* 2:176). By May, the "vast assembly" for reform that *The Mask* conjured into a political vision had gone into reverse: "there is but little unanimity in the mass of the people," he sighed to Peacock, worrying that "a civil war impends from the success of ministers and the exasperation of the poor" (2.193).[50] He wrote *Ode to Liberty* in these months, and put it at the close of the volume named for and opened by *Prometheus Unbound* (published in August). In the last lines, the ideal of Liberty is a receding echo of a great voice, "As waves which lately paved his watery way / Hiss round a drowner's head in their tempestuous play" (XIX)—rhyming with a difference the sonnet's last words, "illume our tempestuous day."

The *Ode* in total, however, leaves open the question whether this tempestuous play marks the retraction of, or a fluctuation within, the theme of the epigraph, Byron's cheer in *Childe Harold's Pilgrimage Canto IV* (1818):

Yet, Freedom! yet thy banner torn, but flying,
Streams like the thunder-storm against the wind.   (xcviii)

"Yet" cries resistance, and Byron's next two lines are so relevant as to count as phantom company: "Thy trumpet voice, though broken now and dying, / The loudest still the tempest leaves behind." This tempest doesn't claim its phonic kin, the trumpet. With the contrast of this stanza's fiercely resistant "opposing mind and will," McGann sees *Ode to Liberty* tracing a "cycle of revolutionary disappointment" as "a general pattern . . . replicated for the individual as well as for society" ("Book of Byron" 271, 270). Keach gives a different measure: reading "a trajectory of commitment to 'Liberty's unfinished cause,'" he respects Shelley's sense of "its historicity, its actuality, as well as its very representational status" (*Arbitrary Power* 158, 157). Both views hang and fluctuate in Shelley's air.

At the front of the volume, in his Preface to *Prometheus Unbound,* Shelley admires the Greek tragedians for refusing to be "bound" by received "national history or mythology" (vii). *Unbound* is the muse and motor of his modern Promethean poetics (xi). The fable is so redundant as to feel synchronic, less a narrative than a platform for Shelley's unbound Promethean poetry. Shelley even transvalues the term of torment, *bound:* "Whatever talents a person may possess . . . he is yet bound to exert them" (xv). The exertion of Promethean poetry is to imagine a future as a presence with poetic agency, synchronic with its narrative. Apparitions of historical change arrive in "scattered lines" (1.668), "sound whirls around" in rhymes with *unbound,* in fresh inspiration (2.3.63), then, in writerly figuring, "radiant lines of morning" (2.5.56). What is "thought" gives "the measure of the Universe" (2.4.73), a proto-poetic pun set to draw "boundless Heaven . . . measureless . . . line through line inwoven" (3.1.113–17) for a "mystic measure" (4.77).

Shelley's unbound poetics project into extremes of imagination, the "loftiest star of unascended Heaven, / Pinnacled dim in the intense inane." This is the very last line of Act III, prepared by that train of subtractions: *Sceptreless, uncircumscribed, unclassed, tireless,* and *nationless* (3.4.194–204). At this climax, *inane* comes as an intensely weird word, not only as this substantive, but also against the customary sense of mere emptiness.[51] No "Bounds" too narrow for "The capacious Mind of Man to expatiate in, which takes its flight farther than the Stars, and cannot be confined by the Limits of the World; that extends its Thoughts" to make "Excursions into that incomprehensible *Inane.*" So Locke, whom Shelley studied attentively, unlocked the constitutive power of words. It is "the Power of Words . . . to imprint complex *Ideas* in the Mind, which were never there before."[52] In this aspect, the mind is the first imprint of unwritten story, the field of its very grammar.

Written for 1819, *Prometheus Unbound* issues both unbound Promethean poetry and, not necessarily in equation, a visionary perspective on historical flux and process. Acts I–III, the drama seemingly completed by spring 1819, unfold the crisis, the unbinding, the new order. Then *The Cenci,* written from August to September in the shade of Peterloo, conjures the nightmare of revenge—a sort of spectral Act IV for *Prometheus Unbound.* The actual Act IV, which Shelley wrote post-Peterloo, counters with a call "To suffer," "To forgive," "To defy," "To love," "To hope." These are the infinitives of its great conclusion (570ff), stretched over, and against, historical knowledge of the turns and cycles of tyranny. What can be the force of such timeless "strong words" (553)? Paul Elmore More complained of bewildering "inconsistencies": "Love is the theme, yet the speeches are full of the gall of hatred: in words Prometheus may forgive his enemy, but the animus of the poem is unrelenting bitterness" (802). To Shelley this *yet/but* was the spirit of the age, and he made no easy, no straightforward, argument about the power of poetry—practical, political, theoretical, lexical—for England in 1819.

> Professors of poetry, apologists for it, practitioners of it, from Sir Philip Sidney to Wallace Stevens, all sooner or later are tempted to show how poetry's existence as a form of art relates to our existence as citizens of society—how it is "of present use." Behind such defences and justifications, at any number of removes, stands Plato, calling into question whatever special prerogatives or useful influences poetry would claim for itself within the polis. Yet Plato's world of ideal forms also provides the court of appeal through which poetic imagination seeks to redress whatever is wrong or exacerbating in the prevailing conditions. Moreover, "useful" or "practical" responses to those same conditions are derived from imagined standards too: poetic fictions, the dream of alternative worlds, enable governments and revolutionaries as well. It's just that governments and revolutionaries would compel society to take on the shape of their imagining, whereas poets are typically more concerned to conjure with their own and their readers' sense of what is possible or desirable or, indeed, imaginable. . . . It is the imagination pressing back against the pressure of reality.

This is Seamus Heaney looking back in 1995 on twentieth-century poets, himself included.[53]

It's also a terrific measure of Shelley's political poetics and his turns of Platonic idealism. Read by the conjuring Heaney describes, Shelley might even freshen an appeal to Raymond Williams, who in 1980 (about 20 years on from "The Romantic Artist") took this (much quoted) measure of idealism and practicality: "It is . . . in making hope practical, rather than despair convincing, that we must resume and change and extend our campaigns" ("Politics" 42). The "maniac maid" ready to martyr herself in Anarchy's triumph figures the question: "her name was Hope, she said: / But she looked more like Despair" (*Mask* 86–89). Despair is the wreck of Hope (*de + sperare*), but the name spoken is a potential, even potent, contradiction. If this didn't materialize in "practical" success, Shelley would try to make hope conceivable in poetry, drafting the unwritten story, again and again, in the illumining of a tempestuous day, its darkness visible, and a phantom of modern Promethean possibility.

* * *

"Can we speak of 'ghosts' without transforming the whole world and ourselves, too, into phantoms?" asks Jean-Michel Rabaté in *The Ghosts of Modernity*. His answer was already under survey: "such a question and the worry within it . . . lies at the very heart of modernity" (xxi). Rabaté poses the extreme manifestation of "modernity" as a haunted world. The Janus-faced *of* in his title (ghosts are part and product of modernity) is the grammatical figure of the crisis he explores: a struggle for an "ethics of mourning," enabling development rather than (inevitably) repeating the past in maneuvers of denial or forgetting.

But what if the project were to embrace, even mobilize, the spectral repetitions that Rabaté's story of modernism registers as a worry? This is the modern grammar, and apparitional glamour, of Byronism. Even in the specters of wordplay, Byron can spring *host* from *ghost*, to entertain ghosts as personal company, and propel their replication as creative energy. His imagination is generously hospitable: spoofs; satire; and haunting history, from the intimately personal to the imperial national, and everything in between.

CHAPTER FIVE

Me and My Shadows

Byron's Company of Ghosts

I. Seeing Ghosts

Byron's boyhood love of Friedrich Schiller's *Ghost-Seer* (*BLJ* 5:203) primed his spirited feeling for actual ghost-sites, especially his ancestral haunt, Newstead Abbey: "worth seeing, as a ruin," he urged Tom Moore in 1814; "The ghosts . . . and the gothics, and the waters, and the desolation, make it very lively still" (August 13; *BLJ* 4:158). He assured Lady Blessington in 1823 that "he was sincere in his belief in supernatural appearances; he assumes a grave and mysterious air when he talks on the subject" (as if miming a ghost)—and he was "fond of doing" this. Byron "has told me some extraordinary stories relative to Mr. Shelley who, he assures me, had an implicit belief in ghosts," said the Lady (*Conversations* 41–42). Even so, she is alert to the sliding scale of Byron, from "sincere" to the affectation of a grave and mysterious air. Byron "likes very much to be listened to, and seems to observe the effect he produces on his hearer" (20). "Grim reader! did you ever see a ghost?" Byron teases, with a witty turn on Grim Reaper, in *Don Juan Canto XV* (95)—part of the latest installment, published March 26, 1824. And last: a few weeks on, Byron was dead.

This chapter is about Byron's production of ghosts, from sociable company, to popular haunts, and ultimately into the performances and deformations of the cultural phenomenon called "Byronism." It arcs from the gothic, ancestral halls of *Childe Harold's Pilgrimage* to the last view of Juan, pale and wan in the nouveau-riche, haunted halls of Norman Abbey, and courses through later cantos of *Childe Harold, Manfred, The Siege of Corinth, The Vision of Judgment,* and the extravagantly apparitional theatrics, and poetics, of the Norman Abbey cantos of *Don Juan*—taking on board the promiscuous life and afterlife of Byron's portraits and Byron's ghosts, his sole visual apparitions in England after April 1816.

Byron relished ghost-story telling. He reviewed his store to publisher John Murray, in 1820 (November 9), ranging from legend to eye-witnessing. Fresh in mind was the apparition in Walter Scott's repertoire, the "White Lady of Avenel." In Byron's view, this was not quite so good as a *real well-authenticated* ("Donna bianca") *White* Lady of *Collalto*—a spectre in the Marca Trivigiana—who has been repeatedly seen—there is a man (a huntsman) now alive who saw her also—Hoppner could tell you all about her—& so can Rose perhaps.—I myself have *no doubt* of the fact, historical & spectral. She always appeared on particular occasions—before the deaths of the family, &c. &c. I heard Me. Benzone [*sic*] say that she knew a Gentleman who had seen her cross his room at Colalto Castle.—Hoppner saw & spoke with the Huntsman who met her at the Chase—and never *hunted* afterwards.—She was a Girl attendant—who one day dressing the hair of a Countess Colalto—was seen by her mistress to smile upon her husband in the Glass.—The Countess had her shut up in the wall of the Castle like Constance de Beverley.—Ever after she haunted them & all the Colaltos.—She is described as very beautiful—& fair.—It is well authenticated. (*BLJ* 7:225–26)

Byron unrolls a trail of tales: Scott's commerce with the "White Lady of Avenel" and *Marmion*'s ghost of "Constance de Beverley," and his own animated rehearsal of the Collalto spectre, with stories of sightings by a Gentleman and a Huntsman (robbed of his very identity), accounts curated by British Consul R. B. Hoppner, writer William Rose, and salon-celebrity Madame Benzoni. The Girl attendant of the tale is a history-revenant, not only a ghost but also a ghost-star in narration, Byron's retail the latest, but not the last.[1]

Byron's reiterated "well authenticated" is meant to credit the genre-blend "historical & spectral." "And now that we may furnish with some matter all / Tastes we are going to try the supernatural," is how the poet of *Don Juan* sets the stage for *Canto XV* (93)—with "the supernatural," the genre du jour, ready for and rhymed to the market-tastes of "all." From the plea of the Ghost of Hamlet to "mark it" (act 1.1), Byron seems to have registered a punning *market*. Just a few years before Blessington's *Conversations* (1834) appeared Mary Shelley's market-cast "Introduction" to *Frankenstein* (1831), with its story of inspiration at Villa Diodati in the summer of 1816.[2] " 'We will each write a ghost story,' said Lord Byron; and his proposition was acceded to," Shelley recalls of the night which gestated both her *Frankenstein* and Polidori's *The Vampyre* (vi–viii). The project was domestic entertainment, but not without thoughts of a market even then. Matthew ("Monk") Lewis's *Castle Spectre*, a sensation at London's Drury Lane in December 1797, had been quickly exported to regional theaters, including one in Bristol, where ghost-minded Wordsworth saw it.

Lewis was expected at Diodati in August, and the group was already battening on "volumes of ghost stories." On June 18, Byron recited Geraldine's ghastly unveiling in *Christabel*, the Coleridge-brand of "supernatural" pressed to a horrific sublime: "Behold! Her bosom and half her side——— / A sight to dream of, not to tell!" (Part I, 246–47). Ghost-believer Percy Shelley freaked out.[3] For Byron, the telling is clearly, sincerely, the thing. Deep dyed ghost-conjurer Shelley pressed the cognitive issue later that summer.[4] "We talk of Ghosts," and if "Lord B" (he wrote in Mary's journal, August 18) did not "seem to believe in them," he would demur: "I do not think that all the persons who profess to discredit these visitations, really discredit them, or if they do in the daylight, are not admonished by the approach of th loneliness & midnight to think more respectfully of the world of Shadows" (*MSJ* 126). This *respectfully* is deftly punning: an attitude of mind and a subject for thought re: *specters*. For this frisson, Shelley's capital "S" casts Shadows as a substantive sensation.

All this is in play between *Byron* and *Shelley*, characters in conversation in a piece in *New Monthly Magazine* 1830.[5] Both historical personages dead for years, the characters are fictional revenants. *Shelley* nags *Byron* about the eerie spectacle of that most famous of ghosts: "But do you not admire the buried majesty of Denmark 'revisiting the glimpses of the moon'?" (329; *Hamlet* 1.1.48, 1.4.54). *Byron* is having none of it, notwithstanding the now famous lunar conjurations at the Coliseum in *Childe Harold's Pilgrimage Canto IV*: "when the rising moon begins to climb / Its topmost arch, and gently pauses there; . . . / When the light shines serene but doth not glare, / Then in this magic circle raise the dead" (cxliv). After 1819, full-moon nights at the Coliseum thronged with eager conjurors, ready to inhabit Byron's scene of conjuring. In the *Magazine* scene, the raised dead is just a burlesque: "Alas! poor ghost!" cries *Byron* (329), camping Hamlet's pity for the revenant's sigh for having to hie back to purgatory at the break of dawn (1.5.3–5).

Byron seems to forget that Shakespeare himself didn't mind mining the comic potential along with the sublimity. The Ghost's caution that his tale will make "each particular hair" on Hamlet's head "stand on end / Like quills upon the fretful porcupine" (1.5) is farce physiology. Hamlet swings (manically) into this mode, with Marcellus and Horatio his audience. When the Ghost rumbles under the stage crying "Swear," Hamlet choruses back: "Ha, ha, boy! say'st thou so? art thou there, true-penny? / Come on,—you hear this fellow in the cellaridge / . . . / Well said, old mole!" (1.5.150–62).[6] It's canny of

Shakespeare to echo "Alas! poor ghost!" in the graveyard bantering in 5.1 when Hamlet, fondling a skull said to be his old jester's, sighs, "Alas, poor Yorick!" Popping *Yorick* into *ghost*-syntax, Shakespeare replays a terrific sublimity as a melancholy farce, a life reduced to and volleyed as a prop.

If *Byron* misses this beat, Byron himself catches the pulse in *Don Juan Canto XIII*, where the ghost-lines of *Hamlet* fuel a satire of social life and death, its assiduous homework, and its perils of performance:

> Kit-Cat, the famous conversationist,
>> Who, in his common-place book, had a page
>> Prepared each morn for evenings. "List, oh list!—"
> "Alas, poor Ghost!"—what unexpected woes
> Await those who have studied their *bon mots!*   (13.97)

"List, list, O list!"—the ghost's plea to Hamlet to listen (1.5.22)—is riffed into a cue-sheet for social success. As a noun, *list!* apostrophizes the prep-sheet; as an imperative, it exhorts its assembly to enter the competitive conversation. The champion is more than conversational; he is an artful conservation*ist*. This word is not in Johnson's Dictionary (nor ECCO). It's fairly new nineteenth-century flash, and Byron has fun with the spectacle. The poor Ghost is recalled and rebranded for Byronic word-play, chimed with *woes*, then *woes* rhymed to *mots*, with a light pun on the verbal aggression at hand, *mows*. Byron himself had entered the lists just two stanzas before, with a punning couplet crafted for dinner-table wit: "Society is now one polish'd horde, / Form'd of two mighty tribes, the *Bores* and *Bored*" (95).

The Ghost of old Hamlet wouldn't have a ghost of a chance at this preview of the Algonquin Round Table:

> Firstly, they must allure the conversation
>> By many windings to their clever clinch;
> And secondly, must let slip no occasion,
>> Nor *bate* (abate) their hearers of an *inch*,
> But take an ell—and make a great sensation,
>> If possible: and thirdly, never flinch
> When some smart talker puts them to the test,
> But seize the last word, which no doubt's the best.   (13.98)

With a glance in *seize* at the trope "carpe diem" (fresh from its meta-poetic play in *Canto XI*, about which more anon), the siege of death is not tomorrow, but the next breath. Byron's ottava rima deftly mimes the strategies of conversation, clapping *occasion* to *sensation*, and winding to the couplet's clever clinch, its last word literally *best*. Spectral Elsinore—all moonlit windings, urgent reports, terrific sensations, and call to courage—is reborn as salon spectacle, the only fear at hand, that of losing command of the conversation, the only ghosts, potential party-crashers, set in a rhyme that literally ingests their *hosts*: "Lord Henry and his Lady were the hosts / . . . / Their table was a board to tempt even ghosts" (99).

In this key, *New-Monthly Byron* treats the Ghost in *Hamlet* as just so much impolite company, answering its haunting "remember me!" with a blithe blow-off:

> the ghost is as whimsical a person as any of the others. It seems to come and go without any reason at all. Why should it make all that bustle in the cellarage when it cries out "Swear!" in echo to Hamlet? Why should it appear so unexpectedly and uselessly in that scene with his mother? But ask not why, seek not reason, or consistency, or art, in the wild rhapsodies of this uncultivated genius. . . . The story, the action, after the first prologue and preparation of this ghost, remain stagnant. (329)

Spoofing the defenses of Shakespeare's "genius" (by Coleridge, inter alia[7]) against the neoclassical cries of rule-flouting, *Byron* won't disagree. *Hamlet* is just a bad, incoherent ghost-story.[8] This whimsy plays into actual Byron's satire of wastrel Prince George, who, on discovering Byron's hand in some verses at royal expense, "chose . . . to be *affected* 'in sorrow rather than anger'" (*BLJ* 4:51)—the pompously pained Prince affecting the pathos of old Hamlet's Ghost (1.2.232).[9]

Yet even Byron's admired Voltaire, famed indicter of Shakespeare's rule-breaking, would cut slack for the Elsinor grandeur: "*Il faut avouer que, parmi les beautés qui étincellent au milieu de ces terribles extravangances, l'ombre du père d'Hamlet est un des coups de théâtre les plus frappants.*"[10] On the same page as Voltaire, *Magazine-Shelley* whips out an unpublished paper for after-dinner recital. Shakespeare's purpose (he takes pains to explain) "to body forth a character so deeply, indeed, and pre-eminently tragic, but most hard to fix and bring down into the definite world of action, as it seemed to lie beyond it in the sphere of thought, silent and invisible," prompted him to invent "the sublime idea of the ghost; an outward and visible sign of the sudden apparitions of the mysterious world within us" (332). The appeal to "us" makes everyone a potential ghost-host.[11] To Hamlet, the ghost embodies a startling epiphany in the material present:

The ghost of his father, clad in complete steel, revisiting the glimpses of the moon, may be considered as a great purpose coming suddenly upon a meditative mind. All the outward circumstance and actual reality, of course, immediately become necessary as the laws and conditions of the visible world into which it is translated. (332)

The formation that *Byron* spoofs on the stage *Shelley* casts on the mind's screen, evoking (ironically for *Byron*) the genre that historical Byron named "mental theatre."[12]

In the realm of mental theatre, *Shelley* also has a bead on Freud's theory of Hamlet's Oedipal agon. When Horatio reports a ghost-at-arms to Hamlet, an out-of-shape, superannuated student, pained by comparison to his father, a "man of action" (says *Shelley*), Hamlet parries his own strong suit: "philosophical . . . questions." As "a man trying to realize completely, in his own mind, the image of the thing" and "strongly" probing the "mysterious contradiction between reality and ideality, one of the most profound questions of ontology" (332), mental exertion is his best manly defense. *Shelley* tracks the agon across act 1, to a sequel crisis, when Hamlet, lecturing his posse on the perversities of national character,

is suddenly visited by the apparition. He breaks off in terror. When the ghost has faded from him, he is left overcome with his feelings, and with the weight of the commanded action. He confuses his external body with his inner self, as if he were nothing but a spirit . . . (333)

—as if the apparition had translated Hamlet into ghost of himself. How terrifically deconstructive, on highest stakes: a king-ghost with substantial weight, his material son left nothing but spirit. *Shelley* triumphantly sums up: "Hamlet is, in itself, a complete and reasonable whole, composed in an harmonious proportion of difference and similitude, into one expressive unity" (336). He could've been ghost-writing for Coleridge on a good day.

But with a wry coda, the *Magazine* scene deflates the achieved unity: "Shelley, as he finished, looked up, and found Lord Byron fast asleep" (336). This is a standard comic bit, one Lord Byron himself used in *Mazeppa*: Mazeppa's tempestuous tale, told to distract a battle-worn king, oversucceeds by putting the king to sleep. The mock-heroic is an honorary ghost in the *Magazine* joke.[13] It is strangely kin to the tonal double-play at the outset of the conversation, where phantasmic horror gets played for laughs— not by *Byron* even, but by *Shelley*. After a morning spent with *Hamlet, Byron* complains of "a nightmare sensation of impotence and vain endeavor," wondering if the failure is his or Shakespeare's. "I understand you!" replies *Shelley*; "'Tis a feeling one but too often feels; when an object stands before one, unintelligible, 'wrapped in its own formless horror like a ghost.'" *Byron* pays *Shelley* the compliment of recognizing the gloss, then turns Oscar Wilde avant la lettre: "I don't wonder you quote that line of yours. It is one of the best you ever wrote. I think it great affectation not to quote oneself" (327–28). The jest elides the horrific context in *The Cenci*, for which no "image" can ever be adequate:

> I, whose thought
> Is like a ghost shrouded and folded up
> In its own formless horror.

So cries Beatrice after she's been raped by her father (3.1.109–11, p. 38), with a prompt for parricide. *Shelley*'s riff and *Byron*'s catch go deep into the "purpose" of *Hamlet*, in ways that Freud's student Ernest Jones analyzed. Hamlet's repressed antagonism to his father recoils as haunting by a murdered father.

II. Byron's Ghost, Writing

Reading *Manfred*, J. W. Croker, recalling that "Voltaire calls Hamlet a 'triste extravagance,'" praises Byron's mental theatre as the embodied etymology: "the very word indeed explains itself he is extravagant Who wanders beyond the beaten track."[14] When Thomas Carlyle learned of Byron's death, he mourned to Jane Welsh, "I dreamed of seeing him and knowing him; but the curtain of everlasting night has hid him from our eyes."[15]

To dream of Byron's ghost, then, was the compensatory Spirit of the age, and it bonded Miss Welsh to Mr. Carlyle. He all but sealed the deal on his courtship when he gave her a letter, sent by Byron to B. W. Proctor (who gifted it to Carlyle): "This, then, was *his* handwriting! *his* whose image had haunted my imagination for years and years," cried Miss Welsh, the handwriting seeming to distill the haunt of her imagination into a palpable presence, and (perhaps disconcerting to her courter) a hot rival romance:

> *he*, then had seen and touched this very paper. I could almost fancy that his look and touch were visible on it! . . . I kissed the seal with a fervour which would have graced the most passionate lover. (*Early Letters* 101–2)

The "image" was less likely any sight of Byron, than a proxy portrait, a site to conjure with. Sitting for Richard Westall in 1813, one year after *Childe Har-*

George Gordon, Lord Byron, painted by Richard Westall in 1813.
© National Portrait Gallery, London.

old's Pilgrimage achieved international fame, Byron was the first conjurer of himself, posing as Hamlet redivivus, taking a cue from Thomas Lawrence's *John Philip Kemble as Hamlet* (1801).[16] Gone from England after 1816, hid from English eyes, Byron throbbed with virtual life. "Believe me," Murray wrote to him in March 1819, "your portrait is engraved & painted & sold in every town t[h]roughout the Kingdom" (*Letters* 267). The year following Byron's death was rampant in conjurings of his spirit, frequently on the template of this portrait. What Tom Mole calls "a visual discourse of Byronism" is revenant in legible signifiers: "a bare throat, a white collar, a curling forelock, a receding hairline, a characteristic pose" (75).

One avatar from 1825 is the illustration for "Lord Byron in the Other World," the first and longest piece in *The Book of Spirits and Tales of the Dead,* a market gambit to blend Byronism into ghost-fiction. This "Lord Byron" is not really a ghost but "Lord Byron" materialized in an "Other World"— and so a canny take on Byron's manner of ghost-presencing. Narrating in first person, "Byron" finds himself "once more in the hall of his ancestors," famed haunt of ghosts. The tale begins in a small comedy, arcing from gothic to Beckett, in the discovery, "I WAS A CORPSE!" (3). This horror musters Byron—resisting the great affectation not to quote oneself—to summon his famous anthem of alienation from *Childe Harold's Pilgrimage III*, "I have not loved the world, nor the world me" (cxiii–iv). Sung from the next world, the poetry swells into a reverie on the ease and freedom of a purely spiritual existence (5).

When the reverie is invaded by a chorus of "brother worms" bruiting the sweet pleasures that "enliven the grave," Byron is gripped by a "fear of annihilation" and cries out "for a voice to tell thee, Nature, how I loathe thy treachery!" The voice is a revenant, of sorts, emanating from another quotable site in *Childe Harold Canto III*, the stanza cries for "one word" of "lightning" to say it all (xcvii). It becomes the voice of Byronism, "my name, many times repeated," along with the sobriquet of fame, "Childe Harold," sounded by "distant voices" in a "hollow, sepulchral tone" of incantation, promising revival (7).

> Up, up from thy dismal shell,
> Thus we break Childe Harold's spell!
> Art thou fond of mystery?
> Come with us and thou shalt see
> Things not made for mortal eyes.
> The spell is broke—arise, arise!

> These words were no sooner pronounced than, to my utter amazement, the whole of my faculties were restored, and I stood forth, once more, an animated being. (7)

The posse conducts the Childe, animated by the spell of his own fame, to the hall of Death, where a convocation of politic skeletons (this scene could have served Beddoes's *Death's Jest-Book*) is debating admissions. Among these skulls, three distinguished by "remarkable thickness"—"Edinburgh Reviewers," whose "agitation" ("Byron" is happy to report) "seemed to increase with my presence" (9). They are soon eclipsed by a band of brothers, "bards of every clime and age," who bestow a gold wreath on "Harold," imaged in repose, in a Westall pose. "Lord Byron in the Other World" renders a new "Vision of Judgment," with Byron as the animated reporter of his own immortal honors, a spirit among spirits.

Lord Byron in the Other World, frontispiece, *The Book of Spirits and Tales of the Dead* (London: ?1825–27). The Carl H. Pforzheimer Collection of Shelley and His Circle, The New York Public Library, Astor, Lenox and Tilden Foundations.

Another ghost-confection, from 1830, *The Spirit of Byron in the Isles of Greece,* doubles the spirit. A terrestrial Byron, portrait-posed, contemplates Byron, portrait-profiled, as the tutelary spirit of Grecian sky, sea, and trees.[17] One needn't go to Greece for the thrill. Drawing on the popular nineteenth-century genre, "Homes and Haunts," L.E.L. worked a conjuration in the 1840 *Fisher's Drawing-Room Scrap-Book,* in the presence of "The Portrait of Lord Byron at Newstead Abbey" (i.e., Westall's, made into a two-tone engraving for readers of *Fisher's*). It was here (as Moore gave the story in 1830) that Byron arose, as if a dynastic revenant, trailing glory's glooms: "young Byron stood forth alone, unannounced by either praise or promise,—the representative of an ancient house, whose name, long lost in the gloomy solitudes of Newstead, seemed to have just awakened from the sleep of half a century in his person" (1:345). On site, L.E.L. performs as skilled reader, exploiting her capital as "the female Byron." This epithet was bestowed by her publisher William Jerdan, to puff her debut volume of poetry,

The Spirit of Byron, in the Isles of Greece. Designed on stone by H. Burn, printed by Englemann & Co. Published by R. Ackermann, No 96, Strand, London, ca. 1830. Private collection.

The Improvisatrice (1824), out just weeks after Byron's death, as the spirit of Byron reborn.

Ace Byronista by 1840, L.E.L. ably wields the signatures—"the constant struggle of the clay and spirit" (p. 11)—to conjure the "youthful poet" out of his portrait, and into Newstead at large. Her tribute goes full-throttle in present-tense immediate sensations:

> His name is on the haunted shade,
>   His name is on the air;
> We walk the forest's twilight glade,
>   And only he is there.   (p. 11)

It's not just that she conjures Byron's ghost at Newstead; she inhabits Byron's own spectral imagination: "The visionary world appears / Girt with fantastic shapes and fears" (p. 14). Her imagination is his imagination, open to any imagination. And so, the inclusive plurals of the spirit-world that she transmits to her readers:

> Here only we recall
> Whatever soothes, subdues, endears
>   In his ancestral hall.
> The deep enchantment we have felt,
> When every thought and feeling dwelt
>   Beneath his spirit's thrall.   (p. 14)

To rhyme *we recall / ancestral hall / spirit's thrall* is conjuration itself.[18]

Stoked up on "the ghost stories with which it abounds" (98), Washington Irving visited Newstead in 1835, publishing his account the same year, freely mixing in *Don Juan*'s poetry of Norman Abbey, as if all of Byron's Abbeys were equivalent, synonymous (111–15). Eager gaze, eager feet, imaginative overdrive, "every sight and sound . . . calculated to summon up touching recollections" (125), Irving is possessed by Byron passion-lore, now fantasizing a lost childhood sweetheart of the region, now a fraternal romance:

> I penetrated the recesses of the mystic grove . . . one of the favorite haunts of the late Lord Byron. . . . I searched the grove for some time, before I found the tree on which Lord Byron had left his frail memorial. It was an elm of peculiar form; having two trunks, which sprang from the same root, and, after growing side by side, mingled their branches together. He had selected it, doubtless, as emblematical of his sister and himself. The names of BYRON and AUGUSTA were still visible. They had been deeply cut in the bark, but the natural growth of the tree was gradually rendering them illegible, and a few years hence, strangers will seek in vain for this record of fraternal affection. (*Newstead Abbey* 122–23)

Irving all but cuts himself in as soul-brother, thrilled by the supernaturalism of the woods and primed by a super-textualism in Byron's ghost-stories (and his own éclat in the genre).[19] "The great lancet window in front of the chapel adjoins the very wall of the chamber, and the mysterious sounds from it at night have been well described by Lord Byron:—" he reports, in a heartbeat quoting the Norman Abbey stanzas in *Don Juan, Canto XIII* (62–64) as if he were at this literary site, too. It's sheer redundancy for him to add, in the wake of this lavish quotation, "Never was a traveller in quest of the romantic in greater luck" in getting lodged in Byron's very material chambers, the "haunted apartment of the Abbey" (197–98).

III. Byron's Ghost-Writing

How unlikely a ghost-hero is Don Juan, then. In the very first installment of his epic, Byron seems to resent his feckless hero for extraordinary spectral-immunity:

> Not even a vision of his former woes
>   Throbb'd in accursed dreams, which sometimes spread
> Unwelcome visions of our former years,
> Till the eye, cheated, opens thick with tears.   (2.134)

Byron first drafted the middle lines above to read "spread / Their loathed phantasmagoria oer the Mind" (*CPW* 5:131n). It is not Juan's blessed dreaming but the poet's categorical Mind that is connected to the ghost-theater of the age. In 1798 Étienne-Gaspard Robertson, a Belgian inventor working in Paris, found international fame with his "Fantasmagorie," featuring "apparitions of Spectres, Ghosts and Revenants, as they must and could have appeared throughout history." Such spectacles appeared at London's Lyceum in 1801 and beamed with success across the Regency stage, sometimes with gothic thrills, and sometimes with the inevitable close company of comedy and farce.[20] Byron will eventually give Juan a ghost or two, in a farce unhaunted by woes of his former years.

Manfred, a drama forever haunted by the woes of former years, would seem *Don Juan's* opposite: a gothic closet-drama, it is all interiority, for reader and hero alike. Byron blazes as a title-page motto Hamlet's dead-serious rebuke to Horatio's skepticism about a ghost on the ramparts of Elsinore:

MANFRED,

A

DRAMATIC POEM.

———

"There are more things in heaven and earth, Horatio,
Than are dreamt of in your philosophy."

———

Stripped of *Hamlet*-markers (except for an incidental Horatio), the motto offers a counter-Enlightenment adage for any reader to entertain. Where ghosts count among the things of earth, it is sober philosophy that is the dubious dream. Yet Hamlet-endorsed as it may be, the spirit world will take some turns in *Manfred* that look like auditions for farce. Of the convocation in the Hall of Aramanes, Thomas Peacock jested, "It is difficult to conceive where this heterogeneous mythological company could have originally met, except at a *table d'hôte.*"[21]

For a sequel to Manfred's serial colloquies with his soul-haunters, and his defiant refusal of serial soul-healers, Byron drafted a last act in this vein, not quite a *table d'hôte*, but serviceable enough.[22] Although he cut it, it is clear he had fun with it—as if he had divined Marx's famous drama-genre metaphor about historical repetition: first tragedy, then farce.[23] Its star is a droll she-demon, Ashtaroth, conjured by Manfred to carry off an abbot who has been pestering Manfred to save his soul. Lightened by "an exorcism or two" (44–45), Ashtaroth takes him away for a night at Shreckhorn, with Manfred's smirk that this holy man "ne'er again will be so near to Heaven" (this fearful Alp yet to be ascended):

> ASHTAROTH *disappears with the abbot, singing as follows:*
> > A prodigal son—and a maid undone—
> > And a widow re-wedded within the year—
> > And a worldly Monk—and a pregnant Nun—
> > Are things which every day appear.   (46–49)

Manfred crabs to himself, "Why would this fool break in on me, and force / My arts to pranks fantastical?" (50–51). The answer is Byron's scripting of the fantastical art, not least in this "irreverent ditty about the ordinariness of evil."[24] The diabolic everyday could have been patter for Peter Cook in *Bedazzled*—or, closer to hand, an entry in Sathan's account-book in *The Vision of Judgment*. By 1817, the tortured, tragic Byronic hero was an outworn hallmark, and Byron himself was fueling the farce-sequel.

Farce-*Manfred,* intended or accidental, flourished. The scene Byron canceled was revived in Moore's *Works of Lord Byron* (1832–33; 11:54). Happy for this resource, the stage took it on, defying the anti-theatrical genre, "Dramatic Poem." When Alfred Bunn brought *Manfred* to Covent Garden (he was its manager) just before Halloween in 1834, he included the canceled episode and added 30 dancing witches in the first act. The shimmer of sublime into silly was irresistible to the reviews. *Morning Chronicle* found the material translation of mental drama "ludicrous"; "such a waste of gauze," complained *Literary Gazette*. Writing for *The London Theatre,* H. C. Robinson crabbed that the invocations "sounded like doggerel . . . a sort of Don Juan without wit or fun."[25] By 1836, *Manfred* was in full farce mode at the Strand, with hero Man-Fred, a haunted, out-of-work chimney-sweep, torturing the famous opening lines:

> This pot must be replenish'd—but I think
> It ne'er would hold as much as I could drink;
> My slumbers—if I slumber—are not sleep,
> But interrupted by a cry of *sweep!*

The metaphysical count, his midnight lamp, and his rogue Spirits are now a quotidian laborer and a pot of spirits.

These events are not so much travesty of *Manfred,* as an extrapolation of its own aspects of travesty, oblique and patent, and with phantoms at hand. By 1817, a vast social text of speculation was spinning on the mysterious "Separation" of Lord and Lady Byron early in 1816. Byron, for whom Lady Byron was a receding ghost of a misbegotten matrimonial past, tweaked the web with the dead-serious phantom, Astarte. She is conjured as a torment to Manfred, threaded with hints of Byron's sexual liaison, before and during his marriage, with his half-sister Augusta, whose name is phantasmically half-lettered into *Astarte:*

> Thou lovedst me
> Too much, as I loved thee: we were not made
> To torture thus each other, though it were
> The deadliest sin to love as we have loved.   (2.4.121–24)

But if this is Manfred's agon, the name *Astarte* also weirdly hooks into Byron's farce-episode: in Eastern lore, *Astarte* is sometimes named *Ashtaroth.* The mordant she-specter and the beloved, torturing phantom twinned in genre-complicated Byronism.[26]

Astarte is both a determined and over-determined name: deepest angst wrought with comic riffs. So, too, are Manfred's serial refusals of patriarchal authority: now high Oedipal agon, now domestic comedy. These strands wind into a scene staged with two down-to-earth castle retainers whose names share a syllable with metaphysical Manfred, Her*man* and *Man*uel.[27] Their conversation turns to the "jocund times" back in the father's day:

> Count Sigismund was proud,—but gay and free,—
> A warrior and a reveller; he dwelt not

> With books and solitude, nor made the night
> A gloomy vigil, but a festal time,
> Merrier than day; he did not walk the rocks
> And forests like a wolf, nor turn aside
> From men and their delights.   (3.3.19–25)

More jaunty than haunty, the father is a patent antitype to his gloomy son. This could be copy for Tom Stoppard's *Rosencrantz and Guildenstern are Dead*, as these schoolmates converse about Hamlet: no man of mystery, just a loner given to talking to himself (p. 52).

In the very midst of this cartoon, phantom Astarte looms on a cue that flirts with the farce formula. Herman has asked Manuel for some back-story, as if they were bored watchers at Elsinore killing time with castle gossip:

> Come, be friendly;
> Relate me some to while away our watch:
> I've heard thee darkly speak of an event
> Which happened hereabouts, by this same tower.   (3.3.30–33)

Manuel obliges with a full-blown recital in gothic-ghost poetry:

> That was a night indeed; I do remember
> 'Twas twilight, as it may be now, and such
> Another evening;—yon red cloud, which rests
> On Eigher's pinnacle, so rested then,—
> So like that it might be the same; the wind
> Was faint and gusty, and the mountain snows
> Began to glitter with the climbing moon;
> Count Manfred was, as now, within his tower,—
> How occupied, we knew not, but with him
> The sole companion of his wanderings
> And watchings—her, whom of all earthly things
> That lived, the only thing he seem'd to love,—
> As he, indeed, by blood was bound to do,
> The lady Astarte, his—————
>   Hush! who comes here?   (3.3.34–47)

Gusty with dashes that signify a suspense of breath and a space for a reader's investment—especially that last one—this report also invites an allusive conjuring (Byron's title-page cues it) from *Hamlet*:

Last night of all,
When yond same star that's westward from the pole
Had made his course t' illume that part of heaven
Where now it burns, Marcellus and myself,
The bell then beating one————

Enter Ghost   (1.1.35–39)

Manuel channels Byron's teasing: "Hush! who comes here?" could easily, on the template of *Hamlet*, cue the ghost of Astarte, awaking with a start, come back to tell all. "Many a real Manfred has trembled as he called up the phantom of Astarte," apparition-theorist Walter Dendy muses, in behalf of how "a shadow of conscience" can take the form of a ghost, and how a formed ghost such as Astarte can cast a shadow of conscience (58). In this "real . . . phantom," literature comes to life as the mode in which the spectral and the determinate can operate simultaneously, as figures called up.

In such a tremble, phantom Astarte emerges from the sorority of Francesca in Byron's *Siege of Corinth*, published the year before *Manfred*, early in 1816, just weeks after Lady Byron had packed up and left for good. The Byronic hero Alp is betrothed to Francesca. When (on a rumor of Alp's perfidy) her father, Corinth's governor, forbids their union, Alp turns renegade, joining the Ottoman forces. On the night before the Ottoman assault on this Venetian stronghold, as Alp ruminates among the ruins outside the city, he hears a "night-wind sigh" when there is not enough wind to wave a blade of grass. At his side distills a sudden, unoriginated "sight," Francesca, unsmiling, pale-eyed and chill (475–87). It is a dreamscaped event in the mind, in the form of psychomachia. "I come from my rest to him I love best, / That I may be happy, and he may be blest," she intones in adages (518–19), urging Alp to reconcile to Venice and Christianity: "thou has done a fearful deed / In falling away from thy father's creed" (530–31). His devotion to vengeance casts her into a shade so immediate as to seem not just a coincidence, but caused by him.

This compressed logic sustains one of Byron's most magnificent stretches of spectral sensation, of life shading into a ghost, without a breath, without a motion, without a pulse, but with an awful sheen of presence in the material world:

Fair but faint—without the ray
Of mind, that made each feature play
Like sparkling waves on a sunny day;
And her motionless lips lay still as death,

And her words came forth without her breath,
And there rose not a heave o'er her bosom's swell,
And there seemed not a pulse in her veins to dwell.
Though her eye shone out, yet the lids were fixed,
And the glance that it gave was wild and unmixed
With aught of change, as the eyes may seem
Of the restless who walk in a troubled dream;
Like the figures on arras, that gloomily glare
Stirred by the breath of the wintry air,
So seen by the dying lamp's fitful light,
Lifeless, but life-like, and awful to sight;
As they seem, through the dimness, about to come down
From the shadowy wall where their images frown;
Fearfully flitting to and fro,
As the gusts on the tapestry come and go.   (564–82)

This real-time sensation of ghost-seeing, like gust-rippled arras-art, is meta-ghostwork. In Byronic revenance, it will be reprised in Juan's nightwalk through Norman Abbey's gallery, where he is frozen in his tracks by a seeming ghost. Alp is drained of life by what he beholds:

The feverish glow of his brow was gone,
And his heart sank so still that it felt like stone,
As he looked on that face, and beheld its hue.   (560–62)

Recovering from this petrification back into his "deep, interminable pride," Alp refuses the lady's plea (609), and she vanishes as suddenly as she came. The next day, her father, meeting Alp in battle, tells him that Francesca died the night before. This news, its spectral logic already condensed, staggers Alp, undone by it before an actual shot takes him down.

In *Manfred*, the guards' gossip-cue to "Astarte" is preempted by a father with a difference. It's that nagging Abbot of St. Maurice, back for one last run at saving Manfred's soul. The latest of the institutional fathers to get no respect from a Byronic hero, he is left to being a straight-man reporter of Byron's most sensational shade ever:

I see a dusk and awful figure rise
Like an infernal god from out the earth;
His face wrapt in a mantle, and his form
Robed as with angry clouds.   (3.4.62–65)

Although an Abbot is trained to manage such a figure ("I do fear him not" [3.4.66]), readers trained on Byronism could tag it as the latest, hyperbolic iteration of the Satanic-Byronic hero.[28] Byron is completely aware that when this Spirit declares itself "The genius of this mortal" (81), it's such old news as to be a comic redundancy. It's a signature shade, the genius of Byron, summoned to be exorcised from a *Manfred* now patently mannerist.[29] "I certainly am a devil of a mannerist," Byron punned to Murray, with a coy addendum, "& must leave off" (9 March 1817; *BLJ* 5:185). The word *mannerist* comes from Old French *maniere* (manner: handling), by way of the Latin *manus,* hand. This is the last word in Manfred's self-accounting: "The hand of death is upon me—but not yours!" so he spurns the Abbot who would save him, then relents: "Give me thy hand—" (149).

But exorcism is an imperfect art. It is not erasure, just ejection from one local habitation into another—and Byron's poetry will not give up its ghosts. Byron had hosted an "Incantation" in 1816 for *The Prisoner of Chillon* volume (pp. 46–59), with a note that it "was a Chorus in an unfinished Witch Drama . . . begun some years ago." When he conjured it into *Manfred* (I.i.192ff), it glowed in the aura of meta-Byronism. With this maneuver Byron contradicts what Marjorie Garber calls the "peculiar characteristic" of a ghost, that it is "both nominally identical to and numinously different from a vanished or unavailable original" (21). Byron's original is a Byronism that puts ghosts into serial production. This is not dialectical (now this, now that) but a relay that thematizes, theatricalizes, and theorizes the interchanges of originality and repetition, authority and dispossession, satire and sincerity, priority and belatedness—and not least, absence and presence.

This is the Byronic relay of a seriocomic interruption in the wicked hilarity of *The Vision of Judgment* (1821–22): the advent of ghost-writer "Junius."[30] The pseudonym conjures Lucius Junius, staunch republican critic in ancient Rome, in the form of his immediate avatar, Junius Redivivus of 1769–72, famous for over 60 anti-Monarchal letters, signed *Stat Nominis Umbra* ("Stands the Shadow of a Name"). Shadow-standing seems to be the case with Byron's signature of revival, too, "Quevedo Redivivus." And the common target is George III. Junius's *Letter 35* earned a prosecution for disrespect, and Byron's *Vision* takes this risk too, aggravating it by including a travesty of Poet Laureate Southey. Yet there is a significant faultline in Byron's alliance with Junius.

The "Shadow of a Name" is intractably opaque, while Byron's pseudonym was decodable, not least because of the *Vision's* ottava rima, Byron's stylistic signature by the 1820s. Junius had no such hallmarks, no flash of lineage or class: "Quick in its motions, with an air of vigour, / But nought to mark its breeding or its birth" (LXXV), he is "a phantasmagoria in / Himself" (LXVII), seeming by turns of surmise everyone and no one.[31] With all efforts to "distinguish whose the features were" thwarted (LXXVI), the words are the event. The "I" of the declaration, "I loved my country, and I hated him" (LXXXIII) is incidental to the syntax of a country loved and a monarch detested. No Byronic expatriate (not to put too fine a point on it), Junius stands in England, and stands by his pen:

> "What I have written, I have written: let
>   The rest be on his head or mine!" So spoke
> Old "Nominis Umbra"; and while speaking yet,
>   Away he melted in celestial smoke.   (LXXXIV)

A shade whose present words are the matter is an Author-function for what has been written, without a display of the historical author. This is left to smoke, or ghost—and so as signature and as mode, is the antithesis of name-invested Byronism.

The paradox in Byron's representation of this Shadow of a Name is its shades of legible Byronism. Notwithstanding the heroism of sheer words in "What I have written, I have written," it echoes Byron's words at the close of *Childe Harold's Pilgrimage, Canto IV* (1818), at the end of its run of spectacular Regency fame: "what is writ, is writ" (clxxxv). The tautology is another signature: "What I have done is done"—so the Poet Laureate of the midnight lamp, Manfred, put it in 1817 (3.4.127). Shadow "Junius" is revived under the survey of Byron's *Vision of Judgment*:

> I've an hypothesis—'tis quite my own;
>   I never let it out till now, for fear
> Of doing people harm about the throne,
>   And injuring some minister or peer
> On whom the stigma might perhaps be blown;
>   It is—my gentle public, lend thine ear!
> 'Tis, that what Junius we are wont to call,
> Was *really, truly,* nobody at all.   (LXXX)

The I-author who appeals (with a riff on Roman Brutus) to the gentle public's ear, and the Laureate Bard Southey, "glad to get an audience" (XC), oddly join in retailing what's "quite my own"— antitypes of the unknown "author" forever in the shadow of a name (LXXXI).

IV. Staging Ghosts

Byron's conjurings from his established company of ghosts marks even a throwaway moment in *Don Juan Canto VI*, when odalisque Katinka tries to wrangle a bed-slot with "Juanna" (Juan's imposed disguise), pretending to a "fear of ghosts":

> I am sure I see
>   A phantom upon each of the four posts;
> And then I have the worst dreams that can be,
>   Of Guebres, Giaours, and Ginns, and Gouls in hosts.   (6.48)

"Giaours" can't help but evoke Byron's notorious *Giaour* (1813), even in this ephemeral farce. Fairly soon Byron updates the ghosts, too, winking at Byronic modernism: "if there be sprites" in this opulent oda, they would follow the fashion of this lucky luxe-haunt:

> They should have walked there in their spriteliest trim,
>   By way of change from their sepulchral sites,
> And shown themselves as Ghosts of better taste
> Than haunting some old Ruin or wild Waste.   (6.64)

This is a world in which "phantoms hovered, or might seem to hover / To those who like their company" (6.70), as if hoping for invitation.

Ghosts of better taste find more welcome in the roster of *Canto XI*, in which the Great World hosts the first singular form, *ghost*. Its first stanza cues Bishop Berkeley's refusal of spirit for matter. By stanza 72, the poet is making this a matter of social life and death:

> Oh, ye ambrosial moments! always upper
>   In mind, a sort of sentimental bogle,
> Which sits for ever upon Memory's crupper,
>   The ghost of vanished pleasures once in vogue! Ill
> Can tender souls relate the rise and fall
> Of hopes and fears which shake a single ball.   (72)

Chiming with *ghost*, *vogue* turns ghostly, in unforgiving recession, from age to age, from moment to moment. The strong rhyme *bogle*/*vogue! Ill* puts the case on the present stage. *Ill* is an adverb, but hung at the end of the line, it invites a ghost, *I'll*: the poet's self-reference, set for vanishing too. This threnody leads to a hilarious, exuberant Englished *ubi est* ("Where is?") across

stanzas 76–80, modulating into the poet's own ledger of changes recorded in
a mere seven years (81–85).

The climax is a pivot into the antidote of "Carpe diem" (11.86), a famous
revenant from Horace's Odes (I.xi.8):

> But 'Carpe diem,' Juan, 'Carpe, carpe!'
>   To-morrow sees another race as gay
> And transient, and devoured by the same harpy.
>   'Life's a poor player,'—then 'play out the play,
> Ye villains!' and above all keep a sharp eye
>   Much less on what you do than what you say:
> Be hypocritical, be cautious, be
> Not what you *seem,* but always what you *see.*   (11.86)

Playing on the warp of revenance, Byron tunes the rhymes of *carpe* to per-
plex its translation to a modern English eye and ear. The stanza's end-rhymes
are such close chimes as to ring into alternative options, a ghostwork in the
micro-stylistics of Byron's anything but careless pen. In strongest rhyme
with its own repetition, *Carpe* tunes the stanza, in a witty scan on the old
adage: *carpe diem, quàm minimùm credula postero* (seize the day, trusting
posterity as little as possible). What is the rhyme posterity of *Carpe*? In
modern English, it sounds with a long *e,* to govern the a-rhymes (*harpy/eye*),
with a plausible claim (against the ottava rima form) on the couplet's *be/see.*
Yet in this chord, *eye* is a tonal rogue, a meta-poetic *eye*-rhyme, torqued into
a long *e* only by antique sounding, or literary quaintness. Sounded more
Latin-wise, the second syllable of *Carpe* leans toward a long *a,* and so plays
into the b-rhymes, in a jesting link with *gay/play (player, play)/say.* What is
being seized in this play?

Into this lively shadow-work of Latin maxims in modern English, Byron's
two quotations summon yet more ghosts. To save the meter, the echo of
Macbeth has to excise *shadow* from "Life's but a walking shadow; a poor
player" (*Macbeth* 5.5). Yet a shadow surely haunts the source text of Falstaff's
protest, "play out the play: I have much to say in the behalf of that Falstaff,"
which he voices as "Prince Hal" against actual Prince Hal's rebuff of "the
play," as he role-plays the reproving King, his father and his future (*Henry IV,
Part 1* 2. 4).[32] Byron seizes the play of the stanza to weave a complicated web:
what seems, what is seen, what the poetry says and what it does, what is in
play and what haunts—and most of all, what is modern-day, against old lore,
old sounds.

Byron's riff on *carpe diem* underwrites Stephen Dedalus's witty declension: "What is a ghost? . . . One who has faded into impalpability through death, through absence, through change of manners" (*Ulysses* 188). New manners are all that's needed to send Falstaff into the shade, and in *Don Juan,* to send a lively ghost into faded glory. Poor Lady Pinchbeck, ever "talked about" when "young, and pretty," survives in a few vendible witticisms:

> But now no more the ghost of Scandal stalked about;
> She merely was deemed amiable and witty,
> And several of her best bon-mots were hawked about.   (12.47)

It's decadent Byronism, the superannuated Lady no match for fresh bait:

> I'd rather not say what might be related
> Of her exploits, for this were ticklish ground;
> Besides there might be falsehood in what's stated.   (14.42)

So hawks the poet of a new, young, pretty, female titillation, her name introduced in a linguistic flirtation with us no less than with Juan: "The Duchess of Fitz-Fulke, who loved '*tracasserie*,' / Began to treat him with some small *agaçerie*" (41). She is more than a Norman Abbey intrigue. She is Regency Byron, rediviva: "Desirable, distinguished, celebrated / For several winters in the grand, *grand Monde*" (42). Norman Abbey stages several material ghost-appearances from Byron's own hawked-about past: Newstead Abbey and his burlesques of its monk-ghosts, his Regency fame, his brand of poetry, his favorite allusions, and everything gossiped and reviewed of him. In the train are revenants from the poetic repertoire: a Junius Redivivus in a Monk's curse, the Spirit of Manfred in masquerade, and Byronic arts in the "freedoms of the female corporation" (14.43).

All come into play in the "story of a ghost" that is launched, but not finished, in *Canto XVI*. This is the legend of a dispossessed, vengeful Black Friar. For such traffic, "Norman Abbey" is a marked open house, its name registering a history of violent possessions and dispossessions: the Norse invasion of northern France, the Norman invasion Anglo-Saxon England, the old Catholic Abbey (priory of the Black Friars) wrested by the Protestant Reformation for English aristocracy (a sore point for Catholic Don Juan). Each rift is loaded with lore: devastations, repressions, and melancholy remains. After the Norman invasion, Norman Abbey endured as an "old, old monastery," then, with the Dissolution, perdured as a "Still older mansion, of a rich and rare / Mixed Gothic" (13.55), sporting a "glorious remnant of the

Gothic pile, / (While yet the church was Rome's)" (59). It then fell to a ruin in the seventeenth-century war "which struck Charles from his throne" (60) and rose again as the country seat of the Amundevilles, their surname bespeaking a French-Norman invasion into English nomenclature.

Byron scarcely needed Marx, or Derrida, to explain haunted hegemony. He had Newstead Abbey for a template.[33] Juan's first ghost-spotting is set in a portrait gallery of ghostly ancestors. At first it is just a chilly sensation: "by dim lights the portraits of the dead / Have something ghastly" (17). But then the images shift into an illusion of spectral life (Alp's ghostly Francesca could be an honorary guest in this company):

And the pale smile of Beauties in the grave,
 The charms of other days, in starlight gleams
Glimmer on high; their buried locks still wave
 Along the canvas; their eyes glance like dreams
On ours, or spars within some dusky cave,
 But death is imaged in their shadowy beams.
A picture is the past; even ere its frame
Be gilt, who sate hath ceased to be the same.   (16.19)

Byron nicely tunes his prepositional phrases between death *in the grave* and animation *in starlight gleams*. Placed at the end of the line, *gleams* shimmers between noun and verb, atmosphere and present action. A shimmer is also in the weirdly phrased "their buried locks still wave": a flicker of a locked grave, then still-life on a canvas, then animation in starlight gleams, with that familiar eerie sensation of actively glancing eyes in the present.

Washington Irving is an ideal register of this effect, adding, as is his wont, the supplement of his experience in the Newstead chamber, stoked on all "the wonderful stories and strange suppositions connected with my apartment." Gazing on its portraits as he "lay in bed at night," its figures "were almost animated by the workings of my imagination . . . almost a spectral effect. . . . In this way I used to conjure up fictions of the brain, and clothe the objects around me with ideal interest and import." He is in such a trance of real interest and import that in summoning Byron's stanza he miswrites "buried locks" as "buried looks" (150–52). Byron's volta at *But death* halts the illusion, *starlight gleams* revoked by *shadowy beams*. The couplet, about inexorable transience and mortality, evokes the graveyard epitaph, *Siste viator* (halt, traveler) that drains viewer (and reader) into a shade. Wilde staged such a moment to generate the most famously unstable of portraits in literature's gallery:

> "How sad it is," murmured Dorian Gray, with his eyes still fixed upon his own portrait. "How sad it is! I shall grow old, and horrid, and dreadful. But this picture will remain always young. It will never be the older than this particular day of June. . . . If it was only the other way! If it was I who were to be always young, and the picture that was to grow old! (*The Picture of Dorian Gray,* chapter 2, p. 19)

Juan, ever the new-one, seems to be granted this wish, without asking.

But this doesn't save him from haunting of another kind, its origin as unknowable as its sensation is immediate:

> No sound except the echo of his sigh
>   Or step ran sadly through that antique house,
> When suddenly he heard, or thought so, nigh,
>   A supernatural agent—or a mouse,
> Whose little nibbling rustle will embarrass
> Most people as it plays along the arras.   (16.20)

Byron has his *Hamlet* and eats it, too. *Hamlet* opens at night on the ramparts, "not a mouse stirring," then traumatized by a supernatural agent; and a flesh-and-blood Polonius plays behind an arras to his end. Byron conjures these hauntings into farce: what plays along *arras* is a rhyme with and lettering into *embarrass*. What emerges, with camp revelation, is something extraordinary, perhaps supernatural, or a venture into phantom-artistry:

> It was no mouse, but lo! a monk arrayed
>   In cowl and beads and dusky garb, appeared,
> Now in the moonlight, and now lapsed in shade,
>   With steps that trod as heavy, yet unheard.   (16.21)

In this gallery, the shifts of alternate shade and moonlight seem to report one of those portraits come to spectral life. Nicely lapsed in this shade is the b-rhyme *unheard,* unheard against *appeared,* a meta-spectral poetry itself. As Juan tries to get a grip back in his chamber by reading a newspaper, Byron slyly conjures ghosts of ghost-stories, especially Hamlet's: "He read an article the king attacking, / And a long eulogy of 'Patent Blacking'" (26). Fashion polish and political peril join, the syllable *king* resounding in both *attacking* and *blacking.*

Up to speed on Juan's thrills, Irving writes his chapter about his night in Byron's chamber, "The Rook Cell" (195–201), in the genre of ghost-story supplement: "to the fancies engendered in his brain in this remote and lonely apartment, incorporated with the floating superstitions of the Abbey, we are, no doubt, indebted for the spectral scene in Don Juan." The prepositions issue the overlays: *in* his brain; *in* this apartment; *in*corporated; *in*debted; *in* Don Juan. Even "spectral scene" could resound as "spectral seen." Irving summons a run of *Juan*'s stanzas (16.17–25) as if he were reporting from Byron's very brain (198–200). With his own present perfect verbs, he dramatizes a readily present haunting:

> As I have lain awake at night, I have heard all kinds of mysterious and sighing sounds from the neighbouring ruin. Distant footsteps, too, and the closing of doors in remote parts of the Abbey, would send hollow reverberations and echoes along the corridor and up the spiral staircase. (201)

And like Byron, he is hospitable to comedy. He brings his chapter to a climax, then a jesting anticlimax, with a ghost of Byronic cast:

> Once, in fact, I was roused by a strange moaning sound at the very door of my chamber. I threw it open, and a form, "black and shapeless with glaring eyes," stood before me. It proved, however, neither ghost nor goblin, but my friend Boatswain, the great Newfoundland dog, who had conceived a companionable liking for me, and occasionally sought me in my apartment. To the hauntings of even such a visitant as honest Boatswain may we attribute some of the marvellous stories about the Goblin Friar. (201)

The quotation "black and shapeless, with glaring eyes" ventriloquizes Byron's own haunting:

> in this chamber Lord Byron declared he had more than once been harassed at midnight by a mysterious visiter. A black shapeless form would sit cowering upon his bed, and after gazing at him for a time with glaring eyes, would roll off and disappear. The same uncouth apparition is said to have disturbed the slumbers of a newly married couple that once passed their honey-moon in this apartment. (198)

Irving's joke, at his own expense, is that his midnight visitor is only a dog. But the joke also turns inside out. In Goëthe's *Faust* (Byron knew Part I, published in 1808), a dog turns out to be the devil. The even friendly Boatswain is still ghostly, bearing the name of Byron's prized, eulogized dog, dead since 1808, reborn in this descendant, famed for accompanying Byron's body from Greece back to England.

Irving's double play of ghost story and comic demystification mirrors the morning-after sequel in *Don Juan*. Still spooked, his gentleman's attire in disarray, Juan appears at breakfast looking like a fresh delivery from a ghost story, "every body wondering" and piqued by his "answers . . . mysterious" (16.30–33). Lord Henry sounds a cue: "'You look,' quoth he, 'as if you had had your rest / Broke in upon by the Black Friar of late'" (35). This divining cues diva Lady Adeline, known to be "half a poetess" (39). Her very name punning *add-a-line*, Lord Henry invites her to "add the words" she has made to the legend she is too ready to sing. Ghost-writing for this Lady poetess, Byron wryly subverts *Lord* Byronism, with his own claims to title and estate. It was no stretch for Irving to cite these stanzas for the ghost at Newstead Abbey and Lady Byron: "Lord Byron pretended to have seen it about a month before he contracted his ill-starred marriage with Miss Milbanke" (146–47)—this "half a poetess" and heiress meant to save Newstead Abbey and the Byron line.

> But beware! beware! of the Black Friar,
>   He still retains his sway,
> For he is yet the church's heir
>   Who ever may be the lay.
> Amundeville is lord by day,
>   But the monk is lord by night.   (16, song-stanza 5)

Playing a part in this exchange of estates—day-lord for night-lord, male poet into female poet—is another event of Byron's linguistic politics, here on the material of the ghost-name itself: how should we hear *Friar*? The rhyme chain (stanzas 2, 5 and 6) is *beware, air, prayer, heir*—in chime with Norman-French *Frère*, the old Catholic order. But it rings doubly, because the Normans were usurpers of the Anglo-Saxon regime. Not for nothing has Lord Henry rhymed *Friar* with *liar*: the epithet of "Fame" that "Tells an odd story" (36), including this one. If you hear a French *Frère* and recall the sequential usurpations, there's the Derridean tale of ghosts in the hegemony. If you hear an English rhyme with *liar* then it's an ironized entertainment, "half believed" in the art of "half a poetess" (36–39).[34] Byron's sound-play is a witty phono-politics of spectral presence.

In the retail of supernatural material, Byron is willing to serve up his own signature fame in the fun, setting the scene in Juan's chamber the next night with a Byronic stamp:

Again—what is't? The wind? No, no—this time
   It is the sable Friar as before,
With awful footsteps regular as rhyme
   Or (as rhymes may be in these days) much more.   (16.113)

The "this time" rhyme of *as before* and *much more* conjures more than the yesternight. It inevitably conjures the famous stanza in *Childe Harold Canto III* (1816) about the dim haunting of the revels at the Duchess of Richmond's ball in Brussels:

Did ye not hear it?—No; 'twas but the wind,
   Or the car rattling o'er the stony street;
On with the dance! let joy be unconfined;
   No sleep till morn, when Youth and Pleasure meet
To chase the glowing Hours with flying feet—
   But, hark!—that heavy sound breaks in once more . . .   (3.22)

It's the artillery being assembled for the battle of Quatre Bras (two days before Waterloo). Byron reprises this herald of a massive military catastrophe in *Don Juan* as a prelude to a conquest of female design. Byronic ghosts and spectral texts are in such intimate relay, each generating the other, that their conflation seems foregone in a conquest of some kind:

The night was as before: he was undrest,
   Saving his night gown, which is an undress;
Completely 'sans-culotte', and without vest;
   In short, he hardly could be clothed with less.   (16.111)

With Juan "undrest," rhymingly "apprehensive of his spectral guest" (111), Byron brings on the ghost: "in the door-way, darkening Darkness, stood / The sable Friar in his solemn hood" (117), with a tip of the hood to Milton's Death: "black it stood as Night" (*PL* 2.670).

   Such terror-powerplay had been theorized by Joanna Baillie in her introduction to *Plays on the Passions*: "how many people have dressed up hideous apparitions to frighten the timid and superstitious!" While she warns pranksters of "the risk of destroying their happiness or understanding for ever" (9), the play's the thing for her. Impressed by her skill, and in the throes of writing *Manfred*, Byron mulled over Voltaire's reply to the question, "why no woman has ever written even a tolerable tragedy": "Ah (said the Patriarch) the composition of a tragedy requires *testicles*." "If this be true," Byron quips to Murray, "Lord knows what Joanna Baillie does—I suppose she borrows them" (*BLJ* 5:203). In *Don Juan*, Lord Byron knows what he'll do with the gender raid—at least in comedy. A woman in male borrowings, deploying an apparition of the Black Friar for erotic adventure, is the ploy in the last stanzas that he saw into publication, "Coined from surviving superstition's mint / Which passes ghosts in currency like gold" (16.22). This isn't Shelley's master-trope of fraud, the Ghost of Gold that is paper-scrip; it is commercial currency that is good as gold. That's the retail superstition about which Juan reminds himself, to allay his portrait-gallery fantods.

The other side of the coin, however, is Juan's gender shift into the imperiled ingenue of ghost-story currency. Capitalizing on Adeline's ballad, "the ghost's fresh operations" (16.111) come in a female design against multiple actors of the patriarchal order: clergy, English nobility, inheritance, masculine self-possession, epic poetry. It is the she-machine in the ghost of Byronism, now in material production for a real spectral presence:

> The ghost, if ghost it were, seemed a sweet soul
>   As ever lurked beneath a holy hood:
> A dimpled chin, a neck of ivory, stole
>   Forth into something much like flesh and blood;
> Back fell the sable frock and dreary cowl,
>   And they revealed—alas! that e'er they should!
> In full, voluptuous, but *not o'er*grown bulk,
> The phantom of her frolic Grace—Fitz-Fulke!   (16.123)

On this alliterated shift from "phantom" to embodied "Fitz-Fulke," Byron ends the Canto, ends the epic.[35] But not Byron's life in ghost-masquerade.

This coup de théâtre issued an invitation to another female erotic adventurer in the "female corporation" (14.43), who wrote up a ghost-story about "Lord Byron." *Don Juan Canto XVI* came out on 25 March 1824. A few weeks later, Byron was dead. In 1825, flagrant courtesan Harriette Wilson published a best-selling memoir that conjured Byron back with a story set at "a masquerade" in 1814. The story itself is a masquerade, confecting a "Byron" from the texts of Regency fame and the sign-system of the portraits.[36] Wilson's story wends into a ghost-scape, one

> still quiet room . . . entirely deserted, save by one solitary individual. He was habited in a dark brown flowing robe, which was confined round the waist by a leathern belt, and fell in ample folds to the ground. His head was uncovered,

and presented a fine model for the painter's art. He was unmasked, and his bright penetrating eyes seemed earnestly fixed, I could not discover on what. "Surely he sees beyond this gay scene into some other world, which is hidden from the rest of mankind," thought I, being impressed, for the first time in my life with an idea that I was in the presence of a supernatural being. His attitude was graceful in the extreme. His whole countenance so bright, severe, and beautiful . . .

A solitary individual, unmasked but no less theatrical for this, bright penetrating eyes mysteriously fixed on "what seemed but space and air": this is iconic "Byron," Byron posing for his portrait, Byron playing "Byron"—or rehearsing his ghost-whisperer Manfred, his eyes holding a "fixed and penetrating gaze on what seemed but space and air," and in this aspect looking like a ghost himself. So stagey is this display that Wilson took it as "a mere masquerade-attitude for effect, practised in an empty room" (2:616–17). She tiptoes up and, playing along, ventures at last (in intimate French), "Who and what are you, who appear to me a being too bright and too severe to dwell among us?" When this being offers her a friendly arm, she's surprised to find "mere solid flesh and blood. I had fancied————" "What?" a voice replies; "'Why,' continued I half ashamed of myself, 'upon my word and honour, I do confess I thought you something supernatural!'" (618). This sounds demystifying, but what she has found is a plausible Shakespearean stage-ghost.

In Shakespeare's day, Wilde proposed, "ghosts were not shadowy, subjective conceptions, but beings of flesh and blood, only beings living on the other side of the border of life, and now and then permitted to break bounds" (Ellmann 251). Freud distinguishes the "poetic reality" of such licensed embodiments—sublime reputation notwithstanding—from uncanny frissons, and in so doing, pretty much describes the dynamic of devoted reading:

> the ghostly apparitions in *Hamlet, Macbeth* or *Julius Caesar,* may be gloomy and terrible enough, but they are no more really uncanny than is Homer's jovial world of gods. We order our judgement to the imaginary reality imposed on us by the writer, and regard souls, spirits and spectres as though their existence had the same validity in their world as our own has in the external world . . . we are spared all trace of the uncanny. . . . Even a "real" ghost, as in Oscar Wilde's *Canterville Ghost,* loses all power of arousing . . . an uncanny horror in us as soon as the author begins to amuse himself. ("Uncanny" 159, 161)

Wilson turns spectral Byronism into a sociable masquerade, the late Lord conjured as a flesh-and-blood ghost in the material world. When he takes his farewell, she speaks to him as if she were Hamlet's friendly ghost: "do you mean to forget me? I may not long continue in the same country with you; but wherever I am, it will console me to know that I am remembered kindly by you" (2:622). A ghost remembered, as Byron and Wilson know in their own media, is remembered better yet in words.[37] Telling of a later visit to her, when she and Byron debate the value of religion against Hamlet-melancholy, Wilson turns material Byron into a living ghost: "his strength and feelings were suddenly exhausted, and his countenance changed to the ashy paleness of death" (635).

This is the pattern for another theatrical encounter with Byron's ghost, *A Spiritual Interview with Lord Byron* (1876), signed by "Quevedo Redivivus," channeling Byron's nom de plume for *The Vision of Judgment*. The narrator has requested this interview from a "Materializing Medium." Stalling for a few days, the Medium obliges with a parlor, dimly gas-lit, and a curtain withdrawn to reveal a seated "Byron." Although "I was too much excited . . . to examine the occupant of the chair very deeply," Quevedo R. reports, the figure before him in the gloom "seemed to be dressed in a long cloak, and had the large collars so well known in Lord Byron's pictures" (4–5). This would have been a no-brainer for Dr. Johnson's Cock-Lane committee. It's clear from the set-up and the residue at its conclusion (clothes on the parlor floor) that "Byron" has been conjured as a style that can be inhabited by an able, opportunistic pretender.[38] "Byron" lives on as a popular commodity in the market for ghost stories told in Romantic shades.

V. Wording's Ghost-Traces

In the last stanzas of the fragment of Canto XVII, which neither Wilson nor Quevedo Redivivus could not yet have read, Byron resumes his ghost-story, its hero at once self-dispossessed and she-possessed:

> Our Hero was - in Canto the Sixteenth -
>   Left in a tender Moonlight situation -
> Such as enables Man to show his strength -
>   Moral or physical; - on this occasion
> Whether his Virtue triumphed - or, at length -
>   His Vice - for he was of a kindling Nation -
> Is more than I shall venture to describe -
> Unless some Beauty with a kiss should bribe. —   (17.12; Nicholson edn., 171)

With narrative and seduction compounded and the ghost world and the official order perplexed, Byron's poet will say only, "I leave the thing a problem like all things" (17.13)—including the thingness of the ghost.

One last problem is, again, the ghost-play of rhyme, in the very stanza that renders Don Juan and Duchess Fitz-Fulke into morning-after ghosts of themselves—the last stanza in the manuscript of Canto XVII. Byron revised to keep a metaphysical shiver in the physical exhaustion; ghosts in multiples seem to be behind all the narrator's speculations:

> best
> Which ~~worst~~ is to encounter — Ghost, or ~~body~~ - None -
> Twere
> ~~Is~~ difficult to say - but Juan looked
> As if he had combated with more than one -
> Being wan - and worn - with eyes <h>that hardly brooked
> The light - that through the Gothic windows shone -
> Her Grace, too, had a sort of air rebuked —
> pale
> ~~Look~~ Seemed ~~grave~~ - and - ~~looked~~
>   had kept
>   shivered, as if she ~~had slept~~
> ~~But little~~
>   dreamt
> A vigil, or ~~dreamt~~ rather more than slept.—   (17.14, p. 173)

Juan is no Manfred of the midnight oil. The look of exhaustion from "more than one" is a hangover from ghost-theater and ghost-sex. The sound of exhaustion is a ghosting of the name *Juan*. No longer chimed to *new one / true one*, it fades to *none* and *wan*; "Juan . . . wan - and worn."[39] This is the only apparition of *wan* in the English cantos.[40] The internal rhyme-word *Man* in 17.12—Juan "in a tender moonlight situation, / Such as enables Man to show his strength"—is no salvation, even with a capital M. Far flung from the Continental icon, *wan*-Juan is the final fallout of the epic poet's anti-invocation, "I *want* a hero." Even in *Canto I*, the sound of old Continental *Hwan* was audible only in the mock-heroics of love: "Young Juan *wan*der'd . . . Thinking unutterable things" (1.90)—old *Juan* unutterable, save in this phonic *wan*dering.[41]

More proximate to Juan in the English cantos is a new rhyme for him: *ruin*. It first sounds in the calculations of Lady Pinchbeck, long lost to any *agaçerie* in the "ghost of Scandal," but sensing its possibility in Juan's history:

> Juan too was a sort of favourite with her,
>   Because she thought him a good heart at bottom,
> A little spoiled, but not so altogether;
>   Which was a wonder, if you think who got him,
> And how he had been tossed, he scarce knew whither.
> Though this might ruin others, it did *not* him.   (12.49)

At the front of the stanza, *Juan* casts a rhyme-line to line 6's mid-line *ruin*, a fate averted here, but on the road toward Lady Adeline, whose heretofore empty heart is set to work

>   its own undoing,
> Its inner crash is like an Earthquake's ruin.   (14.85)

The rhyme-field of *undoing/ruin* summons *Juan*, but it does not get there before Byron blends the signature rhyme, *Juan/new one/true one*, into Lady Adeline's regard of Juan:

> I think not she was *then* in love with Juan:
> If so, she would have had the strength to fly
>   The wild sensation, unto her a new one:
> She merely felt a common sympathy
>   (I will not say it was a false or true one) ...   (14.91)

The enjambment of *fly* and its imperfect rhyme *sympathy* make the *Juan*-rhymes all the more audible. The addition of *ruin* soon arrives in a couplet that couples him with Adeline:

> It is not clear that Adeline and Juan
> Will fall; but if they do, 'twill be their ruin.   (14.99)

As *ruin/undoing* (85 above) shows, *ruin* also holds a ghost-homophone in *ruing*.[42]

The ruin of Juan comes not from a ghost-haunted past, but from the design of ever new plights. By the time Byron was writing Canto XVII, the initial epic call, "I want a hero," was getting answered by Juan's casting into a shade. Byron's first draft for the poet's fondness for "lobster-salad, and champagne, and chat" (1.135) had cast spectral fun: "I'm fond of ... supper—punch—Ghost stories—and such chat" (*CPW* 5:52n). Recall OED's tagging this as the first instance of the genre-phrase "ghost stories." Byron canceled "Ghost stories" for a different spirit, "champagne." The revision allies with the female corporation: "a woman should never be seen eating or drinking, unless it be *lobster sallad & Champagne,* the only truly feminine & becoming viands," Byron advised Lady Melbourne (25 September 1812; *BLJ* 2:208). As with all Byronic exorcisms, however, the meta-form, ghost stories—early and late, male and female, and shades of masquerade between—is not expelled but abides as ready hospitality for Byron's ever evolving company of ghosts.

* * *

What happens when a ghost impinges, with unwanted company, on a poet who means to have exorcised it—more than once, even? Ghosts cannot be exorcised; they always impinge as presences. This is the Long Romanticism of Yeats's apparitional romance with "Keats," a predecessor too intimate to be conjured away on the principles of modernity, proving a persistent haunt in Yeats's thinking and writing a poet.

CHAPTER SIX

Shades of Relay

Yeats's Latent Keats / Keats's Latent Yeats

I. Drawing Yeats / Drawing on Keats

"Shannon . . . has just done a drawing of me which is very charming, but by an unlucky accident most damnably like Keats," grumped Yeats to his friend John Quinn, January 7, 1908, adding, "If I publish it by itself everybody will think it an affectation of mine" (*L* 502). By April, he had come to think the portrait "exceedingly fine," telling Quinn that he was "having it reproduced in the collected edition" of his works (509), one of the four frontispieces by different artists in what amounts to a serial portrait gallery of Yeats-the-poet in the 1908 *Collected Works*.[1] Even so, such initial reluctance about Shannon's Keatsy-Yeats!—a spasm about affectation rather than of any fellow-poet affection, a charm so unlucky as to feel damnable. In his second decade of poetic fame, Yeats, age 42, squirms at a likeness with Keats, dead long ago at 25. It's about more than the luck of the drawing, of course. It's about being taken for Keats, with sensitivity to what he's taken from Keats. "Mr. Yeats . . . occasionally succeeds in 'out-glittering' Keats," wrote Oscar Wilde in *Pall Mall Gazette*, in 1889. Yeats took this glint to heart.[2] He was too keen, too self-conscious, not to have winced at eye-rhymed *Keats/Yeats* as a figural portent (closer in sound to an Irish ear, and west-country English ear, than Anglo long-*e* Keats / long-*a* Yeats).[3] The unlucky rhyme, irritated by a drawing "like Keats," cast an unhappy Keatsian glitter on Yeatsian modernity.

No surprise, then, that when George Williamson invited Yeats to contribute to *The John Keats Memorial Volume* (to be published in 1921, the centenary of Keats's death), Yeats refused, affecting no commerce at all with Keats. "No," he replied; "it is no use. I cannot write on Keats. I have not read Keats during the past five years, and I should have to fill my mind with him." The best he would offer was an appreciation of what Keats was not:

> Of the group of poets at the beginning of the last century, he was the one pure artist, without any intermixture of doctrine of fanaticism, 'so crammed with

life he cannot but grow with life and being,' as Ben Jonson said of some unknown poet, possibly Shakespeare. (Williamson 216)

It's so backhanded that Yeats conveyed it as no more than "an expression of
opinion," quite discardable: "if it is of any use to you, you may use it, of course,
but I don't suppose it is." Yeats's prestige guaranteed its use, and Williamson
published the letter entire, as the last of the English contributions, all on its own
page (216). At this memorial, Yeats and Keats were summarily linked under
the sign of Yeats's not wanting to fill his mind with a Keats who seemed a little
too "crammed with life." Actually, the lines from Jonson's *Poetaster* are in the
voice of Horace, speaking about Virgil (hardly unknown). The end of Horace's
sentence was seemingly forgotten by Yeats, or conveniently amputated.

> And, for his poesy, 'tis so rammed with life,
> That it shall gather strength of life with being,
> And live hereafter more admired than now.   (5.1.137–39)

Yes, Williamson erred in transcribing Yeats's letter, which does read "rammed."
But Yeats did suppress the word *strength* in Horace's praise, as well as the line
about immortal fame—both ghosting too much a compliment to Keats.[4]

It is "not . . . preposterous that the past should be altered by the present as
much as the present is directed by the past," wrote one critic and poet (not
yet 30), in 1917, who admired both Keats and Yeats. Poets who are "aware of
this," T. S. Eliot went on to say, "will be aware of great difficulties and responsibilities" ("Tradition" 45). Such awareness may shape conscious craft; it may
also weave into poetic texture, in workings of, and workings out of, intimate
particulars in words and forms. This chapter takes a long view of Romantic
shades and shadows with a story about Yeats's deflections of and adhesive
reflections of Keats. Keats haunts Yeats in forms of difficult responsibilities
that angle toward a "modernism" drawn and defined at his expense, yet with
latent identifications.[5] In the altering relations of past and present, latency
may tell us more than explicit allusion, more even than exposures of a psycho-
drama of influence, of ravages and resistance, including those unappeasable
hauntings and sensations of belatedness that issue in dialectics of self-
interested misreading.[6]

Yeats's vacillation of charm and unease communicates a larger, under-
reported current in both Keats studies and Yeats studies: a "Long Romanticism" that troubles any "Modernism" (poets' or critics') pivoting on
definitional and historical difference.[7] Keats's writing holds figures to which

W. B. Yeats, detail, by Charles Shannon, 1908. The painting hangs in the reading room of the Houghton Library, Harvard University. The photogravure is from W.B. Yeats, *The Trembling of the Veil* (London: Privately Printed for Subscribers only by T.W. Laurie, ltd., 1922). Kindly supplied by Rare Book Division, Department of Rare Books and Special Collections, Princeton University Library.

Yeats could respond, even correspond.[8] Take his confession in 1888 to fellow poet Katharine Tynan about the arc of his poems, which seemed, as he thought about it, almost always "a flight into fairyland from the real world, and a summons to that flight." To Yeats, this was "not the poetry of insight and knowledge, but of longing and complaint—the cry of the heart against necessity," and he wanted to discipline himself to a long, more worthy goal: "to alter that and write poetry of insight and knowledge" (*L* 63). But this is the very arc, with the same key words and tropes, Keats drew across *Ode to a Nightingale*. Keats's poetry has a way of registering in Yeats's language as an alter ego that is both alter and ego. Yeats's determined refinements of difference, stressed by oblique affiliations, mark out a quarrel for sure—not just with Keats, but with Yeatsian Keats.

John Keats by Joseph Severn, charcoal sketch, 1818, intended for but not used as a frontispiece for *Endymion,* 1818. © Victoria and Albert Museum.

"Though a quarrel in the Streets is a thing to be hated, the energies displayed in it are fine," wrote Keats in 1819, adding that this is "the very thing in which consists poetry" (*K* 243). Yeatsians know an aphorism in this key, almost a century on, from *Per Amica Silentia Lunae* (1918): "We make out of the quarrel with others, rhetoric, but of the quarrel with ourselves, poetry." Whether or not Yeats had checked Keats's scorecard, a common chord is audible:[9] "Unlike the rhetoricians, who get a confident voice from remembering the crowd they have won or may win, we sing amid our uncertainty," Yeats elaborates (29). There is a further Keatsian ring in "amid uncertainty": that receptivity to "uncertainties" Keats strengthened into the aesthetic principle of "negative capability."[10] But if Yeats can sound to us "like Keats" in these wordings, he himself missed the audit in the auditorium of a "Keats" that he needed to disdain for the sake of a modernity reflexively, polemically, signing itself post-Romantic. The operation verges toward "uncanny"—a sensation that Freud sees slipping its prefix to coincide with canny: something "familiar . . . in the mind that has been estranged only by the process of repression" ("Uncanny" 148). This repression of Keats operates differently from the aggressive flexing of Keats's modern "young poets" generation against eighteenth-century protocols.[11] For the more ambivalent "modern" Yeats, the "Romantic" binary was a still haunting, even inalienable, nexus of beauty, ideals, dreams, and aspirations. In shades of wording, Yeats registers what is relative, relational in the estranged differentials of self-definition.

On secure and admired Shelleyan ground—say, the transformative visionary poetry of *Prometheus Unbound*—Yeats's writing can let slip shades of Keats. On the first page of a long and studious essay on "The Philosophy of Shelley's Poetry" (1903), he declares, "I . . . am now certain that the imagination has some way of lighting on the truth that reason has not" (90–91). "I am certain of nothing but . . . the truth of Imagination . . . I have never yet been able to perceive how any thing can be known for truth by consequitive reasoning," wrote Keats to his friend, Benjamin Bailey, in November 1817 (*K* 69), coining the word *consequitive* for what he needed to say to this student of theology. Yeats could have read this letter, even, in R. M. Milnes's *Life, Letters, and Literary Remains of John Keats* (1:64–65) and in later collections. Yeats's "modernity," estranged and warped by its repressions of Keats's wordings, misses such affiliations.

This is because Yeats's conscious project is to read and position "Keats" as the signifier of a puerile sensuousness that a proper "modernist" must purge. In 1902 he blithely satirized Keats's phrasings of "pillowy cleft" and "froth and boil," comparing these to the chaste restraint of young Spenser's love-poetry ("Spenser" 55). Yet the filter of Yeats's distortion is exposed by the actual site in Keats's poetry. These phrases are not the dreamy bubbles that Yeats's synecdoche implies. They percolate in an extended simile housed in a nightmare-stanza that soon-to-be Poet Laureate Robert Bridges had quite admired in 1894, quoting it in full (lxxxiv). In *Isabella; or The Pot of Basil*, Isabella's beloved Lorenzo has been murdered by her brothers. His ghost has come to her in a horrible vision, and departs this way:

> The Spirit mourn'd "Adieu!"—dissolv'd, and left
>   The atom darkness in a slow turmoil;
> As when of healthful midnight sleep bereft,
>   Thinking on rugged hours and fruitless toil,
> We put our eyes into a pillowy cleft,
>   And see the spangly gloom froth up and boil . . .   (XLI)

Keats's simile is immersed in the apparitions of agonized insomnia, and to render the slow turmoil, he may have been the first to make an adjective of "atom" (OED). Yeats's confection of apparent silliness is conspicuously overdetermined.

It is by now a standard narrative, with Yeats's own authority, to map his career as Early/Middle/Late, with "Romantic" progressively on the wane.[12] But even Yeats could defect a bit, identifying himself as "romantic" with proud nostalgia—if Keats could be exorcised from the accounting. In the distresses of the modern world, Late Yeats named himself one of the "last romantics." Though he meant generic cultural forms and ideals, not a gene-alogy from the English poets of the early nineteenth century, by the time he put this phrase in "Coole Park and Ballylee, 1931" (41), the term "roman-tic" had this historical register, too.[13] Yeats not only could not deflect this sense but he seems to have admitted it, along acceptable channels. He could cheer Blake for his "symbolist" mythology, could cheer Shelley for vision-ary dreamers and a "beauty" of Platonic metaphysical import—both modes generating a unifying cosmology that implied a transformative politics, a vigorous, counter-cultural critique of utilitarian mandates and middle-class moralism.[14]

Keats's poetry, which was instinctively and intellectually averse to such macro-polemics, looks deficient in this way to Yeats. As he was writing his essays on Blake and Shelley (1897–1902), he was viewing Keats through the Victorian parlor appreciations that were polished from Matthew Arnold on: skilled in small-bore pictorial vividness, vibrant word-painting, with a "love of embodied things, of precision of form and colouring."[15] Yeats did admire this artistry, and even two decades on, appreciated how islands of Spenser's *Faerie Queene* and colonies of Keats's *Endymion* held on to "certain qualities of beauty, certain forms of sensuous loveliness . . . separated from all the general purposes of life," and he rejected moralizing "indignation" about this sequestration.[16] But this amounts to faint praise, proximate to a weak-ness (Shelley's too) for luxuries drawn from "the impression made by the world upon . . . delicate senses."[17] And it tips into damnable in the part he cast for "Keats" in the poem that serves to preface *Per Amica*.

This is *Ego Dominus Tuus*, a conversation, sometimes a quarrel, between HIC (Latin: this one) and ILLE (that one).[18] In ILLE, Ezra Pound jested at the hint of Yeats's nickname "Willie."[19] It is this anti-Romantic who gets the last word, and more: a call to another, severer antagonist—severer, because he is at once ILLE and a new "other," a paradox that ILLE describes this way:

the mysterious one who yet
Shall walk the wet sand by the water's edge,
And look most like me, being indeed my double,
And prove of all imaginable things
The most unlike, being my anti-self,
And, standing by these characters, disclose
All that I seek . . .   (pp. 14–15)

Some pages on in *Per Amica*, Yeats triplicates his phrasing into "other self, the anti-self or the antithetical self," to say that it "comes but to those who are no longer deceived, whose passion is reality" (30)—and so even more "realist" than ILLE yet is, but aspires to be (he has been tracing "characters" on the sand, in conjuration). "We meet always in the deep of the mind, whatever our work, wherever our reverie carries us, that other Will," Yeats writes, punning himself.[20] (Did he know Wordsworth's *Ode to Duty*?) HIC has his say, but it is plotted for ILLE's modernist correction, a willed "other" of self-improvement.

Yeats's deep worry, however, is that Keats, too, looks like "my double," and Keats is the very last candidate for Yeats's "unlike," revelatory anti-self. "I think he fashioned from his opposite," says ILLE of Dante's severe, tragic art (p. 11). This constitutes Dante's heroism, and it entails a Dante described just three lines above this one, in "hunger for the apple on the bough / Most out of reach" (11). This heroic hunger, weirdly, imprints a near twin, two pages on, namely Yeats's "Keats." The immediate discussion, before the turn to Keats, is relevant. It's about the opposition of self and art in the Dantean mode:

HIC

Yet surely there are men who have made their art
Out of no tragic war; lovers of life,
Impulsive men, that look for happiness,
And sing when they have found it.

ILLE

                                        No, not sing,
For those that love the world serve it in action,
Grow rich, popular, and full of influence;
And should they paint or write still it is action,
The struggle of the fly in marmalade.
The rhetorician would deceive his neighbours,

> The sentimentalist himself; while art
> Is but a vision of reality.   (pp. 12–13)

No art in the fly's struggle in marmalade: Yeats remembered Verlaine's telling him, in 1894, of living, not even struggling, in Paris "like a fly in a pot of
marmalade"[21]—hardly heroic, its only peril its surfeit. ILLE resets the metric
for non-art: artful rhetoric or self-deception rather than self-quarreling. The
correction that "art/Is but a vision of reality" could not be more offhand,
more assured—merely this, and always this for a modernist. Otherwise, art
is decadent, so ILLE elaborates, in the rest of his sentence:

> What portion in the world can the artist have,
> Who has awakened from the common dream,
> But dissipation and despair?   (p. 13)

Yet the poetic shape of this seeming rhetorical question vacillates. The first line,
paused on its comma, seems the question *tout court*. But the "Who"-clause
sequel is an ambiguous complication: is this "the artist" per se, or the artist of
dissipation and despair? And what is the prepositional sense of *from*? One
"Who has awakened [up] from the common dream" might well put a claim on
"a vision of reality," might even have awakened this consciousness [out] from
the dream itself.[22] Yeats wasn't sure: in the text in the 1917 *Wild Swans* (p. 24), the
two commas were gone, to give Who the sense of categorical artist. The question is audibly haunted by the Keatsian poet who asks of his dissipated music,
"Was it a vision or a waking dream?/...Do I wake or sleep?" or the letter-writer
who mapped maturity as an "awakening" from sweetness to "sharpening one's
vision into" the "dark Passages" of life and its answerable poetry.[23]

Yeats's disciplinary modernism, operating against Keats, has to disregard
this Yeatsian Keats. It's a Keats who, in a late-career, blank-verse dialogue of his
own (a long passage in *The Fall of Hyperion, A Dream*) figured a severe mystery, Monéta—at once a "double" in dream-psychology and an anti-self in her
assault on Keats's cherished identity: poet.[24] If there is no allusion in *Ego Dominus Tuus* to *The Fall*, there is a figural, generic affiliation: Dantean dream-
vision.[25] And there is a hard debate, on Yeatsian mandates. The poet of *The
Fall* is an uncommon dreamer, one who might well despair, even dissipate, at
the challenge Moneta issues to dreamer-"vision'ries" (1.161). The visionary
"tribe" that this stern goddess indicts could well include Yeats and the Romantics he valued. In the measure of Keats's Moneta, they're all "dreamers weak,"
distinct from those who serve the world in action and who seek "No music but
a happy-noted voice" (162–64); "thou are less than they," she rules (166):

What benefit canst thou do, or all thy tribe,
To the great World? Thou art a dreaming thing,
A fever of thyself—think of the Earth:
What bliss even in hope is there for thee?   (I.167–70)

Her acid rhyming of *dreaming thing* is a parody of the poet's art. The quarrel of Keats's poet-petitioner with this inquisition could well have set the stage for Yeats's HIC and ILLE.

Yet when HIC cues "Keats," it is not for this severity, but in a script that is loaded against Keats, categorically:

> And yet,
> No one denies to Keats love of the world,
> Remember his deliberate happiness.   (p. 13)

Yeats could have had HIC recall the Keats who said "I scarcely remember counting upon any Happiness," or the Keats who set a nightingale's singing "too happy in [its] happiness" against the poetry of a world "Where but to think is to be full of sorrow / And leaden-eyed despairs"—dead end in sound no less than in sense.[26] Keats's accounting is brutal. Maybe *deliberate* indicates "carefully weighed, carefully considered," a moral discipline in a world that routinely depletes happiness. Yet ILLE seems to endorse HIC's warp on Keats, quarreling only to fine-tune the art of Keatsian happiness as the work of a fevered sensibility in Keats himself:

> His art is happy, but who knows his mind?
> I see a schoolboy, when I think of him,
> With face and nose pressed to a sweetshop window,
> For certainly he sank into his grave,
> His senses and his heart unsatisfied;
> And made—being poor, ailing and ignorant,
> Shut out from all the luxury of the world,
> The ill-bred son of a livery-stable keeper—
> Luxuriant song.   (pp. 13–14)

ILLE's anatomy retails the cartoon voluptuary from the sarcastic reviews of Keats's poetry in 1818: Keats, the immature, pathetic "Cockney," only abject, not even in the sweetshop, let alone Paris. Did ILLE blunder into a twinned "*ill*-bred"? Maybe; by 1919, Yeats revised this to "coarse-bred" (*Wild Swans*, p. 84). ILLE's "Keats" is a class aspirant with no class, his poetry the sign and symptom. That three-line interval between "made" and "Luxuriant song" makes Keats's art a mere appendage to the character-slam, a postscript of hollowed-out desire for material luxury.

Yeats's adhesion to this "Keats" is apparent enough in his elaboration, in his own voice, some pages on in *Per Amica*, marking it the common dream of many first Romantics:

> I imagine Keats to have been born with that thirst for luxury common to many at the outsetting of the Romantic Movement, and not able, like wealthy Beckford, to slake it with beautiful and strange objects. It drove him to imaginary delights; ignorant, poor, and in poor health, and not perfectly well-bred, he knew himself driven from tangible luxury; meeting Shelley, he was resentful and suspicious because he, as Leigh Hunt recalls, "being a little too sensitive on the score of his origin, felt inclined to see in every man of birth his natural enemy." (25)

But the conscription of Keats to this accounting is another one of those Yeats-imaginings warped by bias. Beckford—wealthy from the labors of un-beautiful and strange slaves on his sugar plantations—is a peculiar measure; no less peculiar is the straining of "Keats" through Hunt's filter in 1850 (and not unstrained by class-sensitivity in both Hunt and Yeats). For one thing, Keats was not "poor." For another, as Hunt knows and Keats's letters show, Keats was sensitive less to his middling origins than to Shelley's well-meaning patronage, which could feel patronizing. It wasn't class resentment or suspicion. As Yeats could have read in Hunt's recollection, it was about two "styles in writing," which were "very different": skeptical of Shelley's "universality" and "Archimedean endeavors to move the globe with his own hands," Keats exercised "his unbounded sympathies with ordinary flesh and blood" (2:37). The class bias that irritated Keats's suspicion was in those first reviews, a bias that Yeats's phrase "not perfectly well-bred" so easily endorses many decades on. Excerpting *Ego Dominus Tuus* a few years later in *The Trembling of the Veil*, Yeats seems to have winced, and replaced "The ill-bred son of a livery-stable keeper" with ellipses.[27] But the main line of his story of Keats, drawn from late Hunt, elides and doesn't contextualize, so eager is he to box Keats outside the sweetshop, to make a hallmark of hunger and frustration. The bottom line of Yeats's ledger (entered on the next page of *Per Amica*) is that "Keats but gave us his dream of luxury": sweet-mad boy, desire without fulfillment; no Dantean "conflict" or heart-rending "struggle" (26).

Not willing to credit Keats's art with any undeceived clarity, Yeats con-fects a Keats that deflects felt affiliations—from felicitous phrasings, to dis-enchanted ironies, to measures of the unappeasable depletions of mortal life—that could well disturb a modernist's self-defined difference. The "grav-ity" of art in "awakening from the dream" (29) is yet another common weave. It is a critical thread in Keats's gallery of deluded and rebuked dream-ers, Isabella, Madeline, Lycius, the poet of *The Fall*, and more. So, too, Yeats's contempt of sentimentalists who "find their pleasure in a cup that is filled from Lethe's wharf" (30); this could well have drawn a draught from Keats's "No, no, go not to Lethe" (*Ode on Melancholy*). Yeats prefers, instead, to draft "Keats" as an antitype to a modernist's company of "last romantics." There is no necessity to play into Yeats's gate-keeping, periodizing, stereotyping hands to notice this. The myth of "modernism" is as tendentious as its quarantining of Keats.[28] Keats continues to haunt Yeats with close vibrations.

An audible vibration comes in the praise of "last romantics," the company with whom Yeats proudly identifies in *Coole Park and Ballylee, 1931:*

> We were the last romantics—chose for theme
> Traditional sanctity and loveliness;
> Whatever's written in what poets name
> The book of the people; whatever most can bless
> The mind of man or elevate a rhyme . . .   (41–45)

It was Keats who admired the old Greek poets for "leaving great verses to a little clan"—a line, said Yeats in 1903 (slightly misrecalling it), that had im-pressed him early on as the "happiest fate that could come to a poet," and would be a measure that he "constantly tested" for "my own ambition."[29] It was Keats who praised Wordsworth for elevating "the mind of man" into the haunt and main region of his song (Preface to *The Excursion*), the frontier of his and Wordsworth's modernism.

The Keasian drifts of language and theme in such Yeatsian scenes come on a slant that eludes the sweetshop register. As late as *A Vision* (1938), notwithstanding an appreciative allusion to *Ode on a Grecian Urn* in its opening paragraph (1), passion-tormented Yeats is still busy cordoning off Keats: "little sexual passion, an exaggerated sensuousness . . . intellectual curiosity is at its weakest . . . all is reverie" (134). The poster-boys for Yeats are the moony hero of *Endymion* and the sadly wasting loiterer of "La Belle Dame sans Merci." What Yeats represses is the intellectual, even skeptical pressure in Keats's figurings. *Endymion*, on the arc of its epic ambitions, wanes from springtime hopes to autumnal ironies and sometimes brutal parody. And "La Belle Dame," the autumnal ballad that Keats wrote a year after *Endymion* appeared, while less brutal, is more severe.

II. Keatsian Lines / Yeatsian Lingerings

Even a few turns of close reading can show how far away Yeats thought he needed to keep the reverberations of this storyline from his own agons of sensuous temptation and its defeat. The fatal depletions of "La Belle Dame sans Merci" haunt Yeats's songs far more than the sudden, magical resolution of Endymion's epic wandering.[30] Keats's ballad opens with three stanzas in an unidentified voice interrogating an odd spectacle:

> O what can ail thee knight-at-arms,
>   Alone and palely loitering?
> The sedge has wither'd from the lake
>   And no birds sing.

The caution sounded in *ail thee / palely* is sharpened by the season's report. Then with adjectives pressing at interpretation, the questioner repeats (11):

> O what can ail thee, knight-at-arms!
>   So haggard and so woe-begone?

This is urgent description and emergent narrative. Something has *gone* to produce this *woe*, and *haggard* hints a cause: commerce with a hag, "a wild or intractable person" (usually female) with a " 'wild' expression of the eyes" (OED, adj. 5).

Stanza III issues a diagnosis, implying a back-story:

> I see a lily on thy brow
>   With anguish moist and fever dew,
> And on thy cheeks a fading rose
>   Fast withereth too.

Seamlessly, in the same meters, stanza IV begins, "I met a lady in the meads," to recount a tale of an enchantress "full beautiful," light-footed, wild-eyed, singing and sighing.

> V.
>
> I made a garland for her head,
>   And bracelets too, and fragrant zone;

She look'd at me as she did love,
   And made sweet moan.

VI.

I set her on my pacing steed,
   And nothing else saw all day long,
For sidelong would she bend, and sing
   A faery's song.

VII.

She found me roots of relish sweet,
   And honey wild, and manna dew,
And sure in language strange she said—
   "I love thee true."

Keats's words and syntaxes bare the delusion. The temporal conjunction *as she did love* ghosts a guess, *as if,* to expose *sure* as more wishful than certain, "language strange" strained into fidelity by desire. That the knight's tale enters the ballad so seamlessly, without a punctuated difference between his voice and the questioner's, arguably stages a quarrel of the mind with itself, self-reproach prompting a fevered explanation.[31] The ballad ends where it began, the questioner's voice echoing into the knight's: "And this is why I sojourn here," he trails off (XII).[32] At the core of this tautological "this is why" is an involute of cause and effect: is a faithless "she" the cause, or is a "knight-at-arms" at pains to fabulate a "she" from literary legend to take the rap for the scandal of his truancy from purposeful, manly life? Keats sounds *man* in the ballad only, and tellingly, as a syllable of that honey-poison *man*na, the drug that entrances manhood unto death.

In 1902 Yeats was all too ready to label Keats a singer "of a beauty so wholly preoccupied with itself that its contemplation is a kind of lingering trance" ("Spenser" 82–83), implying that he's no Keats. All too ready, because his *Song of the Wandering Aengus* looks like, sounds like, just such a preoccupied, lingering trance—and gorgeously. Its host volume is *The Wind Among the Reeds* (1899), a title consonant with Pan's music, played on a pipe fashioned from the reeds into which harried, hotly desired nymph Syrinx was transformed, seemingly in the gods' compassionate protection but, alas, vulnerable to Pan's artful appropriation. Yeats's title-word *Wandering*, though glancing at Latin *errant,* is more audibly keyed to the Pan-reed named a *wand*—and by its effects, a poet's instrument:

I went out to the hazel wood,
Because a fire was in my head,
And cut and peeled a hazel wand . . .   (1–3)

The wand becomes a fishing rod, and the silver trout it catches becomes a *glimmering girl*—a very soundscape of poetic music and poetic vocation:

. . . something rustled on the floor,
And some one called me by my name:
It had become a glimmering girl
With apple blossom in her hair
Who called me by my name and ran
And faded through the brightening air.   (11–16)

If this glimmering girl seems a little too kin to La Belle Dame, Yeats's safety is to plot his bright singer against Keats's fading knight, bending a sad addiction to a femme fatale into a noble visionary quest.[33]

Yet what ensues bodes a distinction without a difference. A gap of time across one of the most stunning interstanzaic spaces in English poetry exposes the raptured, ruptured logic of a wandering that turns out to be perpetual, its hope for ever futuring. The glimmering girl does fade, and the wanderer is never more, and never less, than "winning near the goal" (the plight of the eager, arrested lover on Keats's Grecian Urn):

Though I am old with wandering
Through hollow lands and hilly lands,
I will find out where she has gone,
And kiss her lips and take her hands;
And walk among long dappled grass,
And pluck till time and times are done,
The silver apples of the moon,
The golden apples of the sun.   (17–24)

It's a phenomenal song, enflamed by its very poetry: a fire in the head issuing a glimmering girl, a brightening air, and, in vision, those silver apples of the moon, those golden apples of the sun. "The passionate feed their flame in wanderings and absences, when the whole being of the beloved, every little charm of body and of soul, is always present to the mind, filling it with heroical subtleties of desire." This is Yeats writing in 1902 of what Spenser is not, and does not do ("Spenser" 71).

It is also what Yeats does do for the Wandering Aengus, with heroic sympathy. On the lure to wander, passionate Keats had exercised more irony in "La Belle Dame" and had imposed a more cautious halt in the run of enchantment to the end of "I stood tip toe" (1817):

> Was there a Poet born?—but now no more,
> My wand'ring spirit must no further soar.——   (241–42)

In the syllabled contraction *wand'ring* Keats rings and all but hands Yeats that link of *wand* to *wandering*. Yeats wants to stress Keats's errancy but Keats, with poetry such as this, ironizes the Latin ghost of error in the spirit of Yeatsian wandering. Needing a forlorn Keats, Yeats tracks the Spenser of immediately "delighted senses" to the trickle-down Keatsian melancholy of "*Belle Dame sans Merci* and his 'perilous seas in faery lands forlorn'" ("Spenser" 235): the poet of depletion, betrayed of delight. Yeats writes his wanderer's *Song* not only not in the major key of "forlorn" but so sonically seductive in its visionary devotion as to enlist readers as co-conspirators. Who could not be enchanted by the rhymes, entranced by the hypnotic quatrains of *abcb*, seduced by the anaphora of *And* and its echoing in *ran, lands, hands*? The poetry presents an echo chamber, ever resounding:

> *something / some one / become / blossom*
> *something / glimmering / brightening / wandering*
> *hollow / hilly / I will / till*
> *apple blossom / dappled / silver apples*
> *golden apples / old / golden.*

The music sustains what Helen Vendler calls a "reduplicative spell-casting" (108).[34]

"This sort of 'self-generating' poetry is meant to mimic absolute command," Vendler adds. Appreciating the force of this illusion, I want to suggest a qualification, even an alternative, to "absolute," in a stress by privately coded grievance. The song's "I will find out where she has gone" vocalizes, with significant pronouns, the names *Will* and *Gonne* (in Irish sounding, *gone* and *Gonne* are homophones).[35] The year 1899, when *Song* appeared in *The Wind Among the Reeds*, was also when Maud Gonne refused Will Yeats's proposal of marriage—for a second time. Here again, is nomen-ghosting, authorized from Petrarch's pun-mad celebration of Laura—*l'oro, l'aura, lauro* (gold, aura, laurel), into Shakespeare's *Will* sonnets, and the transparent masquery of *The Picture of Dorian Gray,* Wilde-peppered with "wild"-

tempered characters. In Yeats's *Song*, "Apple blossom" amplifies the hint of naming autobiography: after first meeting Maude Gonne (Yeats said) she glowed in his head "like a goddess" and "luminous, like that of apple blossom through which the light falls." After this recollection went public in 1922 (*Trembling* I.V.13), it became the *Song*'s default paratext, its words whispering Yeats's most intimate trance.

"All visionaries have entered into such a world in trances, and all ideal art has a trance for warranty," wrote Yeats in 1906. The logic is entrancingly circular. Like Keats's abject loiterer, Yeats's wanderer sings a romance that suspends everything else. Such "delight," Yeats said, is conditioned by world-"weariness."[36] And it is dangerous "to sojourn there" without an "ideal . . . warranty."[37] Yeats knew this in his original title, "A Mad Song."[38] "A fire was once within my brain," sings Wordsworth's "Mad Mother" (21). "And this is why I sojourn here, / Alone and palely loitering" is the Keats-worded ghost in the malady. What Yeats deflected was Keats's critique: the delusions of the knight in the ballad, and the self-listening alertness to "fairy lands forlorn" in *Ode to a Nightingale*: "Forlorn! that very word is like a bell / To toll me back from thee to my sole self" (70–72). This toll is a sensation just as immediate in Keats's *Ode* as the song's trance.

No small part of the seduction of Yeats's *Song* is its phonic richness and fluidity, a music that feels enchanted rather than enchained. Decades on, in 1937, describing his need for "a passionate syntax for passionate subject-matter," Yeats included the syntax of "traditional metres": not formal laws, but not "free verse" either.[39] There was good Keatsian alliance in this critical pulse, which Yeats himself could sense in 1936 when he wrote in the Introduction to *The Oxford Book of Modern Verse*, "I see Pope as . . . Keats saw him." Keats saw him this way in a cheeky satire of Pope's mechanical meters, for which he took a lot of heat in those sneering first reviews. Yeats had quoted Keats's very lines back in 1922 (without naming Keats), to explain his own disdain, in his early twenties,

of leaning towards the eighteenth century

> "That taught a school
> Of dolts to smooth, inlay, and clip, and fit
> Till, like the certain wands of Jacob's wit,
> Their verses tallied."

> (*Trembling* 56, about *Sleep and Poetry* 196–99)

Refusing this kind of hazing wand, Keats undertook his own schooling with a form marked by tallies and fits, and for which he had a career-long affection, the sonnet.

With no aim at publication, Keats wrote a sonnet in 1819 to work out, for himself and a few correspondents, the difficult fascinations of a form unbolted of prescribed patterns, prescribed business, yet still formed:

> If by dull rhymes our English must be chain'd,
> And, like Andromeda, the Sonnet sweet
> Fetter'd, in spite of pained loveliness;
> Let us find out, if we must be constrain'd,
> Sandals more interwoven and complete
> To fit the naked foot of Poesy;
> Let us inspect the Lyre, and weigh the stress
> Of every chord, and see what may be gain'd
> By ear industrious, and attention meet;
> Misers of sound and syllable, no less
> Than Midas of his coinage, let us be
> Jealous of dead leaves in the bay wreath crown,
> So, if we may not let the Muse be free,
> She will be bound with garlands of her own.[40]

Irked by the "pouncing rhymes" of the "legitimate" sonnet (Petrarchan), Keats was no warmer to Shakespeare's liberal variations. No free-verser, Keats works meta-sonnetry, punning its cues: *the naked foot of Poesy* is meter blank of rhyme (in this very line, even); *attention meet* audits meter; the *chord* of sounds, the constraints of rhyme-pattern traditions.

Keats's verse is unruly, spinning its puns to make its points. Take the first rhyme, *chain'd/constrain'd*. It's figuratively fit (picking up *pained*) for a Petrarchan quatrain. But Keats fuels his syntax against this promise, with a re-launch of the *If*-clause at line 4, driving on the stressed syllables of the trochees at the front of lines 3 and 4, *Fetter'd/Let* us, with a charge from *to fit* (as if this verb had sprung from *Fetter'd*). The sentence does not come to rest, aptly, until *Poesy*. And this keyword is either boldly no rhyme at all, or a conspicuously weak one, tripping up even the iambic pentameter.[41] "What moves me and my hearer is a vivid speech that has no laws except that it must not exorcise the ghostly voice" of "lyric metres" as "an unconscious norm." Except for "unconscious," this sounds like Keats theorizing his sonnet-practice, not giving up its formal ghosts. But it's Yeats, on the contrapuntal relay of pattern and passion in decision about distributing stresses in the opening line of *Paradise Lost.*[42]

Keats's master-simile is chained Andromeda's liberator, Perseus, whose winged steed Pegasus is iconic poetic imagination. In that satire of neoclassical prosody that Yeats liked, Keats mimics versifiers who "sway'd about upon a rocking horse, / And thought it Pegasus" (*Sleep and Poetry* 186–87). How apt that a trapped Pegasus is the fallen star of Yeats's *The Fascination of What's Difficult*, composed in 1910—but in no composed sensibility. "Metrical composition is always very difficult to me," he sighed in pride in 1922 (*Trembling of the Veil*, 86). In April 1910, he chided a younger poet, Thomas MacDonagh, about dodging "the difficulty of rhyming" by resorting to "certain words in poetry which we do not use in speech" and turns to syntactic "inversion" of no "positive value," just "because they get us out of a difficulty" (*Unpublished Letters* 1326). "You do not work at your technic," he scolded another poet (and lover) in April 1936:

> you take the easiest course leave out the rhymes or choose the most hackneyed rhymes, because—damn you—you are lazy. . . . When your technic is sloppy your matter grows second-hand there is no difficulty to force you down under the surface difficulty is our plough. (*Unpublished L* 6532)

And so *The Fascination of What's Difficult.*

Yeats's Diary holds a prompt for the poem so titled: "To complain of the fascination of what's difficult. It spoils spontaneity and pleasure, and wastes time" (September 1909; Jeffares 106). Yet Yeats will take time for a "complaint," a well-ploughed poetic genre. His title's ambiguous grammar is no small blade in Yeats's plough. But what's its edge? Is it a fascination on what's difficult? Or is what's difficult a fascinating addiction? Might fascination even be the perverse modernist muse?

> The fascination of what's difficult
> Has dried the sap out of my veins, and rent
> Spontaneous joy and natural content
> Out of my heart. There's something ails our colt
> That must, as if it had not holy blood,
> Nor on Olympus leaped from cloud to cloud,
> Shiver under the lash, strain, sweat and jolt
> As though it dragged road metal. My curse on plays
> That have to be set up in fifty ways,

On the day's war with every knave and dolt,
Theatre business, management of men.
I swear before the dawn comes round again
I'll find the stable and pull out the bolt.   (*The Green Helmet,* pp. 20–21)

In this energetically crabby poem, some undifficult couplets do Yeats's business: *plays/ways* (echoed by *days*); *men/again.* But how do you hear *rent/content*: is it this hard rhyme (as in "Are You Content")? Or is Yeats meta-poetically shifting the sound-casing of substance into a trochee, *content*: nature's content—a usage in the singular that was obsolete (OED) well before 1910? It's difficult enough to say.

The question registers in the main-rhyme fits of all those *t*-ended words. In his notebook, Yeats assigned himself a *difficult* task on this field, as if redeeming for modernism that eighteenth-century parlor game of *bouts rimés* (cited in ridicules of Keats's rhymes):[43] "Repeat the line ending difficult three times and rhyme on bolt, exalt, coalt, jolt."[44] Yeats does *difficult* only once, and slant rhymes with three on this list: *coalt, jolt, dolt* (*rent* and *content* may also count). Line 4's *colt* intensifies the play with its double duty: closing a first quatrain-rhyme and initiating, especially with the assist of enjambment, the next (Vendler, *Our Secret Discipline* 163). But where did that new rhyme-word, *dolt,* come from? I think it is the ghost-writing of Keats's satirized "school / Of dolts."

In this pique, Yeats forgot one rhyme on his list, *exalt,* but it's there in spirit in this not-sonnet—perversely a line short, to be difficult about a formal expectation: the fugitive *exalt* may have flown in a 14th line to a world elsewhere.[45] That's one way to ghost a sonnet. Another is to allow the title as a 14th line. Its resounding in line 1 will then perform a fastening troped to fascination, as if Yeats were staging etymology, and in this production securing his claim as Poet Laureate of What's Difficult. The missing rhyme, *exalt,* returns, slant, as *exult/difficult,* at the conclusion of Yeats's 16-line cheer, *To a Friend Whose Work Has Come to Nothing*:[46]

Be secret and exult,
Because of all things known
That is most difficult.

The next step would seem a vision beyond material frustration.

This is *Sailing to Byzantium* (1927), the opening poem of *The Tower.* Yeats concludes his great early essay, "The Philosophy of Shelley's Poetry" (1900),

with a surmise that looks like a dress-rehearsal for *Sailing*: "voices would
have told him how there is for every man some one scene, some one adventure, some one picture that is the image of his secret life," sufficiently potent
to "lead his soul, disentangled from unmeaning circumstance and the ebb
and flow of the world, into that far household where the undying gods await
all whose souls have become simple as flame" (140–41). And so the disentan-
gling from unmeaning to undying, 27 years on, in an ottava rima of sonnet-
like crafting:

> That is no country for old men. The young
> In one another's arms, birds in the trees,
> —Those dying generations—at their song,
> The salmon-falls, the mackerel-crowded seas,
> Fish, flesh, or fowl, commend all summer long
> Whatever is begotten, born, and dies.
> Caught in that sensual music all neglect
> Monuments of unageing intellect.   (1–8)

This poet has left one world for another, defined by the negations toward
which Yeats's reconstituted Shelley is pointed: *disentangled, undying.* The
opening of *Sailing* is strung on, sung on, patterned polarities: *young/old;
dying generation/unageing monuments.* The first and last lines of the stanza
array the argument: "That is no country for old men. The young" versus
"Monuments of unageing intellect." Yet for all the formal force of the un-
summery summary couplet, the stanza's center swells an ode to sensual life,
however timed out. In such contradiction, the poet's disdain of "those dying
generations" sounds no less spiteful than self-important. "Why should they
think that are for ever young?" is Yeats's thinking in "Her Vision in the
Wood" (*A Woman Young and Old*, XIII). In this spite, Yeats managed to
echo Keats on the illusion of eternity imaged in an ancient urn's static art:
lovers "for ever young" among "forest branches" in an eternity that teases the
poet "out of thought" (*Ode on a Grecian Urn*, stanzas 3 and 5).

If the ageing sailor would rather be a monument than a mackerel, it is
distinctly brave of Yeats to describe the unageing monument-world as "the
artifice of eternity" (24). Brave, because the word *artifice* is overproductive:
denoting grand art and artwork—and reflexively, the artistry of *Sailing to
Byzantium*—it can't quite rub off a smudge of *artificial.* The "artifice of eternity," moreover, holds another one of those double-dealing *ofs*: the fabrica-
tion of an eternity, and eternity's own fabrications. As carefully plotted as

Yeats's vision is, the poetry is in the disturbances. The romances of Keats's Odes fissure on sighs of "faery lands forlorn" (*Nightingale,* stanza 7), or more monumentally, "Cold Pastoral" (*Grecian Urn,* stanza 5), *forlorn* and *Cold* retracting romance-art, in rhyme of a different order. Both poets, brilliantly, devastatingly, involve a quarrel of artifices: the artifice of eternity romanced by the speaker (with a hint that eternity is in love with artifice, too) against the artifice of poetry that ironizes the romance. Blakean Yeats would know this "Proverb of Hell": "Eternity is in love with the productions of time" (*The Marriage of Heaven and Hell,* plate 7). The ironizing artificer of the temporal is the proto-modernist Keats that would become more visible to Keats's modernist readers, Yeats's contemporaries.

Keats's aesthetic ironies were imprinting Yeats as early as 1906, as he was searching for "some dynamic and substantializing force as distinguished from the eastern quiescent and supersensualizing state of soul" (he coined that extravagantly heptasyllabic adjective); his hunch, he told Florence Farr, was that this force would come in "a movement downwards upon life, not upwards out of life" (*L* 469). He was tracing here, without caring to recall, Keats's arc of disenchantment with nightingale-song and art's cold pastoral. *Ode to a Nightingale* moves from a desire to fly away with the nightingale to a recognition that this is just so much passage to fairy lands forlorn; *Ode on a Grecian Urn* imagines a better world, "far above" human life, then turns back to the world of "woe" that generates such fantasies.

In Yeats's own enchantments he can warp Keats to his purposes, even substantializing what Keats's wit marks as fantasy. This is the case with the ghost-town in *Ode on a Grecian Urn:* some "little town by river or sea shore, / Or mountain-built with peaceful citadel" (stanza 4). In the opening paragraph of *A Vision* Yeats cites "the little town described in the *Ode on a Grecian Urn*" as apt for Rapallo, a town in the material world of Italy (1). In a letter to Lady Gregory, written from Rapallo itself, 24 February 1928 (ten years before *A Vision*), Yeats had summoned Keats's image to communicate his pleasure in this world: "This is an indescribably lovely place—some little Greek town one imagines—there is a passage in Keats describing just such a town" (*L* 738). By 1916, he was suggesting to his father, anyway, that Keats might even be "greater than Shelley . . . because he makes pictures one cannot forget and sees them as full of rhythm as a Chinese painting" (*L* 608)— makes these pictures with the power of words. Ranging in his letter to Lady Gregory from "indescribably" to a "describing" by Keats's poetry, Yeats concedes an imagination pleasantly haunted by Keats's imagination. On this ledger, he is more sentimental than Keats, eliding a critical difference from Keats's stanza 4. This little town isn't a real place (or its simulacrum). It is a retrojected surmise, with a sequel of rueful wit that Yeats's allusion neglects: its "folk" for ever on a Grecian Urn's artifice, their history is irrevocably silent, desolate, in the bargain with art's eternity, never to "return" (the stanza's last word rhymes with Keats's title, its lettering spelling the medium that prevents return, ret*urn*). Nor is there any speaking from the Urn's presence: it is a "silent form" that can only "tease us out of thought / As doth eternity" (44–45).

The reciprocal of Yeats's "just" Keats (the poet whose art could imagine the town of Rapallo) is the eternity-minded voyager of *Sailing to Byzantium*, heading for a city famed for Grecian artistry in singing forms. He has begun the transition by singing his soul out from a dying, heartsick body, and into an imagination of a holy city, holy sages, eternal soul-song—released, he will hope, from the pained eros of golden apples of the sun:

Once out of nature I shall never take
My bodily form from any natural thing,
But such a form as Grecian goldsmiths make
Of hammered gold and gold enamelling
To keep a drowsy Emperor awake;
Or set upon a golden bough to sing
To lords and ladies of Byzantium
Of what is past, or passing, or to come.

A rhyme-thread gives desire's perfection: the poet at the end of stanza II, "come / To the holy city of Byzantium," now sings, in chiasmus, in "Byzantium / Of what is past, or passing, or to come" (IV)—the final infinitives poised and posed for infinite possibility. Yet this ideal of song from a golden bird is also a cartoon of a beautiful toy (a poetic one, too, in the phonic chiasmus of "hammered gold and gold enamelling"), set out to amuse an imperial court. In such a world, Grecian art is not a tease of eternity but an artifice of material luxury, a bit of a fly in golden marmalade.

Amid the passionate syntax of an ideal, Yeats doesn't sort out the ironies any more than Keats does. The poet of Keats's Odes desires and knows better, but with no finality: the enchanted imagination is haunted by what reflective thinking is moved to resign. The poet of *Ode to a Nightingale* may have struggled more, even, than Yeats's Byzantium-minded poet. Keats's poet finds the "full-throated ease" of the nightingale's song (10) only a realization that his own romance is "half in love with easeful Death" (52). And the poet of *Ode on a Grecian Urn* comes to recognize the Urn's illusion of song and love "for ever young" as a condition of "Cold Pastoral": static, indifferent marble survival midst a perpetual human history of "woe" (47).

III. Mortal Lingerings

Yeats's severest conversation with eternity comes in another poem, rehearsed in the same lexicon as *Sailing to Byzantium* and marked out in similar, but not identical, eight-line stanzas. It is set in *Byzantium* (1930), and it is art with a vengeance:

> Miracle, bird or golden handiwork,
> More miracle than bird or handiwork,
> Planted on the starlit golden bough,
> Can like the cocks of Hades crow,
> Or, by the moon embittered, scorn aloud
> In glory of changeless metal
> Common bird or petal
> And all complexities of mire or blood.   (stanza 3)

Yeats's syntax is itself a test of complexities when it comes to "by the moon embittered." Shining on gloriously changeless metal, the changeful moon may be what *embittered* as an adjective modifies (*by* is positional): the moon is bitter at miracle of art. But the syntax is not so decidable.[47] The paced lines allow a suggestion that the voices from the golden handiwork, embittered by moon-glow from on high (*by* is agency), scorn aloud to assert pride in their own medium. The verb in the last stanza of *Sailing to Byzantium*, "sing," is nowhere in this Byzantium: its golden birds crow or scorn aloud.

This complexity, and irony, descends from the first stanza, which sets the scene this way, setting up repetitions in stanza 3:

> A starlit or a moonlit dome disdains
> All that man is,
> All mere complexities,
> The fury and the mire of human veins.   (5–8)

Man, the maker of art, is *mere* in *mire*. Stanza 3 shifts the counterpoint of moon and man to a counterpoint of golden bird and common bird. But "handiwork" concedes a hand that has worked this difference. However mired, this is the condition in which artists of human vein, "the golden smithies of the Emperor" (35), do their work. Golden handiwork may, but Yeatsian poetry does not, polish off these conditions. If the voice of disdain is wound up, mechanically, to outlast human "complexities," it is human complexities, Yeats insists, that generate such golden art, and are the furious throb of the artwork titled *Byzantium*.[48] Keats tips this hand in *Ode on a Grecian Urn*, as the poet imagines the pictured men and maidens "All breathing human passion far above" (28). This, too, is complex syntax, what poetry does. Keats's line conjures the Urn's figures, "all" of them, breathing human passion in a realm miraculously "far above" human life, and in a twinned syntax, values this realm as superior to the mire of "all breathing human passion." In both registers, "breathing" is a categorical difference: sensuous human life and human inspiration. Pressed to a limit, both Yeats's and Keats's wordings of art's perfection reverse into a counter-argument for the messy complexities of human life.

What artifice, then, not of eternity, but of presence in the world, can a poet craft? Both Keats and Yeats answer with an artifice of mortality: the pre-posthumous epitaph that begets readers into its duration. Stanley Plumly has conjured the "Posthumous Keats" that haunts Keats throughout his career, and Jahan Ramazani has identified Yeats's perfected genre of "self-elegy." To read this spectral consciousness in young Keats and late Yeats is to confront a rhetorical and dramatic power in a figural ethics nearly too intimate for wording. Nearly. If, as Yeats wrote in 1913–14, "Works of art are always begotten by previous works of art" ("Art and Ideas," *E&I* 352), both he and Keats beget pre-posthumous self-elegies from their own antecedence, with Yeats unearthing Keatsian materials and implications.

Here is Keats's gesture, a fragment (first published in 1898) that overrides elegy into a begetting agency:

> This living hand, now warm and capable
> Of earnest grasping, would, if it were cold
> And in the icy silence of the tomb,
> So haunt thy days and chill thy dreaming nights
> That thou would[st] wish thine own heart dry of blood
> So in my veins red life might stream again,
> And thou be conscience-calm'd—see here it is
> I hold it towards you.[49]

Revising the legal burden, *mort-main*, Keats writes a living hand as both somatic and scriptive. How can we know the hand writing from the handwriting?

Keats manuscript, "This living hand." Photolithograph from *John Keats, Poetry Manuscripts at Harvard: A Facsimile Edition*, ed. Jack Stillinger. Cambridge, MA: Harvard UP, 1990, p. 259, with permission from Houghton Library, Harvard University, which holds MS Keats 2.29.2.

A warm living hand becomes a cold dead hand, then handwriting coolly handed out, to leave *thy dry* a destined rhyme. Keats's mercilessly unfolding single sentence dilates its subjunctive ("would, if it were") to absorb its addressee ("that thou would"), with a double-thrust "So" (intensely; in consequence). Working the proposition into stark immediacy ("see here it is"), blending a stagey eloquence into colloquial intimacy, chastening the accreting syntax into spare monosyllables, Keats's lines conjure the present of writing into the future (or every-present) of reading: "here it is / I hold it towards you." Twice-told, this *it* grabs all the referents in the poetic field: living hand, cold hand, writing hand, handwriting. No wonder that Marjorie Garber summoned these lines for the movement figured by Shakespeare's ghosts (xxvi). Keats knew Hazlitt's stunned admiration for Edmund Kean's acting of Richard III's death (at the end of *Richard III*): "the attitude in which he stands with his hands stretched out, after his sword is wrested from him, has a preternatural and terrific grandeur, as if his will could not be disarmed, and the very phantoms of his despair had power to kill" (*Characters* 229–30). Keats's lines revive to survive in a claim staked with more than uncanny frisson. It is vampiric power. While holy bodies exude miraculous oil, "under heavy loads of trampled clay / Lie bodies of the vampires full of blood / . . . their lips are wet" (Yeats's "Oil and Blood," *Variorum* 483). Red life streams again as read life, a gothic rival to Keats's sadly self-sentenced epitaph on his deathbed, "Here lies one whose name was writ in Water."[50]

Change the surface to paper, or stone, and you come to the hard-hearted end of Yeats's *Under Ben Bulben* (*Variorum* 636–40). In the penultimate stanza (V), Yeats's percussive tetrameters command a making in mimesis of poetry itself: "Irish poets learn your trade, / Sing whatever is well made." Yet Yeats's most determined poems, remarks Michael Wood, tend to "a certain edginess in the formal activity," with "an intense feeling for form" in the haunts of loss (*Yeats* 92–93). If Yeats's aim at "well made" edges into *poet-maker*, the pre-posthumous epitaph that caps *Under Ben Bulben* is beyond well made. It is an inscription that sends poetry into rhetoric, even a rhetoric of poetry. It abjures the spectral legends of Grecian Urns, disdains the polite, meaningless words that traffic in Wordsworthian epitaphs with a pretense of tribute and memorial.

No marble, no conventional phrase;
On limestone quarried near the spot
By his command these words are cut:

> *Cast a cold eye*
> *On life, on death.*
> *Horseman, pass by!*

> *September 4, 1938*

Yet not for nothing is Yeats the master of complexities in rhetoric and poetry. Command notwithstanding, the italic words arrest the eye and ear, not the least for the halts of the percussive meter, with only one (arguably) of these 12 syllables unstressed: "a." The last line especially (first drafted as *Horse man* for four beats) refuses clip-clop dimeter.[51] The italics of this tercet in the newspapers of 3 February 1939 command all eyes to stop.

Some drafts show a provisional quatrain-making first line: "Draw rain / rein; draw breath."[52] In this double-draw—pause your journey, hold your breath—the draft speaks the *Siste viator* trope of mortal epitaph, the halt that haunted Wordsworth and then de Man. Whether by accident or design, this line in Yeats's draft did not get into print, and Yeats approved, endorsing the

Yeats's tombstone, Drumcliff churchyard, Sligo, Ireland.
Photograph by Susan Wolfson.

antonym. *"Pass by, and curse thy fill; but pass, and stay not here thy gait"* is
the literary genealogy, the scornful iteration of Shakespeare's Timon on his
"grave-stone."[53] Back in 1910, Yeats described Timon's self-epitaphing as one
of those "moments of comedy" in Shakespearean "tragic-comedy" in which
"character is defined" (*Tragic Theatre* 199–200). Tuned to the formal call of
Yeats's version for chiseling and print, Vendler describes the sensation of a
quatrain (*abab*) stopped short of a fourth line that seemed primed to rhyme
with "death" (97). Is this a rhetoric forbidding mourning? or is it poetry's
bidding? or is it a distinction overridden? For the living to cast a cold eye on
life is to be a bit dead-hearted; for the living to cast a cold eye on death is to
defy its dominion. Not the indifferent equation, in 1919, of the Irish Airman's
imminent farewell "In balance, with this life, this death" (*Wild Swans* 13),

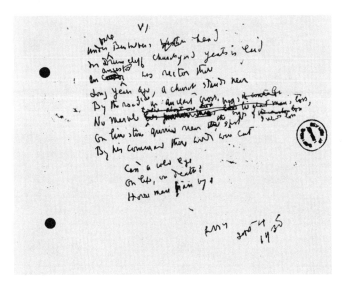

WBY, manuscript detail, last page of *Under Ben Bulben*. 14ʳ (see *Last Poems* xix–xx, 234–35). By kind permission of the National Library of Ireland 13,593 [52]. NLI 13,593 [52], 14ʳ.

Yeats's command from the grave is a rhetoric of contradiction. To read *pass by!* is not to pass by.

Roland Barthes's famed "death of the author" gets skewed with a difference, with a vengeance: not the fall of author to wayward reading, but an author invoking, constituting readers on the way, at his material tomb, and ultimately on his material page.[54] The total text includes that final date-inscription, *September 4, 1938,* a fourth line of sorts, poised, or scored, between the writing of poetry and the record for history. This ghost of poetry did not get translated onto the tombstone. Another ghost of a fourth line appears on the manuscript (see above). Slantwise, below the tercet that would be cut in stone, just left above the date, is written *WBY*, a last self-marking, and with a poetic punch: the *BY* repeats the epitaph's last word *by!*—an authorial self-rhyme for the reading eye.[55] What a return for a poet inheriting an eye-rhymed *Yeats/Keats*! Just two years before, Yeats declared, "I have spent my life in clearing out of poetry every phrase written for the eye, and bringing all back to the syntax that is for ear alone"—what he called, a few sentences on, "character in action."[56] He means "character" as dramatic persona. But "character" is also, in its earliest sense and etymological core, chiseling or engraving, and in its evolved sense, writing or signature

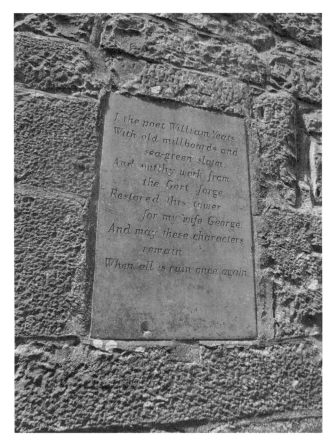

Carved in stone on Thoor Ballylee. Photograph by Susan Wolfson.

handwriting—and so nicely witted for the epitaph-dictation.[57] "And may these characters remain," Yeats writes in his only other poem (also an object in the material world) with the name "Yeats": "I, the poet William Yeats" in *To be carved on a Stone at Thoor Ballylee*. "In Drumcliff churchyard Yeats is laid" is the self-naming in *Under Ben Bulben*. Both are also carvings on slate, in the spots designated. Yeats set his chisel to the hardest stone.

"It is time that I wrote my will," Yeats began the final section of *The Tower* (1928), blending his forename into scriptive volition and its posthumous extension (p. 12)—sensing a legacy in the name-word, as Wordsworth had, in his self-writing. The temporal frames for all Yeats's will-inscriptions are double-crafted: "these characters" and "these words" (and "my will") are in the poetic present, and cast into an unclosed future. Even as words cut in limestone in County Sligo under Ben Bulben arrest and exhort readers not to read, Yeats writes the words to be read, cut in stone, in books, in volumes, on the pages left behind. The most severe, most vivid, meeting of Yeats and Keats may be in these lively textures: a command to read that is embedded in and remanded to an uncertain, ultimately unknowable, temporality— now and in time to be.

In a kinship of generic unearthing by self-estrangement, both Yeats and Keats, at the end of their mortal history, conjure poetry's most self-invested language, the auto-epitaph, to produce characters in action. To read this relay on the field of literary history (how poets and poetry may survive) is to undertake the particulars of juxtaposition rather than hew to master-narratives. A latent Yeats in Keats and a latent Keats in Yeats stir in conceptual figurings that the main current of reception for nineteenth-century "Keats" has rinsed from general recognition. Long Romanticism cannot be trumped or curtailed, then, as easily as Yeats in prose and pose might wish. His poetry knows better. And poetry survives in these particulars of shades and shadows. Such are the circuitous routes—and bypasses—of literary history that there remain debts that cannot be acknowledged or repaid in kind but get productively reinvested in both the haunts and the visible grain of making new.

After Wording

Writing of Apparitions

What Milton staged with the specter Death—an awful sensation of "substance . . . that shadow seem'd / For each seem'd either" (*PL* 2.669–70)—Keats humanized for the poet of *The Fall of Hyperion*. This is a dream with no awakening, arrested under the load of mortality: "And every day by day methought I grew / More gaunt and ghostly.—" (1.395–96)—not all at once, but by unceasing increments of consciousness. Keats would need no dreaming imagination for his own register of wasting into spectrality. Just days before his death on February 21, 1821, after a long, agonizing deterioration, Keats was speaking as if he had already grown into a shade, become his own ghost. He asked "how long is this posthumous life of mine to last," with a look that was more than his doctor and his friend Joseph Severn could bear: "the extreme brightness of his eyes—with his poor pallid face—were not earthly" (*LJK* 2:378).

Ever since he left England (for ever, he sensed), Keats was haunted by ghosts of the living, and his own existence at the limit-point. "I eternally see her figure eternally vanishing," he wrote to his friend Charles Brown on his way to Italy at the end of September 1820, about beloved Fanny Brawne (2:345). Her fading from person to figure, from figure to ghost, has Keats feeling himself fading into a ghost. His syntax suspends *eternally* between "I" and "her figure": she is eternally vanishing and he eternally sees this—a special kind of Orphic torture on an Infernal Urn, with Keats's other urn's "for ever happy, for ever young" haunting about the shape of this pained antithesis. Eternally vanishing, this is a deathwards progressing to no death, or even into medial stasis. Keats lives on, unresolved into absence or presence, teased into thought by the pained sensation of becoming lost, the cruelest parody of enchantment.

In September 1818 he had written that "the voice and the shape of a Woman has haunted me," his imagination taunted and haunted by the pleasant presence of this unnamed captivator (*K* 201). On November 1, the first day of Keats's 26th year, Fanny Brawne (was she the woman of September 1818?) is so vivid in his imagination ("I see her—I hear her") that to "see her hand writing would break my heart" (*LJK* 2:351–52). The sight of handwriting is haunted by the hand writing, then in metonymy, by the writer, lost in time. If "This living hand" is a practiced, even campy, ghost-writing against this sensation, the sentence from this letter may mark out the most canny, the most anguished sequel, a recession of the living writing into its phantasmal script. "I cannot bear the sight of any hand writing of a friend I love so much as I do you," Keats writes to Brown, as well.[1] He felt like a ghost-reader:

> I have an habitual feeling of my real life having past, and that I am leading a posthumous existence. God knows how it would have been — but it appears to me — however, I will not speak of that subject. (f.34–f.35 [seq. 69, 71])

In the first publication of this letter, R. M. Milnes emended *past* to *passed* (*Life, Letters* 2:282); but Stanley Plumly respects the fine-grained "posthumous tense" of Keats's *having past* (294). This is the ghost-form of "I have an habitual feeling of . . .": "real life" turned apparitional, "how it would have been," ached by the presence of "it appears to me." Keats pushes his writing to give and then give up its ghost: "I will not speak of that subject." But like patience to prevent that murmur, "posthumous existence" is the oxymoron that cannot forbid the writing:

> Write to George as soon as you receive this, and tell him how I am, as far as you can guess; — and also a note to my sister —who wh walks about my imagination like a ghost — she is so like Tom. I can scarcely bid you good bye even in a letter. I always made an awkward bow. (f.36 [seq. 73])

Tom, the brother dead for almost two years; brother George and sister Fanny, so far away as not to seem in real time: all in Keats's mind and in his writing as present ghost-forms. The pained formality of the sentence that abides as Keats's very last writing, "I always made an awkward bow," has to be what Christopher Ricks calls the least awkward bow ever made (*Keats* 219). It is surely grace under pressure, reading the self in its last act of habit.

Taking leave of what has already left, and is left, Keats knows what it is to think through ghosts. This is the spectral effect of a still present, not gone, life. "A phantom is an act of thinking," apparition-theorist Walter Dendy was willing to argue (56), translating Hobbes's *Phantasma est sentiendi actus*.[2] This is because thinking is an act like conjuring:

> It is as easy to believe the power of mind in conjuring up a spectre as in entertaining a simple thought: it is not strange that this thought may appear

embodied, especially if the external senses be shut: if we think of a distant friend, do we not *see* a form in our mind's eye, and if this idea be intensely defined, does it not become a phantom? (55)

How deft of Dendy to conjure (in present tenses, even) his reader's assent to this conjecture. No less felicitous is his conjuring of Hamlet's ghost-thinking with the phrase "our mind's eye":

Hamlet: My father———methinks I see my father.
Horatio: Where, my lord?
Hamlet: In my mind's eye, Horatio.   (1.2.184–85)

Thinking hosts phantoms, and writing responds, corresponds: recall Wordsworth's yearning to write his "phantoms of conceit" (1805 *Prelude* 1.130), with *conceit* doubling in the grammar as both the phantom-idea and the phantom-figure. For Wordsworth, a mental specter can even usurp a material presence: "In my mind's eye I seem'd to see him," he writes of a Leech-Gatherer talking futilely before him (1807 *Poems*, 1:97)—words so haunted by Hamlet's ghost-seeing as to register an allusion. If "between an idea and a phantom," as Dendy proposes, "there is only a difference in degree" (56), then writing gains an apparitional and a determinate logic. Dendy's recurring term *impression* registers this verbal-scriptive imprint, and his citation of "the intense . . . ideas of a Shakspere, a Milton, or a Dante" (56) gives present literary proofs.

Tennyson casts an extreme, where thinking of a world far distant in space and time is so close to phantomizing it that the only exorcism seems to be not thinking at all. Or at least that's the impossible phantomology for the Lotos-Eaters. In languorous Lotos-land, the war-weary veterans' memory of a world elsewhere has been fading into apparition. After those ten long years in Troy and the long toiling back to Ithaca that feels like another decade of war, they sing in chorus about a home that feels ever more ghostly, and in which they can imagine themselves only as ghosts:

Dear is the memory of our wedded lives,
And dear the last embraces of our wives
And their warm tears: but all hath suffer'd change;
For surely now our household hearths are cold:
Our sons inherit us: our looks are strange:
And we should come like ghosts to trouble joy.

                    (*The Lotos-Eaters*, stanza 6; 1842 version, p. 181)

Ariel's song in *The Tempest* is a faint, cruel echo of rhyme and reason in the song of these fathers. When Ariel sings to a son about a father lost in shipwreck to "suffer a sea-change / Into something rich and strange" (1.537–38), it is secretly tuned for their reunion, with the prospect of a future family line. The poignancy of memory in Lotos-land is its awful reversal of *change* and *strange* into distant homes, shades of history clinging in the present tense of imagination's affections: "Dear *is* . . . ," embracing the phantoms of *our* (five times) and *are*. The idea of a palpable absence is more than a shadow; it feels like an expression of a felt presence.

Phantasmics in this register and resonance tell a different story from the plot-lines mapped out in Seymour Chatman's narratological theory: "The working out of plot" is "a process of declining or narrowing possibility . . . choices become more and more limited, and the final choice seems not a choice at all, but an inevitability" (46). The choice made by the Lotos-Eaters comes in negations that speak regret as much as resolution. These are etched more sharply in the first version (1832):

> Oh! islanders of Ithaca, we will not wander more.
> Surely, surely slumber is more sweet than toil, the shore
> Than labour in the ocean, and rowing with the oar.
> Oh! islanders of Ithaca, we will return no more.   (p. 117)

That's the last line, sung in yearning, haunted by a still felt identity as islanders of Ithaca.[3] The rhymes give it a chord that accumulates from *wander more* to *the shore* to *the oar* to *no more,* with *shore,* in the midst, suspended, at the cusp of a phantasmal space beyond. In the shades of this Long Romanticism, spectral histories close, but do not foreclose: alternatives haunt and linger in present imaginations. Tennyson subtly registers this force with syntax that oscillates between saying and shading, a modal rhetoric that also sounds through litotes and double negatives—all specters that expose and contest what is, ostensibly, being contained and controlled.

In a late poem, *Constancy to an Ideal Object,* Ghost-Theorist Coleridge works toward, and dilates, a middle mode that hosts, gorgeously, a specter of negation with a shimmer of hazy presence. "And art thou nothing?" the poet sighs of an "Ideal Object" (the beloved who will never be more than a phantom of delight). The poetry answers (as if cued) by analogy, investing in a phantom under the cover of illusive, maybe elusive, ironizing. It is a figural phenomenology that remains suspended between enchantment and explanation:

And art thou nothing? Such thou art, as when
The woodman winding westward up the glen
At wintry dawn, where o'er the sheep-track's maze
The viewless snow-mist weaves a glist'ning haze,
Sees full before him, gliding without tread,
An image with a glory round its head;
The enamoured rustic worships its fair hues,
Nor knows he makes the shadow he pursues!   (25–32)

In this mini-epic-simile, Coleridge unfolds one of those optical illusions that look like a material presence. The *w*-chord—*woodman winding westward . . . viewless snow . . . weaves . . . without . . . knows . . . shadows* (undertoned by *weaves . . . sees*)—accumulates a sensate accrescence (to recall his remark on the Ghost in *Hamlet*). Snow-mist seems "viewless" only in the illusion of another substance. The text above is the 1834 one (2:91), which Coleridge carefully revised for this sensation. In an earlier form, line 32 was "Nor knows, he *makes* the shadow, he pursues!" (1828. 2:95; 1829. 2:93). This rustic is self-enchanted, making and mistaking his shadow for an independent glory. Coleridge's commas and italics make all the difference, implying, on the slant of irony and the frame of analogy, a poet-reader—and a poet's reader— who are illusion-savvy. The revision to an unpunctuated "nor knows he makes the shadow he pursues" nicely blurs the distinction between alluring appari- tion and marked delusion by allowing a spectral grammar ("shadow [that] he pursues") to underwrite a poet's sensation—not declined, not narrowed to the sidelines—of what it would be like to inhabit a mind that sees, loves, and reveres an image with this glory.

Coleridge's contemporary, medical philosopher John Ferriar was fasci- nated by this kind of apparitional epistemology, "imagination assisted by physical causes" (21–29), and refers to a figure that Coleridge had in mind as he wrote of the *Ideal Object*: the Brocken-Specter that appears on this high Alp at dawn.[4] Another contemporary, De Quincey, whose writing is deeply inwrought with ghosts, summoned both Coleridge's poem and the "famous" Alpine phenomenon to describe the logic of the illusion. The grammar of De Quincey's title, "The Apparition of the Brocken," aptly shimmers between indicating a thing and a specter.[5] The story he tells is of imagination physi- cally assisted into ghost-seeing, then recognizing the optical illusion:

> The spectre takes the shape of a human figure . . . At first, from the distance
> and the colossal size, every spectator supposes the appearance to be quite in-

dependent of himself. But very soon he is surprised to observe his own motions and gestures mimicked; and wakens to the conviction that the phantom is but a dilated reflection of himself. (748n)

Mirroring *spectre* in *spectator*, De Quincey will soon supplement *reflection*
with *reflex*, a wry recognition of psychology, even physiology: "the apparition is but a reflex of yourself" (749). But his double-sounded "is but a" does
not deflect the phantasmics. Noting that Coleridge, with some eagerly expec-
tant English students from Goettingen ascended the Brocken in 1799, on
Whitsunday—the day that celebrates the apparition of the Holy Spirit to
Christ's disciples—"but failed to see the phantom," De Quincey implies that
the poet satisfied himself by confecting an English iteration for the vehicle of
his "ideal object." Not quite recollecting Coleridge's last line, he gives it in his
own refraction: "And *makes* (not knowing) that which he pursues" (748n, his
italics). Like the Ghost in *Hamlet*, the apparition is a call into present language from psychic shadowlands—so recognizable a reflex that De Quincey's
summoning of the phantom shifts his pronouns to a second-person, read-
erly collaboration in a present tense: "in uttering your secret feelings to *him*,
you make this phantom the dark symbolic mirror for reflection to the daylight what else must be hidden forever" (749).

For the shadow-play that Coleridge stages in *Constancy to an Ideal Object*
and that De Quincey theorizes into the dark mirror of general psychology (a
"Dark Interpreter"), Gerald Prince coins the term "disnarrated." He distinguishes this mode both from what is regarded as "unnarratable" (unmention-
able) and from the mere contingency of being "unnarrated" (unmentioned)
(1–2). The "most important function" of the disnarrated is a "rhetorical/inter-
pretive" signal on the level of "narrating" itself: "it foregrounds ways of creating a situation or ordering an experience, emphasizes the realities of representation as opposed to the representation of realities." I like this refinement, but
why not a conjunction instead of a binary deconstructive inversion? In its
"tellability," the disnarrated is a present ghost, neither pure reality nor pure
representation. In a more appealing formulation, Prince argues that what
isn't told exposes the "the logic at work in narrative": "every narrative function opens an alternative . . . choices not made, roads not taken, possibilities not actualized, goals not reached" (5). Chatman likes the term *antistory*
for this opened alternative, and cites J. L. Borges's *Garden of the Forking
Paths* as a parable (57–58). But there is a subtle distinction between the *anti*-
prefixing of "attacks" on narrative convention, and the uncanny palimpsest

of Prince's *dis-*. The issue has bearing on the way Borges's plot of forking paths plants a temporal labyrinth of returns: the uncanny doubling of a person-name and a place-name, and relatedly, the narrative method of the fable titled *The Garden of the Forking Paths*.

Prince's "disnarrated" reads a foreground against a phantom, not a cleared ground. A tacit allusion, and a canny glance, for him is Robert Frost's *The Road Not Taken*. This poem is my parable. In the woodland of the poet's mind is a tacit notation (a ghost-mode characteristic of Frost) of the epic topos that launches Dante's *Divine Comedy: In the middle of the road of our life, / I found myself within a shadowy wood.*[6] For Frost, it's a quotidian *comedia*, retrospectively amped into a heroism of choice that *"made all the difference."* Yet for all this vaunted totalizing, the road taken and the one not taken are only nominally distinguishable:

> the passing there
> Had worn them really about the same,
>
> And both that morning equally lay
> In leaves no step had trodden black.

I took / Not Taken: the verbs echo to narrate and disnarrate. The doubling is the ghost-effect of the mode of repetition "based upon difference" described by J. Hillis Miller. Difference takes the form of "simulacra" or "phantasms": "the second is not the negation or opposite of the first, but its 'counterpart,' . . . the subversive ghost of the first, always already present within it as a possibility."[7] Frost glimpses this ghost not only in the arbitrary differential of *Not* but also in distributions of "I" that subvert the heroics of unified consciousness:

> I shall be telling this with a sigh
> Somewhere ages and ages hence:
> Two roads diverged in a wood, and I——
> I took the one less traveled by,
> And that has made all the difference.

The "I" moves forward in time ("I shall be telling") and doubly backward in time ("I / I took"). While the disnarrated road is left behind experientially, it lingers in the mind, and in the poem. It may be counter-factual, but it is not counter-actual.

It is perfectly consonant that an intimate, formative ghost in the poem's moment of telling is Frost's strange anecdote (and strangely present in the writing of it) of a slant meeting with his "own image," with shades of a spectral Dantean dreamscape in its "lonely" setting "in the wilderness" and "at nightfall" (*Letters* 1:61–62):

> Two lonely crossroads that themselves cross each other I have walked several times this winter without meeting or overtaking so much as a single person on foot or on runners . . . neither is much travelled. Judge then how surprised I was the other evening as I came down one to see a man, who to my own unfamiliar eyes and in the dusk looked for all the world like myself, coming down the other, his approach to the point where our paths must intersect being so timed that unless one of us pulled up we must inevitably collide. I felt as if I was going to meet my own image in a slanting mirror. . . . I verily expected to take up or absorb this other self and feel the stronger by the addition for the three-mile journey home. But I didn't go forward to the touch. I stood still in wonderment and let him pass by; and that, too, with the fatal omission of not trying to find out by a comparison of lives and immediate and remote interests what could have brought us by crossing paths to the same point in the wilderness at the same moment of nightfall. Some purpose I doubt not, if we could but have made it out. I like a coincidence almost as well as an incongruity.

Reflected by this tale of coincidence, the poem's totalized *"all the difference"* seems more arbitrary yet, arbitrary to the point of an ironizing subversion. A slant mirroring poises its cross-linear repetition, *"and I— / I took the one"*: more than a dramatic flux and reflux, *I— / I* is a ghost-double at a crossroads of coincidence. The dash between the two marks of "I" is intensely loaded: a hesitation, a stutter, a pause that reaches and then redounds in its repetition.[8] The crossroads are doubled just before this crux: "Two roads diverged in a yellow wood" and "Two roads diverged in a wood." Doubled in sight and doubled in the poem, these roads are marked *about the same* and *equally lay* (says the letter, "neither is much travelled"). Even the poem's present-perfect of *"has made all the difference"* gives an ongoing sensation, in which the road not taken repeats in apparition. This is imagination in the mode to which Frost accorded deepest value: "doubleness, double entendre, and duplicity and double play" ("Being Let In").

At such crossroads, from such play, Wordsworth could draw an epic map. So obsessively did he revise *The Prelude*'s "road" (1.669) of options taken or deferred, of provisional choices and things chosen, of choices made for him, of accidents and divergences, that revision looms as its spectral narratology:

not just rewriting, but re-vision, the difference read in every revisiting to his road, and from his road.[9] This may be because "All stories are, more or less, ghost stories," as Julian Wolfreys proposes; and by extension, "all forms of narrative are . . . haunted" (3). Or, as Michael Wood puts the case for "conflicting stories," each, "as Empson might say, casts a correcting shadow on the other . . . and also suggests something else, something that moves us, once again, beyond historical faith and into speculation: that all stories inhabit both real and virtual worlds and the ghosts even of unperformed actions never go away" ("Time" 204). As Wood's sentences also show, we like to write about our reading in the present tense. "Such a procedure is simultaneously the most commonplace . . . and yet the most irrational," Wolfreys comments; "We accord writing—that which, strictly speaking is neither alive nor dead, neither simply material nor immaterial—life and volition . . . make believe that the writer continues to speak to us" (xii–xiii). He sees this make-believe as a reflex of the reader's "complicity in acts of uncanny revivification" (xiii), but I'd call this make-believe the canny life of any engaged "reading."

Apparitions are writing's recurrence, in figural effects that repeat, and haunt, as real-time effects in reading. Advocates of "Surface Reading," a practice (also called "just reading") paved with flat declarations, are predictably either/or about spectral reading. "Just reading sees ghosts as presences, not absences, and lets ghosts be ghosts, instead of saying what they are ghosts *of*," advise Stephen Best and Sharon Marcus (13). To proclaim that we don't need to speculate about what apparitions might be the appearance *of* is to miss the way reading turns up depths that are not the opposite of surface but continuous with it. Ghosts are not mere elements to be managed by a shallow suspension of disbelief. Coleridge's case for a *willing* suspension of disbelief is a response to word-power already present, with force for cognitive belief. The disturbance of ghosts in what wordings are "saying" (how I've been reading) involves absence and presence, absence felt as presence— not only in reading, but in the differentials of *re*reading.

The corporate regime of "The Way We Read Now," by contrast, makes no allowance for the pressure of rereading. It administers an untroubled surface for "just reading"—*just* seeming to mean (in dictionary terms) the "weakened sense" of "neither more nor less than, no other than; simply, merely; limiting the degree or extent." What *just* seems not to mean is "judiciously curious."[10] A claim about what a "surface" communicates, moreover, is itself scarcely disinterested, unilateral, or immune to question by other readers. If you are going to submit literary formations and textures, literary language and nuance, to distant or surface reading, then you have to allow literary language and nuance to read these paradigms: if distinctive literary effects are invisible to "just reading" or the scope of "distant reading," then one might question the justice of just reading and the limits of its theory.

"I could not so easily get rid of my hideous phantom; still it haunted me," writes Mary Shelley, on the verge of shifting her verbs from historical past to the real-time of writing: "I must try to think of something else. I recurred to my ghost story" (xi). The recurrence (we know) issued *Frankenstein*. The meta–ghost-story unfolds in her "Introduction" to the 1831 reissue. But it's not so much an introduction as a post-script to a novel that was by then well known—and so, a retrospect on its genesis inflected by the fame since generated.[11] It's about rereading, a return that is both inspired and haunted by time past and time passed, and so less than and more than, mere recurrence. Shelley writes her envoi in this spirit, with campy affect: "And now, once again, I bid my hideous progeny go forth and prosper. I have an affection for it . . ." (xii). Go little book and go large. But it's a valediction haunted by mourning: "I have an affection for it, for it was the offspring of happy days, when death and grief were but words, which found no true echo in my heart" (xii). The reiteration *for it, for it*—a grammatical slide from the object for affection to the logic of affection—is a heart-breaking repetition in historical recurrence, wrought along a flux and reflux of reading.

The manuscript of 1816–17 ended on Robert Walton's report of the Creature: "he was carried away by the waves and I soon lost sight of him in the darkness & distance."[12] It's a perceptual limit. Shelley then canceled the "I" to leave a scene of dreamlike dissolve: "he was soon borne away by the waves, and lost in darkness and distance."[13] In this evanishment, how right is her change, too, from *carried* to *borne,* with a slight shade, by a pun on *born,* of unknown consequence. Her 1831 "Introduction" adds a sequel of darkness and distance that could not be known in 1818. Having reveled in the vitality of her progeny, Shelley suddenly sighs of days so lost that she is now "alone," bereft of company that "I shall never see more." Her final words, that her revision of the novel is "leaving the core and substance of it untouched," is a leaving in the shade of this loss. In the poetry of her prose, *core* echoes the absence of *never more,* and makes its own "echo in my heart," sounding both *coeur* (heart) and *core* (body). Shelley's final inscription gives both the pulse and the body of her writing, figuring the new birthday, *"October* 15, 1831," and a haunting by historical difference from its original company (xi)—the writing of a ghost.

I am haunted by the last sentences of Norman Maclean's *A River Runs through It.* Vividly modulating from the past tense of deep history to the present tense of haunted memory, Maclean speaks to the endurance of words that call through depths, under the surface, in timeless close presence.

> The river was cut by the world's great flood and runs over rocks from the basement of time. On some of the rocks are timeless raindrops. Under the rocks are the words, and some of the words are theirs.
>
> I am haunted by waters. (104)

A professor of English at the University of Chicago, Maclean loved teaching the Romantic poets and, like any good Romantic-Romanticist, Shakespeare, too. "Shakespeare . . . must have known more about writing than anybody else ever did. Every year I said to myself, 'You better teach this bastard so you don't forget what great writing is like.'" When it came to *Hamlet,* he pretty much realized the Ghost's command, "Remember me . . . do not forget" (1.5, 3.4). He might even have been haunted, happily, by the notion of Shakespeare voicing this Ghost. "I taught him technically, two whole weeks for the first scene from *Hamlet.* I'd spend the first day on just the first line, 'Who's there?'" (Dexter 91).

It's not a ghost—but then it is.

I am happily haunted. For encouragement and sharp advice on every chapter, I thank Garrett Stewart. The chapters on Hazlitt and Byron have been improved by Andy Elfenbein's expert attention, Duncan Wu's depth of knowledge, and Christopher Ricks's friendly rigor. Andy was my go-to on the nuances of Wordsworth and words, and Nick Roe with wonky Keats questions. Peter Manning's long friendship, his gifts of time, care, and sharp intelligence are reflected whenever I write on Byron and Wordsworth. He was most helpful, too, at critical phases in my work on Yeats's Keats. So was Dan Blanton. William Keach's critical energy courses everywhere in my chapter on Shelley, and his careful advice improved my chapter on Wordsworth; his encouragement and friendship have mattered immensely. Doug Mao, friend, editor, and the embodiment of polite rigor, urged me to better clarity in the chapter on Wordsworth. Billy Galperin, always my reliable cartographer and sounding board, managed a timely review, with full critical acumen. Alan Bewell was very encouraging at critical moments. Stan Plumly was an amazing interlocutor. And Ron Levao's steady focus, generous attention, sympathy, and unerring judgment, as always, are resources that are as much fun as they are incredibly valuable.

For various kinds of material help, I thank Kevin Mensch and AnnaLee Pauls at Princeton University, as well as Geoffrey Bond, Jeff Cowton, Leslie Morris, Nicholas Roe, and Christopher Rovee. Discussions in some chapters had earlier or partial iterations in *ELH, PMLA* and the *Oxford Handbook of Percy Bysshe Shelley*. I am grateful for these venues and to my editors—also for the generous attention of several audiences: at the Byron conference in St. Andrews, the Wordsworth Conference at Rydal (especially Nick Roe and Jamie Castell), Brown University, Harvard University, Cornell University, Georgetown University, University of Connecticut, the Fordham Romantics Group, Queen Mary's College, University of Minnesota, University of Chicago and the Yeats Summer School. While I write for colleagues and students, I am always impressed by, and grateful for, how much I keep learning from them.

Chapter 1 · Setting the Stage

1. To R. B. Cunninghame Graham, August 5, 1897 (*Letters* 46). Garrett Stewart directed me to this pregnant communication (*Dear Reader* 393).

2. See Dr. Samuel Johnson's *Dictionary* for both words. CONCEIT: 1] "Conception; thought; idea; image in the mind"; 2] "Understanding; readiness of apprehension." PHANTOM: 1] "A spectre; an apparition"; 2] "A fancied vision."

3. William writes to Dorothy in September 1790 of being at the Grand Chartreuse (*EY* 32–33). See *The Thirteen-Book Prelude* 2.104 for the first draft and the actual historical event (for this notation, editor Mark Reed credits Mary Moorman, p. 136).

4. "Yet at this very moment do tears start / Into mine eyes . . . / . . . In memory of the fare-wells of that time," Wordsworth writes in recollection of "the bravest youth of France" in 1792 "posting on / To meet the war upon her frontier-bounds" (9.269–76). The blur of parti-san discrimination (are these youths royalists or republicans?) indexes the stronger posses-sion of the compositional present by tears, marked in present tense in 1804–5, and still in *1850* (9.268–70).

5. Shakespeare's poetry, it is fair to say, trained close-reading in the Romantic era, on track to Stephen Booth's edition of the sonnets and the sequel of his critical monograph. I was directed to Coleridge's notebook by Bate and Engell (*BL* 2:19). Keats's remark is from a note in his *Paradise Lost* (*K* 235).

6. The foundational statement is McGann's critique with this title.

7. Derrida's *Specters of Marx* gives the grammar of "hauntology": "Ontology opposes it only in a movement of exorcism. Ontology is a conjuration" (161). Inspired by Derrida, David Simpson's *Wordsworth, Commodification and Social Concern* reads spectral forms as a "death in life" reflecting the material conditions of modernity: mass warfare, mechanization of labor, urbanization, and the rapid expansion of commodity form over economic and social change.

8. OED's first citation is from a draft of *Don Juan* 1.137, published in Byron's *Works* (1833) 15:165n.

9. Fred Botting's first chapter gives a great account of excess and transgression in the gothic mode.

10. Buss (1804–1875) is best known for *Dickens' Dream* (1870), a fantasia, on the news of Dickens's death that conjures the novelist in his study at Gad's Hill Place, with figures from his fictions swirling about, some fully realized, some in two-tone wisps.

11. Scarcely revising from its first writing in 1799, Wordsworth recalls the poetry to *Book First*, there to pivot into a recovery from the long bout of writer's block that beset high hopes and promises.

12. For this evocative tense in Wordsworth's poetry, see Julian Boyd and Zelda Boyd. *Book Fifth* holds another episode (one that was in its first draft, about himself) in this tense. A verse paragraph that begins "There was a boy" (389) modulates into a report of how "a gentle shock of mild surprise / Has carried far into his heart the voice / Of mountain torrents" (407–9). In MS JJ S^r (with the first-person), the verb was past-habitual, "Would carry" (*The Prelude, 1798–1799*, 86–87). It shifted to "Has carried" in the 1800 *Lyrical Ballads*, a tense car-ried into the poet's haunted visitings to the Boy's grave: "I have stood" (2:15–16). How apt that Thomas De Quincey would echo the present perfect progressive in his appreciation of *far into*: " 'far,' by which space and its infinities are attributed to the human heart, and to its ca-pacities of re-echoing the sublimities of nature, *has always struck me* as with a flash of sub-lime revelation" ("William Wordsworth" 94, my italics).

13. See MS JJ X^v and MS V 3^r (*The Prelude, 1798–1799*, pp. 108–9, 232–33).

14. As De Quincey comments, "Wordsworth was a profound admirer . . . of the higher geometry"; but the reason he offers (citing the Arab dream of *Book Fifth*)—"the antagonism between this world of bodiless abstraction and the world of passion" ("William Wordsworth" 97)—is subverted in the interplay of passion and abstraction in the illusion that besets the rowing boy. In new lines in *1850*'s *Book Fourteenth* Wordsworth has higher geometry in mind, still writing about "More rational proportions" relaxing the "overweening grasp" of "fear" (maybe this terror) (283–85).

15. "There is a suggestion here from the pause at the end of the line that he had not merely 'a feeling of' these unknown modes but something like a new 'sense' which was partly able to apprehend them—a new *kind* of sensing" (Empson, "Sense in *The Prelude*" 290).

16. Superstition "taught the Weak to bend, the Proud to pray / To Pow'r unseen, and mightier far than they" (*Essay on Man*, "Epistle III" vi.252–53; p. 17).

17. The words in quotation are from an oft-cited paragraph in *The Statesman's Manual* (1816) on the spiritual importance of not confusing "SYMBOLS with ALLEGORIES"—the latter a dead-letter proxy (36–37). Paul de Man deconstructs this distinction to propose that Coleridge's "symbol" is also an allegorical operation of displaced signifieds ("Rhetoric of Temporality"). Coleridge's effort to "desynonimize" the two figures may be a belated corrective to the affective conflations and haunting aftereffects of how he had read Radcliffe.

18. Coleridge is after something more liberal in "willing suspension" than what Margaret Russett regards as this flaw in Radcliffe's art: to suspend "both will and judgment" about "laws of nature and probability" (159–60) is to embarrass the "standard for regulating the slippage from novelistic to real-world conventions, or from books to readers" (175). Coleridge argues the difference between naïve slippage and a willing contract with "illusion," this "contradistinguished from delusion" (*BL* ch. 22; 2:219). Russett, doubting this difference, also sees Coleridge begging a question of origin.

19. After a train of dissolution, Restoration dramatist Nathaniel Lee spent five years in Bedlam Hospital. Byron jested to his publisher John Murray that *Manfred* in three acts was "as mad as Nat. Lee's Bedlam tragedy—which was in 25 acts & some odd scenes" (March 3, 1817; *BLJ* 5:179)

20. Dr. Johnson's supposing that readers are delusion-proof, argues Coleridge, "makes no sufficient allowance for an intermediate State, . . . Illusion"; "in the perusal of a deeply interesting Novel," we choose to entertain "a negative reality" (Lecture I (1818–19), on *The Tempest*, *Lectures 1808–1819* 2:266).

21. Castle, "Phantasmagoria" 51–52. The project of scientific rationalists to replace theological supernaturalism with a psychology of spectral phenomena, she argues, did not so much exorcise ghosts as reformulate them for apparitional imagination. (I do not concede, however, that "the invention of the uncanny" has an "Eighteenth-Century" patent, as the subtitle of her book states.) Botting comments nicely on the migration of "gothic" superstructure from haunted houses, crypts, dungeons, labyrinths, chasms, desolate mountains, and deep forests into "the murky recesses of human subjectivity" (11); I don't, however, see this subjectivity excluding or usurping "the social fold" (92). Subjectivity is at once haunted by and projects its own energies into social anxiety.

22. Hartman, "Words, Wish" 194.

23. From Carlyle's journal, 15 July 1835 (Froude, *Thomas Carlyle . . . 1834–1881* 1:54).

24. See Claudia Johnson's foundational reading of this situation (34–35). William Galperin provides a sharp analysis of Catherine's humiliation as the engine of the marriage plot, even as the novel itself dramatizes "the degree to which the gothic, as a species of writing for and about women, has a *relevance* that is perfectly warranted: that gothic dread, although seemingly contained by genre, is sufficiently justified by experience" (149).

25. While one effect of *Northanger Abbey* was to remand *The Mysteries of Udolpho* to precincts for parody, recent attention to the everyday gothic in *Northanger*—the labyrinths of Bath's social scheming, dark plots of the marriage market, shadows of patriarchal tyranny, the periphery of state surveillance—has returned sociological credibility to the mysteries of *Udolpho* (Botting 70–71). Critical consensus these days is that Catherine Morland ably gauges, on the basis of *Udolpho* and her experience of her world, shades of villain Montoni in courtly, controlling, forbidding, anger-flashing General Tilney.

26. See George Bernard Shaw's discernment of a virtual Marxian treatise on capital (175–76), and my elaboration of the economic basis of the gothic marriage plot (*Reading John Keats* 51–54).

27. See Benjamin Bailey to R. M. Milnes (Rollins, *Keats Circle* 2:275). Edgy about Keats's skepticism with regard to the consolations of religion, clergyman Bailey insisted Keats was a faithful Christian. Late in 1817, Keats formulated the aesthetic of "Negative Capability," the openness of "Literature" to "being in uncertainties, mysteries, doubts" against, say, Coleridge's "inability to remain content with half knowledge" (*K* 78). He seems to have had *Biographia Literaria* at hand, but oddly missed Coleridge's notion of the "*negative* faith" given to reading, "without either denial or affirmation," outside any "immediate neighbourhood to words and facts of known and absolute truth" (ch. 22; 2:148).

28. *In all acts of perception imagination is involved.* When Coleridge summoned this phrase for an essay on ghosts and apparitions in *The Friend* (first in 1809 [no. 8; October 5] 2:124, then in 1818, 1:248), he cited the German rationalist philosopher "WOLFE"—i.e., Christian von Wolff, *Psychologia rationalis* (Logic) (1725). See Coleridge, *Lectures* 2:208n52.

29. In 1987, 30 percent of *Shakespeare's Ghost Writers* was about *Hamlet* and its ghost. The second edition (2010), with a new 30-page chapter on *Hamlet*, brings the total to about 40 percent. The ghost of *Hamlet* is the romance in her long engagement with Shakespeare, as she happily concedes. As a teacher of and writer about Shakespeare myself, I'm grateful for this capacious, mobile study (and for directing me to the comment of Edward Gordon Craig [xvii]).

30. "Question it" is not the reading in *Dramatic Works;* it in the first folio and first quarto, substituted for a repeated "Speak to" (*Hamlet* ed. H. Jenkins p. 168).

31. This is not *sous rature* (the mark of linguistic inadequacy that plays against the illusion of presence in the chain of signification) but is more akin to the way litotes evokes what is averted or absent.

32. "On the English Novelists" (250), a well-attended lecture in London, 1818, with Keats in the audience.

33. I use the text in *The Friend* (1818) because it introduces the term "Ghost-Theory" (Coleridge, Essay III, 245). While Orrin Wang is belated in putting his signature on this term, I like his suggestion that its significance "lies not least in [its] redundancy": "Ghost theory is a theory about ghosts, theorized by ghosts—by a discourse structured around . . . spectral entities and phantasmic thought" (203–4). Coleridge's essay sets out this very grammar: a ghost makes sign and meaning equivalent; it signifies itself.

34. Christopher Ricks (pers. comm.) noted Bob Dylan's reverse play in "Spirit on the Water": "You ever seen a ghost? No, / But you have heard of them" (*Modern Times*).

35. "If this joking envelope is removed, we have: 'it is much easier to get rid of a fear of ghosts intellectually than to escape it when the occasion arises.' This is no longer in the least a joke, though it is a correct and still little appreciated psychological discovery" (Freud, *Jokes* 108).

36. For this project, see also *Lectures* 1:131n. In her essay "On Ghosts" (about which more, soon), Mary Shelley cites Coleridge's jest to the lady (apparently much repeated) but she wants to sort out reports of "real ghosts" from the "shadows, phantoms unreal" known to be a

"delusion," analogous to "optical deception" (254). Yet the more she works at the distinction, the more it is deconstructed by her very medium: ghost stories and their deep psychology, grief, and remorse (254–56).

37. Dendy may have known Keats. He closes a chapter, "Poetic Phantasy, or Frenzy," with an anecdote about seeing Keats scribbling a "quaint fragment" of prose, "Whenne Alexandre the Conqueroure," during an evening lecture at Guy's Hospital; he gives the text in full, its only source and attribution (99–100). (In this amusing satire, when Alexandre discovers a sleeping beauty, the narrator's powers of description fail to do justice to her fair breast.) Noting the dates of Dendy's likely lecture attendance and of Keats's, Nicholas Roe and Hrileena Ghosh (pers. comm.) doubt the authenticity of this quarter-century-later anecdote about Keats. See also B. Ifor Evans, who thinks the fragment is "a piece of invention manufactured for the occasion" (391) and indicates some material on which Dendy could have drawn. To my ear, Dendy's manufacture—Keats "soon chilled to death by the icy finger of criticism" (99)—draws on the lore of Shelley's *Adonais*. Might Dendy have concocted a "Keats," unhealthily enchanted by "the phantom of his waking dreams" at the expense of "science" (99), as a front for his own exercise of dreamy erotic writing?

38. Cicero, *De oratore* II.lxxxvi, 351–54, quoted by Frances Yates (2) in a discussion of classical mnemonics.

39. The parental grief in the affliction of ghost-calling was profoundly admired by Coleridge (*BL* ch. 22; 2:231). The poem was first published in the 1807 *Poems* (1:45–49); in the 1815 *Poems*, it appears in "Poems Founded upon the Affections," XIX (1:155–59). When Byron (unsigned) reviewed the 1807 *Poems* in *Monthly Literary Recreations*, July 1807 (just before a mostly praising review of his own *Hours of Idleness*), he picked out "The Affliction of Margaret ——— of ——— " as a poem of particular beauty (65).

40. Cicero, *De oratore* II.lxxxvi, 351–54, quoted in Yates (2). For Quintilian, this is a resource for oratory, a mnemotechnics. I respect Yates's refusal to regard as any mere technique Cicero's curation of "impressions of almost incredible intensity," a "piercing inner vision" that makes a mysterious subject of the "art of memory" in its most immediate manifestation (4).

41. See Eleanor Cook, "*Methought* as Dream Formula in Shakespeare, Milton, Wordsworth, Keats."

42. De Man, *Rhetoric of Romanticism* 78. David Simpson, even though he cites Garber's later text, reproduces her miswording (122). De Man does slip in quoting "Dost make us marble" as "Doth make ..." (see *MLN* 928 and again, *Rhetoric of Romanticism* 78), though I think this a poetic slip, a lapse into an auxiliary consonant with "Death."

43. Susan Stewart reads "Lyric Possession" as the antagonist of "poetic will": "It is an anxiety that affects poet and reader alike," in "a concern that one of these positions might contaminate the other. When actors become the recipients of actions, when speakers speak from the position of listeners, when thought is unattributable and intention wayward, the situation of poetry is evoked" (34).

44. For the definitional contours, see my essay "Our Puny Boundaries." The question of "Romantic"/"Modern" binarism will be taken up in my last chapter. Fred Botting ranges valuably over the Gothic terrain. Geoffrey Hartman's "Gods, Ghosts" focuses on a population of lesser spirits, performing on a wide stage of conceptual, epistemological, and modern-theological issues in Romantic-era lyrics. See also his brilliant essay on "spectral symbolism" in Keats's *Fall of Hyperion*.

45. On ghost-theory eluding both the logic of materialism and the antidote of idealism, see Wang 204–5. After I completed my book, John Hollander's Clark Lectures were published (posthumously) as *The Substance of Shadow: A Darkening Trope in Poetic History,* a rich and lucid meditation on the poetics of shadow in multiple formations as "the substance of poetry

itself" (editor Kenneth Gross, x). Although not the kind of study I work out in the present volume, it is very good company, especially in its sense of the paradoxical lights in various shadows of imagination.

46. This is Eleanor Cook's nice term for possibilities of full rhyme that hover around slant rhyme-words, a chime that "is not there, and yet is there as a ghost" ("Ghost Rhymes" 224).

47. These are salient, provocative attempts to accommodate our rapidly expanding canons and technologies of reading. "Distant Reading" is Franco Moretti's project of data-driven, abstractly charted "morphological transformations"; the front cover of the book so titled says it all: it's a network diagram of the dramatis personae of *Hamlet* (by Joon Mo Kang of the Stanford Literary Lab founded by Moretti). The polemic for "Surface Reading" (grandly subtitled "The Way We Read Now") is waged by Stephen Best and Sharon Marcus (9, 11). While I share their interest in literary formation, nuances of meaning, and complexities of structure, I question the assumption of what is said to be "evident, perceptible, apprehensible," lodged on the surface of "what the text says about itself"—mere "description," needing "no thickness . . . no depth," nothing "hidden" or "hiding" (9). For a careful critique of these manners of reading, and the assumed binaries of surface/depth, critical overdrive / plain description, see Linda Shires (xii–xiv), and the essays she cites. The "limits of critique" is Rita Felski's banner, with no patience for reading against the grain or between the lines (1); there are only obvious grains, clear lines. Her critique is of "a *thought style* that slices across differences of fields and discipline" (2, her emphasis), with a dismissal of how field and discipline may join or disjoin thought and style, reading practices from reading effects. I appreciate her critique of the we-know-better mode of militant, suspicious revelatory "critique" leveled at unwitting texts (2–3), but I find phases of her own critique too often flaunted in this same mode (see my next note).

48. This is Felski's conceited cartoon, with assurance that she has "no desire to reverse the clock and be teleported back to the good old days of New Critical chitchat about irony, paradox, and ambiguity" (5). No better for me is her retail in a long surpassed view of "romantic": "bursts of romantic hope coexist with the deciphering of ideological subtexts" (4). As anyone who has studied the Romantic era could point out, ideological subtexts are also what its writers read and write about.

Chapter 2 · Shades of *Will* + *Words* + *Worth*

1. Accordingly, for this chapter I use *1850* for the dream-text of *Book Fifth*. In *1805*, the dream is a friend's. In this respect, then, I reverse the position taken by Timothy Bahti: "Rather than being the relation of a dream which is significant because it is Wordsworth," this passage in *Book Fifth* is most important as "a *text* which floats from narrator to narrator, and of which the primary importance is that it be introduced, narrated, and interpreted" ("Figures" 608). My proposal is that Wordsworth anchors this float as his own relation, narration, and (such as it is) interpretation.

2. As Jane W. Smyser has discovered (270–72), this dream is neither the poet's nor his friend's but a loose purchase on Cervantes-lore, cross-fertilized with René Descartes' well-known third dream (10 November 1619). Coleridge was familiar with this, and it is related in Adrien Baillet's *La Vie de Monsieur Descartes* (1691). Two books figure into Descartes' dream: a dictionary of sciences and *Corpus Poetarum*, a work fraught with Descartes' crisis of vocation. For smart work with these biblio-involutions, see Jacobus, "Wordsworth and the Language of the Dream" 637–38.

3. In *1805*, Wordsworth had named "dreamers" as "lawless" forgers (5.548).

4. This debut was "Sonnet, on seeing Miss Helen Maria Williams weep at a Tale of Distress" (*European Magazine*, March 1787).

5. The etymon *logos* (vs. *logus*) would have made it all Greek.

6. The name-word populates lines 4–8 and 11–14 of this sonnet.

7. The first quip is quoted by John C. Reid (7); the second is reported by William Henry Hudson (25). My archive of name-puns will open again in my last chapter on Yeats.

8. For the several events, with increasing frequency, in the *Morning Post* and the *Courier*, 1801–3, see David Erdman, ed. 1:376, 390, 391, 400, 427, 436; 3:292–96. *Dejection: An Ode* (*Morning Post* 4 October 1802) also has this signature.

9. *Letters* 2:867. Coleridge is remembering, with elision, St. Paul's admonition, "Wherefore let him that thinketh he standeth take heed lest he fall" (1 Cor. 10:12, KJV). Richard Rand briefly discusses Coleridge's name-alphabetics ("Geraldine" 93–95).

10. *CL* 4:902 (30 December 1818); see also the puns on the Greek phonetics of his initials in his letter to J. H. Green (*CL* 6:962–833) It is "myself, Samuel Taylor Coleridge, beneficially abridged Esteese[e] (εστησ[ε]) i. e. S. T. C.," he signs a note to James Gillman (Gillman 9; my brackets correct mistranscriptions).

11. For the manuscript title, see Collier, *Diary* 4:56 (20 October 1833), itself a printing "for strictly private circulation" (so reports its cover).

12. Hazlitt's pained outrage is the focus of my next chapter. His notices on Coleridge's publications appeared in *The Examiner*, 8 September 1816 (prompted by an advertisement for *A Lay Sermon*) and 29 December 1816 (his review of *The Statesman's Manual*), and a letter to the editor of *The Examiner*, 12 January 1817—all collected in *Political Essays* (1819): 118–39. He also had a scathing article on *The Statesman's Manual* in *Edinburgh Review* (December 1816).

13. My text is from its first publication, in Coleridge's 1834 *Poetical Works* (rpt. 1835) 2:139. For these lines (70–73), I correct the placement of the opening quotation mark in line 73, with reference to the editions of E. H. Coleridge (453) and J. C. Mays (1.972). For line 72, E. H. Coleridge also notes the British Museum's manuscript reading: "In symbol just his name ΕΣΤΗΣΕ" (453n).

14. "Punic Greek" describes the translation of a massive work in Punic by general Mago, rendered sometime after 146 BCE by Cassius Dionysius of Utica (his name indicating a Greek man owned by a Roman of *gens Cassia*). Coleridge's signaled retro-idiom may give a dicey spin to his word-game and its figural import: Punic Greek is an exile's literary labor with no national standing.

15. *CL* 6:963. Morton D. Paley offers the double-reading of "better known" (130). Coleridge seems to have been the first to use the verb "Graecized" in this sense of transliterated (the OED has no entry).

16. To J. G. Lockhart, 5 November 1833 (*CL* 6:973). Coleridge, who died 25 July 1834, placed this as the last piece in his 1834 *Poetical Works*, a position it held through many later editions. For various texts, with the Graecized letterings, see Mays's edition, 1:1145 and 2:1360–63.

17. Despite the alluring title of Hugh Sykes Davies's keyword study, *Wordsworth and the Worth of Words*, weirdly (but luckily for me), *worth* and *words* are absent. I was glad to discover good, if brief, company for my venture in Andrew Bennett's pausing over a few of our shared spots of attention in his introduction to *Wordsworth Writing* (1).

18. De Man, "Autobiography as De-facement," 920–23.

19. Jacobus, "The Writing on the Wall," 6–7; her essay adeptly unfolds the lines of the crisis-argument, enlisting critical allies.

20. LION gives the 1850 *Prelude* as the first instance in print; OED has no listing at all.

21. Raymond Williams comments that by the eighteenth century, "in versions of the laws of God or of Nature," the sense of *determined* "extended to . . . a notion of 'inevitable' determined process." Yet, as the scare-quotes indicate, this notion is imposed on a "consequence which whether derived from some inherent or, as possibly, accidental element," is "seen as inevitable" (*Keywords* 99).

22. Here and following, italics that display the name-field of *William Wordsworth* are my own, unless otherwise indicated.

23. On the "numerous accidents" (*1799* 1.280) that claim *The Prelude* (*numerous* glancing at a poetic numbers, too), see chapter 4 of my *Formal Charges*. In "The Accidents of Figuration," Cynthia Chase reads a "dilemma for the interpreter" in events in which literal designations are not distinguished from the figural modes on which meaning depends—a coincidence of "surface features of style and the sense and significance of the referents" (especially in chance puns) (27). I read homonym-convergences of name elements and ordinary words as fortuitous accidents for self-reflection.

24. "Co-relative" may be Wordsworth's coinage, appearing first in "Epitaphs" (*Friend* 25, p. 405) and *Excursion* (p. 433). The hyphenated word is not in Dr. Johnson's *Dictionary*. ECCO shows only accidental end-line hyphens (incorrectly listed as substantives in OED).

25. Preface to *Poems* (1815) 1:xxxii–xxxii, on the untitled lines that begin "There was a Boy," the opening poem of the subsection "Poems of the Imagination" (1:297). This was first published in *Lyrical Ballads* 1800 (2:14–15) then transplanted into *Book Fifth* as third-person only. The phrase "gentle shock of mild surprise" is line 382 (see also *1805* 408).

26. *The Prelude, 1798–1799*, pp. 86–87.

27. Peter McDonald's comment on Wordsworth's motivation of repetition into a "semantically charged" path maps nicely onto my interest in the accidental semantic potential in the paths of name-words: "Wordsworth writes verse which tends to listen closely to its own sounds, and the intentness of this listening is inseparably a part of the intention of the poetry." Such self-consciousness "works subtly against the generic and formal distinctions of writing itself" (103).

28. Garrett Stewart, *Deed* 105–41, with debts to Stanley Cavell on Poe; I quote also from Stewart's brilliant *Reading Voices* 29.

29. I quote from Prynne's report on Saussure's post-*Cours* investigation of anagrams ("Stars" 19–20). Saussure's 99 notebooks on this project were published in 1971 as *Les mots sous les mots* ("words beneath words"), with commentary by Jean Starobinski. As translator Olivia Emmet describes the lure for Saussure, "He hoped to find, buried in the words deployed on the page by a text in verse or even in prose, the hypograms which constituted the point of departure of literary composition" and "which—hypothetically—directs the elaboration of the poem: the poem would take as its foundation a succession of theme words and would, literally, construct its discourse *on top* of them by repeating their phonic substance" (Starobinski xi). In Starobinski's paraphrase, the "theme word" or hero-name was "a material *donnée*" that "quickly evolved into a mnemonic supportive device for a poetry of improvisation and then a regulatory process inherent in writing itself. . . . Saussure never claimed that the developed text pre-existed in the theme-word: the text is *based* on the theme-word, which . . . simultaneously *opens* and *limits* the scope of the developed line"—the extreme of Wordsworth's array of name-charged syllables (Emmet trans., 45; I reverse the publisher's italics and romans).

30. All the quotations are from Prynne (21), the last riffing untagged on Coleridge's famous phrase in *Biographia Literaria* 2:2. Saussure's anagram project, remarks Jonathan Culler, offers a "practical dramatization of the tension between finding and positing meaning" (*Ferdinand de Saussure* 134). Even in *Cours*, Saussure's explication of the "arbitrary" linguistic sign is troubled by "a lower category of puns based upon the ridiculous confusions which may result from pure and simple homonomy"; on this point, Saussure summons a nonarbitrary register: what the mind "naturally" desires for intelligibility and its resistance to what "beclouds" it (126–27n10).

31. "Ancient Epitaphs," in Grosart's edition, 2:45–46.

32. Not spelling it out, Wordsworth paraphrased "Lamb": "From the most gentle Creature nursed in fields / Had been derived the Name he bore" (MS 2 pp. 16–17, in *Last Poems*, ed. Curtis, p. 297). He puns his sister in *The Prelude*, recalling their reunion after an absence so long that "she seemed / A gift first bestowed" (*1805* 6.218; *1850* 6.203; Dorothy: "gift of god"). Coleridge, with his ear for Greek name-puns, had played the name-pun in a letter to Wordsworth, 28 July 1803 (*CL* 2:957)—and Wordsworth plays it back to him in this verse.

33. In a letter to Tom Moore, Byron masked "Turdsworth" with five sly asterisks (*BLJ* 8:68). While these held in Moore's *Letters and Journals of Lord Byron: with Notices of His Life* (1830; 2:442) and *The Works of Lord Byron* (1832–33; 5:122), "Wordsworth" got spelled out in the edition of 1832 (12:322), this repeated in *Literary Gazette*'s notice of vol. 12 (758). By 1835, Paris editions were printing the name (Galignani, 902; Baudry's, 498), and by 1837 Murray's *Miscellanies by Lord Byron* had relented (3:247). Wordsworth wasn't clueless, writing in 1847, "I never spoke with acrimony of Lord Byron, notwithstanding the noble poet's public poetic attacks—perhaps the worst, because the most enduring of all" (*LY* 4:841). "Turdsworth" did not come to public light until the Earl of Rosebery purchased the letter in 1885, 35 years after Wordsworth's death.

34. Coleridge, *Unpublished Letters* 1:291. OED gives this as the first instance of "Self-involution." Perhaps winking at Coleridge and Wordsworth, De Quincey put the world in play to describe Turkish opium-eaters (*Confessions* Part II, p. 359).

35. This "valuable quality" (or worth) is second only to "*clearness*" (Cobbett, *Grammar* 89).

36. The evolution of compounds gets this explanation in Lindley Murray's *English Grammar* (1798): as two closely associated words evolve into a hyphenated word, the hyphen then "may be dispensed with in cases where the association has been long established and is become familiar" (138). Here is Eric Partridge's iteration of this philology in his twentieth-century *Concise Usage and Abusage*, into which I interpolate *Wordsworth* as site for excavation: "(1) two separate words [*words worth*]; (2) a hyphenated compound [*words-worth*]; (3) a single word [*Wordsworth*]" (87).

37. *Notebooks*, 4 January 1804 (1:1801). In 1797, William Taylor (no shy word-coiner himself) wondered whether "Self-biography" was a legitimate "word" in English, even as he thought the new-fangled "autobiography" too fey: "it is not very usual in English to employ hybrid words partly Saxon and partly Greek: yet *autobiography* would have seemed pedantic" (375). For an account of the career of the genre-word from 1799 to 1809, see James M. Good. In 1817, *Literary Gazette* summoned the questionable compound, ironically, for a scathing notice of *Biographia Literaria*: "Self-Biography is a difficult task. It bespeaks a sort of egotism in the writer" (83). Forgoing the hyphen, *New Monthly Magazine* opened in the same key: "Self biography is a very delicate undertaking and few instances can be mentioned wherein it has yielded satisfaction" (50). Hazlitt allowed "Auto-Biographer" into his review of *Biographia* in the *Edinburgh Review* (August 1817, p. 488). By 1821, having read *The Prelude* in manuscript, De Quincey used "auto-biographers" in his genre-allied *Confessions* (*London Magazine* 4, p. 360). By the 1820s "autobiography" was settling into an acceptable genre-term. *Edinburgh Magazine* featured an essay in its June 1822 issue titled "On Auto-Biography." Christopher Wordsworth noted in 1832 his brother hard at work on a "long autobiographic poem" (*Prelude*, Norton edn., 536); the first publication was titled *The Prelude, or Growth of a Poet's Mind; An Autobiographical Poem*.

38. Romantic-era interest in the thingness of words gets a penetrating exposition in William Keach's chapter in *Arbitrary Power*, "Words are Things." Concerned with how "the specific historical materiality of writing" exposes the "contradictory working" in words "both through and beyond conscious human agency" (45), Keach's genius (fortunately for me) did not scoop my terrain: his track is Wordsworth's anxiety about words as "perishable materi-

ality," or as ultimately secondary to "the mind's privileged work in giving all things, including words, life" (30).

39. Though not on pun-names, Catherine Bates's essay nicely presents a meta-discussion on a critic-reader's hospitality to pun potential.

40. As Catherine Bates puts the case: if some readers "may be more playful than others, more hospitable, more receptive to the pun," a pun still has to make sense, be readable in "a system of signification" (427–28). Readers are not on the same page in deciding whether the associations of primary and homonymically reverberated meanings are arbitrary and anarchic, or purposeful and pointed, or ambiguously suspended. While Hartman is famously hospitable, Umberto Eco objected to his audit of "subliminal punning" in Wordsworth's "A slumber did my spirit seal" (60–62). Christopher Ricks is more scrupulous about admissions requirements.

41. Both folk etymologies and puns motivate chance effects of wording into figures of new meaning (Culler, *On Puns* 3). Saussure will allow a pun under the radar of intelligibility in this aspect, but only when a "fortuitous" association by homonymy "is supported by an association of ideas," giving "one member of the pair . . . a new interpretation," as in the case of "Folk etymologies" (127n10).

42. Wordsworth, Note to *The Thorn* (1800 *Lyrical Ballads* 1:213); his italics on *things*.

43. Coleridge has Wordsworth redeeming Jeremiah's caution to those who have "eyes, and see not . . . ears, and hear not" (Jer. 5.21).

44. In a chapter titled "The Signification of Words," Locke proposes that "*there comes by constant use*, to be such a *Connection between certain Sounds, and the* Ideas *they stand for*, that the Names heard, almost as readily excite certain *Ideas*, as if the Objects themselves, which are apt to produce them, did actually affect the Senses" (*Essay* Book III, Chapter II §6 (p. 160).

45. "Essay Upon Epitaphs," *The Excursion* (1814), pp. 434–35. With this Sage is the Greek lyric poet Simonides, who accords the corpse a proper burial and is rewarded when its ghost warns him away from travel on a ship fated to be wrecked. Famed for the art of memory, Simonides is remembered in kind by a sonnet that Wordsworth published on the anecdote, "I find it written of Simonides," *Morning Post*, 10 October 1803.

46. *Poems, in Two Volumes* (1807) 1:91. It was drafted 1802; see DC MS 41 10ᵛ (*Poems, in Two Volumes*, ed. Curtis, p. 319).

47. MS 89 (1828), in *Last Poems*, ed. Curtis, 691. *On the Power of Sound* is the closing poem, with its own title page and all-capitals title, in *Yarrow Revisited, and Other Poems* (309–22).

48. For this midstage, see MS D, Book V, p. 14 (Owen, ed., *The Fourteen-Book Prelude* 602–3).

49. Ricks, *The Force of Poetry* 99–100, on *fleet* in 1850's *Books*. Ricks coins the term "antipun" (100) to describe the double operation for the reader in considering and then rejecting a pun. This aligns with Saussure's low regard for sound-doublings as "abnormal" intrusions, to be refused for the sake of intelligibility (*Cours* 126, 126–27n10).

50. In the Preface to *Poems* (1815), Wordsworth means the naval sense when he comments on the grand simile of Satan's soaring (1:xxi–xxiii): "As when far off at sea a fleet descry'd, / Hangs in the clouds" (*PL* 2.636–37). See also his letter, 28 August 1811, to George Beaumont, which mentions this simile, with the endorsement of having seen a similar illusion off the coast himself (*MY* I, 1:509)

51. MS V 17ʳ (1799), in *The Prelude, 1798–1799*, pp. 294–95: Second Part, lines 262–67.

52. MS D Book XIII, p. 14 (*Fourteen-Book Prelude*, ed. Owen, pp. 1094–95). In *1805* (12.215–19) only *forth* is at a line-end (216). Ricks is the solar force of attention to such figurings;

"Wordsworth: A Pure Organic Pleasure from the Lines," especially section II. The essay's running head is "The Prelude's Line-endings."

53. MS V 7ʳ (1799), in *The Prelude, 1798–1799*, pp. 254–55.

54. MS RV/DC MS 33 (1799), 10ᵛ; compare DC MS 33:50ʳ (*The Prelude, 1798–1799*, pp. 206–7, 164–65).

55. Coleridge urged *The Recluse* to Wordsworth, 12 October 1799: "of nothing but 'The Recluse' can I hear patiently" (*CL* 1:538). Still delinquent decades on, Wordsworth shifted the determined "I will forthwith" to mere futurity, "forthwith shall" (MS D, p. 42, *Fourteen-Book Prelude*, pp. 414–15). For a historically nuanced report on *will/shall* and Wordsworth's precision with the difference, see Elfenbein, *Romanticism and the Rise of English* 56–71. But where he slots Wordsworth's *will*-modes as temporal and worldly, compared to a grandly aspirational *shall* (68–69), I see *will* (here and elsewhere in *The Prelude*) in the aspirational mode, and *shall* as diminished promise.

56. Personifications of "abstract ideas" will appear only "in a very few instances" because a fidelity to "the very language of men" will "not find that such personifications make any regular or natural part of that language" (Preface to *Lyrical Ballads* 1800; 1:xx–xxi).

57. I was happy to see U. C. Knoepflmacher catch the name-glint in "Composed Upon Westminster Bridge, September 3, 1802": "'Will' Wordsworth has invested the river that 'glideth at his own sweet will' with a power he suddenly felt within himself" (14).

58. For a theoretically astute, contextually thick reading of this event, see Cynthia Chase, "The Ring of Gyges and the Coat of Darkness" 67–76.

59. *Lectures on Shakespeare* 2:265–66; *desynonimize* is Coleridge's coinage, minted in *BL* chapter 4 (1:87).

60. Saussure's method of name-scouting would surely magnetize *wil . . . ima* [*gination*] *worth.*

61. For all his canny titling, "Words, Wish, Worth: Wordsworth," and the subtitle of section IX, *There darkness makes abode* (199), Hartman doesn't pause at this abode of writing.

62. In conversation with me, Andy Elfenbein suggested a self-possessed counterpoint to Vaudracour on the template of Wordsworth's name-syllables: Iago's last words, "From this time *forth* I never *will* speak *word*" (*Othello* 5.2.371).

63. For this emphatic revision to MS A (1805) 253ʳ, see *The Thirteen-Book "Prelude"* (ed. Mark Reed) 1:1011, 2:847.

64. 1799 *First Part* 321; MS V 8ᵛ (*The Prelude, 1798–1799*, ed. Parrish, pp. 260–61). Compare *1850* 12.255.

65. Wordsworth rather liked this litotes for poetic self-esteem and, in tune, bestowed it on those whom he admired. There are ten instances in the 1893 poetic works. Near the close of "Epitaphs" (*The Excursion* 1814), he remarks that the "mighty Benefactors of mankind" need no more memorial than "an intuition, communicated in adequate words, of the sublimity of intellectual Power . . . the only offering that upon such an Altar would not be unworthy!" (445–46). While the case in point is Shakespeare, the relay from *words* to *not unworthy* enlists an apparition of *Wordsworth.*

66. Wordsworth's earliest hope was that his audience "will think with me" of the past times he relates (*Two-Part Prelude, Second Part* 2.41 [MS U 80ᵛ]; *The Prelude, 1798–1799*, pp. 276–77). The *Conclusion's* rings of *we will*, in collaboration with Coleridge, join volition to vocation: "we to them will speak / A lasting inspiration . . . / . . . / . . . what we have loved / Others will love, and we may teach them how" (13.442–45). Even after the partnership crumbled, *we will* could replace *we may* in *1850* (14.449).

67. Milton's "To the Parliament of England" (the address heading *The Doctrine and Discipline of Divorce*) disdains the moralism that would "set straiter limits to obedience than God

hath set, to enslave the dignity of man, to put a garrison upon his neck of empty and over-dignified precepts" (Hughes edn., 699).

68. DC MS 44 (1804) shows the revision to "will" (*Poems, in Two Volumes*, ed. Curtis, 107n). For the inception of "Ode to Duty" early in 1804, see Pinion, *Wordsworth Chronology* 56.

69. See McDonald's nuanced reading of "Ode to Duty" as "provid[ing] a design for 're-pose' rather than achieving it," against a self that weighs with stubborn persistence (74). Reading otherwise, David Bromwich gives the Ode a Burkean spin: the poet's "willing his own subjection" to a "doctrine" of better "will" shows a "spirit of self-sacrifice" in the long-ing "to be finished as an individual mind" (12–14). This is a poet, Bromwich contends, "fin-ished" with "a kind of self-knowledge" (14). To me, the poet of *The Prelude* (and plausibly the Ode, too) is productively un-"finished" within a (creative) haunting by a self-knowledge in-commensurate with self-discipline.

70. "Ad Vilmum Axiologum" was first published in E. H. Coleridge's edition (1893); he dates it 1805, the year S. T. Coleridge heard Wordsworth read the epic at Grasmere. Subse-quent editors propose the later dates (see Keach edn., 578).

71. "To a Gentleman" 10–11 (*Sibylline Leaves*, p. 197). The "Intimations" *Ode* was first pub-lished in 1807, in *Poems, In Two Volumes* (the last line is on 2:158). It had summary place in all Wordsworth's lifetime publications, first again in 1815 (last line, 2:355). Coleridge's readers in 1817 would be ably primed for his revisionary allusion.

72. Translating Derrida's "une chose ou un nom commun. L'érection-tombe. Pas d'homme" (57), Rand opts for *noun* (56), less rich than *name/noun*, both denoted by *nom*. Derrida's French is richer yet for the pun-prone phonics across the whole phrase. Rand trans-lates the last two sentences as "The erection-tomb falls. Step, and stop, of man"—the basic sense, but losing the vibe from compacting *tomb* and *fall* into *tombe* and of *step* and *not (no more)* into *pas*. Here, too, Derrida's metrical lilts and flirtation with rhyme-sounds intensify the already intimate logic.

73. MS B 4^r (Dorothy Wordsworth's hand) and MS C, p. iii (Mary Wordsworth's hand); *The Thirteen-Book "Prelude"* 1:1168, 1217.

74. "'The Prelude,' had not been fixed on by the author himself: the poem remained anon-ymous till his death," reports his nephew Christopher Wordsworth (*Memoirs* 1.313).

75. Cavell 179, and Jacobus, "Language of the Dream" 618; my italics in both.

76. MS JJ (1798–1799) Z^v; *The Prelude, 1798–1799*, pp. 116–17.

Chapter 3 · Hazlitt's Conjurings

1. I was directed to Drayton's headnote by Joseph Pucci.

2. Pucci's interest in how allusion is "codified into a coherent rhetorical system" (xviii) for a reader's grasp is amplified by Andrew Elfenbein's reading of allusion as a design to "reflect cultural practices" by signaling membership in group skills. Hazlitt is surely alert to the ef-fect Elfenbein describes: "an author draws on quotations from prestigious works that are part of the assumed common ground between author and audience" ("Discrimination" 486–87).

3. The working of allusion, writes Wasserman, must "include a creative act by the reader," whose "ready knowledge" is activated into a "rich interplay" with the full contexts aroused, the "resonances" "not peripheral but functional to the meaning" (427, 429, 443–44). See also Reuben Brower on Pope's "Poetry of Allusion." James Chandler describes these accounts as "intentionalist and historicist" ("Romantic Allusiveness" 464). This is also Hazlitt's strong suit.

4. For a reader or recipient, allusion and the uncanny are "characterized by the unex-pected presence of the known and familiar within a new . . . context" (3). But by extending the range to intertextuality and echo, Brown elides, or deactivates, complex intentions, and

so accords with Chandler's account of "Romantic lyricism" as part of "an emerging doctrine of unconscious association" in the form of "literary influence"—a flow toward rather than activated by an author ("Romantic Allusiveness" 497). So, too, Jonathan Bate reads allusions to Shakespeare in the Romantic generations as "a process in the imagination . . . not a consciously contrived artistic effect" (35–36). Eleanor Cook attempts a typology of allusion, echo, and intertextuality, but pretty much gives up on any secure definition, preferring just to consider instances that focus "Questions of Allusion" (her title).

5. Swift's phrase is no praise, however. The site is a letter to Pope, 23 July 1737, grumbling about "the corruption of English by those Scribblers who send us over their trash in Prose and Verse, with abominable curtailings and quaint modernisms" (*Letters* 252).

6. "Dr. Warburton's Preface," in Shakespeare, *Dramatick Writings* (1788) 1:79, 1:81. The extravagances often cover "common thoughts" or "some latent conceit not unworthy of his Genius" (1:lxiv).

7. Hazlitt, *Lectures on the English Poets* (1818) 228 and *TT* III (1820) "Conversation of Authors" 258.

8. Talfourd, "Thoughts" (1836) xxxvii, xxxviii.

9. Talfourd, "William Hazlitt" (1848) 157–58; see also 161.

10. Planning to follow his father into the Unitarian ministry, Hazlitt studied for about two years at the New College, in Hackney (East London), then quit "an avowed infidel" just after his seventeenth birthday (Henry Crabb Robinson 1:6).

11. Wu, *William Hazlitt* 15–16, 445n60.

12. See Shakespeare, *Coriolanus* 5.634–35; "Salopians" are residents of Shropshire.

13. Elfenbein deftly extends this figural field in ways that are relevant to Hazlitt's personal historiography: "the more the reader recognizes that an allusion describes core causal events in both earlier and later texts, the more salient the allusion" and "the greater the likelihood that the reader will notice plot-based connections between the two texts" ("Discrimination" 491).

14. Stewart honed this term in his reading of Christopher Ricks's remarkable *Allusion to the Poets*; see 593–94. See also Stephen Hinds: "Certain allusions are so constructed as to carry a kind of built-in commentary, a kind of reflexive annotation, which underlines or intensifies their demand to be interpreted *as* allusions" (4–5).

15. The "numbers that conclude this stanza are of so burlesque and ridiculous a kind, and have so much the air of a drinking song at a county election, that one is amazed and concerned to find them in a serious ode," scoffed Warton, finding the verse more apt to a "travesty" by John Dennis, Joseph Addison, or "some hero of the Dunciad" (1:54–55); for "a drinking song" the first edition had "an Hudibrastic song" (1:56).

16. For both Shelley and Hazlitt, the figure of "winged words" (Elfenbein reminds me) alludes to ἔπεα πτερόεντα (Latin: *Epea pteroenta*; English: *Winged Words*), the main title of John Horne Tooke's philological treatise, better known as *The Diversions of Purley*. Near the end of chapter 1, Tooke endorses the trope, with qualification: words deserve to be "called *winged*" in comparison with speech, but "compared with the rapidity of thought, they have not the smallest claim" (28). Shelley ordered *Diversions* in December 1812, and would have found this measure "entirely consistent with his own convictions about the relation of verbal to mental operations . . . words can never fly as fast as the mind that discovers and uses them" (Keach, *Shelley's Style* 181–82). Shelley and Hazlitt both admired Tooke's political courage in facing down the Crown during the dark days of Prime Minister William Pitt's Gagging Act prosecutions. For Hazlitt, see Wu, *William Hazlitt* 66.

17. Hazlitt's love of Coleridge's poetry draws on the era of *My first Acquaintance*. In "On the Living Poets" (1818) he cites this *Ode* and "Ancient Mariner" as reflections of his "great natural powers" (327). In *The Spirit of the Age* (1825) he defends this last fantasia against a tide

of ridicule: "it is unquestionably a work of genius—of wild, irregular, overwhelming imagination" (69). He was also haunted by "one fine passage" in *Christabel* about broken male affection.

18. *RT* 2:110–11. Quoting from memory and plausibly in a mnemonic of alliteration, Hazlitt transposes *glory* and *splendour*; the lines he misremembers are in Wordsworth's 1807 *Poems* 2:157.

19. Wu, *William Hazlitt* 288.

20. *My first Acquaintance* was sent to press in late February 1823 and published in late April. *Liber Amoris* appeared May 9 (Wu 333–34; Wu, ed. 9:232). Hazlitt had been reading Shelley (including *Prometheus Unbound*), and in 1821 ridiculed the poet as the antitype of "People of Sense" (370–71) and satirized his extravagance ("On Paradox and Common-place" 354–55). Even so, he reviewed *Posthumous Poems* with qualified admiration in 1824, and included several extracts by Shelley (and some complete poems) in *Select British Poets* (1824) 745–53. I think he read *Epipsychidion*, in secret sympathy with both its desiring poet-hero and its exquisitely despairing poetry.

21. Hazlitt was still spinning this romance in March 1822. "I have begun a book of our conversations," he tells P. G. Patmore, giving his title, *Liber Amoris* (*L* 246; this very letter gets into *Liber* 116–17).

22. "H." was transparent (Wu, ed. 9: 232; Wu, *William Hazlitt* 336–38). Within weeks, on 22 June, *John Bull* (p. 198) gleefully published in full a purloined letter, from "W.H." (naming himself "Mr. Hazlitt" within) to "Sarah Walker" that had been redacted for *Liber* (42–44). *Dictionary of National Biography* would treat *Liber* "without demur as an autobiography" (Butler 217).

23. Mme. d'Houdetôt, Rousseau's "Julie": "je vis ma Julie en Mad^e d'Houdetôt" (cited by Barnard 190). Barnard traces Rousseau's imprint on *Liber Amoris:* fueled by "a sentimental training in Rousseau," H. misreads S. "entirely on artistic and literary prototypes" (191–92).

24. See Rousseau, *Confessions*, Seconde Partie, Livre IX : "je trouvai, pour rendre les mouvemens de mon cœur, un langage vraiment digne d'eux" (391).

25. Barnard's essay capably searches the field (see especially 188–89), not only to discuss the allusions but also the wealth of quotations, some of which shall interest me in this section.

26. For Napoleon as idea and icon in *Liber Amoris,* see Sonia Hofkosh's incisive essay.

27. Shelley's Preface cast (fatally typecast) Keats as kin-prey to Tory reviews: "The savage criticism on his *Endymion* which appeared in the *Quarterly Review* produced the most violent effect on his susceptible mind." In Hazlitt's essays, "Mr. Keats" is often foil to his own self-possession, especially "On living to one's self" (1821)—even though Hazlitt despised the class politics that at once abused Keats and cut Byron large slack for similar phrasings.

28. For comic riffs, see Frederick Reynolds, *The Dramatist* (p. 8) and Thomas Moore, *M. P. or the Blue-Stocking* I.iii (p. 18). For melodramatic sounding, see Charlotte Smith, *Emmeline* (2:XII, p. 266; 4:IV, p. 79) and *The Old Manor House* (1:III, p. 59); Mary Hays, *Emma Courtney* (2:197); Francis Jeffrey, review of *Manfred* (Astarte's "fatal attachment") 420. Reviews of *Liber* ridiculed Hazlitt as a despicable, liberal, Cockney fool (see *Blackwood's*, and for more, Wu, ed. 7:xiii–xix).

29. *Don Juan* Canto XI.60 (1823), much repeated.

30. Hazlitt is sharp on "the deep workings of treachery under the mask of love and honesty" ("Othello," *Characters* 58–59). For brilliant work with this keyword, see Empson, "Honest in *Othello.*"

31. *Liber Amoris* has the cast of a commonplace book of Shakespeare's passion-tormented heroes: Troilus (46), Othello (61, 100, 146) and deluded rival Roderigo (122), Macbeth (65), Richard III (118, though a cynic), King Lear in a rage (96), and (by turns) the adoring, abject,

and bitter lover of the Sonnets. For Hazlitt's life during this romantic pursuit, including his agonizing three months in Scotland to secure a divorce from the first Sarah, his wife, see Wu, *William Hazlitt,* chapter 19.

32. Elfenbein smartly comments on the latent narratology of allusioning ("Discrimination").

33. Soon after (we find out later in the essay), Tom Wedgewood's offer of an annuity would enable Coleridge "to devote himself entirely to the study of poetry and philosophy" (31).

34. The sentences that he quotes are from Saint-Preux's reply to Julie in Cinquieme Partie, Lettre VII, which begins, "JULIE! une lettre de vous! . . . après sept ans de silence!" (253). W.H. compresses noncontiguous sentences from further on in this letter: "O Julie! il est des impressions éternelles que le tems ni les soins n'effacent point. . . . Dussai-je vivre des siècles entiers, le doux tems de ma jeunesse ne peut ni renaître pour moi, ni s'effacer de mon souvenir" (254–55).

35. Hazlitt, "On the Character of Rousseau."; the Englished tribute to Rousseau is in *Round Table* 2:52. On his 200-mile walk to accept Coleridge's invitation to visit in the spring, Hazlitt read this novel (in French) on his twentieth birthday (Wu, *William Hazlitt* 7).

36. Garber's witty phrase (70) refers to the explicit form of allusion that is quotation.

37. The legend is given in Ovid's *Metamorphoses* X.214–16. See *John Milton,* ed. Hughes 123n103.

38. Replying to Coleridge's regard of Caliban as a caricature Jacobin (lecture, February 1818), Hazlitt countered with derision of "the bloated and rickety minds and bodies of the Bourbons, cast as they are, in the true *Jus Divinum* mould" (Hazlitt, "Mr. Coleridge's Lectures," *Yellow Dwarf,* 14 February 1818).

39. *Semper ego auditor tantum? numquamne reponam* (Ever must I be a listener only? never reply?)

40. Coleridge, *Christabel* 396–418, in *Christabel & c* (32). A briefer reference in Hazlitt's *The Spirit of the Age* (69) effects an allusion to the full passage, linked to another allusion: "Alas! Frailty, thy name is *Genius!*" (67)—Hazlitt rivaling Coleridge in Hamlet-alluding, with *Genius* replacing *woman* and, with this gender-palimpsest, edging the lament with a charge of unmanly betrayal of fidelity. For his part, Coleridge felt the pain of "Hazlitt's notorious frantic hatred of me, who was Father, and Brother to him in one" (the era of 1798); letter to Daniel Stuart, 8 July 1825 (*L* 5:475).

41. *Julius Caesar* 2.1.242. This is what Talfourd was riffing on, as he complains about the diversions of Hazlitt's allusiveness. Hazlitt does not draw his Republican father into the politics of the murderous Roman Republicans.

42. *The Task* II.699–733 (pp. 81–82). The allusions return a compliment to Coleridge's admiration of Cowper: "the best modern poet," W.H. recalls him saying (*My first Acquaintance* 44).

43. These sentences take an edge as an averted allusion to Hazlitt's censure of Coleridge: "He has a thousand shadowy thoughts that rise before him, and hold each a glass, in which they point to others yet more dim and distant. He has a thousand self-created fancies that glitter and burst like bubbles" ("Coleridge's *Lay-Sermon*" 446).

44. On the call of apostrophe against, and reversing, historical distance or loss, see Jonathan Culler's splendid "Apostrophe," especially 66–67.

45. Coleridge completed his tragedy *Remorse* in 1813; it was staged on 23 January 1813 at Drury Lane. He was writing a first version, *Osorio,* in 1797, just before the era of *My first Acquaintance.*

46. At the top of "On going a Journey" (*New Monthly Magazine* 4:73), Hazlitt quotes another bookish line from the first poem in the 1800 *The Farmer's Boy* ("The fields his study, nature was his book"; "Spring," p. 5).

47. In his "Verses to the Memory of Bloomfield" (1824), Bernard Barton would use "quaint" to praise the poet for not truckling to the "unletter'd mind" with "quaint and local terms" (81–88, p. 62).

48. The long train of error is reiterated most recently in Wu's edition (8:391n34, 9:238n81).

49. Hazlitt had read the poem entire in the last of his lectures on the English poets (311–18) before proceeding to a hilarious satire on Wordsworth's egotism.

Chapter 4 · Shelley's Phantoms of the Future in 1819

1. Titles in quotation are not Shelley's but derive, by editorial tradition, from first publications, most of these crafted in the post-Reform 1830s (with some manuscript variants) by Shelley's cousin Thomas Medwin (*Athenæum*) and his widow, Mary Shelley, 1839.

2. Spurred by the Manchester demonstrations, the Acts outlawed weapons training except by government officials; allowed local officials to seize weapons and arrest their owners; limited bail and accelerated trials; curtailed public assembly; heightened penalties for blasphemy and sedition; and increased the financial burdens on publishers, especially the radical press.

3. For the persecutions, see Holmes 539–41; Foot, *Red Shelley* 34–36, 220–21. Shelley was following the ordeal of Richard Carlile in 1819 for publishing Tom Paine's works, as well as post-Manchester anti-government invectives. Already depleted of thousands of pounds by bail, he was fined another £1,500 and sentenced in October to three years in prison.

4. Foot, *Shelley's Revolutionary Year* 16; *Red Shelley* 219. The "little volume" in Shelley's sights was realized in 1990, with *Shelley's Revolutionary Year*, a "marvellous, cheap volume" (Redwords; £3.95), to meet "the enthusiasm of members of the SWP [Socialist Workers Party] for Shelley's revolutionary writings" (9) and to use in "duty to their children to bribe or bully them to learn the poetry which carries revolutionary ideas through the centuries" (26). Foot includes *A Philosophical View of Reform* (first published in 1920) and two "high-flown" lyrics (18) from *Prometheus Unbound & c* (1820): *Ode to the West Wind* (written October 1819) and *Ode on Liberty* (written spring 1820).

5. This Radical activist and charismatic orator (b. 1773) was not related to Leigh and John Hunt.

6. Edwards 165–66. The scene in *The Mask* (344–55) corresponds to the advice in *A Philosophical View of Reform* that the leaders should exhort Englishmen "peaceably to defy the danger, and to expect without resistance the onset of the cavalry, and wait with folded arms" and "unshrinking bosoms" whatever comes. Shelley is confident that the soldiers will relinquish the instinct of their trade and not "massacre an unresisting multitude of their countrymen drawn up in unarmed array before them, and bearing in their looks the calm, deliberate resolution to perish rather than abandon the assertion of their rights" (80–81).

7. *Spectator* 150, p. 366. Stephen Goldsmith says as much about *The Mask*: "the transformation from silence to speech, from death to life . . . ends oppression automatically, as if the dismantling of power on the terrain of political discourse were somehow a *generic* dismantling of domination itself," which "appears to be insubstantial, a mere language effect that evaporates the moment one brings to an end its monopoly over representation" (256).

8. Milton, *Reason of church-government* I.III, p. 11.

9. Blackstone hastens to add that by force of long custom, *leges non scriptae* have the binding power and force of written law (I.64).

10. The official success of the Crown's prosecution of Carlile, for instance, had to contend with both the public theater of the courtroom and publications of the proceedings. The Crown, remarked Keats to his brother, was "affraid to prosecute" Carlile, "affraid of his defence: it ~~will~~ would be published in all the papers all over the Empire: they shudder at this: the Trials would light a flame they could not extinguish" (18 September 1819; *LJK* 2:194). Laclau

explains the dynamic of dislocation, aptly enough, in a chapter with a *Hamlet*-tuned title: "The Time is Out of Joint" (67).

11. For a deft and subtle reading of how the arc of the *Defence* wrests this argument along the stresses of Shelley's thinking about language and potency, see Keach, *Shelley's Style* 27–28.

12. This comment was published in 1913, on the cusp of a career in wartime journalism; "fiery" Brailsford was "the best socialist writer in Britain" in the 1930s, said Foot ("*New States-man*" 21).

13. Shelley's fragmentary *Essay on Christianity* (261), circa 1812–19. Connecting this to the negative theology of Thomas Aquinas, Timothy Webb sees *A Defence* pointed toward "the possibility of a realm in which the seemingly negative is caught up, transformed, redeemed, or even regenerated by some high reality" ("Unascended Heaven" 57, 37).

14. Stewart, *The Deed of Reading* 87, with reference to Giorgio Agamben's "Philosophy and Linguistics." Webb reads this lexicon as bearing on the revolutionary structure of *Prometheus Unbound* (40–45).

15. Social activist and subtle literary critic Keach stresses the need, "politically as well as critically," to press on "things that do not fit, or that fit only uneasily, with the 'enthusiasms' that Foot so engagingly transmits." He hears Shelley registering the complications and contradictions involved in "powerful political protest" ("Rise Like Lions?"—his question mark is important).

16. The "*discipline* of the sixty or a hundred thousand who assembled' aroused alarm about the emergence of "a disciplined *class*" (Thompson 682, his emphasis).

17. *Manchester Observer*, 28 August 1819. See Thompson 681–89; Holmes 529–31; Behrendt, ed., 74–115; and the eyewitness accounts in Bruton. Slated to speak next after Hunt, Carlile escaped arrest and published the first detailed eyewitness report in *Sherwin's Weekly Political Register* (18 August). When the Crown shut this down, Carlile rebranded the paper *The Republican,* and on 27 August called for the "massacre" to "be the daily theme of the Press until the MURDERERS are brought to justice" (1:1, 3). It was the sequel that worried Shelley and other moderates: "Every man in Manchester who avows his opinions on the necessity of Reform, should never go unarmed—retaliation has become a duty, and revenge an act of justice" (1:1, 83).

18. With a tip of the hat to the Jacobin Cockade in the streets of Revolutionary Paris, the Manchester paraders donned a "Cap of Liberty"—also the name of a radical periodical in 1819 (Thompson 695). In September 1819, Keats assessed the ongoing force of the "french revolution": reactionary alarm halted "the rapid progress of free sentiments in England; and gave our Court hopes of turning back to the despotism of the 16 century. They have made a handle of this event in every way to undermine our freedom" (*LJK* 1:194).

19. A durable folk etymology is "out-rage," but the root is excess (French *outré*): here, beyond words.

20. For the abuse of Henry Hunt, see the eyewitness accounts in Bruton 20, 68–69.

21. Shelley's *Ode to Liberty* uses *Anarchs* as a synonym for official tyrants (43). For a sharp genealogy of "anarchy" from Milton to Shelley, see Keach, "Radical Shelley?"

22. "The whole distance . . . was lined with Multitudes," perhaps 3,000 (*LJK* 2:194). *Gentleman's Magazine* guessed at least 200,000 ("Occurrences in London" 269), and the *Times* put it at 300,000 (Thompson 689). *Monthly Magazine* said it looked like "the entire population of the metropolis" ("Incidents" 280). Hunt and his comrades were convicted of sedition at the York Assizes in March 1820, with Hunt given a 30-month prison sentence.

23. This is a type in William Empson's *Seven Types of Ambiguity* (v, and chapter 2).

24. "Disturbances at Manchester" 30; the article began on page 1. Hunt may have remembered that in 1818, the year before Peterloo, Keats had described "regalities" as "gilded masks"

(*Endymion* III, 22), a trope that had *Blackwood's* Z crying "sedition," an actionable offense ("On the Cockney School" 524).

25. Shelley regarded "Masque" as a satiric title (to Leigh Hunt, November 1819, *L* 2:152). Hunt's edition of 1832 uses this word. For Shelley's shrewd play with the seventeenth-century genre, see Curran, *Shelley's Annus Mirabilis* 186–88.

26. Eldon to Sir William Scott (August 1820), in Twiss 2:340.

27. Viscount Castlereagh (Robert Stewart), Foreign Secretary and Tory leader in the House of Commons, was reviled for his violent suppression of Ireland and his alliance with reactionary European monarchies. Shelley despised Lord Chancellor Baron Eldon (John Scott) in general, and in particular for depriving him of his children by his first wife. Home Secretary Viscount Sidmouth (Henry Addington) fostered programs of religious instruction to mollify workers, and set *agents provocateurs* on the intractable, luring them into actions that were prosecuted into death sentences.

28. So convincing is Shelley's *as-if* that Anne Janowitz elides it, hearing "female Earth" (94–95) as directly authorizing the "communitarian" mode (89). This is the mode of *Ode to Liberty* (1820): "there came / A voice from out the deep: I will record the same" (14–15).

29. For the historicity of the rhetorical strata, see Behrendt, *Shelley's Audiences* 199–202.

30. While ECCO does show instances of *unclassed*, these do not refer to to social hierarchy (rather, systems of classification). Its one instance of *nationless* is a degraded sense, synonymous with *barbarian*. OED rightly marks *sceptreless* and *tribeless* as Shelley's innovations and also gives him coining-credit for "destroyingly" (1.781) and "inter-transpicuous"—words to convey "unimaginable shapes" (4.244–46).

31. Hunt set * * * for "Sidmouth" (still alive), but allowed "Lord E" to code Eldon (also still alive). Castlereagh (d. 1822) could be (and was) named without libel (his suicide attenuated the protections). In her edition, Mary Shelley followed Hunt's typography.

32. Stanzas LXXXI–LXXXIII (pp. 42–43; Norton Critical Edition 327–39). The "old laws of England" counterpoints, with rhyme stress, the "laws . . . sold" in modern England (231–32).

33. Keach, "Rise Like Lions?" The demographic sense of *masses* emerged in the post-Reform 1830s. In *The Fudges in England* (1835), Thomas Moore writes of "that new Estate, 'the masses'" ("Letter IV" line 102, p. 37), followed by Thomas Fessenden's *Terrible Tractoration* (1836): "The mounting mobocratic masses / May over-top US UPPER-CLASSES" (535–36, p. 34). Moore may have noticed this, since he's mentioned on the same page (lines 513–16). In Charles Dickens's *The Posthumous Papers of the Pickwick Club* (1837), Mr. Slurk grumbles about his unappreciated "years of labour and study in behalf of the masses"; "no enthusiastic crowds . . . greet their champion" (chapter 50, I.281). In April 1837, Moore comments that the popularity of Dickens's persona "Boz" "appears one of the few proofs of good taste that 'the masses,' as they are called, have yet given" (*Journal* 5:1850).

34. The anecdote is from G. B. Shaw, "Shaming the Devil about Shelley" (1892). Shelley's tone troubles Keach, who notes K. N. Cameron (*Golden Years* 343) "puzzling" over it, too: "sardonic" in mood, "shaming" in intent. I appreciate Behrendt's hearing "a calculated challenge" in the "bitter irony" (*Shelley's Audiences* 195–96).

35. While the lettering may be muted in oratory, the print is legible. My thanks to John Kerrigan for the remark on the oath.

36. For the collective, see Keach, "Rise Like Lions?"—a formation that he also describes in *Prometheus Unbound* ("The political poet" 140–41).

37. Reiman, *Facsimile* 32. While the draft was "not intended as press copy" (1), Mary Shelley's press-copy (which P. B. Shelley reviewed) also lacks a closing quotation mark. It has a terminal period, then below, "The End" (50), as does Hunt's text (47).

38. Medwin's headnote (p. 554) hewed to Hunt's tact, naming Castlereagh but masking the other name. Mary Shelley used Medwin's title (*1839* 3:188), but her decision not to name anyone could have the effect of a general indictment. Otherwise she followed Medwin, with minor variants (deleting the first two dashes; *hue* for *yew* at 7).

39. My thanks to Rick Bogel for noting this. The medical icon was a much later development.

40. In this mode, Prometheus senses liberty in "lovely apparitions,—dim at first,/Then radiant—as the mind, arising bright/From the embrace of beauty (whence the forms/Of which these are the phantoms) casts on them/The gathered rays which are reality" (*Prometheus Unbound* 3.3.49–53). Keach gives a nuanced reading of how the syntax of *as* enriches the comparisons with a hint of temporal processes already at work ("The political poet" 137; *Shelley's Style* 76–77).

41. "England in 1819" is the categorical crisis-title devised by Mary Shelley (*1839* 3:193).

42. Coleridge, *Statesman's Manual*, appendix, ix–x. In pre-Napoleonic France, iterations of "liberticide factions," "liberticide machinations," "liberticide maneuvers," and "liberticide conspiracy" helped justify the executions of Louis XVI, Marie Antoinette, and Mme. Roland. See Roland's *Appeal* 127, 141; *Chronologist* 244; Gifford 663. Helen Maria Williams's *Letters* (1796) indicted the "liberticide factioners" who threatened to discredit the Revolution (1:70). In 1790s England, Frances Burdett, champion of popular rights and opponent of Pitt the Younger's ministry and the war against France, railed against severe taxation on the manufacturing and laboring classes as a "liberticide war" (3 January 1798, *Parliamentary Register* 4.543). William Cobbett called the war against U.S. independence "liberticide" (*Works* 39). Closer to the temper and era of Shelley's *Mask*, Jeremy Bentham's *Plan of Parliamentary Reform* (1817) indicted "the late liberticide Acts" (cccxxix).

43. If Wordsworth's works amount to "one of the greatest literary revolutions the world has ever seen," the "nerve and purpose to work it were braced and formed under the influence of a corresponding convulsion in politics" (466). This reviewer takes seriously the analogy of formal defiance and political revolution satirized by Hazlitt in his lecture *On the Living Poets* (*Lectures on the English Poets*, 318–19).

44. For Paine's famous sentence, see *Rights of Man* 24. Shelley printed 20 copies. In 1843 Thomas Rodd (most likely a proxy for Shelley's usual publisher, Ollier) issued a limited facsimile "reprint." The address was not widely published until 1888 (following the founding of the Shelley Society), in Shepherd's edition of Shelley's *Prose Works*. The shadow of the Pentridge tract on the Peterloo indictment is historically measured: "the repression of 1817 provoked . . . an accession of strength to the radical reformers" that in turn provoked conservative anxiety about "the growing weakness of the English *ancien régime*" and the violent counteractions at Peterloo (Thompson 671).

45. Text from Foot, *Shelley's Revolutionary Year* 105–6.

46. Arnold imaged this "Shelley" at the end of the Preface to his 1881 edition of Byron's poetry (xxxi), also printed in *Macmillan's Magazine* 53 (March 1881). He elaborated and amplified for the conclusion of his essay on Edward Dowden's *Life of Percy Bysshe Shelley* (1888), figuring Shelley as one of his own glorious phantoms: "The Shelley of actual life is a vision of beauty and radiance, indeed, but availing nothing, effecting nothing. And in poetry, no less than in life, he is 'a beautiful *and ineffectual* angel, beating in the void his luminous wings in vain'" (39). In *Essays in Criticism, Second Series*, the angel-Shelley sentences appear on 203–4 ("Byron") and 251–52 ("Shelley").

47. In standard usage, "phantom" denotes "illusion," "delusion of imagination," "deception," merely phantasmic (OED 1, tagged *Obs.* but in Shelley's aura of counter-definition).

48. Their base was University of Ingolstadt, young Victor Frankenstein's school of science, 1789–92.

49. Coleridge did not collect this sonnet (published on 10 January), but it was probably known to Shelley, a disciple of Godwin in his college days and son-in-law after 1816. The *Chronicle* leaned Whig-radical after 1789.

50. In 1822, a test case brought against the Manchester Yeomanry resulted in a vindication.

51. Shelley would also coin *Unapparent* as a substantive, to name the place where those of "unfulfilled renown" reign (*Adonais* XLV).

52. Locke, *Essay*, Book II, Chap. vii (1:94–95) and Book III, Chap. iv.12 (2:29). For Shelley's formative interest in Locke, see Keach, *Shelley's Style* (15–16, 37).

53. Heaney, *The Redress of Poetry* 1 (the opening paragraph of the essay that titles this book).

Chapter 5 · Me and My Shadows

1. Moore refreshes the lore in *Life of Lord Byron* (5:30–31), noting that the "ghost-story . . . forms the subject of one of [Samuel] Rogers's beautiful Italian sketches," referring to "Coll'alto" in *Italy* (1830 edn., p. 43). I wonder if Murray, who published the first edition of *Italy* with this story (1823), passed along a Byronic hint to Rogers. On the wings of Rogers's popular volume, the story figured into an opera, *The White Lady*, at Drury Lane in 1826 (translating *La Dame Blanche*, Paris in 1825), and was popular in repertoires throughout the nineteenth century.

2. On September 3, 1831, the front page of *The Morning Chronicle* advertised "Mrs. Shelley's popular Romance, Frankenstein, Revised by the Author, with a New Introduction explanatory of the origin of the Story"—a front-page advertisement repeated on October 29, with an article within (on Moore's *Life of Byron*) that quoted Byron on the genesis in 1816: "The most memorable result, indeed, of their story-telling compact, was Mrs. Shelley's powerful romance of 'Frankenstein'—one of those original conceptions that take hold of the public mind at once, and for ever" (4). *Court Journal* (published by Colburn) ran advertisements throughout September, and pre-published Shelley's "new Introduction" on October 22 (724). *Frankenstein* was primed for the ghost-market of its Halloween-launch, paired in the Bentley and Colburn Standard Author series (vol. IX) with Byron's boyhood favorite, Schiller's *Ghost-Seer*.

3. In *Biographia Literaria* (1817), Coleridge registered *Christabel* in his supernatural list (2.2–3). For Byron's recital in 1816 and Shelley's reaction, see Polidori's diary (128). "I won't have you sneer at Christabel," Byron wrote from Diodati to Murray (whom he had persuaded to publish it); "it is a fine wild poem" (September 30, 1816; *BLJ* 5:108). The volume containing it had come out in May.

4. For such conjurings, see Shelley's *Hymn to Intellectual Beauty* (written at Geneva 1816): "while yet a boy I sought for ghosts, and sped / Through many a listening chamber, cave and ruin, / And starlight wood, with fearful steps pursuing / Hope of high talk with the departed dead" (stanza 5), the last line with a shade of gothic literature in the Scrope Davies Notebook: "Hopes of strange converse with the storied dead" (P. B. Shelley, *Poetry and Prose* 95).

5. I follow *New Monthly* in italicizing the names. The unknown author is likely Mary Shelley; some of *Shelley's* ghost-descriptions (332) echo her Introduction to *Frankenstein* (vii–viii). The case for Mary Shelley is informatively made by Charles Robinson, *Shelley and Byron* 270n30.

6. Hamlet's Ghost was popular in Romantic-era ghost-shows—at the Taunton Theater in 1802–3; in 1807 at the Temple of Apollo in the Strand, where the spectacle was the thing. On the Taunton, see Owen Davies 237; on the Temple, see Castle, "Phantasmagoria" 38–39. The trap-door for the Ghost's entries and exits was open for farce. When a corpulent actor got stuck therein at the Manchester Theater, grinding the machinery to a halt, several stagehands

were required to extract him, giving everyone in the theater a good laugh. See the Liverpool *Mail* and the London *Times*, October 2, 1838 (Davies 237).

7. "Are the Plays of *Shakespear* works of rude uncultivated Genius in which the splendor of the Parts compensates . . . for the barbarous Shapelessness & Irregularity of the Whole?" Coleridge opens a lecture of 1812 (*Lectures 1808–1819* 1:494).

8. Byron refused to have the serious address that he wrote for the reopening of the Drury Lane in 1812 delivered by Raymond, its stage manager and sometime player of the Ghost in *Hamlet*, the play staged for the reopening (*BLJ* 2:204–5).

9. Byron adds another Shakespeare-riff for Moore's delectation: "would he had been only angry! but I fear him not," he writes of the Prince's affectation (51), riffing Caesar (soon to be a ghost) taking the measure of Cassius's "lean and hungry look," and the portly Prince's ineligibility for Caesar's sequel: "Would he were fatter, but I fear him not" (*Julius Caesar* 1.2).

10. "I will insist that among the beauties that glisten in the midst of these terrible extravagances, the ghost of Hamlet's father is a most striking *coup de theatre*" (Voltaire 570).

11. Christian ears might even catch a riff on the Catechism on the Sacrament of the Holy Ghost: "an outward and visible sign of an inward and spiritual grace given unto us" (*Book of Common Prayer*, ca. 1808; 181). I thank Andy Elfenbein for hearing this echo.

12. Byron named his genre to Murray (August 23, 1821; *BLJ* 8:187), and then to (estranged) Lady Byron (September 14; 8.210).

13. The frame-poet reports in the last line: "The king had been an hour asleep" (869). For Byron's joking at his own expense, see Manning 103.

14. Croker to Murray, April 14, 1817, in John Murray, *Letters* 225n3.

15. He was replying to her letter of May 20, 1824: "If they had said that the sun or the moon had gone out of the heavens, it could not have struck me with the idea of a more awful and dreary blank in creation than the words: 'Byron is dead!' " (Froude, *Thomas Carlyle . . . 1795–1853* 1.220–21).

16. So, too, Thomas Phillips's "cloak" portrait of Byron in 1814 was mindful of George Henry Harlow's painting of Charles Mayne Young as Hamlet (1801), the observed of all observers.

17. A lithograph by E. Burn (ca. 1830) was printed by Englemann & Co., published by R. Ackermann, and offered for sale in his print shop. There is a gorgeous plate (11) in Kenyon-Jones, discussed by Tom Mole in the same volume (75–76).

18. Byron was not the only ghost in the 1840 *Fisher's*. Editor William Howitt's pained foreword is titled, as if tombstone chiseling, "L.E.L." to report this poet's "early and melancholy death." At the volume's front, readers confronted a full-page portrait (by Daniel Maclise) of self-possessed "L.E.L.," signed "Cape Coast Castle, October 12"—now a ghostly avatar. Below the portrait is verse by her that is not only Byronic but could conjure Byron as a participant in its *we*:

Alas! hope is not prophecy. — we dream
But rarely does the glad fulfillment come:
We leave our land — and we return no more!

And so this *Scrap-Book* drew a recession of ghosts.

19. Irving's *Legend of Sleepy Hollow*, written in England, had been published in 1820.

20. See Owen Davies, *Haunted* 194 and, more generally, Castle, "Phantasmagoria."

21. Peacock, *Nightmare Abbey* 48n (end of chapter 4), noted by Charles Robinson, *Shelley and Byron* 47.

22. For the draft, see *BCPW* 4:467–69.

23. Referring to Napoleon Buonaparte and his nephew Louis Napoleon (Napoleon III), Marx opens *The Eighteenth Brumaire of Louis Napoleon*: "Hegel says somewhere that all great

historical facts and personages recur twice. He forgot to add: 'Once as tragedy, and again as farce'" (9).

24. McGann, *Byron and Romanticism* 183.

25. For the farcical stage afterlives of *Manfred* (including *Man-Fred*, and the reviews I cite), see Howell 97–106.

26. In the Latin Vulgate Bible, the name is Astharthe (singular) / Astharoth (plural), the last also in the KJB, perhaps a version of Astarte (DuQuette and Hyatt 52). Compare to *Paradise Lost*: "*Astoreth*, whom the *Phoenicians* call'd /*Astarte*, Queen of Heav'n" (1.438–39), also named *Ashtaroth* (422).

27. This mirroring is helped in the 1817 publication, from the first page to the last, by the abbreviation of Manfred as "MAN."

28. McGann comments nicely on the tonal layering of "awful" in *Manfred* as sublime and despicable (*Byron and Romanticism* 186); here the mixer is not despicable but sublime-parodic. The other tonal layering is pointedly ironic: Manfred insists that his "mind which is immortal makes itself / Requital for its good or evil thoughts— / Is its own origin of ill and end— / And its own place and time—" (3.4.129–32) in poetry legibly not his "own," but ghost-written by Milton for Satan: "The mind is its own place, and in it self / Can make a Heav'n of Hell, a Hell of Heav'n" (*PL* 1.254–55).

29. For a deft anatomy of this Spirit as an "aspect of Byron's confrontation with himself," see Stuart Sperry, who reads this last scene of *Manfred* as Byron's liberating "divestiture" from this type.

30. I cite *The Vision* by stanza. For my fuller discussion of authorship and spectrality, see my "*The Vision of Judgment* and the Spectres of 'Author.'"

31. Castle nicely notes the redundancy of a "phantasmagoria in / Himself," but errs in assigning the Shadow to George III ("Phantasmagoria" 44).

32. For a smart analysis of Falstaff as Byron's ghost-double, see Levao 127–35.

33. With a comment on "the ghost stories with which it abounds," Washington Irving gives a resonant, brief history ("Newstead Abbey: Historical Notice" 109–11).

34. "The appearance of a ghost (it is immaterial whether it is a real ghost or an aristocrat in drag)" is "the mark of repression . . . within the walls of what dialectic had hoped to contain through artistic representation," comments Jerome Christensen, with a Derridean gloss (331). Byron's artistry of rhyme makes the containment its theme, troping expression over repression.

35. The fragment of Canto XVII was first published in 1903, thereafter usually.

36. The fabricating is exposed by Wilson's reference (2:615) to Caroline Lamb's *Glenarvon*, published 1816, two years after the memoir-scene, a masquerade at Watier's Club in 1814 (*BLJ* 9:36). On Wilson's Byronic "pastiche," composed by "the mechanisms of textual replication" for a "salable simulacra," see Nicola Watson's smart essay (197–200).

37. Wilson's *Memoirs* proved a hot seller, 30 editions in its first year and quickly pirated. Along with her investment in spectral Byronism, she solicited hush-money from living referents, a gambit that failed with the Duke of Wellington, said to have retorted, "Publish and be damned!"

38. For a sharp reading of this spoof of Byronic imitation and conjuring, see Townshend.

39. Byron's imperfect chime of *wan* with Spanish *Hwahn* is a semantically rich cross-current in the rhyme field. Even as he insists on rhyming *Juan* in its two-syllable English sound, he frequently parries the ghost of the Continental name. Christopher Ricks and Andy Elfenbein helped me audit this sound-play. OED has no entry on "Juan" or cognates, so no history of pronunciation. Verse dramas prior to Byron do *Juan* in two syllables, implying the trochee *Joo-uhn* (see Mitford 1.502 and 534, 4.470; and Warren 1.1.76, 1.5.77, 2.1.62, 2.1.76, 3.5.34, 3.5.40, 3.5.79, 4.4.38, 4.5.21). Bernard Beatty tells me that to English ears *Hwahn* would be the

foreign sound, and *Joo-uhn* is not Anglicizing, just English. Even so, *Juan* is not an English name, so Byron's refashioning is still a satiric effect.

40. Donna Julia's tirade to a suspicious Don Alfonso is enhanced by "her wan cheek" (1.158). More poignantly, Haidée's "wan fingers" symptomize madness and death (4.66). Although Potemkin is fatally "worn and wan" (7.36), the stanza's end-rhyme with *man* and *span* is not a Juan-punning.

41. My thanks to Ron Levao for this note.

42. On the homophones *ruin* and *ruing*, see Walker's *Critical Pronouncing Dictionary*: "our best speakers do not invariably pronounce the participle *ing*, so as to rhyme with *sing, king,* and *ring*" (49). Byron may have known this volume: he jested about Walker's *Rhyming Dictionary* (1775) in 1814 (*BLJ* 4:108), and then in 1817 in *Beppo* 411 12. In *Evolution in English Pronunciation,* H. C. K. Wyld describes the *in'* sound as the early nineteenth-century pronunciation, *ing* not sounded among the educated until the 1820s or 1830s (21). Hear, for instance, in *Don Juan*: *about in/doubting* (9.17); *illumine us/consuming us* (9.35); *Erin/wearing* (11.38); *Juan/brewing/new one* (12.23); *off-ing /scoffing/coffin* (12.435), and the meta-enunciatory *speaking/Greek in* (2.161).

Chapter 6 · Shades of Relay

1. All the portraits, all "romantic" in aspect, were rendered in photogravure by Emery Walker. Vol. I has a charcoal sketch (1908) by John Singer Sargent, R.A., featuring a dreamy downcast gaze, tousled hair, and black neckwear flounced into a bow; vol. III (dedicated "To Maude Gonne") has the Shannon portrait; vol. V has a drawing (1907), arty and wistful, by Antonio Mancini; and vol. VII has a drawing by his father, J. B. Yeats. This last, done in 1896, is youthful Yeats, "poetic" (dreamy-eyed, with the same silk neckpiece and white collar, tousled hair).

2. So conscious was Yeats of Wilde's judgment that he never forgot Wilde's disapproval even of the color of his shoes (Ellmann, *Yeats* 78).

3. "Keats's west-country father possibly sometimes wrote and quite probably often pronounced his name 'Kates' " (Gittings 63).

4. The ALS at Princeton reads "rammed with life." It has other sentences about not wasting his time thinking about Keats that editor G. C. Williamson excised. See also Yeats, *Unpublished Letters* 3833.

5. For my account of another, but not unrelated, angle on Keats's gender trouble and gender liberalism for nineteenth-century writers, including Wilde, see *Borderlines,* chapter 8.

6. Such are the master-narratives of Harold Bloom's *The Anxiety of Influence* and *A Map of Misreading*. For a subtly differential refinement of "influence," "allusion," and "intertextuality," see Elfenbein, *Byron and the Victorians.*

7. On the self-interested fabrications of "literary modernity," see de Man, "Literary History and Literary Modernity." *Romantic/Modern* are of course no reifications but variable, relational descriptors. The vast discussion of what is and isn't "Romantic"—whether genre, sensibility, initial periodizing, latest anthologizing—may be encountered in Lovejoy's prescient, controversial essay, "On the Discrimination of Romanticism" (1924); McGann, *The Romantic Ideology;* Wolfson and Manning, Introduction to *The Romantics & Their Contemporaries;* and Wolfson, *PMLA* forum on periodizing "Our Puny Boundaries."

8. Li Ou's chapter, "Modernist Heritage of Negative Capability" (153–71), surveys some "echoes," "parallels," and "reminiscent" situations in Yeats of Keatsian formulations, to develop an account of heritage without haunting.

9. Keats's remarks are in a letter (March 1819), which Yeats could have read in Colvin's 1891 edition (237) and Forman's 1895 edition (304–5); see also *K* 243.

10. Letter, December 1817, first published 1848 (*K* 78); it is also in Forman's 1895 edition of *Letters* (57).

11. A signal broadcast was Leigh Hunt's essay in *The Examiner,* December 1816, "Young Poets" *The Examiner,* 1 December 1816 (761–62), featuring Keats, Shelley, J. H. Reynolds, and a nod to Byron's affinity.

12. James Pethica rehearses this consensus in his Introduction to the Norton Critical Edition of *Yeats's Poetry, Drama, and Prose.*

13. Unless otherwise indicated, quotations of Yeats's poetry follow Richard Finneran's edition, *The Poems,* vol. 1 of *The Collected Works of W. B. Yeats.* I supply original dates and sites of publication where these are critically relevant.

14. See "William Blake and the Imagination" (*Ideas* 173) and "William Blake and his Illustrations to *The Divine Comedy*" 176–77. Yeats's "Shelley" is delineated in "The Philosophy of Shelley's Poetry" (begun July 1899, partly published in 1900, and entire in *Ideas of Good and Evil,* 1903). An essay on *Prometheus Unbound* (1932; published in 1933, then *Essays,* 1937) hews to the same Shelleyan potential (though Yeats is vexed by Demogorgon's "incoherent" metaphysics). For Yeats's "Romantic" filterings, see Bornstein's chapter in *Transformations,* chiefly on Blake and Shelley (developing *Yeats and Shelley*), with a few pages on Keats.

15. Yeats, "The Philosophy of Shelley's Poetry" 133.

16. Yeats, *The Trembling of the Veil* 189. For "beauty" as a protected aesthetic in Yeats (with a Spenser-Keats genealogy), see Leighton, *On Form* 150–51.

17. Yeats, "Art and Ideas" (1913; *E&I* 347). Yeats reads delicate sensibility in Shelley too (drawing on Hallam's essay of 1831 on Tennyson as a "poet of sensation"), but he writes this up as a counter-cultural aesthetic principle.

18. I cite the poem by page number. Dated here "*December* 1915" (15), it was previously published in 1917, in *Poetry* (October), and in November in *The New Statesman* and *The Wild Swans at Coole.*

19. For Pound's wit, see Ellmann, *Yeats* 201. For Willie-naming, see (just for example), Maud Gonne's letters in White and Jeffares, *Gonne-Yeats Letters.*

20. This sentence concludes the next section, "Anima Hominis" VIII (*Per Amica* 40), which opens with yet another Will, Goëthe's *Wilhelm Meister* (38).

21. "The Tragic Generation," *Trembling,* Book IV:XVIII.215. Matthew Campbell pointed me to Yeats's record of Verlaine's remark (197). "The Tragic Generation" of fin-de-siècle poets (Edward Dowson and Lionel Johnson) fell to dissipation and despair, with no modern creative capital (*Trembling* 189, where Yeats quotes the inset poetry's question for them). The title of Yeats's book reflects his sense that the cultural climate of the 1920s was being "disturbed" by "the trembling of the veil of the temple" (portent of revelation)—recalling what Stéphane Mallarmé had said of his own epoch (191; cf. Preface).

22. A notably tricky Yeatsian *from* pivots the climactic question of *Among School Children*: "How can we know the dancer from the dance?": *apart from, in distinction from,* or, contradictorily, *in derivation from?* For this productive ambiguity, see Hollander, *Melodious Guile* 37; Cavell, "Politics of Interpretation" 45–47.

23. *Ode to a Nightingale* (79–80) and letter, 3 May 1818, Milnes, *Life, Letters* 2:99 (also *K* 130).

24. Delving into other aspects of the dream, Hartman reads a "Spectral symbolism" in the dream of the Titan gods (however fallen, "not human, or not entirely so"): "spectral" because these are psychogenetic, the "parental or ancestral" formations of poetic ambition and existential trauma ("Spectral Symbolism" 57–58).

25. In Dante's *La Vita Nuova,* a "Lord of Terrible Aspect" (Amore) brings "a new life" to the dreamer, announcing, "ego dominus tuus" (I am your master). Yeats quotes this passage in *Per Amica* 19, from Dante Rossetti's translation, which he admired (26).

26. Keats to Benjamin Bailey, 22 November 1817 (*K* 71), in print since Milnes, *Life, Letters* 2:54; *Ode to a Nightingale* 6, 27–28.

27. The excerpt at the end of *The Trembling of the Veil*, Book III, was the text from "What portion" to "Luxuriant song" (154).

28. Even Yeats's mapping of "the transition from past to present as a literary shift from Romantic to modern," notes Jahan Ramazani, forgets that "relinquishing youth's dreamy innocence for a chastened maturity" is itself a "Romantic" paradigm (*Yeats* 138).

29. *CL* 406; *Trembling of the Veil* 10. The phrase that struck Yeats is from "Mother of Hermes," Keats's irregular sonnet, first published in 1848 (Milnes, *Life, Letters* 2:97). Milnes actually italicized the line praising the old bards for "Leaving great verse unto a little clan" in his 1854 memoir for *The Poetical Works of John Keats* (xix). In this spirit, Yeats did pair Keats honorably with Shelley in an essay for *Samhain* (1904) titled "First Principles": these "creative" minds "are among the moulders of their nation and are not made upon its mould" (*Irish Dramatic Movement* 64).

30. I use the text, based on a manuscript, as first published in 1848 by R. M. Milnes (2:268–70), "La Belle Dame sans Merci. A Ballad. 1819" because this was the version best known in the nineteenth century, retained by Milnes (Lord Houghton) for his edition of 1891. H. B. Forman's 1895 edition of Keats (446–49) recovered the version in Leigh Hunt's magazine, *The Indicator* 31 (10 May 1820), with notes on the variants (chiefly, "wretched wight" for "knight-at-arms"), gleaned from Sidney Colvin's transcription of Keats's letter-text, April 1819 (see *K* 247–49) in his article in *Macmillan's Magazine* (August 1888): 316. In his biography of Keats (1917), Colvin polemically reprised the letter-text as the "right version" (351–52; index, 581)—contradicting Forman's regard of *The Indicator* version as an authoritative correction, a decision endorsed by Arthur Symons's edition (1900), p. 125. These days, both versions are considered legitimate.

31. For the ballad as a self-questioning, see my *Questioning Presence* 296–300, and, more recently, *Reading John Keats* 83–86.

32. There is a slight variation on two words ("*Though* the sedge *is* wither'd . . .").

33. Bornstein hears Keats's ballad in *Song of the Wandering Aengus* and in another poem in its volume, *He Hears the Cry of the Sedge*: "I wander by the edge / Of this desolate lake / Where wind cries in the sedge" (*Yeats and Shelley* 56, 58). I'd add to his list *He Tells of a Valley Full of Lovers* (compare the knight's dream, stanzas 10–11), *The Lover Mourns for the Loss of Love,* and *He Remembers Forgotten Beauty;* and from *The Rose* (1893), *The Man Who Dreamed of Faeryland.*

34. I admire Vendler's whole account of phonic texturing, *Our Secret Discipline* 105–8.

35. The homophones would become more plangent than when the song was first published in *The Sketch* (1897). Ramazani's subtitled chapter, "A Woman Dead and Gon(n)e," though (phew!) missing the mirroring here, catches *gone/Gonne* elsewhere (*Yeats* 17–26). In *Fallen Majesty* (1912), the poet twice declares, "this hand alone / . . . records what's gone. / . . . I record what's gone" (2, 4, 6); then, more sadly in *Her Praise* (1916): "I have gone about the house, gone up and down" (2), looking for anyone to whom to speak her name, which he does in the homonyms.

36. Yeats implies this link in *An Irish Airman Foresees His Death:* the Airman's "delight" in tumult among the clouds is inseparable from indifference about the war, about whether he lives or dies.

37. Yeats, "Religious Belief . . . Religious Art" 109–10. This is the logic of Bornstein's harsh sentence on *Song of the Wandering Aengus:* the "metallic garden" of the vision issues "more a wishful thought than a possible form for [the singer's] exhausted imagination" (78).

38. *The Sketch,* August 1897. That madness is unmanning is sensed by Yeats's similizing to hysteria, *the* female ailment. The narrator of Yeats's *Rosa Alchemica* (1914) experiences trances in which he "felt fixed habits and principles dissolving before a power, which was *hysterica passio* or sheer madness" (*Stories* 209), and playwright Yeats insisted, "I have never

'produced' a play in verse without showing the actors that the passion of the verse comes from the fact that the speakers are holding down violence or madness—'down Hysterica passio.' All depends on the completeness of the holding down, on the stirring of the beast underneath" (5 August 1936; *Unpublished Letters* 6630)—not a specifically female beast here, but unmanning in alliance with deposed patriarch King Lear, "*Hysterica passio!* down, thou climbing sorrow!" (2.4.55)

39. "General Introduction" (1937), *E&I* 522–24.

40. I use H. B. Forman's text (*Letters of John Keats*), the one most historically proximate to Yeats. The sonnet was first widely published in 1848 (Milnes 2:303). For Keats's letter-text and poetry (May 1819), see my *John Keats* 254–55.

41. For the muscular work-out of Keats's sonnet, see Hollander, *Melodious Guile* 93–96; and my *Formal Charges* 170–72, or more briefly, *Reading John Keats* 87–89.

42. "A General Introduction" (1937), *E&I* 524.

43. In *bout-rimés* players receive a set of words to craft into couplets. Keats was abused in the *Quarterly Review*, as Yeats might know, for "amusing himself and wearying his readers" with poetry in *Endymion* that not only read like "an immeasurable game at *bouts-rimés*" but violated the "indispensable" rule that the result must "have a meaning" (19 [September 1819] 205–6).

44. Jeffares 106. Ramazani is sharp on how conflicts in Yeats's aesthetic self-reflection go to extremes in *Fascination*: constraint and chaos, rhymes and slants, lines and enjambment, demotics and high-art allusions ("Self-Theorizing Poetry" 68–69).

45. This is Vendler's fine perception about a sonnet completed in "airborne escape out the unbolted stable door of poet and Pegasus together" (*Our Secret Discipline* 164).

46. *Responsibilities* (1914) p. 34. It follows *September 1913* 32–33, with the famous refrain "Romantic Ireland's dead and gone."

47. Vendler beautifully glosses the verbal drama. Although the one long sentence feels "fundamentally unstoppable," it is "constantly interrupted by subordinate units of qualification, as the poet thinks his way through the moral attitudes of an artifact" (*Our Secret Discipline* 42).

48. That Yeats composed this poem in 1929, in dire illness ("Malta fever" or brucellosis) is the logic for its longing for a life purged of mortal agonies; but it is also these agonies that motivated the composition.

49. Editors date this mysterious fragment late 1819; see H. B. Forman, *Keats* (1898) 417. I give Forman's transcription, because it is contemporaneous with Yeats's possible attention.

50. Reported by Joseph Severn, 1 June 1823; Rollins, *Keats Circle* 1:273. Keats was ruefully echoing Shakespeare: "Men's evil manners live in brass, their virtues / We write in water" (*King Henry VIII* 4.2; *Dramatick Writings* 15:100)—"in water" seeming the surface and the ink at once.

51. Pethica scans dimiter (*Last Poems* xli); Vendler, too (*Our Secret Discipline* 97).

52. Yeats, *Last Poems: Manuscript Materials* 18–19, 24–25. The draft on 18–19 reads, "Draw rain. Draw breath," as if a command to revivify.

53. *Timon of Athens*, near the end of act 5 (*Dramatick Writings* 17:102). Yeats's echoing was noted by H. J. Oliver (140).

54. Describing a genre of "self-elegy," Ramazani reads a speaker of "disembodied" authority, "outside of time," radically "self-alienated," in contradiction to the "rhetorical structure upon which the fiction of lyric self-identity is founded" (*Yeats* 148–49). I read a gambit of identity in rhetorical presence.

55. *Last Poems* 34–35; NLI 13,593 [52], 14ʳ. "WBY" is a signature autograph (e.g., *Per Amica* 98). "NLI" is National Library of Ireland.

56. Yeats discusses this notion in "An Introduction for My Plays" (1937), *E&I* 529–30.

57. For the etymology and earliest denotation, see OED. Yeats uses this sense of handwriting in the "characters" that I L L E traces on the sand in *Ego Dominus Tuus* (*Per Amica* 14–15). The sense of "engraving" appears in *Timon* as a mysterious "character" on a tomb (act 5).

After Wording

1. Quotations from Keats's letter follow Brown's transcription in *Life of John Keats,* f.34–f.36 (seq. 69, 71, 73). This sentence is on f.35 (seq. 71). This letter is also printed in *LJK* 2:359–60 and Rollins, *Keats Circle* 2:85–86.

2. Castle's "Phantasmagoria" (66–67) brought these pages to my attention. The Latin phrase, which she doesn't quote, is a conjuring from Thomas Hobbes, *De Corpore,* part IV, chapter 25, section 2. How apt that Dendy would translate *sentiendi* as "thinking" (rather than sensation).

3. The last lines in the 1842 version (1:184) and later delete the mention of Ithaca, and substitute "not wander more" for "return no more"—"return" seeming ever more ghostly a prospect in wandering.

4. De Quincey cites another authority, Sir David Brewster's *Letters on Natural Magic* ("Apparition" 748n). "Among the wonders of the natural world," writes this celebrated optic scientist and inventor of the kaleidoscope, "some are occasionally displayed which possess all the characters of supernatural phenomena," including "the Spectre of the Brocken." Brewster gives two reports, elaborated with a sketch marking out sun, Alps, cloud-mist, human figures, and spectral emanations, to show how the optical illusion is produced (127–30).

5. Johnson's Dictionary (p. 145) covers these bases: (1) appearance, visibility; (2) the thing appearing; (3) a spectre—this with a citation from *Hamlet:* "Horatio says 'tis but our phantasy, / Touching this dreaded sight twice seen of us; / Therefore I have intreated him, / That if again this *apparition* come, / He may approve our eyes, and speak to it" (compressing 1.1.30–36 in Johnson's edition of Shakespeare [18:8]).

6. I thank Ron Levao for catching this epic shade. I translate Dante's famous first lines, *Nel mezzo del cammin di nostra vita / mi ritrovai per una selva oscura,* to mirror Frost's situation.

7. Miller, "Two Forms of Repetition" 6, 9. Elsewhere Miller reads verbal negatives in Wordsworth's lyrics as forms of "double saying," the "unarticulated" indicated in "the articulate" through "devices of differentiation that are basic to poetry" ("Wordsworth" 68).

8. I thank Stan Plumly for getting me to pause over the dash.

9. Not alone in studying this dynamic in detail, I survey the territory, at least up to the end of the last century, in the first part of my chapter in *Formal Charges* on Wordsworth's thematizing of this compositional call.

10. I'm resorting to the OED: "Just," adv. 6a (for the regime of limitation).

11. By 1831, there had been a decade of reviews, popular reception, and stage versions, as well as other publications by Shelley: several novels and a posthumous edition of Percy Shelley's poems in 1824.

12. Charles Robinson, *Frankenstein Notebooks* 2:642–43. Alas, Robinson has just left our world (November 2016). He abides as a generous ghost for all our *Frankenstein* studies.

13. *Frankenstein* (1818) 3:192.

Bracketed attributions, when not self-evident, are derived from various scholarly editors, or later editions of the author.
Pseudonyms are given after a known author: [Last name, First name] Pseudonym.
&c in title: and other works
&c in publisher: and partners
edn.: edition
When a periodical is the primary citation, the listing is by periodical title. If a cross-reference is relevant, this is supplied.

Abrams, M. H. "The Correspondent Breeze: A Romantic Metaphor." 1957; revised for *English Romantic Poets: Modern Essays in Criticism*. Ed. M. H. Abrams. New York: Oxford UP, 1960. 37–54.
Aikin, Anna Laetitia (later Barbauld). "On the Pleasure Derived from Objects of Terror." J. and A. L. Aikin, *Miscellaneous Pieces, in Prose*. London: J. Johnson, 1773. 119–27.
Arnold, Matthew. "Byron." *Macmillan's Magazine* 53.257 (March 1881): 367–77.
———. *Essays in Criticism, Second Series*. London: Macmillan, 1888. "Byron" 153–204. "Shelley" 205–52.
———. Preface. *The Poetry of Byron*. London: Macmillan, 1881. vi–xxxi.
———. "Shelley." *The Nineteenth Century* 23 (1888): 1–39.
———. "Stanzas on the Grande Chartreuse." *Fraser's Magazine* 51 (April 1855).
Athenæum 252 (25 August 1832): 554–55. "Memoir of Shelley."
———. 262 (3 November 1832): 705. Review of Percy Bysshe Shelley, *The Masque of Anarchy*.
———. 267 (8 December 1832): 794. "Original Papers: 'LINES / Written during the Castlereagh Administration' / By the Late Percy Bysshe Shelley."
[Austen, Jane]. *Emma: A Novel in Three Volumes*. London: John Murray, 1815.
———. *Northanger Abbey*. 1818. *The Annotated Northanger Abbey*. Ed. Susan J. Wolfson. Cambridge, Harvard UP, 2014.
Bahti, Timothy. "Figures of Interpretation, The Interpretation of Figures: A Reading of Wordsworth's 'Dream of the Arab.'" *Studies in Romanticism* 18 (Winter 1979): 601–27.
———. "Wordsworth's Rhetorical Theft." *Romanticism and Language*, ed. Arden Reed. 82–124.
[Baillie, Joanna]. "Introductory Discourse." *A Series of Plays in Which it is Attempted to Delineate the Stronger Passions of the Mind*. London: T. Cadell Jr. and W. Davies, 1798.
[Barbauld, Anna Letitia]. "Washing-Day." *Monthly Magazine* 4 (December 1797): 452.
Barnard, John. "Hazlitt's *Liber Amoris; or, the New Pygmalion* (1823): Conversations and the Statue." *Translating Life: Studies in Transpositional Aesthetics*. Ed. Shirley Chew and Alistair Stead. Liverpool: Liverpool UP, 1999. 181–99.
Barthes, Roland. "La mort de l'auteur." 1968. Trans. Stephen Heath as "The Death of the Author." *Image-Music-Text*. London: Fontana / Glasgow: Collins, 1977. 142–48.
Barton, Bernard. "Verses to the Memory of Bloomfield, The Suffolk Poet." *Poetic Vigils*. London: Baldwin, Cradock, and Joy, 1824. 59–64.
Bate, Jonathan. *Shakespeare and the English Romantic Imagination*. Oxford: Clarendon P, 1986.
Bate, W. Jackson, and James Engell, eds. *Biographia Literaria*, by Samuel Taylor Coleridge. 2 vols. Princeton: Princeton UP, 1983.
Bates, Catherine. "The Point of Puns." *Modern Philology* 96.4 (May 1999): 421–38.
Bateson, F. W. *Wordsworth: A Re-Interpretation*. London: Longmans, Green, 1954.

Behrendt, Stephen C. *Shelley and His Audiences*. Lincoln: U of Nebraska P, 1989.

Bennett, Andrew. *Wordsworth Writing*. Cambridge: Cambridge UP, 2007.

Bentham, Jeremy. *Plan of Parliamentary reform in the form of a Catechism, with Reasons for Each Article, with an Introduction Showing the Necessity of Radical, and of the Inadequacy of Moderate, Reform*. London: R. Hunter, 1817.

Best, Stephen, and Sharon Marcus. "Surface Reading: An Introduction." *Representations* 108.1 (Fall 2009): 1–21.

Blackstone, William. *Commentaries on the Laws of England*. 4 books. Oxford: Clarendon P, 1765.

Blackwood's Edinburgh Magazine 13 (1823): 640–46. On [Hazlitt], *Liber Amoris*.

———. 16 (August 1824) 162–78. "Celebrated Female Writers. No I. Joanna Baillie."

Blake, William. *The Marriage of Heaven and Hell*. Printed c. 1790.

Blessington, Marguerite. *Conversations of Lord Byron with the Countess Blessington*. London: Henry Colburn, 1834.

Bloom, Harold. *The Anxiety of Influence: A Theory of Poetry*. New York: Oxford UP, 1973.

———. *A Map of Misreading*. New York: Oxford UP, 1975.

Bloomfield, Robert. *The Farmer's Boy; A Rural Poem*. 2nd edn. London: Vernor and Hood, 1800. "Spring," 4–23. "On Revisiting the Place of My Nativity," 100.

Book of Common Prayer, and Administration of the Sacraments and other Rites and Ceremonies of the Church. Cambridge stereotype. Cambridge University: R. Watts, 1808.

Booth, Stephen. *An Essay on Shakespeare's Sonnets*. New Haven: Yale UP, 1969.

———. ed., with analytic commentary. *Shake-speare's sonnets*. 1977; revised, New Haven: Yale UP, 1978.

Borges, Jorge Luis. "The Garden of the Forking Paths." Trans. Donald A. Yates, 1958. *Labyrinths: Selected Stories & Other Writings*. Ed. Donald A. Yates and James E. Irby. New York: New Directions, 1962. 19–29.

Bornstein, George. *Transformations of Romanticism*. Chicago: U of Chicago P, 1976.

———. *Yeats and Shelley*. Chicago: U of Chicago P, 1970.

Boswell, James. *The Life of Samuel Johnson, LL.D.* 2 vols. London: Henry Baldwin, 1791.

Botting, Fred. *Gothic*. New York: Routledge, 1996.

Boyd, Julian, and Zelda Boyd. "The Perfect of Experience." *Studies in Romanticism* 16 (1977): 3–13.

Brailsford, H. N. "Shelley." *Shelley, Godwin, and their Circle*. London: Williams and Norgate, 1913. 212–51.

Brewer, Rev. E. Cobham. *Character Sketches of Romance, Fiction and the Drama*. Vol 5. New York: Selmar Hess, 1892.

Brewster, David. "Letter VI. Natural phenomena marked with the marvelous." *Letters on Natural Magic*. London: John Murray, 1832. 127–56.

Bridges, Robert. "Critical Introduction." 1894. *The Poems of John Keats*. 2 vols. Ed. G. Thorn Drury. London: Lawrence and Bullen, 1896. 1:xiii–cv.

Bromwich, David. *Hazlitt: The Mind of a Critic*. New York: Oxford UP, 1983.

———. "The 'Ode to Duty' and the Idea of Human Solidarity." *The Wordsworth Circle* 40.1 (2009): 9–16.

Brooks, Cleanth. *The Well Wrought Urn: Studies in the Structures of Poetry*. 1947. San Diego: Harcourt Brace Jovanovich, 1975.

Brower, Reuben. *Alexander Pope: The Poetry of Allusion*. Oxford: Oxford UP, 1959.

Brown, Charles Armitage. *Life of John Keats*. A.MS.signed, no pn. 1836–1840. Harvard Keats Collection. MS Keats 4.3.27.

Brown, Sarah Annes. *A Familiar Compound Ghost: Allusion and the Uncanny*. Manchester: Manchester UP, 2012.

Bruton, F. A. *Three Accounts of Peterloo By Eyewitnesses.* Manchester: U of Manchester P / London: Longmans, 1921.

Bulwer-Lytton, Edward. "*Romance and Reality.* By L.E.L." *New Monthly Magazine* 32.132 (December 1831): 545–51.

Burdett, Francis. Comments, 3 January 1798. *Parliamentary Register.* 12 vols. London: J. Debrett, 1797–1802. 4:543.

Burke, Edmund. "Letter I: On the Overtures of Peace." *Two Letters Addressed to A Member of the Present Parliament, on the Proposals for Peace with the Regicide Directory of France.* 2nd edn.. London: Rivington, 1796.

———. *A philosophical enquiry into the origin of our ideas of the sublime and beautiful.* London: R. and J. Dodsley, 1757.

———. *Reflections on the Revolution in France.* 2nd edn. London: J. Dodsley, 1790.

Butler, Marilyn. "Satire and the Images of Self in the Romantic Period: The Long Tradition of Hazlitt's 'Liber Amoris.'" *Yearbook of English Studies* 14 (1984): 209–25.

Byron, George Gordon, Lord. *Byron's Letters and Journals.* 12 vols. Ed. Leslie A. Marchand. London: John Murray, 1973–82.

———. *Childe Harold's Pilgrimage, Canto the Fourth.* London: John Murray, 1818.

——— *The Complete Poetical Works.* 7 vols. Ed. Jerome J. McGann. Oxford: Clarendon P, 1980–93.

———. *Complete Works of Lord Byron.* Paris: Baudry's European Library, 1835.

——— *Complete Works of Lord Byron.* Paris: A. and W. Galignani, 1835.

———. *Don Juan. Complete Poetical Works*, ed. McGann, Vol. 5. 1986.

———. *Don Juan, Cantos X, XI, XII and XVII Manuscript.* Ed. Andrew Nicholson. New York: Garland P, 1993.

———. *Letters and Journals of Lord Byron: with Notices of His Life.* 2 vols. London: John Murray, 1830.

———. *Manfred, A Dramatic Poem.* London: John Murray, 1817. Line numbers from McGann, ed., *Complete Poetical Works*, vol. 4. 1986 .

———. *Mazeppa, A Poem.* London: John Murray, 1819.

———. *Miscellanies by Lord Byron.* 3 vols. London: John Murray, 1837.

[———]. Review of Wordsworth's *Poems, In Two Volumes. Monthly Literary Recreations* 13 (July 1807): 65–66.

———. *The Siege of Corinth, A Poem. / Parisina. A Poem.* London: John Murray, 1816. 1–57.

[———] Quevedo Redivivus. *The Vision of Judgment. The Liberal, Verse and Prose from the South* 1. 2nd edn. London: John Hunt, 1822. i–v and 1–39.

———. *The Works of Lord Byron.* 17 vols. Ed. Thomas Moore. London: John Murray, 1832–33.

———. *The Works of Lord Byron, with His Letters and Journals, and His Life.* 14 vols. Ed. Thomas Moore. London: John Murray, 1832.

Cadava, Eudardo. *Words of Light: Theses on the Photography of History.* Princeton: Princeton UP, 1998.

Cameron, Kenneth Neill. *Shelley: The Golden Years.* Cambridge: Harvard UP, 1974.

Campbell, Matthew. *Irish Poetry Under the Union, 1801–1924.* Cambridge: Cambridge UP, 2013.

Carlyle, Jane Welsh. *Early Letters of Jane Welsh Carlyle.* Ed. David George Ritchie. London: Swan Sonnenschein, 1889.

Castle, Terry. *The Female Thermometer: Eighteenth-Century Culture and the Invention of the Uncanny.* New York: Oxford UP, 1995.

———. "The Gothic Novel." *Cambridge History of English Literature, 1660–1780.* Cambridge: Cambridge UP, 2005.

———. "Phantasmagoria: Spectral Technology and the Metaphorics of Modern Reverie." *Critical Inquiry* 15.1 (1988): 26–61.

Cavell, Stanley. *The Claim of Reason: Wittgenstein, Skepticism, Morality, and Tragedy.* Oxford: Oxford UP, 1979.

———. "The Politics of Interpretation." *Themes Out of School: Effects and Causes.* Berkeley: U of California P, 1984. 27–59.

Chandler, James. *England in 1819: The Politics of Literary Culture and the Case of Romantic Historicism.* Chicago: U of Chicago P, 1998.

———. "Romantic Allusiveness." *Critical Inquiry* 8.3 (1982): 461–87.

Chase, Cynthia. "The Accidents of Figuration: Limits to Literal and Figurative Readings in Wordsworth's 'Books.'" *Decomposing Figures: Rhetorical Readings in the Romantic Tradition.* Ithaca: Cornell UP, 1986. 13–31.

———. "The Ring of Gyges and the Coat of Darkness: Reading Rousseau with Wordsworth." *Romanticism and Language,* ed. Arden Reed. 50–85.

Chatman, Seymour. *Story and Discourse: Narrative Structure in Fiction and Film.* Ithaca: Cornell UP, 1978.

Christensen, Jerome. *Lord Byron's Strength: Romantic Writing and Commercial Society.* Baltimore: Johns Hopkins UP, 1993.

The chronologist of the present war. Containing a faithful series of the events which have occurred in Europe, from the commencement of the year 1792, to the end of the year 1795. London: J. W. Myers, 1796.

Cobbett, William. *A Grammar of the English Language.* London: Thomas Dolby, 1819.

———. *The Works of Peter Porcupine.* Philadelphia: Thomas Bradford, 1795.

Coleridge, Samuel Taylor. "A Character." *Poetical Works.* 1834. 1835 edn. 2:137–39.

———. "Ad Vilmum Axiologum." *Complete Poetical Works,* 1893. 391–92.

———. *Aids to Reflection, in the Formation of a Manly Character.* London: Taylor and Hessey, 1825.

———. *Biographia Literaria; or, Biographical Sketches of My Literary Life and Opinions.* 2 vols. London: Rest Fenner, 1817.

———. *Christabel, Kubla Khan, and The Pains of Sleep.* London: John Murray, 1816.

———. *The Collected Letters of Samuel Taylor Coleridge.* Ed. Earl Leslie Griggs. 6 vols. Oxford: Clarendon P, 1956–71.

———. *The Collected Works of Samuel Taylor Coleridge: Poetical Works.* Ed. J. C. C. Mays. 2 Parts. Princeton: Princeton UP, 2001.

———. *The Complete Poetical Works of Samuel Taylor Coleridge: Including Poems and Versions of Poems now Published for the First Time.* Ed. Ernest Hartley Coleridge. Oxford: Oxford UP, 1893.

———. "Constancy to an Ideal Object." *Poetical Works,* 1834.

———. "Epitaph." *Poetical Works,* 1834. 1835 edn. 2:152.

———. Essay III ("my Ghost-Theory"). *The Friend: A Series of Essays in Three Volumes, to Aid in the Formation of Fixed Principles in Politics, Morals, and Religion, with Literary Amusements Interspersed.* 3 vols. London: Rest Fenner, 1818. 1:244–50. Developed from Essay V, *The Friend* 8 (5 October 1809): 114–28.

———. *Lectures 1808–1819, On Literature.* Ed. R. A. Foakes. 2 vols. Princeton: Princeton UP, 1987.

———. Lecture XII: "Dreams, Apparitions, &c." 1818. *The Literary Remains of Samuel Taylor Coleridge.* 4 vols. Ed. Henry Nelson Coleridge. Vol. 1. London: William Pickering, 1836. 201–16.

———. *Notebooks.* Ed. Kathleen Coburn. 2 vols. Princeton: Princeton UP, 1957.

———. *The Poetical Works of S. T. Coleridge.* 3 vols. London: W. Pickering. Vol. 1, 1828. Vol 2, 1829. Vol. 3, 1834 (actually published 1835).

[———.] Review of Ann Radcliffe's *The Mysteries of Udolpho. The Monthly Review or Critical Journal* 15 (November 1794): Article VIII: 278–83.

———. "Sonnet: To William Godwin, Author of *Political Justice.*" December 1794. *Morning Chronicle*, 10 January 1795.

———. *The Statesman's Manual; or The Bible The Best Guide to Political Skill and Foresight: A Lay Sermon, Addressed to the Higher Classes of Society.* London: Gale and Fenner, 1816.

———. "To a Gentleman." *Sibylline Leaves: A Collection of Poems.* London: Rest Fenner, 1817. 197–203.

———. "To William Wordsworth." Wordsworth, *The Prelude,* ed. Wordsworth, Abrams, and Gill, 542–45.

———. *Unpublished Letters.* Ed. Earl Leslie Griggs. London: Constable, 1933.

Collier, John Payne. *An Old Man's Diary, Forty Years Ago.* 4 Parts. Part 4: *For the Last Six Months of 1833.* London: Thomas Richards, for private circulation, 1872.

Colvin, Sidney. *John Keats/His Life and Poetry/His Friends Critics and After-Fame.* London: Macmillan, 1917.

———. "On Some Letters of Keats." *Macmillan Magazine* 58 (August 1888): 311–20.

Conrad, Joseph. *Joseph Conrad's Letters to R. B. Cunninghame Graham.* Ed. C. T. Watts. Cambridge: Cambridge UP, 1969.

Cook, Eleanor. *Against Coercion: Games Poets Play.* Stanford: Stanford UP, 1998.

———. "Ghost Rhymes and How They Work." Cook, 223–34.

———. "*Methought* as Dream Formula in Shakespeare, Milton, Wordsworth, Keats, and Others." *English Language Notes* 32.4 (1995): 34–46.

———. "Questions of Allusion." Cook, 99–106.

Cornwall, Barry [Bryan Waller Procter]. *A Sicilian Story.* 2nd edn. London: C. and J. Ollier, 1820.

Cowper, William. *The Task, a poem in six books.* London: J. Johnson, 1785.

Craig, Edward Gordon. "The Ghosts in the Tragedies of Shakespeare." *On the Art of the Theatre.* Chicago: Brown's Book Store, 1911.

Culler, Jonathan. "Apostrophe." *diacritics* 7.4 (1977): 59–69.

———. "The Call of the Phoneme." *On Puns: The Foundation of Letters.* Ed. Jonathan Culler. New York: Basil Blackwell, 1988. 1–16.

———. *Ferdinand de Saussure.* 1976; revised, Ithaca: Cornell UP, 1987.

Curran, Stuart. *Poetic Form and British Romanticism.* Oxford: Oxford UP, 1986.

———. *Shelley's Annus Mirabilis: The Maturing of an Epic Vision.* San Marino: Huntington Library, 1975.

Davies, Hugh Sykes. *Wordsworth and the Worth of Words.* Ed. John Kerrigan and Jonathan Wordsworth. Cambridge: Cambridge UP, 1986.

Davies, Owen. *The Haunted: A Social History of Ghosts.* New York: Palgrave Macmillan, 2007.

De Man, Paul. "Autobiography as De-facement." *MLN* 94.5 (1979): 919–30.

———. *Blindness and Insight: Essays in the Rhetoric of Contemporary Criticism.* 2nd edn. Minneapolis: U of Minnesota P, 1983. 142–65.

———. "Literary History and Literary Modernity." 1971. *Blindness and Insight,* 142–65.

———. *The Rhetoric of Romanticism.* New York: Columbia UP, 1984.

———. "The Rhetoric of Temporality." 1969. *Blindness and Insight,* 187–228.

Dendy, Walter Cooper. *The Philosophy of Mystery.* London: Longman & c, 1841.

[De Quincey, Thomas]. "The Apparition of the Brocken." *Suspiria de Profundis: Being a Sequel to the Confessions of an English Opium-Eater. Blackwood's Edinburgh Magazine* 47 (June 1845): 747–50.

———. *Autobiographic Sketches, 1790–1803.* Edinburgh: Adam and Charles Black, 1852.

[———]. *Confessions of an English Opium-Eater, Being an Extract from the Life of Scholar.* Part II. *London Magazine* 4.22 (October 1821): 353–79.

[——] The English Opium-Eater. "Lake Reminiscences, from 1807 to 1830: William Wordsworth." *Tait's Edinburgh Magazine* 6.39 (February 1839): 90–103.

[——]. *North British Review* 9.18 (August 1848): 163–82. Article I: review of W. Roscoe's 8 vol. 1847 edition of *The Works of Alexander Pope*. Attribution: Vol. 8, *De Quincey's Works*. Edinburgh: Adam and Charles Black, 1862.

Derrida, Jacques. *Signéponge /Signsponge*. Trans. Richard Rand. New York: Columbia UP, 1984.

——. *Specters of Marx: the state of debt, the work of mourning, and the New International*. Trans. Peggy Kamuf. New York: Routledge, 1994. Originally published as *Spectres de Marx: l'état de la dette, le travail du deuil et la nouvelle Internationale*. Paris: Éditions Galileé, 1993.

De Selincourt, Ernest, ed. *The Prelude; or, Growth of a Poet's Mind, by William Wordsworth.* 1926; revised edn. Mary Moorman. Oxford: Oxford UP, 1959.

Dexter, Pete. "The Old Man and the River." *Esquire Magazine* 95.6 (June 1981).

[Dickens, Charles] Boz. *The Posthumous Papers of the Pickwick Club.* 1837. 2 vols. Paris: A. and W. Galignani, 1838.

Donne, John. "A Hymne to God the Father." 1623. *Poems by John Donne*. London: Iohn Marriot 1633. 350.

Drayton, Michael. *Poly-Olbion: A Chronologic Description of Great Britain*. 1612. Stratford Upon Avon: Shakespeare Head Press by Blackwell, 1961.

DuQuette, Lon Milo, and Christopher S. Hyatt. *Aleister Crowley's Illustrated Goetia*. Tempe: New Falcon, 1992.

Eco, Umberto. "Overinterpreting Texts." *Interpretation and Overinterpretation*. Ed. Stefan Collini. Cambridge: Cambridge UP, 1992. 45–66.

Edinburgh Magazine and Literary Miscellany 10 (June 1822): 742–45. "On Auto-Biography."

Edinburgh Review 28.56 (Aug. 1817): 418–31. [Francis Jeffrey], Art. VII: on Byron's *Manfred*.

——. 28.56 (August 1817): 488–515. [William Hazlitt], Art. X: on Coleridge's *Biographia Literaria*.

Edwards, Thomas R. *Imagination and Power: A Study of Poetry on Public Themes*. New York: Oxford UP, 1971.

Elfenbein, Andrew. *Byron and the Victorians*. Cambridge: Cambridge UP, 1995.

——. "On the Discrimination of Influences." *Modern Language Quarterly* 69.4 (2008): 481–507.

——. *Romanticism and the Rise of English*. Stanford: Stanford UP, 2009.

Eliot, T. S. *A Choice of Kipling's Verse*. London: Faber and Faber, 1941.

——. "Tradition and the Individual Talent." 1917. *Essays on Poetry and Criticism*. New York: Alfred A. Knopf, 1921. 42–53.

Ellmann, Richard. *Oscar Wilde*. New York: Vintage, 1987.

——. *Yeats: The Man and the Masks*. 1948; New York: Norton, 1978.

Empson, William. "Honest in Othello." *Complex Words*, chapter 11, 218–49.

——. *Milton's God*. London: Chatto and Windus, 1961.

——. "Sense in *The Prelude*." *Complex Words*, chapter 14, 289–30.

——. *Seven Types of Ambiguity*. 1930. Cleveland: World, 1955.

——. *The Structure of Complex Words*. London: Chatto and Windus, 1951.

Erdman, David V. "Wordsworth as Heartsworth." *The Evidence of the Imagination: Studies of Interactions between Life and Art in English Romantic Fiction*. Ed. Donald H. Reiman, Michael C. Jaye, and Betty T. Bennett. New York: New York UP, 1978. 12–41.

Erdman, David V., ed. *Samuel Taylor Coleridge: Essays on His Times in* The Morning Post *and* The Courier. 3 vols. Princeton: Princeton UP, Bollingen, 1978.

Evans, B. Ifor. "Keats as a Medical Student." Letter to *TLS*, 31 May 1934. 391.

Examiner 608 (August 22, 1819): 529–31. [Leigh Hunt], "Disturbances at Manchester."

Favret, Mary A., and Nicola J. Watson, eds. *The Limits of Romanticism: Essays in Cultural, Feminist, and Materialist Criticism.* Bloomington: Indiana UP, 1994.

Felski, Rita. *The Limits of Critique.* Chicago: U of Chicago P, 2015.

Ferguson, Frances. *Language as Counter-Spirit.* New Haven: Yale UP, 1978.

Ferriar, John, M.D. *An Essay Towards a Theory of Apparitions.* London: Cadell and Davies, 1813.

[Fessenden, Thomas Green] Christopher Caustic. *Terrible Tractoration and Other Poems.* 4th American edn. Boston: Samuel Colman, 1837.

Fisher's Drawing-Room Scrap Book for MDCCXL. London: Fisher, Son & Co., 1840.

Foot, Paul. "*New Statesman,* Decline and Fall." *Socialist Review* 201 (October 1996): 21.

———. *Red Shelley.* London: Sidgwick and Jackson, 1980.

———. *Shelley's Revolutionary Year: The Peterloo Writings of the Poet Shelley.* London: Redwords, 1990.

Freud, Sigmund. *Jokes and Their Relation to the Unconscious.* 1905. Trans. James Strachey, 1960. New York: Norton, 1963.

———. "The Uncanny." First published as "Das Unheimliche." *Imago.* 1919. Trans. Alix Strachey, 1925. *On Creativity and the Unconscious: Papers on the Psychology of Art, Literature, Love, Religion.* New York: Harper & Row, 1958. 122–61.

Frost, Robert. "Being Let In On Symbols." Lecture, Bread Loaf School of English, 25 June 1953. Tape, with typographical transcription by India Tressault. Abernethy Manuscripts, Middlebury College, Middlebury, Vermont.

———. *The Letters of Robert Frost: The Early Years: 1886–1912.* Ed. Donald Sheehy, Mark Richardson, and Robert Faggen. Cambridge: Harvard UP, 2014.

———. "The Road Not Taken." *Mountain Interval.* New York: Henry Holt, 1916. 9.

Froude, James Anthony. *Thomas Carlyle: A History of First Forty Years of his Life, 1795–1835.* 2 vols. London: Longman, 1891.

———. *Thomas Carlyle, A History of His Life in London 1834–1881.* 2 vols. London: Longmans, 1885.

Galperin, William H. *The Historical Austen.* Philadelphia: U of Pennsylvania P, 2003.

Garber, Marjorie. *Shakespeare's Ghost Writers: Literature as uncanny causality.* 1987. New expanded edn. New York: Routledge, 2010.

Gentleman's Magazine and Historical Chronicle 32 (February 1763): 81–82. "An Account of the Detection of the Imposture in Cock-Lane." [Dr. Samuel Johnson].

———. "A Present to the renowned Society of ghost-mongers, and particularly to the Clergyman their Secretary." 82–84.

———. 89 [126] Part 2 (September 1819) 269. "Occurrences in London and its Vicinity."

Gentleman's Magazine and Historical Review 34 (November 1850) 459–68. "Wordsworth's Autobiographical Poem."

Gifford, John, Esq. *The reign of Louis the Sixteenth; and complete history of the French Revolution. With notes, critical and explanatory.* London: C. Lowndes, 1794.

Gillman, James. *The Life of Samuel Taylor Coleridge.* London: William Pickering, 1838.

Gittings, Robert. "Keats and Cats." *The Happy Fireside: Romantic Poems about Dogs and Cats.* Selected and introduced by Duncan Wu. Rome: Keats-Shelley House, 2011. 63–76.

Goldsmith, Stephen. *Unbinding Jerusalem: Apocalypse and Romantic Imagination.* Ithaca: Cornell UP, 1993.

Good, James. M. "William Taylor, Robert Southey, and the Word 'Autobiography.'" *The Wordsworth Circle* 12.2 (1981): 125–27.

Goodson, A. C. *Verbal Imagination: Coleridge & the Language of Modern Criticism.* New York: Oxford UP, 1988.

Gray, Thomas. *The Bard: A Pindaric Ode.* 1757. *Poems by Mr. Gray.* London: J. Murray, 1776. 65–79.

Grosart, Alexander B., ed. *The Prose Works of William Wordsworth, for the first time collected, with additions from unpublished manuscripts.* 3 vols. London: Edward Moxon, 1876. Vol. 2: *Aesthetical and Literary.*

[Hallam, A. H.]. "On Some of the Characteristics of Modern Poetry, and on the Lyrical Poems of Alfred Tennyson." *The Englishman's Magazine* 1.5 (August 1831)· 616–28.

Hartman, Geoffrey H. "Gods, Ghosts, and Shelley's 'Atheos.'" *Literature & Theology* 24.1 (March 2010): 4–18.

——. "Spectral Symbolism and Authorial Self in Keats's *Hyperion.*" 1974. *The Fate of Reading and Other Essays.* Chicago: U of Chicago P, 1975. 57–73.

——. "The Voice of the Shuttle." 1969. *Beyond Formalism.* New Haven: Yale UP, 1970. 337–55.

——. "Words, Wish, Worth: Wordsworth." *De-Construction & Criticism.* New York: Continuum, 1979. 177–216.

——. *Wordsworth's Poetry, 1787–1814.* 1964. New edn.; New Haven: Yale UP, 1975.

Hays, Mary. *Memoirs of Emma Courtney.* 2 vols. London: G. G. and J. Robinson, 1796.

Hazlitt, William. *The Characters of Shakespear's Plays.* London: several booksellers, 1817.

—— *The Collected Works of William Hazlitt.* Ed. A. R. Waller and Arnold Glover. 12 vols. London: J. M. Dent, 1904.

[——]. *Edinburgh Review, or Critical Journal* 27.54 (December 1816): 444–59. Article VIII: on S. T. Coleridge, *The Statesman's Manual.*

[——]. *Edinburgh Review* 28.56 (August 1817): 488–515. Article X: "Coleridge's Literary Life." Attribution: *BL*, ed. Bate and Engell. lxv.

[——]. *Edinburgh Review* 40.80 (July 1824): 494–514. Art. X: on Shelley, *Posthumous Poems*, ed. Mrs. [Mary W.] Shelley.

[——]. *The Examiner,* 8 September 1816. "Literary Notices No. 11": on the advertisement of Coleridge, *A Lay-Sermon on the Distresses of the Country, Addressed to the Middle and Higher Orders.* Reprinted in *Political Essays,* 118–24.

[——]. *The Examiner,* 29 December 1816. "Literary Notices No. 21": on Coleridge, *Statesman's Manual.* 125–36.

——. *Lectures Chiefly on the Dramatic Literature of the Age of Elizabeth Delivered at the Surrey Institution.* London: Stodart and Steuart, 1820.

——. *Lectures on the English Poets. Delivered at the Surrey Institution.* London: Taylor and Hessey, 1818.

——. *The Letters of William Hazlitt.* Ed. Herschel Moreland Sikes, with Willard Hallam Bonner and Gerald Lahey. New York: New York UP, 1978.

[——]. *Liber Amoris; or, The New Pygmalion.* London: John Hunt, [9 May] 1823. Hazlitt's authorship was transparent to the first reviewers.

——. "On the Living Poets." *Lectures on the English Poets.* 283–331.

[——] SEMPER EGO AUDITOR. "Mr. Coleridge's Lay-Sermon." To the Editor of *The Examiner,* 12 January 1817. Reprinted in *Political Essays,* 137–39.

——. "Mr. Coleridge's Lectures." *Yellow Dwarf,* 21 February 1818. *Fugitive Writings,* in *Collected Works of William Hazlitt,* ed. Waller and Glover. 11:416–19.

[——] W.H. "My first Acquaintance with Poets." *The Liberal: Verse and Prose from the South* III. London: John Hunt, [ca. 23–26 April] 1823. 23–46.

——. W.H. "On the Character of Rousseau." *The Examiner,* 14 April 1816. Reprinted in *Round Table* 2:45–55.

[——] T. "On the Conversation of Authors." *Table-Talk* No. III. *London Magazine* 1.7 (September 1820): 230–62.

——. "On the English Novelists." Lecture VI, *Lectures on the English Comic Writers.* London: Taylor and Hessey, 1819. 208–65.

[——] T. "On going a Journey." *Table-Talk* No. I. *New Monthly Magazine* 4 (January 1822): 73–79.

——. "On living to one's self." *Table-Talk* (1821). 211–33.

[——] W.H. "On Mr. Wordsworth's *Excursion.*" *The Examiner*, 28 August 1814. 555–58. Reprinted as "Observations on Mr. Wordsworth's Poem, 'The Excursion.'" *The Round Table* 2:95–112.

——. "On Paradox and Common-place." *Table-Talk* (1821). 349–72.

[——] T. "On People of Sense." *Table-Talk* No. IX. *London Magazine* 3.16 (April 1821): 370–71.

[——] T. "On the Qualifications Necessary to Success in Life." *Table-Talk* No. I. *London Magazine* 1.6 (June 1820): 646–54.

[——] T. "On Reading Old Books." *Table-Talk* No. VII. *London Magazine* 3.14 (February 1821): 128–34.

——. "On the Living Poets." *Lectures on the English Poets*, 283–331.

——. "Othello." *Characters of Shakespear's Plays.* 1817. London: Taylor and Hessey, 1818. 42–60.

——. *Political Essays, With Sketches of Public Characters.* London: William Hone, 1819.

——. *The Round Table: A Collection of Essays on Literature, Men, and Manners.* 2 vols. Edinburgh: Archibald Constable, 1817.

——. *Select British Poets: Or New Elegant Extracts from Chaucer to the Present Time: With Critical Remarks.* London: Wm. C. Hall, 1824.

——. *The Spirit of the Age, or Contemporary Portraits.* London: Henry Colburn, 1825.

——. *Table-Talk; or, Original Essays.* London: John Warren, 1821.

Heaney, Seamus. *The Redress of Poetry.* London: Farrar, Straus, and Giroux, 1995.

Hinds, Stephen. *Allusion and Intertext: Dynamics of Appropriation in Roman Poetry.* Cambridge: Cambridge UP, 1998.

Hofkosh, Sonia. "Broken Images." *Nineteenth-Century Prose* 36.1 (2009): 27–54.

——. *Sexual Politics and the Romantic Author.* Cambridge: Cambridge UP, 1998.

Hollander, John. *The Figure of Echo: A Mode of Allusion in Milton and After.* 1981. Berkeley: U of California P, 1984.

——. *Melodious Guile: Fictive Pattern in Poetic Language.* New Haven, CT: Yale UP, 1988.

——. *The Substance of Shadow: A Darkening Trope in Poetic History.* Ed. Kenneth Gross. Chicago: U of Chicago Press, 2016.

Holmes, Richard. *Shelley: The Pursuit.* 1974. New York: E. P. Dutton, 1975.

Hopps, Gavin, ed. *Byron's Ghosts.* Liverpool: U of Liverpool P, 2013.

Howe, P. P., ed. *The Complete Works of William Hazlitt.* 21 vols. 1930–34. New York: AMS P, 1967.

Howell, Margaret J. "Manfred Transformed." *Byron Tonight: A Poet's Plays on the Nineteenth Century Stage.* Windlesham, Surrey: Springwood, 1982. 95–120.

Hudson, William Henry. "Thomas Hood: the Man, the Wit, and the Poet." *A Quiet Corner in a Library.* Chicago: Rand McNally, 1915. 1–58.

Hunt, Leigh. *The Autobiography of Leigh Hunt, with Reminiscences of Friends and Contemporaries.* 2 vols. London: Smith Elder, 1850.

[——]. "Disturbances at Manchester." *Examiner* 608. 22 August 1819: 529–31.

——. *Lord Byron and Some of his Contemporaries.* London: Henry Colburn, 1828.

[——]. "Young Poets." *Examiner* 466, 1 December 1816. 761–62.

Hunt, Leigh, ed. *The Masque of Anarchy. A Poem. By Percy Bysshe Shelley*/NOW FIRST PUBLISHED. London: Edward Moxon, 1832.

[Irving, Washington]. *Newstead Abbey.* London: John Murray, 1835. *The Crayon Miscellany*, No. 2. Philadelphia: Carey, Lea, and Blanchard, 1835. 95–230.

Jacobus, Mary. "'That Great Stage Where Senators Perform': 'Macbeth' and the Politics of Romantic Theatre." *Studies in Romanticism* 22.3 (1983): 353–8.

———. "The Art of Managing Books." *Romanticism and Language*. Ed. Reed. 215–46.

———. "Wordsworth and the Language of the Dream." *ELH* 46 (1979): 618–44.

———. "The Writing on the Wall: Autobiography and Self-Inscription in *The Prelude*." *Romanticism, Writing, and Sexual Difference: Essays on* The Prelude. Oxford: Clarendon P, 2002. 3–32.

Jameson, Fredric. *Marxism and Form: Twentieth-Century Dialectical Theories of Literature*. Princeton,: Princeton UP, 1971.

Janowitz, Anne. "'A Voice from across the Sea': Communitarianism at the Limits of Romanticism." Favret and Watson, eds. 83–100.

Jeffares, A. Norman. *A Commentary on the Collected Poems of W. B. Yeats*. Stanford: Stanford UP, 1968.

[Jeffrey, Francis]. *Edinburgh Review* 28.56 (August 1817): 418–31. Article VII: on Byron's *Manfred*.

Johnson, Claudia L. *Women, Politics, and the Novel*. Chicago: U of Chicago P, 1988.

Johnson, Samuel. *A Dictionary of the English language . . . illustrated in their different significations by examples from the best writers*. 2 vols. London: Longman, 1755.

[———]. "An account of the Detection of the Imposture in *Cock-Lane*." See *Gentleman's Magazine* 32 (February 1763).

Jones, Ernest. "Œdipus-complex as an Explanation of Hamlet's Mystery: A Study in Motive." *The American Journal of Psychology* 21 (January 1910): 72–113. Developed into *Hamlet and Oedipus* (1949).

Jonson, Ben. *Poetaster or His Arraignment: A Comical Satire. Works*. Ed. H. C. Hart. 2 vols. London: Methuen, 1906. 2:93–174.

Joyce, James. *Ulysses*. 1922. New York: Random House, 1961.

Keach, William. *Arbitrary Power: Romanticism, Language, Politics*. Princeton: Princeton UP 2004.

———. "The political poet." *The Cambridge Companion to Shelley*. Ed. Timothy Morton. Cambridge: Cambridge UP, 2006. 123–41.

———. "Radical Shelley?" *Raritan* 5.2 (1985): 120–29.

———. "Rise Like Lions? Shelley and the Revolutionary Left." *International Socialism* 2.75 (1997). https://www.marxists.org/history/etol/newspape/isj2/1997/isj2-075/keach.htm. Accessed August 22, 2017.

———. *Shelley's Style*. London: Methuen, 1984.

———. "Words are Things." *Arbitrary Power*, 23–45.

Keach, William, ed. *The Complete Poems of Samuel Taylor Coleridge*. London: Penguin, 1997.

Keats, John. *Endymion, A Poetic Romance*. London: Taylor and Hessey, 1818.

———. *John Keats: A Longman Cultural Edition*. Ed. Susan J. Wolfson. New York: Pearson, 2007.

———. *The Letters of John Keats*. Ed. Hyder E. Rollins. 2 vols. Cambridge: Harvard UP, 1958.

———. *The Letters of John Keats: Complete Revised Edition*. Ed. H. Buxton Forman. London: Reeves and Turner, 1895.

———. *Letters of John Keats to His Family and Friends*. Ed. Sidney Colvin. London: Macmillan, 1891.

———. *Life, Letters, and Literary Remains of John Keats*. Ed. R. M. Milnes. 2 vols. London: Edward Moxon, 1848.

———. *Poems of Keats*. Selected by Arthur Symons. Edinburgh: T. C. and E. C. Jack, 1900.

———. *The Poetical Works of John Keats*. Ed. Lord Hughton [R. M. Milnes]. London: George Bell, 1891.

———. *The Poetical Works of John Keats, Given from His Own Editions and Other Authentic Sources and Collated with Many Manuscripts*. Ed. H. Buxton Forman. 1895; 6th edn., London: Reeves and Turner, 1898.

———. MS. Keats's marked copy of *The Dramatic Works of William Shakspeare*. 7 vols. London: Chiswick P, 1814. Harvard Keats Collection. *EC8 K2262 Zz814s.

Kenyon-Jones, Christine, ed. *Byron: the Image of the Poet*. Newark: U of Delaware P, 2008.

Kirsch, Adam. Review of Christopher Ricks, *True Friendship*. *New York Review of Books* 57.6 (8 April 2010): 75–80.

Knoepflmacher, U. C. *Victorians Reading the Romantics: Essays of U. C. Knoepflmacher*. Ed. Linda Shires. Columbus: Ohio State UP, 2016.

L.E.L. [Letitia Elizabeth Landon]. "The Portrait of Lord Byron at Newstead Abbey." *Fisher's Drawing-Room Scrap-Book*. London: Fisher, 1840. 11–14.

Laclau, Ernesto. *Emancipation(s)*. New York: Verso, 1996.

Lamb, Charles. *The Letters of Charles and Mary Lamb*. Ed. Edwin W. Marrs Jr. 3 vols. Ithaca: Cornell UP, 1975–78.

Leavis, F. R. "Revaluations VIII: Shelley." *Scrutiny* 4.2 (1935): 159–61.

Leighton, Angela. *On Form: Poetry, Aestheticism, and the Legacy of a Word*. Oxford: Oxford UP, 2007.

Levao, Ronald. "'They Hate Us Youth': Byron's Falstaff." *Literary Imagination* 11.2 (2009): 127–35.

Levine, George. "Translating the Monstrous: *Northanger Abbey*." *Nineteenth-Century Fiction* 30 (1975): 335–50.

L[ewes], G. H. "Percy Bysshe Shelley." *Westminster Review* 35 (April 1841): 154–74.

The Literary Gazette, Journal of Belles Lettres, Politics, and Fashion 29 (9 August 1817): 83–85. On Coleridge's *Biographia Literaria*.

The Literary Gazette, and Journal of the Belles Lettres, Arts, Sciences, &c 167 (1 April 1820): 209–11. On P. B. Shelley, *The Cenci*.

——— 828 (1 December 1832): 758–59. On vol. 12, Thomas Moore, *Life and Works of Lord Byron*. London: John Murray, 1832.

Locke, John. *Essay Concerning Human Understanding, / In Four Books*. 2 vols. 1690. London: several printers, 1775.

London Magazine 9 (March 1824) 253–56. "On Ghosts." See Mary Shelley.

"Lord Byron in the Other World." [?by W. Davenport]. *The Book of Spirits, and Tales from the Dead*. London: William Charlton Wright [?]1825–27.

Lovejoy, Arthur O. "On the Discrimination of Romanticisms." *PMLA* 39.2 (1924): 229–53.

Maclean, Norman. *A River Runs Through It and Other Stories*. Chicago: U of Chicago P, 1976.

Mahoney, Charles. "*Liber Amoris*: Figuring Out the Coquette." *European Romantic Review* 10.1 (1999): 23–52.

Manning, Peter J. *Byron and His Fictions*. Detroit: Wayne State UP, 1978.

Marx, Karl. *The Eighteenth Brumaire of Louis Napoleon*. 1852. Trans. Daniel De Leon. 1897. 3rd edn. Chicago: Charles H. Kerr, 1913.

Marx, Karl and Frederick Engels. *Manifesto of the Communist Party*. 1848. Trans. Samuel Moore, 1888. Ed. Frederick Engels. Chicago: Charles H. Kerr, 1905.

Maxwell-Stuart, P. G. *Ghosts: A History of Phantoms, Ghouls & Other Spirits of the Dead*. Gloucestershire: Tempus: History P, 2007.

McDonald, Peter. *Sound Intentions*. Oxford: Oxford UP, 2012.

McGann, Jerome J. "The Book of Byron and the Book of a World." *The Beauty of Inflections: Literary Investigations in Historical Method & Theory*. 1985. Oxford: Clarendon P, 1988. 255–93.

———. *Byron and Romanticism*. Ed. James Soderholm. Cambridge: Cambridge UP, 2002.

———. *The Romantic Ideology*. Chicago: U of Chicago P, 1983.

Melchiori, Barbara. "Lord Byron Among the Ghosts." *Arte e Letteratura: Scritti in ricordo di Gabriele Baldini*. Roma: Edizioni di Storia e Letteratura, 1972. 241–57.

Miles, Robert. *Gothic writing: A Genealogy 1750–1820*. 1993. Manchester: Manchester UP, 2002.

Miller, J. Hillis. "Two Forms of Repetition." *Fiction and Repetition*. Cambridge: Harvard UP, 1982. 1–21.

———. "Wordsworth." *The Linguistic Moment*. Princeton: Princeton UP, 1985. 59–113.

Milnes, Richard Monckton. "Memoir of John Keats." *The Poetical Works of John Keats*. London: Edward Moxon, 1854. i–xl.

Milton, John. *Areopagitica; A Speech of John Milton for the Liberty of Unlicensed Printing, to the Parliament of England*. London, 1644.

——— *The Doctrine and Discipline of Divorce*. John Milton, 696–715.

———. *Complete Poems and Major Prose*. Ed. Merritt Y. Hughes. New York: Odyssey P, 1957.

———. *Paradise Lost. A Poem in Twelve Books*. 2d edn., revised and augmented. London 1674. *Poetical Works*, ed. Beeching.

———. *Poetical Works*. Ed. H. C. Beeching. 1900. Oxford: Oxford UP, 1922.

———. *The reason of church-government urg'd against prelaty*. 2 books. London: E. G. for Iohn Rothwell, 1641.

Mitford, Mary Russell. *Blanch; A Poem in Four Cantos. Narrative Poems on the Female Character, in the Various Relations of Life*. London: Rivington, 1813. 1–160.

Mole, Tom. "Ways of Seeing Byron." Kenyon-Jones, ed., 68–78.

Monthly Magazine (August 1797): 102–3. "Terrorist System of Novel-writing." Letter from "A Jacobin Novelist."

Monthly Magazine, or British Register 48. Part 2 (October 1819): 280. "Incidents . . . in and near London."

Monthly Review; or Literary Journal 15 (1794): 278–83. Art. VIII: on Radcliffe, *The Mysteries of Udolpho*.

Monthly Review. 2nd ser. 94 (February 1821): 162. Review of Shelley, *The Cenci*.

[Moore, Thomas] Thomas Brown, the Younger. *The Fudges in England*. 2nd edn. London: Longman &c, 1835.

Moore, Thomas. *The Journal of Thomas Moore*. 5 vols. 1836–42. Ed. Wilfred S. Dowden. Cranbury: Associated UPs, 1988.

———. *Letters and Journals of Lord Byron: with Notices of His Life*. 2 vols. London: John Murray, 1830.

———. *M. P. or the Blue-Stocking, A Comic Opera, in Three Acts*. London: J. Power &c, 1811.

———. *The Works of Lord Byron, With His Letters and Journals, and His Life*. 14 vols. London: John Murray, 1832. 17 vols. London: John Murray, 1832–33. Reprinted at least through 1848.

Moorman, Mary. *William Wordsworth: A Biography. The Early Years, 1770–1803*. Oxford: Clarendon P, 1957.

More, Paul Elmore. "The Wholesome Revival of Byron." *Atlantic Monthly* 82.494 (1898): 801–11.

Moretti, Franco. *Distant Reading*. London: Verso, 2013.

Murray, John. *The Letters of John Murray to Lord Byron*. Ed. Andrew Nicholson. Liverpool: Liverpool UP, 2007.

Murray, Lindley. *English grammar, adapted to the different classes of learners*. 1795. York: Wilson, Spence, and Mawman, 1798.

New Monthly Magazine 43.8 (1 August 1817): 50. On S. T Coleridge's *Biographia Literaria*.

———n.s. 29.2 (1830): 327–37. [? Mary Shelley], "Byron and Shelley on the Character of Hamlet."

New Statesman, 27 June 2017. http://www.newstatesman.com/politics/uk/2017/06. " 'Rise like lions after slumber': why do Jeremy Corbyn and co keep reciting a 19th century poem? How a passage from Percy Shelley's *The Masque of Anarchy* became Labour's battle cry."

Norris, Christopher. "Names." *London Review of Books,* 20 February 1986. 10–12.

Oliver, H. J., ed. William Shakespeare, *Timon of Athens.* Arden Edition. London: Methuen, 1963.

Ou, Li. *Keats and Negative Capability.* London: Continuum, 2009.

Paine, Thomas. *Rights of Man: Being an Answer to Mr. Burke's Attack on the French Revolution.* London: J. Johnson, 1791.

Paley, Morton D. *Coleridge's Later Poetry.* Oxford: Clarendon, 1996.

The Parliamentary register; or, history of the proceedings and debates of the House of Commons. 12 vols. London: J. Debrett, 1797–1802.

Partridge, Eric. *The Concise Usage and Abusage: A Modern Guide to Good English.* 1951. London: Hamish Hamilton, 1954.

Peacock, Thomas. *Nightmare Abbey.* London: T. Hookham, 1818.

Pethica, James. Introduction. *Yeats's Poetry, Drama, and Prose: A Norton Critical Edition.* New York: W. W. Norton, 2000. xi–xx. See also Yeats, *Last Poems.*

Phillipson, M. "Byron's Revisited Haunts." *Studies in Romanticism* 39 (2000): 303–22.

Pinion, F. B. *A Wordsworth Chronology.* Boston: G. K. Hall, 1988.

Plumly, Stanley. *Posthumous Keats.* New York: Norton, 2008.

Poe, Edgar Allan. *An Essay on the Poetic Principle.* 1849. *The Poetical Works of Edgar Allan Poe.* New York: J. S. Redfield, 1858. 217–47.

Polidori, John. *The Diary of John Polidori.* Ed. William Michael Rossetti. London: Elkin Mathew, 1911.

Pope, Alexander. "Epistle to Robert, Earl of Oxford and Earl of Mortimer, Prefixed to Parnelle's *Poems.*" *Works of Alexander Pope.* 9 vols. London: A. Millar & c, 1760. 6:41.

———. *An Essay on Man.* 1732. Dublin: S. Powell, 1733.

———. *Ode for musick on St. Cecilia's Day.* 3rd edn. London: Bernard Lintot, 1719.

Prince, Gerald. "The Disnarrated." *Style* 22.1 (Spring 1988): 1–8.

Prynne, J. H. *Stars, Tigers and the Shape of Words.* London: Birkbeck College, 1993.

Pucci, Joseph. *The Full-Knowing Reader: Allusion and the Power of the Reader in the Western Literary Tradition.* New Haven: Yale UP, 1998.

Quevedo Redivivus, *A Spiritual Interview with Lord Byron: In which His Lordship Gave His Opinion and Feelings about His New Monument, and gossip about The present day, with some Interesting Information about the Spirit World, With Notes Explanatory and Elucidatory.* London: Samuel Palmer and Sons, 1876.

Rabaté, Jean-Michel. *The Ghosts of Modernity.* Gainesville: U of Florida P, 1996.

Radcliffe, Ann Ward. *The Mysteries of Udolpho, A Romance.* 2nd edn. 4 vols. London: G. G. and J. Robinson, 1794.

———. *A Sicilian Romance.* 2 vols. 1790. London: Hookham and Carpenter, 1792.

———. "On the Supernatural in Poetry." *New Monthly Magazine* 16.1 (1826): 145–52.

Ramazani, Jahan. "The Elegiac Love Poems: A Woman Dead and Gon(n)e." *Yeats & the Poetry of Death,* 17–26.

———. "The Self-Elegy." *Yeats & the Poetry of Death,* 134–99.

———. "Self-Theorizing Poetry: Yeats's Ars Poetica in *The Green Helmet and Other Poems.*" *Poems and Contexts: Yeats Annual* 16. Ed. Warwick Gould. New York: Palgrave Macmillan, 2005. 53–69.

———. *Yeats & the Poetry of Death: Elegy, Self-Elegy, and the Sublime.* New Haven: Yale UP, 1990.

Rand, Richard A. "Geraldine." *Glyph* 5 (1978): 74–97.

Redfield, Marc. *The Politics of Aesthetics: Nationalism, Gender, Romanticism.* Stanford: Stanford UP, 2003.

Reed, Arden, ed. *Romanticism and Language.* Ithaca: Cornell UP, 1984.

Reed, Mark L., ed. *The Thirteen-Book "Prelude."* 2 vols. Ithaca: Cornell UP, 1991.

Reid, John C. *Thomas Hood.* London: Routledge and Keegan Paul, 1963.

Reiman, Donald H. *The Mask of Anarchy: A Facsimile Edition.* New York: Garland P, 1985.

Reiman, Donald H., and Neil Fraistat, eds. *Shelley's Poetry and Prose.* New York: Norton, 2003.

Reynolds, Frederick. *The Dramatist: or Stop Him Who Can! A Comedy.* London: T. N. Longman &c, 1793.

Ricks, Christopher. *Allusion to the Poets.* Oxford: Oxford UP, 2002.

———. *The Force of Poetry.* Oxford: Oxford UP, 1987.

———. *Keats and Embarrassment.* 1974. London: Oxford UP, 1976.

———. "Wordsworth: 'A Pure Organic Pleasure from the Lines.'" *Essays in Criticism* 21.1 (1971): 1–32.

Robinson, Charles E. *The Frankenstein Notebooks: A Facsimile Edition of Mary Shelley's Manuscript Novel, 1816–1817.* 2 vols. New York: Garland P, 1996.

———. *Shelley and Byron: The Snake and Eagle Wreathed in Fight.* Baltimore: Johns Hopkins UP, 1976.

Robinson, Henry Crabb. *Recollections of Books and Writers.* 3 vols. Ed. Edith J. Morley. London: J. M. Dent, 1938.

[Rogers, Samuel]. "Coll'alto." *Italy: A Poem.* London: John Murray, 1823. 53–58.

Roland, Mme. (Marie-Jeanne). *An appeal to impartial posterity, by Citizenness Roland, wife of the Minister of the Home Department: or, a collection of pieces written by her during her confinement in the prisons of the Abbey, and St. Pélagie: Published for the Benefit of her only Daughter.* Part 1. Trans. from the French. London: J. Johnson, 1795.

Rollins, Hyder E., ed. *The Keats Circle: Letters and Papers.* 2 vols. Cambridge: Harvard UP, 1965.

Rossetti, D. G., trans. *The Early Italian Poets, Together with Dante's Vita Nuova.* 1861. London: J. M. Dent, 1894.

Rossington, Michael, ed. *The Cenci. The Poems of Shelley, Volume Two. 1817–1819.* Harlow, England: Longman, 2000.

Rousseau, J.-J. *Confessions.* Neuchatel, 1790.

———. *Julie, ou la nouvelle Héloïse: Lettres de deux Amans, Habitans d'une petit Ville au pied des Alpes.* 3rd corrected edn. Amsterdam: Marc-Michel Rey, 1772.

Russett, Margaret. "Narrative as Enchantment in *The Mysteries of Udolpho.*" *ELH* 65 (1998): 159–86.

Sales, Roger. *English Literature in History 1780–1830: Pastoral and Politics.* New York: St. Martin's P, 1983.

Saussure, Ferdinand de. *Cours de linguistique générale.* (A posthumous construction from the notes of Charles Bally and Albert Sechehaye, with Albert Reidlinger, 1916). Trans. Wade Baskin as *Course in General Linguistics.* New York: Philosophical Library, 1959.

Scrivener, Michael Henry. *Radical Shelley: The Philosophical Anarchism and Utopian Thought of Percy Bysshe Shelley.* Princeton: Princeton UP, 1982.

Shakespeare, William. *The Dramatick Writings of Will. Shakspere.* Based on the edition of Samuel Johnson and George Steevens. 20 vols. London: John Bell, 1788. *Coriolanus* vol. 15; *Cymbeline* vol. 20; *Hamlet* vol. 18; *Julius Caesar* vol. 16; *Macbeth* vol. 10; *Othello* vol. 19; *Romeo and Juliet* vol. 20; *Tempest* vol. 3; *Timon of Athens* vol. 17. With more than one play in several volumes, page runs begin anew for each, and so plays are cited by act.scene. line(s); if relevant, volume and page are given.

———. *Hamlet*. Ed. Harold Jenkins. Arden Edition. London: Methuen, 1986.

———. *The Poems of William Shakspeare*. London: Edward Jeffery, ?1798.

———. Sonnets. *The Poetical Works of Shakspeare*. London: C. Cooke, 1797.

———. *Shake-speares Sonnets* (quarto). London, 1609.

Shaw, George Bernard. "Keats." Williamson, ed., 173–76.

———. "Shaming the Devil about Shelley." *The Albemarle* 2 (September 1892): 91–98.

[?Shelley, Mary]. "Byron and Shelley on the Character of Hamlet." *New Monthly Magazine* n.s. 29.2 (1830): 327–37.

[Shelley, Mary]. *Frankenstein; or, The Modern Prometheus*. 3 vols. London: Lackington, 1818.

Shelley, Mary W. *Frankenstein*. London: Colburn and Bentley, 1831. "Introduction." 1:ix–xii.

———. *The Journals of Mary Shelley*. Ed. Paula Feldman and Diana Scott-Kilvert. Baltimore: Johns Hopkins UP, 1987.

———. *The Letters of Mary Wollstonecraft Shelley*. Ed. Betty T. Bennett. 3 vols. Baltimore: Johns Hopkins UP, 1980–88.

———. "Note on Poems of 1819." *The Poetical Works of Percy Bysshe Shelley*. Ed. [Mary] Shelley. 4 vols. London: Edward Moxon, 1839. 3:205–10.

[———] / Σç. "On Ghosts." *London Magazine* 9 (March 1824): 253–56. For my attribution, see *Journals*, 55, 126, 230.

Shelley, Percy B. *Adonais*. Pisa: private printing, 1821.

———. *The Cenci: A Tragedy, in Five Acts*. Italy and London: C. and J. Ollier, 1819. My text is from the corrected version in Reiman and Fraistat, eds., *Shelley's Poetry and Prose*.

———. *A Defence of Poetry*. In *Essays, Letters from Abroad, Translations and Fragments*. Ed. [Mary] Shelley. 2 vols. London: Edward Moxon, 1840. 1:1–57.

———. "England in 1819." *Poetical Works*. Ed. [Mary] Shelley. 3:193.

———. "England in 1819." Based on P. B. Shelley's fair copy, Reiman and Fraistat, eds., *Shelley's Poetry and Prose*. 326–27.

[———]. *Epipsychidion: Verses Addressed to the Noble and Unfortunate Lady, Emilia V———, Now Imprisoned in the Convent of ———*. London: C. and J. Ollier, 1821.

———. *Essay on Christianity. Shelley Memorials: From Authentic Sources*. Ed. Lady [Jane] Shelley. London: Smith, Elder, 1859. 255–90.

———. *Letters of Percy Bysshe Shelley*. Ed. Frederick L. Jones. 2 vols. Oxford: Clarendon P, 1964.

———. "LINES / Written during the Castlereagh Administration." *Athenæum* 267 (8 December 1832): 794.

———. *The Mask of Anarchy*. 1819. Press copy, reviewed by P. B. Shelley, with corrections from an intermediate stage. *Shelley's Poetry and Prose*, 316–26.

———. *The Masque of Anarchy: A Poem*. London: Edward Moxon, 1832.

———. *Ode to Liberty*. In *Prometheus Unbound &c*. 207–17.

———. *Percy Bysshe Shelley: A Longman Cultural Edition*. Ed. Stephen C. Behrendt. New York: Pearson, 2010.

———. *A Philosophical View of Reform*. 1819. Ed. T. W. Rolleston. Oxford: Humphry Milford, 1920.

———. *Prometheus Unbound: A Lyrical Drama in four acts, With Other Poems*. London: C and J Ollier, 1820.

———. *The Prose Works of Percy Bysshe Shelley*. Ed. Richard Herne Shepherd. 2 vols. London: Chatto and Windus, 1888.

———. *Shelley's Poetry and Prose*. Ed. Donald H. Reiman and Neil Fraistat. New York: W. W. Norton, 2002.

———. "Similes." *Athenæum* 252 (25 August 1832): 252.

[——] The Hermit of Marlow. "*'We Pity the Plumage, But Forget the Dying Bird': An Address to the People on the Death of Princess Charlotte.*" November 1817. *Prose Works,* 1:367–80.

Shires, Linda. "Reading Knoepflmacher Now." Knoepflmancher, ed. Shires. vii–xvi.

Simpson, David. *Wordsworth, Commodification and Social Concern: The Poetics of Modernity.* Cambridge: Cambridge UP, 2009.

Smith, Charlotte. *Emmeline, the Orphan of the Castle.* 4 vols. London: T. Cadell, 1788.

——. *Manon L'Escaut: or, The Fatal Attachment* (after A. F. Prévost). 2 vols. London: T. Cadell, 1786.

——. *The Old Manor House: A Novel, in Four Volumes.* London: J. Bell, 1793.

Smyser, Jane Worthington. "Wordsworth's Dream of Poetry and Science: The Prelude, V." *PMLA* 71.1 (1956): 269–75.

Soderholm, James. *Fantasy, Forgery, and the Byron Legend.* Lexington: U of Kentucky P, 1996.

Sperry, Stuart M. "Byron and the Meaning of *Manfred.*" *Criticism* 16.3 (Summer 1974): 189–202.

Starobinski, Jean. *Les mots sous les mots.* Translated by Olivia Emmet as *Words/upon/Words:/ The Anagrams of Ferdinand de Saussure.* New Haven: Yale UP, 1979.

Stewart, Garrett. *Dear Reader: The Conscripted Audience.* Chicago: U of Chicago P, 1996.

——. *The Deed of Reading.* Ithaca: Cornell UP, 2016.

——. "Metallusion: The Used, the Renewed, the Novel." *MLQ* 65.4 (December 2004): 583–604.

——. *Reading Voices: Literature and the Phonotext.* Berkeley: U of California P, 1990.

Stewart, Susan. "Lyric Possession." *Critical Inquiry* 22 (1995): 34–63.

Stillinger, Jack, ed. *John Keats, Poetry Manuscripts at Harvard: A Facsimile Edition.* Cambridge: Harvard UP/Belknap, 1990.

Stoppard, Tom. *Rosencrantz & Guildenstern are Dead.* New York: Grover, 1967.

Swift, Jonathan. *Letters to and from Dr. J. Swift, D. S. P. D. from the Year 1714, to 1738.* Dublin: George Faulkner, 1741.

Tait's Edinburgh Magazine 17.201 (September 1850): 521–27. "*The Prelude.*"

Talfourd, Thomas Noon, Sergeant. "Thoughts Upon the Intellectual Character of the Late William Hazlitt." By Mr. Sergeant Talfourd M.P. *Literary Remains of the Late William Hazlitt.* Ed. E. L. Bulwer and Sergeant Talfourd. London: Saunders and Otley, 1836. xxxiii–lxix.

——. "William Hazlitt." *Final Memorials of Charles Lamb . . . With Sketches of Some of His Companions.* 2 vols. London: Edward Moxon, 1848. 2:156–78.

[Taylor, W.]. Article IV: review of Isaac D'Israeli, *Miscellanies. Monthly Review, or Literary Journal,* 2nd ser. 2.24 (December 1797): 374–79.

Tennyson, Alfred Lord. "The Lotos-Eaters." *Poems.* 1832. London: Edward Moxon, 1833. 108–17. Revised, *Poems, in Two volumes.* London: Edward Moxon, 1842. 1:175–84.

"Terrorist System of Novel-Writing." See *Monthly Magazine* (August 1797).

Thompson, E. P. *The Making of the English Working Class.* London: Gollancz, 1963.

Thomson, James. *The castle of indolence: An allegorical poem. Written in imitation of Spenser.* 2nd edn. London: A. Millar, 1748.

Tooke, John Horne. *The Diversions of Purley.* 1786. 2nd edn. London: J. Johnson, 1805.

Townshend, Dale. "Conjuration and Exorcism: Byron's Spectral Rhetoric." Hopps, ed., 97–130.

Twiss, Horace. *The Public and Private Life of Lord Chancellor Eldon, with Selections from His Correspondence.* 3 vols. London: John Murray, 1844.

Vaihinger, Hans. *The Philosophy of "As if": A System of the Theoretical, Practical and Religious Fictions of Mankind.* 1911. Trans. C. K. Ogden, 1924. London: Routledge and Kegan Paul, 1949.

Vendler, Helen. *Invisible Listeners: Lyric Intimacy.* Princeton: Princeton UP, 2005.

———. *Our Secret Discipline: Yeats and Lyric Form.* Oxford: Oxford UP, 2007.

———. "Technique in the Earlier Poems of Yeats." *Yeats Annual* 8. Ed. Warwick Gould. London: Macmillan, 1991. 3–20.

Voltaire. *Dissertation sur la tragédie ancienne et moderne.* 1748. Vol. 2, *Oeuvres Completes de Voltaire.* Paris: Libraire de L. Hachette &c, 1859.

Walker, John. *Critical Pronouncing Dictionary of the English Language.* London: G. G. J. and J. Robinson and T. Cadell, 1791.

Wang, Orrin N. C. "Ghost Theory." *Studies in Romanticism* 46 (Fall 2007): 203–25.

Warburton, Dr. [William]. "Preface." *The Plays of William Shakespeare . . . with . . . various commentators; to which are added notes by Sam. Johnson.* 8 vols. London: J. and R. Tonson & c, 1765. I.lvi–lxii.

Warren, Mrs. M [Mercy Otis]. *The Ladies of Castile. Poems, dramatic and miscellaneous.* Boston: I. Thomas and E. T. Andrews, 1790. 97–278.

Warton, Joseph. *An essay on the genius and writings of Pope.* 2 vols. London: M. Cooper, 1756. 2nd edn., 2 vols. London: R. and J. Dodsley, 1762.

Wasserman, Earl R. "The Limits of Allusion in *The Rape of the Lock.*" *JEGP* 65 (1966): 425–55.

Watson, Nicola. "Trans-figuring Byronic Identity." Favret and Watson, eds., 185–206.

Webb, Timothy. *Shelley: A Voice Not Understood.* Atlantic Highlands: Humanities P International, 1977.

———. "The Unascended Heaven: Negatives in *Prometheus Unbound.*" *Shelley Revalued: Essays from the Gregynog Conference.* Ed. Kelvin Everest. Leicester: Leicester UP, 1983. 37–62.

White, Anna MacBride, and A. Norman Jeffares, eds. *The Gonne-Yeats Letters 1893–1938.* New York: W. W. Norton, 1992.

Whiter, Walter. *A specimen of a commentary on Shakspeare. Containing . . . An attempt to explain and illustrate various passages, on a New Principle of Criticism, Derived from Mr. Locke's Doctrine of the Association of Ideas.* London: T. Cadell, 1794.

Wilde, Oscar. *The Picture of Dorian Gray. Lippincott's Monthly Magazine* (July 1890): 8–100.

———. "Three New Poets" (including notice of W. B. Yeats, *The Wanderings of Oisin and Other Poems* [1889]). *Pall Mall Gazette,* 12 July 1889. 3, column 2.

Williams, Helen Maria. *Letters containing a sketch of the politics of France, from the thirty-first of May 1793, till the twenty-eighth of July 1794, and of the scenes which have passed in the prisons of Paris.* 2 vols. London: G. G. and J. Robinson, 1795.

Williams, Raymond. "Determine." *Keywords: A Vocabulary of Culture and Society.* New York: Oxford UP, 1985. 98–102.

———. "The Politics of Nuclear Disarmament." *New Left Review* 124 (November-December 1980): 25–42.

———. "The Romantic Artist." *Culture and Society, 1780–1850.* New York: Columbia UP, 1958.

Williamson. G. C., ed. *The John Keats Memorial Volume.* London: John Lane, 1921.

Wilson, Harriette. *The Memoirs of Harriette Wilson Written by Herself.* 2 vols. London: Private printing, 1825.

Wolfreys, Julian. *Victorian Hauntings: Spectrality, Gothic, the Uncanny and Literature.* New York: Palgrave, 2002.

Wolfson, Susan J. *Borderlines: The Shiftings of Gender in British Romanticism.* Palo Alto: Stanford UP, 2006.

———. *Formal Charges: The Shaping of Poetry in British Romanticism.* Stanford,: Stanford UP, 1997.

———. "Our Puny Boundaries: Why the Craving to Carve Up the Nineteenth Century?" *PMLA* 116.5 (October 2001): 1432–41.

———. *The Questioning Presence.* Ithaca: Cornell UP, 1986.

———. *Reading John Keats.* Cambridge: Cambridge UP, 2015.

———. "*The Vision of Judgment* and the Spectres of 'Author.'" *The Cambridge Companion to Byron.* Ed. Drummond Bone. Cambridge: Cambridge UP, 2004. 256–74.

Wolfson, Susan J., and Peter J. Manning. Introduction to *The Romantics and Their Contemporaries.* 5th edn., New York: Pearson, 2012. 1–33.

Wollstonecraft, Mary. *An Historical and Moral View of the Origin and Progress of the French Revolution; and the Effect It Has Produced in Europe.* London: J. Johnson, 1794.

Wood, Michael. "Time and Her Aunt." *The Blackwell Companion to Jane Austen.* Ed. Claudia Johnson and Clara Tuite. London: Blackwell, 2009. 195–205.

———. *Yeats & Violence.* Oxford: Oxford UP, 2010.

Woolf, Virginia. "William Hazlitt." *The Common Reader: second series.* London: Hogarth, 1932. 17–85.

Wordsworth, Christopher. Letter to Christopher Wordsworth Jr. 18 April 1832. British Museum Add. MSS. 46137.

Wordsworth, Christopher Jr. *Memoirs of William Wordsworth.* 2 vols. London: Edward Moxon, 1851.

Wordsworth, William. "The Affliction of Margaret———of———." *Poems* (1807), 1:45–49; "Poems Founded Upon the Affections," XIX. *Poems* (1815) 1:155–59.

———. *Autobiographical Memoranda.* Christopher Wordsworth, *Memoirs of William Wordsworth, Poet-Laureate.* 2 vols. London: Edward Moxon, 1851. 1:7–17.

———. "Celebrated Authors Considered." Ms. essay "Upon Epitaphs." *Prose Works.* Ed. Grosart. 2:60–75.

———. *The Complete Poetic Works of William Wordsworth.* London: Macmillan, 1893.

———. "The Country Church-yard, and Critical Examination of Ancient Epitaphs." Ms. essay, "Upon Epitaphs." *Prose Works.* Ed. Grosart. 2:41–59. Cited as "Ancient Epitaphs."

———. "Epitaphs." *The Friend* 25 (22 February 1810): 401–16.

———. "Essay Upon Epitaphs." *The Excursion* (1814). 431–46.

———. *The Excursion, Being a Portion of The Recluse, A Poem.* London: Longman & c, 1814.

———. *The Fourteen-Book "Prelude."* (MS D). Ed. W. J. B Owen. Ithaca: Cornell UP, 1985.

———. *Last Poems, 1821–1850.* Ed. Jared Curtis. Ithaca: Cornell UP, 1999.

———. "Lines, Written a few miles above Tintern Abbey, on revisiting the banks of the Wye, during a tour, July 13, 1798." *Lyrical Ballads* (1798), 201–10. Cited as *Tintern Abbey* with line numbers added.

———. W[illiam]. *Lyrical Ballads, with Other Poems.* 2 vols. London: T. N. Longman and O. Rees / Bristol: Biggs, 1800.

———. *Lyrical Ballads, with Pastoral and Other Poems.* 3rd edn. London: T. N. Longman and O. Rees, 1802.

———. "The Mad Mother." *Lyrical Ballads* (1798), 141–46.

———. MS/MSS. For MSS JJ, RV, U, V see *The Prelude, 1798–1799*; for MSS A, B, C, see *The Thirteen-Book "Prelude"*; for MS D, see *The Fourteen-Book "Prelude."* For a brief census, see *The Prelude*, Norton Critical Edition, 507–9, and for the ms. history, 510–26. MSS in the Dove Cottage archives, Grasmere, England, are presented in various Cornell UP editions, marked DC by number. The Norton Critical Edition presents some of these, in selection.

———. "Nutting." *Lyrical Ballads* (1800) 2:132–35.

———. *Ode. Poems, In Two Volumes.* 2:147–58.

———. "Ode to Duty." *Poems, In Two Volumes.* 1:70–74

———. *Poems.* London: Edward Moxon, 1845.

———. *Poems by William Wordsworth, including Lyrical Ballads and the Miscellaneous Pieces of the Author, with Additional Poems, a New Preface, and a Supplementary Essay*. 2 vols. London: Longman & c., 1815.

———. *Poems, In Two Volumes*. London: Longman & c., 1807.

———. *"Poems In Two Volumes" and Other Poems, 1800–1807*. Ed. Jared Curtis. Ithaca: Cornell UP, 1983.

———. *Poetical Works of William Wordsworth: A New Edition*. 6 vols. London: 1836 (vols. 1–2); 1837 (vols. 3–6).

———. *The Prelude, 1799, 1805, 1850*. Ed. Jonathan Wordsworth, M. H. Abrams, and Stephen Gill. New York: W. W. Norton, 1979.

———. *The Prelude, 1798–1799*. Ed. Steven M. Parrish. Ithaca: Cornell UP, 1977.

———. *The Prelude, or Growth of a Poet's Mind; An Autobiographical Poem*. London: Edward Moxon, 1850.

———. "Resolution and Independence." *Poems, In Two Volumes*. 1:89–97. *Poems* (1815) 2: 27–34.

[———] Axiologus. "Sonnet, on seeing Miss Helen Maria Williams weep at a Tale of Distress." *European Magazine, and London Review* 11 (March 1787): 202.

———. "Stanzas on the Power of Sound." *Yarrow Revisited, and Other Poems*. London: Longman & c and Edward Moxon, 1835. 309–22.

———. "There Was a Boy." *Lyrical Ballads* (1800), 2:13–14.

———. *The Thirteen-Book "Prelude."* Ed. Mark L. Reed. 2 vols. Ithaca: Cornell UP, 1991.

———. "Three years she grew in sun and shower." *Lyrical Ballads* (1800), 2:136–38.

Wordsworth, William, and Dorothy Wordsworth. *The Letters of William and Dorothy Wordsworth*. Ed. Ernest de Selincourt. *The Early Years, 1787–1805*, 2nd edn., revised Chester L. Shaver. Oxford: Clarendon P, 1967. *The Middle Years, Part I: 1806–1811*, 2nd edn., revised Mary Moorman. Oxford: Oxford UP, 1969. *The Later Years, Part 4, 1840–1853*. 2nd edn., revised Alan G. Hill. Oxford: Clarendon P, 1988.

Wu, Duncan. *William Hazlitt: The First Modern Man*. Oxford: Oxford UP, 2008.

Wu, Duncan, ed. *The Selected Writings of William Hazlitt*. 9 vols. London: Pickering and Chatto, 1998.

Wyld, Henry Cecil Kennedy. *Evolution in English Pronunciation: a public lecture delivered at the University of Liverpool, on November 21st, 1913*. Liverpool: UP at Liverpool, 1913.

Yates, Frances A. *The Art of Memory*. Chicago: U of Chicago P, 1966.

Yeats, William Butler. / Yeats. W. B. "Art and Ideas." *The New Weekly*, 20 and 27 June 1914. *The Cutting of an Agate* (1924). *E&I*. 346–54.

———. "Byzantium." *The Winding Stair*.

———. *The Collected Letters of W. B. Yeats*. General Ed. John Kelly. Oxford: Oxford UP, 1986–. *Unpublished Letters (1905–1939)*. Ed. Ronald Schuchard, 1994. Charlottesville: InteLex Electronic Edition, 2002 (cited by item number).

———. *The Collected Works of William Butler Yeats*. 8 vols. Stratford-on-Avon: Shakespeare Head Press, 1908.

———. *The Cutting of an Agate*. New York: Macmillan, 1912.

——— "Edmund Spenser." October 1902. *Cutting of an Agate* (1912), 213–55. Cited as "Spenser."

———. *Essays*. London: Macmillan, 1924.

———. *Essays and Introductions*. London: Macmillan, 1961.

———. "The Fascination of What's Difficult." *Green Helmet*, 20–21.

———. "A General Introduction for My Work." 1937. *Essays and Introductions*, 509–36.

———. *The Green Helmet and Other Poems*. London: Macmillan, 1912.

———. "Her Vision in the Wood." *The Winding Stair*, 93.

———. *Ideas of Good and Evil*. London: A. H. Bullen, 1903.

———. *The Irish Dramatic Movement*. Eds. Mary FitzGerald and Richard J. Finneran. *Collected Works of W. B. Yeats*. Vol. 7. New York: Scribner, 2003.

———. *Last Poems: Manuscript Materials*. Ed. James Pethica. Ithaca: Cornell UP, 1997.

———. "A Letter from W. B. Yeats." Williamson, ed., 216.

———. *The Letters of W. B. Yeats*. Ed. Allan Wade. London: Rupert Hart-Davis, 1954.

———. "A Mad Song." *The Sketch* 19:236. 4 August 1897. 52.

———. *Per Amica Silentia Lunae*. New York: Macmillan, 1918.

———. "The Philosophy of Shelley's Poetry." Part I, *The Dome* 7 (May–July 1900); entire in *Ideas of Good and Evil* (1903) 90–141. Quotations from *Ideas*.

———. *The Poems*. Vol. 1, *The Collected Works of W. B. Yeats*. Ed. Richard J. Finneran. 1983; revised, New York: Macmillan, 1989. Except where noted, quotations follow this edition.

———. "Poetry and Tradition." August 1907. *The Cutting of an Agate*, 116–38.

———. "*Prometheus Unbound*." 1932. *The Spectator* 150.5464 (17 March 1933): 366–67. Reprinted in *E&I* (1937).

———. "Religious Belief Necessary to Religious Art." 1906. *The Cutting of an Agate* (1912), 109–12.

———. *Responsibilities and Other Poems*. Churchtown: Cuala P, 1914; London: Macmillan, 1916.

———. *Stories of Red Hanrahan*. New York: Macmillan, 1914.

———. *The Tower*. New York: Macmillan, 1928.

———. "The Tragic Theatre." August 1910. *The Cutting of an Agate* (1912), 196–207.

———. *The Trembling of the Veil*. London: Private subscription printing, T. Warner Laurie, 1922.

———. *Unpublished Letters (1905–1939)*. Ed. Ronald Schuchard. 1994. Charlottesville, VA: InteLex Electronic Edition, 2002. Cited by item number.

———. *The Variorum Edition of the Poems of W. B. Yeats*. Ed. Peter Allt and Russell Alspach. New York: Macmillan, 1957.

———. *A Vision*. 1938. New York: Macmillan, 1956.

———. *The Wild Swans at Coole*. New York: Macmillan, 1919.

———. *The Wild Swans at Coole, Other Verses and a Play in Verse*. Churchtown: Cuala P, 1917.

———. "William Blake and His Illustrations to *The Divine Comedy*." 1897. *Ideas of Good and Evil*, 176–225.

———. "William Blake and the Imagination." 1897. *Ideas of Good and Evil*, 168–75.

———. *The Wind Among the Reeds*. London: Elkin Mathews, 1899.

———. *The Winding Stair, and Other Poems*. New York: Macmillan, 1933.

Z. "On the Cockney School of Poetry. No IV." *Blackwood's Edinburgh Magazine* 3 (August 1818): 519–24.

INDEX

Note: Short titles are keyed to Works Cited

Williamson, G. C. (editor of *Keats Memorial Volume*), and Yeats, 158–59, 222n4
Wilson, Harriette, and Byronic ghost-pastiche, 152–54, 221nn36–37
Wolfreys, Julian, on spectral reading, 10, 196
Wood, Michael: on ghost story narratology, 196; on Yeats, 183
Woolf, Virginia, on Hazlitt, 79, 96
Wordsworth, William (chapter 2): "Axiologus" (pen-name, pun-name), 39, 65, 205n4; and Byron, 204n39, 208n33; and Coleridge, 65, 208n34, 211nn70–71; on epitaph-names, 33, 45, 50, 58, 65–66, 81, 209n45, 210n65; and Milton, 13, 210–11n67; personification-poetics, 14, 57, 67, 210n56; phantoms of conceit, 1–2; spectral "sense" in, 14, 24, 42, 55, 59, 201n15; and Shakespeare, 50–51. *See also under* accidents; allusion; apparition-poetics; "as if"; author; Coleridge; De Quincey; dream-apparition; ghosts; grammar; Hamlet; haunting; Hazlitt; Keats; *Macbeth*; litotes; name-apparitions; negative prefixes; optical illusion; revenants; rhymes; supernatural
—WORKS: "Affliction of Margaret," 31–32, 204n39; *Brothers*, 31; *Excursion*, 22, 168; "Mad Mother," 173; *Ode: Intimations of Immortality*, 24–25, 65, 213n18; "Ode to Duty," 63–64, 211nn68–69; "On the Power of Sound," 52, 209n47; *Resolution and Independence*, 23, 51, 190; "Three years she grew," 80–81; *Tintern Abbey*, 20–22, 31
  Prelude, 4–5, 22–23; as genre, 65–67, 195–96, 208n37, 211n74, 226n9; key episodes and passages: boat-theft, 14–15; Boy of Winander ("There was a Boy"), 43, 201n12, 207n25; Cave of Yordas, 3; Convent of Chartreuse, 2, 34; discharged veteran, 22; dog-ghost, 12; dream of the Arab's stone and shell, 22, 38–39, 50–53, 202n14, 205nn1–3; gibbet-trauma, 61–62; glad preamble (opening lines), 12, 46, 54, 67–68; London's shows, 58–59, 210n58; mystery of words, 53–54; nest-robbing, 12–13; Paris in "The Terror," 18; Sarum Plain, 59–60;

trap-theft, 12–13; Vaudracour, 60–61; waiting for horses, 24–25
"Wordsworth's Elements," 39, 56, 66
Wu, Duncan, on Hazlitt, 212n11, 212n16, 213n22, 213n28, 214n31, 214n35

Yates, Frances A., on memory, 204n40. *See also* mental images
Yeats, W. B.: anti-self ghost, 163–64; apparitional syntax, 183, 223n22; on Blake, 163, 223n14; on Dante (in *Per Amica*), 164, 167, 223n25; on *Endymion* (Keats), 163; and Maud Gonne, 172–73, "Gonne"-play, 172, 224n35; on hysteria, 224–25n38; and Keats (chapter 6); and *Keats Memorial Volume*, 158–59, 222n4; and Ben Jonson, 158–59; as "last romantic," 162; on meter, 173–75, 183; periods in career, 163, 224n28; on Pope, 173; portrait of, 158-60, 222n1; on rhyme, 175–76, 184 (eye-rhyme, 186); rhymed with *Keats*, 158, 222n3; on Shelley, 162–63, 176–78, 223nn14–15, 223n17; on Spenser's poetry, 162–63, 171–72; on Timon of Athens's epitaph, 184; and Wilde, 222n2. *See also under* author; dream-apparition; epitaph; ghosts (&c); grammar-shades; name-puns, negative prefixes; prosopopoeia; rhymes; Shelley; Vendler; Wilde; Wood
—WORKS: "Byzantium," 180–81; "Coole Park and Ballylee," 163; "Coole Park and Ballylee, 1931," 163, 168; *Ego Dominus Tuus*, 163–67, 223n18, 226n57; "The Fascination of What's Difficult," 175, 225nn44–45; "Her Vision in the Wood," 177; "Mad Song," 173, 224n38; *Per Amica Silentia Lunae*, 162–64; *Philosophy of Poetry*, 162; "Sailing to Byzantium," 176–80, 225nn47–48; "Song of the Wandering Aengus," 170–73, 224n37; "To a Friend Whose Work has Come to Nothing," 176, 225n46; "To be carved on Stone at Thoor Ballylee," 186; *The Trembling of the Veil*, 160, 173, 223n21, 224n27; "Under Ben Bulben," 183–86, 225nn51–54; *A Vision*, 168, 178; "A Woman Young and Old," 177